यथाग्नेर्दाहिकाशक्ति रामकृष्णे स्थिता हि या ।
सर्वविद्यास्वरुपां तां सारदां प्रणमाम्यहम् ।।

Eternally Talented India
108 Facts

VIVEKANANDA INSTITUTE OF HUMAN EXCELLENCE
Ramakrishna Math, Domalguda, Hyderabad - 29.
e-mail : publication@rkmath.org | website: www.rkmath.org

Eternally Talented India — 108 Facts

First Impression (Jan, 2008) & Second Impression (Nov, 2009)
from Vivekananda Life Skills Academy, Hyderabad.

Third Impression (May, 2013)

Editorial Team:

Main Contributors:

J. Chandra Sekhar, *Chartered Accountant, Hyderabad.*

M. Gangadhar Prasad, *Journalist & Sys. Administrator, Chennai.*

Supported by :

Dr. L. Srinivas, BAMS (Ayurveda), M.A.(Saṁskṛta), Hyderabad.

Sri Prathap Jaisimha, Medical Transcriptionist, Hyderabad.

Smt JK. Manonmani, M.A, B.Sc. B.Ed, Retd Teacher, TTD, Tirupati.

Sri N. Lakshman Rao, Consultant (Infira - Projects), Hyderabad.

Advisory Team: (that Guided and Corrected us)

Dr. K.Subrahmanyam, Retd, Principal, Vivekananda College, Madurai. T.N.

Dr. Paran Gowda, Doctorate in Nuclear Physics, (IIT Bombay) & Social Activist., and

Rev . Swami Satchidananda Puri, Kailash Ashram, Rushikesh.

Published by

Adhyaksha
Ramakrishna Math
Domalguda, Hyderabad - 29

From 2008 to 2017: 23,300 copies
Eighth Impression: 6,000 copies (October 2018)

ISBN 978-93-83142-34-7

Printed in India at :
Sravya Grafics
Hyderabad

First words of Introduction & Inspiration . . .

India's Eternal Contribution to the World's Progress

By Swami Vivekananda

If there is any land on this earth that can lay claim to be blessed Punya Bhūmi.. the land where humanity has attained its highest towards gentleness, towards generosity, towards purity, towards calmness, above all the land of introspection and of spirituality, it is India.

We find that the Indian race never stood for wealth. Although they acquired immense wealth, perhaps, more than any other nation ever acquired, yet the nation did not stand for wealth. It was a powerful race for ages, yet we find that nation never stood for power, never went out of the country to conquer.

The debt, which the world owes to our motherland, is immense. As I look back upon the history of my country, I do not find in the whole world another country, which has done quite so much for the improvement of the human mind. Therefore, I have no words of condemnation for my Nation. I tell them, "You have done well; only try to do better."

India has given to antiquity the earliest scientific physicians (Suśruta & Charaka) and according to Sir William Hunter, she has even contributed to modern medical science by discovery of various chemicals and by teaching you how to reform misshapen ears and noses.

Even more it has done in Mathematics, for Algebra, Geometry, Astronomy and the triumph of modern science-mixed mathematics - were all invented in India, just so much as the ten numerals, the very cornerstone of all present civilization, were discovered in India and are in reality, Saṁskṛta words.

In philosophy we are even now head and shoulders above any nation, as Schopenhauer, the great German philosopher has confessed.

In music, India gave to the world her system of notation with the seven cardinal notes and the diatonic scale.

In philology, our Saṁskṛta language is now universally acknowledged to be the foundation of all European languages.

In literature, our epics and our poems and dramas rank as high as those of any language; Our "Shakuntala" was summarized by the German greatest poet as "heaven and earth united." India has given to the world the fables of Aesop, which were copied by Aesop from an old Saṁskṛta book; it has given the Arbaian Nights, yes, the story of Cinderella and the Bean Stalks.

In manufacture, India was the first to make cotton and purple (dye), it was proficient in all works of jewellary and the very word sugar as well as the article itself is the product of India.

Lastly, she invented the game of chess and the cards and the dice.

Three-quarters of the wealth of the world has come out of India, and does even now. The commerce of India has been the turning point, the pivot, of the history of the world. Whatever nation got, it became powerful and civilized. The Greeks got it and became the mighty Greeks; the Romans got it and became the mighty Romans.

India has been the one country to which every nation that has become strong wants to go and conquer - it being reputed to be very rich. The wealth of the people had become a fable, even in the most ancient history. [Many foreign invaders] rushed to become wealthy in India and conquered the country.

Every one of these invasions destroyed one or more of these families, burned many libraries and houses. And when that was so, much literature was lost. It is only within the last few years that ideas have begun to spring up about the retention of these various religions and books.

So great, in fact, was the superiority of India in every aspect that it drew to her borders the hungry cohorts of Europe and thereby indirectly brought about the discovery of America.

And I challenge anybody to show one single period of her national life when India was lacking in spiritual giants capable of moving the world. But her work is spiritual and that cannot be done with blasts of war trumpets or the march of cohorts.

Her influence has always fallen upon the world like that of the gentle dew, unheard and scarcely marked, yet bringing into bloom the fairest flowers of the world.

The education that you are getting now has some good points, but it has a tremendous disadvantage, which is so great that the good things are all weighed down. In the first place, it is not a man-making education, it is merely and entirely a negative education. A negative education or any training that is based on negation is worse than death.

The child is taken to school, and the first thing he learns is that his father is a fool, the second thing that his grandfather is a lunatic, the third thing that all his teachers are hypocrites, the fourth that all the sacred books are lies! By the time he is sixteen he is a mass of negation, lifeless and boneless. And the result is that fifty years of such education has not produced one original man in the three Presidencies. Every man of originality that has been produced has been educated elsewhere, and not in this country or they have gone to the old Universities once more to cleanse themselves of superstition

A nation that has no history of its own has nothing in this world; Out of the past is built the future. Look back, therefore as far as you can, drink deep of the eternal foundations that are behind and after that, look forward, march forward and make India brighter, greater and much higher than she ever was. Our ancestors were great. We must recall that.

The more, therefore, the Indians study the past, the more glorious will be the future and whoever tries to bring the past to the door of everyone is the great benefactor to the nation.

For a complete civilization of the world is waiting, for the treasures to come out of India; waiting for the marvelous spiritual inheritance of the race. Little do you know how much of hunger and thirst there is outside of India for these Wonderful Treasures of our Fore-Fathers ?

The more you go out and travel among the nations of the world, the better for you and for your country. I went to America and Europe, to which you so kindly allude; this reviving national life, expanding inside, threw me off and thousands will be thrown off in that way. Mark my words, it has got to come if this nation lives at all.

But one vision I see clear as life before me that the ancient Mother has awakened once more, sitting on her throne- rejuvenated, more glorious than ever. Proclaim her to the entire world with the voice of peace and benedicition.

ARISE, AWAKE! STOP NOT TILL THE GOAL IS REACHED

(Compiled from Complete works of Swami Vivekananda — Vol-3, 321)

Message

"As I look back upon the history of my country, I do not find in the whole world another country which has done quite so much for improvement of human mind. Therefore I have no words of condemnation for my nation. I tell them "You have done well; only try to do better."

"India has given to antiquity the earliest scientific physicians...she has even contributed to modern medical science by discovery of various chemicals and by teaching you how to reform misshapen ears and noses. Even more it has done in mathematics, for algebra, geometry, astronomy and the triumphs of modern science-mixed mathematics- were all invented in India, just so much as the ten numerals, the very cornerstone of all present civilization, were discovered in India and are in reality, Saṁskṛta words."

Swami Vivekananda
(C.W.Vol-2-511-512)

Foreword

We are glad to publish *Eternally Talented India – 108 Facts* featuring the numerous fields in which our motherland has excelled from time immemorial. The readers will be amazed to find that India has surpassed every nation through the ages in all the possible branches of study, investigation and action that the western world is credited with in recent times. It is not just for spirituality that the west has looked up to India. Our mother land is the birth place of many a field such as—sciences, mathematical concepts, medicine, astrology, astronomy just to mention a few.

As Swami Vivekananda said, "Drink deep the eternal foundations that are behind us and then march forward, and make India brighter, greater and much higher than She ever was." There have been "wonderful treasures of our forefathers" in store for us. However we the legal heirs of these treasures instead of claiming them and realizing that the roots of the tree are here are enticed by the fruits borne in foreign lands. We hope this book while facilitating us acknowledge the million milestones we have touched will help us awaken our Mother after a long lull once more, and see her "rejuvenated and more glorious" thus fulfilling Swamiji's dream.

The first and second edition of this book was published by Vivekananda Life Skills Academy, and now the copyright of the same has been given to us. We are thankful to them. The present edition is the revised edition and we hope that readers will get pleasure and benefit by reading this book.

-Publisher

Our Words

Two thousand years ago, India was at its pinnacle of prosperity and peace. It was at its height of material learning and spiritual advancement. India remained as a beacon of wisdom & learning. The World looked at India as the Guru- the preceptor. Great universities like Taxshila & Nalanda; Universal spread of Indian culture; India's commercial links; Vedic scriptures; splendid granite marvels, galaxy of spiritual giants all stand as a testimony of India's ancient glory.

But, for the past 1000 years, India was enslaved and draped into darkness. As India neglected its material prosperity, India lost its balance between spirtuality and materialism and soon became the victim of foreign invasion and plunder. Without India being materialistically assertive, India lost its spiritual vigour and strength and freedom.

Many great souls descended on this holy land in the last two hundred years, to restore to India, its lost individuality. India was awakened socially and roused politically; today India is beaming with material wealth. Unfortuanately, the politically independent material India is becoming a cultural slave of the Western influence. This agony of cultural degradation had become rampant during the last sixty years. We as a nation are distancing ourselves from spirituality- where the cultural roots of India lie. India's cultural roots are centered in spirituality. We are losing them fast. Also, we are falling down into the valley of darkness by neglecting our spiritual/cultural values. Modern Independent India is a success story materialistically, yet ethically, culturaly & spirtually, it had slipped from the prime postion it had occupied in the past. It has to be awakened and had to be rejuvenated again. If we look into the mirror of past glory, we are sure to regain our self-confidence. Ancient India flourished with more advanced material and secular knowledge than what is being revealed by modern science. This truth has to reach the youth of this country, who constitute 60% of its population. This will end blind imitation of the West for everything. Then the Indian youth shall understand the glory of Indian culture and spiritual values. The vibrant, resurgent, confident, sublime & Satvik India shall soon regain its position as the world teacher, to play its role of preaching "the art and science of living" - i.e balancing the spiritual and material aspects of life i.e balance of Dharma, Artha and Kama without losing sight on moksha, the ultimate goal of human life.

Our effort of compiling this book into 108 facts, covering eighteen chapters, is to reach the youth of India, by exposing them to ancient India's achievements & eternally talented India.

- Editorial Team

O India! Forget Not Your Ideals

O India ! Forget not that the ideal of thy womanhood is Sita, Savatri, Damayanti; forget not that the God thou worshippest is the great Ascetic of ascetics, the all-renouncing Shankara, the Lord of Uma; forget not that thy marriage, thy wealth, thy life are not for sense-pleasure, are not for thy individual personal happiness; forget not that thou art born as a sacrifice to the Mother's altar; forget not that thy social order is but the reflex of the Infinite Univesal Motherhood; forget not that the lower classes, the ignorant, the poor, the illiterate, the cobbler, the sweeper, are thy flesh and blood, thy brothers. Thou brave one, be blod take courage, be proud that thou art an Indian, and proudly proclaim, " I am an Indian, every Indian is my brother." Says, "The ignorant Indian, the poor and destitute Indian, the Brahmin Indian, the Pariah Indian, is my brother." Thou, too, clad with but a rag round thy lions proudly proclaim at the top of thy voice: "The Indian is my brother, the Indian is my life, Indian's gods and goddesses are my God. India's society is the cradle of my infancy, the pleasure-garden of my youth, the sacred heaven, the Varanasi of my old age." Says, brother; "The soil of India is my highest heaven, the good of India is my good," and repeat and pray day and night , "O Thou Lord of Gauri, O Thou Mother of the Universe, vouchsafe manliness unto me! O Thou Mother of Strength, take away my weakness, take away my unmanliness, and make me a Man!"

Contents

Eternally Talented India-108 Facts

1. The Significance of 108 1

✦ **Astronomical Talents**

2. Spherical Earth— Who knew it first? 7
3. Many Apples had fallen before Newton's Gravity Laws 9
4. Who goes around whom, Earth vs Sun? 11
5. Seven Colours of Sun Light 13
6. Measuring the Speed of Light 14
7. Scaling the Eternal Time 15
8. Jantar-Mantar, a place for monitoring Heavens 20
9. Comets 22

✦ **Medical Talents**

10. Pioneering the Surgery— World's First Surgeons 24
11. Āyurveda—A Therapeutical Treasure 26
12. Hṛdayam— for Healthy Heart Beats 29
13. Test Tubes Babies 31
14. Benefiting from the Cow 32
15. Tulasi— The Wonder Herb 35
16. Long drawn battles for Turmeric and Neem 37
17. Copper shields our Health 41
18. Successful Jai-"Poor" Foot 42

✦ **Green Skills of Eternal India**

19. Traditional Agricultural Expertise 47
20. Father of Botony—Sage Parāśara 51
21. Indian Cattle Science 53

✦ **Scientific Talents**

22. Genius of Indian Mathematical Brains 56
23. Indian Chemistry through Ages 62
24. Ship Building Skills 65
25. Machine Science of India 68
26. Hijacked Indian Aeronautics 70
27. Sound Secrets 75
28. Hidden Knowledge in Naṭarāja's Cosmic Dance 78
29. Finding the Basic Building Blocks of the Universe—Atomic theory. 80
30. String Theory 86
31. Time-Space & Relativity—Einstein Vs India's Perspective 88
32. Evolution theory—Animal-human-God or reverse, Which is true? 91

✦ **Technological Talents**

33. Sage Agastya's way of Generating Electricity 99
34. Building Technology of India 100

35. Indian Town Planning Skills 101
36. World's First Constructed Dam 103
37. "Paper" made in India-first 104
38. Technique of predicting Earth Quakes 106
39. Finding the underground Water Resources 107
40. A metallurgical marvel— Delhi Iron pillar 109
41. Origin of Lens 110
42. Art of Brightening Diamonds 111
43. Magnet & Its Varieties 113
44. Marconi's wire "Less" values 115
45. Textile technology of India 117

✦ **Vedic Cultural Excellence**

46. Vedas— The Creator's Manual 122
47. Great bluff of Aryan Invasion Theory 131
48. Saraswati River & once Glorious Civilisation 136
49. Under-water city of Lord Kṛṣṇa 139
50. Landmarks of Rama's Bridge on Indian Ocean 141
51. World's Oldest Port— Lothal 143
52. The Eighteen Purāṇas 145
53. Vedic Chandas & its Excellence 149
54. Transport System During Vedic Times 152
55. Ancient Scientific Texts of India 153

✦ **Modern Indian Talents**

56. Indian Elephant Dancing its way to become an Economic Superpower 162
57. Modern Indian Scientists 174
58. Indian Industrial Giants 184
59. Indian Multinational Companies 190
60. Massive Indian Railways 192
61. Success Story of Indian Space Technology 193
62. Largest Postal Network of the World 198
63. Ingineous Tank Irrigation System in India 201

✦ **Spiritual Excellence**

64. Ṛṣis — Great Seers of India 206
65. Global Influence of Indian Spiritual Gurus 215
66. The Grandeur of Indian Spiritual Excellence 235
67. Prophecies of Swami Vivekananda 240

✦ **Talented Nonresident Indians**

68. Nonresident Indians— Scientists & Intellectuals 244
69. NRI— Millionaires, Industrialists, Business & Political Leaders 252
70. NRI— Contributions to America's Progress 256

✦ **Educational Talents**

71. World's First Universities 258
72. Ancient Indian Libraries 260
73. Pāṇini's Logic & Computer Languages 262
74. Saṁskṛta Words in English 264
75. Maculay's Game Plan of Westernizing Indian Generations 267

76. Indian Educational Scene When British Entered India 272
77. Replicating Indian Teaching Methods in England 275

✦ **Ancient Indian Global Influence**

78. Ages ago Indians reached American Shores 278
79. India, The China's Teacher 284
80. Indians Inspired Greeks 291
81. South Asian Cultural Bondage 294
82. Influencing East Asian Countries 304
83. Ties with Rome & Egypt 308

✦ **Indian Military Skills**

84. Indian Science of Warfare 312
85. History's First Atomic Explosion at Harrappa 316
86. Inventing Gun Powder 319
87. World's First Rocket Launches 321

✦ **Governing Skills of Ancient India**

88. Dharma Śāstras— The Science of Ethics 324
89. Nyāya Śāstra—The Science of Logic/ Reasoning 326
90. India— The Cradle of Democracy 328
91. Indian Governing Principles Through Ages 332

✦ **Talents in Mystical Sciences**

92. The Science of Vāstu for Harmonious Living 344
93. Yoga— The World's Craze of the Day 347
94. Mantra Science & its Application 352
95. The Samudrika Śāstra— The Science of Body Language 355
96. Jyotiṣa—The Science of light that Correlates Planetary Influence on Human Behaviour 358

✦ **Artistic Excellence**

97. Indian Sculpture & Painting 362
98. Nāṭya Śāstram 366
99. Musical Melody of India 371
100. Beauty of Saṁskṛta Literature 377
101. Avadhānam—The Language Gymnastics 382

✦ **Exemplary Indian Womanhood**

102. Women Ṛṣis 386
103. Women Rulers Through Ages 387

✦ **Talents in Sports**

104. Indian Sports & Sports Legends 392

✦ **Other Indian Glories**

105. Taj Mahal—A Wonderful Mystery 400
106. Eternal Fragrance of Indian Perfumes 404
107. Natural Dyes —Eternal India in Flying Colours 405
108. Sugar's Sweet History 408

The significance of "108"

1 The significance of "108"

"Ekaṁ sat viprā bahudhā vadanti"
Truth is one, but wise people say it in different ways.

Indian knowledge echoes it throughout. The ultimate truth is that the creation is manifested from God, sustained within God and gets dissolved in God.

The whole of creation, which includes heavens, galaxies, planets, stars, human beings, and other creatures, is created, sustained and merged accordingly in that divine principle. There is a rhythm, a pattern, and a discipline in the whole universe. Ancient Indians knew that. That rhythm is symbolized as "108 factor or number".

The mystic number 108 is so sacred to ancient Indians. In all spiritual practices 108 is given utmost importance.

There are 108 beads on a "Japa mālā", that are counted while repeating a mantra and the equal number of names of a God or Goddess chanted during Pūjā while offering flowers.

In explaining the number of beads on a Japa Mālā, it is said that 108 are the number of steps a soul takes to reach the Divine within us. With this sacred number appearing in so many intersections between the Divine and the human, it is no wonder that all Indians including Hindus, Buddhists, Jains, Sikhs and Taoists find that offerings of 108 help us remain in harmony with God's perfect universe.

In Astronomy, Vedic seers calculated that :

- The distance between the Earth and Moon is 108 times the diameter of the Moon

- The distance between the Earth and Sun is 108 times the diameter of the Sun
- The diameter of the Sun is 108 times the diameter of the Earth.

These numbers are remarkably close to the results of calculations based on modern scientific measurements using the average distances between Earth and the Moon and Earth and the Sun.

Āyurveda tells us that there are 108 "Marma"* points in the body, where consciousness and flesh intersect to give life to the living being. The chain of 108 'links' is held together by 107 joints, which is the number of marmas, or Vital points, of the body in Āyurveda.

Similarly, the lines of the mystical, mesmerizing Śri Cakra Yantra intersect in 54 points, each with a masculine and feminine quality, totalling 108.

Vedic Astrology divides the heavens into 27 moon signs, called Nakṣatras, each with 4 padas, making 108 padas in all, giving 108 basic kinds of human nature. The pada occupied by the moon at the time of birth indicates the nature of one's career, pleasures, family and path to liberation.

In Indian Astrology, there are 12 houses and 9 planets. 12 times 9 equals 108.

Tantra estimates the average number of breaths per day at 21,600, of which 10,800 are solar energy, and 10,800 are lunar energy. Multiplying 108 by 100 is 10,800. Multiplying 2 x 10,800 equals 21,600.

The Nāṭya Śastra of Bhārata speaks of the 108 kāraṇas — combined movements of hand and feet — of dance

There are 18 Purāṇas, 108 Upanishads, 18 Chapters of Bhagavad Gītā, many great literary Saṁskṛta works have 108 verses and many saints prefix their name with 108, 1008.

> "There is a rhythm, a pattern, and a discipline in the whole universe. Ancient Indians knew that. That rhythm is symbolized as 108 factor or number."

* secretly hidden vital points

There are 54 letters in Saṁskṛta . Each letter is mentioned as masculine (Śiva) and feminine (Śakti) aspects, i.e 54 times 2 are 108.

According to Ancient Indian Time measure, one day of Brahma is equal to 43,20,000 years covered by four yugas, which is factor of 108.

In numerology, the 108 number breaks down to 1 + 0 + 8 = 9. Nine is a mystically-charged number, and the sum of the digits resulting from any number multiplied by 9 always returns to 9. It is said that 1 stands for God or higher Truth, 0 stands for emptiness or completeness in spiritual practice, and 8 stands for infinity of space in eight directions.

Powers of 1, 2, and 3 in Maths: 1 to 1st power=1; 2 to 2nd power=4 (2x2); 3 to 3rd power=27 (3x3x3). 1x4x27=108 i.e 1*1*2*2*3*3*3=108.

As 108 reveals us the connection between the Creation and the Creator, our effort of compiling 108 truths about Indian greatness into one book is also by Divine ordination and is in tune with cosmic rhythm.

Astronomical Talents
Antarikṣa Pratibhā

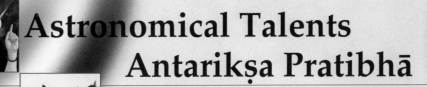

The picture above shows the Navagraha Devatās. In the center is Sūrya (Sun). In the front corner of the picture is Candra (Moon), and clockwise from there are: Kuja or Maṅgala (Mars), Rāhu (northern nodal point of the moon), Śani (Saturn), Ketu (southern nodal point of the moon), Guru or Bṛhaspati (Jupiter), Budha (Mercury), and Śukra (Venus).

Ancient India's contribution to knowledge of Astronomy is immense.

★ Vedas and Indian Astronomical texts proclaim Earth is round.

★ Indians calculated with Precision
  Occurence of eclipses.
  Circumference & diameter of Earth.
  Speed of Light.

★ Indians observed skies with the help of well-developed observatories and Instruments.

★ Indians placed sun as the centre of the solar system.

★ Ages before Newton, Indians evolved and applied Laws of Gravitation.

★ Calculus , Trignometry and Advanced Mathamatics used in Astronomy are of Indian origin.

2 Spherical Earth – Who knew it first?

Who had discovered that Earth is a sphere?

Our books teach us that it was Kepler, Copernicus, and Galileo. They all belong to 16th & 17th century AD. What was ancient India's Knowledge in this regard? Don't they know that earth was round? Yes, they do. Indians knew this fact for ages, even from ancient times.

Here are a few references to substantiate this fact…

The renowned Indian Astronomer Āryabhatta (476AD) had said:

- **"Bhūgolaḥ sarvato vṛtaḥ"- the earth is round from all sides.**

(Āryabhaṭṭiyam, Golapada, sixth śloka)

He had also accurately calculated the diameter of the Earth.

(Āryabhaṭṭiyam, Chapter 1- śloka five)

Another Indian Astronomer Varahamihira (6th century AD) in his text *"Pañca Siddāntika"* said as under

- **Pañca mahābhūtamayastrārāgaṇa pañjare mahi1golaḥ**

("Pañca Siddāntika" ***13Ch-śloka1)***

The "spherical" Earth that is made up of Pañca Bhūtas (five elements) is hanging in the space, studded by twinkling stars like an iron ball hanging in a cage.

Let us observe this Vedic mantra of Ṛgveda

- **Cakrāṇāsaḥ parīṇahaṁ pṛthivyā** (*Ṛ*ig veda 1.33.8)

It says "people who reside on the surface of the Earth's circumference."

There are many Vedic verses; many of them proclaim the spherical shape of the Earth.

Sūrya Siddhānta, an ancient Indian astronomical text reveals that truth.

- **Madhye samantāṇḍasya bhūgolo vyomni tiṣṭhati** (12th Ch-32 śloka)

"In the midst of Universe (Brahmāṇḍa), the spherical earth stands firm in the space."

Bhaskaracharya (11th century AD), the famous Mathematician, in his book titled *"Leelavathi"*, answers a question posed by the little girl Leelavathi,

- "Whatever your eyes see is not the reality. Earth is not flat as you see it. It is a sphere. If you draw a very big circle and look at the one fourth of its circumference, you see it as a straight line. But in true sense it is a circle. Similarly earth is spherical in shape."

Aryabhatta- Indian Astronomer

Āryabhaṭṭiyam the book written by Āryabhatta had been translated into Latin during 13th century. This book would have influenced the Western Astronomers.

Āryabhatta had even explained in his book the reasons for eclipse:

- **Chādayati śaśi sūryam śaśinaṁ mahati ca bhūchāyā**

(Āryabhaṭṭiyam, Golapada, śloka 37)

"When moon shadows the Sun, solar eclipse occurs, when earth shadows the Moon, lunar eclipse occurs."

He had also calculated the accurate occurrences of the eclipses; number of days Earth takes to revolve round the Sun (365 days six hours 12 minutes and 30 seconds) and number of hours that earth takes to revolve around itself (23 hours, 56 minutes, 4.1 seconds).

Even today in most of the Indian languages the term "Geography" means BHŪGOLA ŚĀSTRA. The very word "Bhūgola" means spherical earth. This shows that ages ago Indians knew that earth was spherical in shape.

Then why do we teach our children in schools that Western scientists had discovered this great truth about the shape of the Earth?

3 Many Apples had fallen before Newton's Gravity Laws

Yes, many apples, especially many Indian apples had fallen down before Newton had discovered Laws of Gravitation. Ancient Indian Astronomical texts are replete with Gravitational laws. It is not fair to say that Newton had discovered them first without giving due recognition to great Indian Astronomers.

Let us get into the facts…

- *Sūrya Siddhānta*, the classical Indian Astronomical text says "because of the *dhāraṇātmika śakti*, Earth is standing firm in the space without falling away.

  madhye samantāṇḍasya bhūgolo vyomni tiśṭhati
  bibhraṇaḥ paramām śaktim brahmaṇo dhāraṇātmikam

  (Sūrya Siddhānta 12th chapter 32 śloka)

- Varahamihira (6th century AD) had said "it is an experience of everyone that on any part of the earth, that the flames of the fire go up and the objects that were thrown up fall down.

  gaganamupaiti śikhiśikha kṣiptamapi kṣitimupaiti guru kincit
  yadvadiha mānavānām a surāṇam tadvadevājghaḥ

  (Pañca Siddhānta, 13th chapter 4th śloka)

- Bhaskaracharya (11th Century AD), the famous Indian mathematician in his text *"Leelavathi"* explains, "Earth has *guruthvākarṣṇa śakti* (Gravitational force). Due to mutual attraction between the planets, they (planets) are able to hold themselves firmly in space.

- In his other text, *"Siddhānta Shiromani,"* Bhaskaracharya reveals that, "Earth naturally attracts every object in the space towards itself. Because of this attracting force, all objects fall on the earth. When there is balance in attraction among planets where would they fall?"

> "Ancient Indian Astronomical texts are replete with Gravitational laws. It is not fair to say that Newton had discovered them first..."

ākṛṣṭa śaktiśca mahī tayā yat svastham guru svābhimukham svaśaktyā
ākṛśyate tatpatatīva bhāti same samantat kva patatviyam khe

(Siddhānta Shiromani, Bhuvanakośa, sixth śloka)

Brahmagupta (7th century AD), renowned Mathematician in his famous text *"Brahma Sputa Siddhāt,"* discloses " like water having natural downward flow, Earth also has similar attraction power, because of which all objects get attracted towards it."

- Jagad Guru Sri ĀdiŚaṅkara in his commentary on *Praśna Upaniṣat* had said, " as earth attracts the up going (thrown up) objects, so do the ever elevating *Prāṇaśakti* in the body, is being pulled down by the Apānaśakti.

  tathā pṛthivyāmabhimānini yā devatā prasidtha saiṣā
  puruṣasya apāna vṛttimavaṣṭabhyā kṛṣya vaśikrityādha eva
  apakarṣena anugraham kurvatī vartata ityarthaḥ
  anyathā hi śarīram gurutvāt patet sāvakaśe vodgacchet

  (Commentary of Ādi Śankara for 3Ch-8th śloka of Praśnopaniśat)

Many Indian texts had similar references about Gravity Laws. All these facts were revealed centuries before Newton.

4 Who goes around whom, Earth vs Sun?

Heliocentric theory of our solar system was first propounded by Copernicus in 1543. He propounded that the Sun is the centre of our universe and all the planets revolve around it. He died as soon as his book(De revolutionibus orbium coelestium) was published .As it was against the views of the holy Bible, his book had been considered as an act of persecution and was bannedin the year 1616. Afterwards in the year 1632 Galileo, supported this view and became a sinner in the eyes of Church(was condemned by inquisition and put under house arrest).

But, Indian perception about our solar system is clearly stated in Vedas and other oriental Astronomical texts. Ancient Vedic knowledge is very lucid in its expression about Sun being the centre of our Universe (Solar system).

Let us analyse few Vedic verses in this regard,

mitro dādhāra prthavīmutadyāṁ mitraḥ kṛṣṭīḥ *(Rigveda 3..59.1)*

Sun, with his attracting force is holding this earth and the other celestial bodies.

Trinābhicakramajaramanarvaṁ yenemā viśvā bhuvanāni tasthuḥ

(Ṛgveda 1.164.2)

All the celestial bodies (Planets) are moving in elliptical orbits.

āyam gauḥ pṛṣnirakramīt asadanmātaraṁ puraḥ pitaraṁ ca prayantsvaḥ

(Ṛgveda 10.189.1)

Moon being the sub-planet of earth, is revolving around its motherly planet earth and earth is revolving around its fatherly planet sun.

Sun never sets or rises, (because of earth's movements, it appears to us as sun rising in the east and setting in the west. *(Ṛgveda- Aitareya Brahman)*

Aryabhatta, had clearly explained this phenomenon with a logical principle called, **"Laghu- Guru Nyaya."** Laghu means small or light weighted object, Guru means big or heavy object. It implies that a small object revolves around a big object, like a disciple going around a Guru or Teacher. He had also stated that Moon gets Light from the Sun and so shines. He is the first person to propound that each planet moves around itself and he had accurately calculated the time taken for Earth's rotation around itself and Earth's revolution around Sun. **Sri Nilakanta Somayaji , a great mathematician of Kerala(1444-1544),even spelt out the positons of planets from the sun and depicted clearly thier orbits of motion**.In the Indian view, the Sun and the moon were also considered to be "Graham" (The meaning of the word should not be mistaken for Planet). "Graha" in Saṁskṛt means that which influences or which gets influenced.

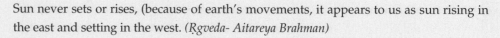

Many Astronomical and Astrological calculations of various Indian Astronomers were based on the relative positions of various celestial bodies. Hence these calculations should not be interpreted as "Earth centered universe". There was a crystal clear clarity among Indians that Sun is the centre of solar system. The Vedas, and the above-referred Indian Astronomical texts, substantiate this fact. *(Source for slokas : Ancient Indian Science and its relevance to modern world P-27; Published by Rashtriya Sanskrit Vidyapeeth, Tirupathi)*

5 Seven Colours of Sun Light

Seven colours mix together to become an intense glow of white rays of the Sun. Sir Isaac Newton, the renowned scientist of 16th century had been accredited with this Discovery. World believes this with all fanfare.

Ages before Newton, the ancient Indian Vedic knowledge had revealed that the sunlight consists of seven colours.

> **sapta tvā harito rathe vahanti deva sūrya śoacikṣeśam vicakṣaṇa** *(Ṛigveda 1.50.9)*
>
> **ava divastārayanti sapta sūryasya raśmyaḥ** (Atharvaveda 17-10-17-1)
>
> Sun's seven coloured rays are making a day.

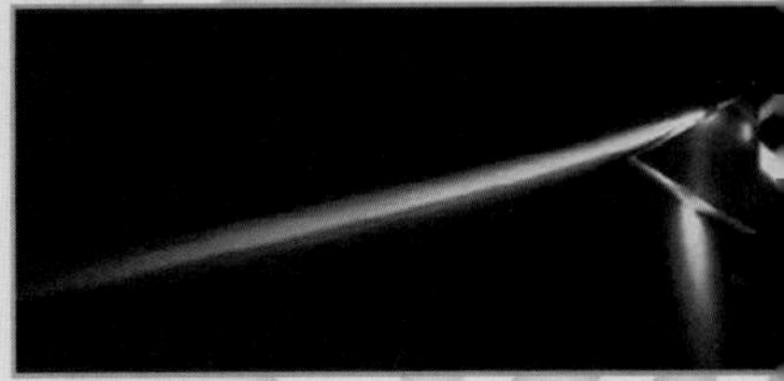

Does that mean sun has only seven rays? No, sun emits millions and millions of rays. But each ray of light has seven colours embedded in it. The Vedic terminology often refers to word "sapta aśva rūḍa". It actually means seven coloured white sunrays. The Vedic meaning of word "aśva" also means "light rays".

The *Taittirīya araṅyakam* says "eko-aśva vahati sapta namāḥ" *(Ṛg veda 1-164-2)*

It means sun Light is one (white) but called as seven; figuratively the above śloka can be expressed as sun being carried by one horse called with seven names.

Interestingly in *Chāndogya Upaniśat* there is a śloka (8-6-1); it says that sun's ray has three colours; they are blue, yellow and red. Infact this is also true in the sense that three colours are the basic colours, which diversify into other colours.

6 Measuring the Speed of Light

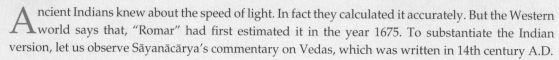

Ancient Indians knew about the speed of light. In fact they calculated it accurately. But the Western world says that, "Romar" had first estimated it in the year 1675. To substantiate the Indian version, let us observe Sāyanācārya's commentary on Vedas, which was written in 14th century A.D.

taraṇirviśvadarśato jyotiśkṛdasi sūrya viśvamā bhāsi rocanam *(Ṛig veda 1.50.4)*

For the above Ṛg Vedic śloka-verse, he had written an explanation, revealing the speed of sunlight.

yojanānaṁ sahasraṁ dve dve śate dve ca yojane
ekena nimiśārdhena krama māṇa namostu te

It means that the sunlight travels 2202 yojanas in half nimiṣa. Here yojana means 9.11 miles. According to traditional Indian calculations in one full day (including night) there are 8,10,000 half -nimishas. That means for one second there are 75/8 half nimishas(i.e. 9.375 half nimishas).

Then the speed of light should be 2202 X 9.11 X (9.375)=1,88,064 miles per second.

The above calculation is very close to the modern value estimated by the 19th century scientists' Michelson and Morley i.e 1,86,300 miles per second. The above fact had been clearly mentioned in Maxmūller's compilation of Ṛgveda, (1890), as he had taken Sāyana Bhāṣya as authority for his work of translating Vedas. Maxmüller had referred to the manuscript of Sāyanācārya's commentary (1395 AD) copy of which is now available in Baroda library for our reference.

Note: Yojana according to *Arthaśāstra* is equal to 9.11 miles, which is equal to 8000 *dhanuṣa*. One *Dhanuṣa* is equal to average man's height that is six feet. But Indian Astronomers like Āryabhatta and Brahmagupta had considered one *yojana* as equal to four *krosas*, which is equal to five miles. Thank God, they have defined their unit of measurements in their works.

7 Scaling the Eternal Time

As Time flies eternally, events fly with it and get absorbed in it. Every moment of this eternal time remains precious and puzzles us in every way. The Western world had tried to scale the time in many ways and times (occasions), but stumbled, faltered and corrected their calendars quite often.

Even ancient Indians measured time; their methods of measurement varied, but their calculations remained precise, systematic and accurate. From smallest unit of time *"liptha"* to the largest unit of time 'Yugas' and 'kalpas", our ancestors had calculated and measured time with all aptness and skill.

In the Western concepts of time, only the measure of year had been logically deduced; other units of time like day, week, month etc, are not precisely determined. Indians measured the time by relatively determining the movements of celestial objects, like planets, stars against the Earth's motion and thus evolved the unit of measurements of time. Based on celestial movements of sun and moon, Indians had invented additional measures like "Adhika māsa" (additional months) for making adjustments and for maintaining accuracy.

Day or Divas

Earth is moving around itself at the speed of 1600kms per hour. At this speed, to revolve around itself, it takes 24 hours. In this rotation, 12 hours is considered as day and remaining 12 hours is considered as night.

According to Indian measurement of time, one full day consists of 24 "horo"s. This Saṁskṛta word "horo" has become "hour" in English. This 24 horo period or 24 hour period is being called as day or *Pṛthvi divas.*

Earth revolves around the sun at the speed of one lakh kms per hour. One-degree movement of earth around sun had been considered as a solar day or sūrya divas. Moon revolves around the earth (27.3 Earth Days). Twelve-degree movement of moon in its orbit around the earth is called as lunar day or tithi or Chandra divas.

> "Indians measured the time by relatively determining the movements of celestial objects, like planets, stars against the Earths motion and thus evolved the units of measurement of time."

Week or Vaara:

Throughout the world, the week is considered as a seven-day period. This had been adopted from Indian mode of measurement. The planetary names of the days had been adpoted from India. The moon is considered to be the nearest celestial object to the earth and Saturn is the far-off planet (graham) according to Indian perspective. The sequence of planets from the earth is Moon, Mercury, Mars, Venus, Sun, Jupiter and Saturn.

During a 24-horo period or 24-hour period, each of the seven planets becomes the lord (influences most; vibrations effect more) for a period of one hour. One after another, each of the seven planets dominates for a period of one hour. Once the cycle of 24 hours gets completed, the second day starts with the continuing sequence of planetary dominance of first hour. The second day had been named after the planet, which gains the lordship in a sequence after the completion of 24-horo period or 24-hour period.

For example, Sunday or Adivar had been named after Sun (Sun and moon are also grahas according to Indian school of thought) because it occupies the first hour of the 24-horo or 24-hour period. Monday or Somavar had been named after Moon because it occupies the first hour of 24-horo or 24-hour period after the completion of first day. The sequence follows.

Fortnight & Month or Pakṣha & Māsa

During the day of Amavasyā, the moon shall be at the centre in between the Earth and the Sun. This straight-line position is taken as zero degrees. The moon's movement of 12 degrees from that position is considered as tithi or a day. During the period of such fifteen lunar days, the moon completes 180 degrees. This period is called Sukla Pakṣa and the fifteenth day is Pūrṇimā. The remaining 15-day period of Moon's motion is called Kṛṣṇa Pakṣa, which ends with Amavasyā. The two Pakṣas or two fiteen-day periods together become a lunar month or māsa of 30-day period. Two months become one season or Ṛtu and twelve months become one full year.

Our ancestors had identified 27 stellar constellations (Nakṣatra Maṇḍal) in the space and each of them had been classified into four parts or Padas. These 108 padas are divided into groups of Nine. So there are 12 such groups called Rāśis or Zodiac signs. They are Mīna Rāśi, Meṣa Rāśi, Vṛṣhabha Rāśi, Kanyā Rāśi etc. Based on these Rāśis the solar months have come into existence.

Lunar months that are in vogue are formed based on twelve stellar constellations. These stellar constellations are visible throughout the night sky, starting from dusk to dawn. Each month is named after a star that is visible throughout the night sky during that month begining from the full moon day. The following table indicates the visibity of the star throughout the night and the respective name of each month, derived from it.

Month –Star	**Month –Star**	**Month-Star**
Chitram- Chitra	*Sravanam- Sravanam*	*Margasira-Mrigasira*
Vaisaka- Visaka	*Badrapada- Purvabhadra*	*Pushya- Pushya*
Jyestham- Jyesta	*Asvayuja- Aswini*	*Maagha- Magha*
Ashadham- Ashada	*Karthika- Krithika*	*Phalguna- Phalguni*

"According to Indian measurement of time, one full day consists of "24" "horos". This Sanskrit word "horo" has become "hour" in English. This 24 horo period or 24hour period is being called as day or Pruthvi divas."

Earth is slanting by $23^1/_2$ degrees towards north–west. Sun's rays fall perpendicularly on both sides of the equator by the $23^1/_2$ degrees between north–south directions.

The line transcending $23^1/_2$ degrees from north of equator is called Karkaṭaka Rekhā; the line transcending $23^1/_2$ degrees from south of equator is called Makara Rekhā.

The six-month period of travel of Sun's Rays from Makara Rekhā to Karkaṭaka Reka is called Uttarāyaṇa and the vice versa is called Dakshinayana. The point of transition is called Sankranti. There would be two sankrantis in a year.

Year

Sun travels at a speed of one lakh kmph, the distance of 96,60,00,000 kms in 365 days. This period of travel is called a year.

Yugas

Once in 4,32,000 years all the seven planets group together.

The span of 4,32,000 years had been considered as Yuga. Period of Kali Yuga is 4,32,000 years.

Span of two Kali Yugas is one Dvāpara Yuga.

Span of three Kali Yugas is one Tretā Yuga.

Span of four Kali yugas is one Satya Yuga.

The period of four yugas is one ChaturYuga or Mahā Yuga. It is a period of 43,20,000 years.

72 such Mahā yugas are equal to one Manvantaram.

14 such Manvantarams are equal to one bright day of Brahmā (excluding night) means 1000 Mahā yugas, i.e 432,00,00,000 years. This is called one kalpa. One full day of Brahmā i.e (bright day +night)

is equal to 864 crore years. Brahmā has such 365 days as one year and one hundred years of life span. One life span of Brahmā is equal to one day of Vishnu. The cosmic age is equal to Brahmā's life span.

Let us analyse how wonderfully the knowledge of time had been intermingled in the daily rituals of Indians. The Saṇkalpa of Hindus goes as under by which, Second October 2006 had been explained, herewith,

"By the order of *Sri MahaViṣṇu,* I take this resolve and make prayer, as on Brahmā's 51 year, *(Dwithiya parardhay)* of *Sweta Varaha kalpay* (kalpa is one day for Brahmā), which is in the ruling period of *Vaivaswata Manu* during the first part of *Kali Yuga,* in *Jwambu Dwipa*, in *Bharata Varsha*, in *Bharata khaṇḍa,* in the southern side of meru mountains, towards the north eastern side of Srisailam ranges, in the land embedded between Krishna and Cauvery rivers, at my residing house, in the presence of all deities, Brahmanas, Gurus and family members, by following the lunar measurement of time, in the year named *"vyaya"* during the southern part of six months (*Dakshinayanam*), in the *Sarad Ruthu* (season), *Aswyayuja masa* (lunar month) during the receding fortnight of moon (*krishnapakshay*) on the Tenth day of fortnight (*Dasami tithi*), Monday (*Somavara*), *Uttarashada* (stellar constellation) and let all the *Subha yogas* and *Subha karanas* be bestowed during this auspisicious time as I perform my actions."

Are we not struck with awe, as we look at the above saṅkalpa, wherein we find a perfect blend of time & space to reveal the identity of an event. Our seers had wonderful knowledge of time and the way it had been intermingled in the daily rituals clearly proves beyond doubt about their ingeniousness, their systematically perfected outlook and scientifically evolved perspective. The above example, confirms the fact that Indians considered Time & space as relative to each other.

"Our seers had wonderful knowledge of time and the way it had been intermingled in the daily rituals like "Sankalpa" clearly proves beyond doubt about their ingeniousness, their systematically perfected outlook and scientifically evolved perspective."

8 Jantar – Mantar, a place for monitoring Heavens

At least in the field of ancient Indian Astronomy, we are left with certain classical Astronomical texts. Thanks, to the efforts of ancient Indian Astronomers.

Āryabhattiyam, Siddhānta-śiromaṇi, Bhṛhat-samhitā, Sūrya-siddhānta Brahmaspuṭa-siddhānta, Śiśyādhivridhida, etc are the texts that stand today as credentials of advanced Astronomical Knowledge of India.

The facts and concepts that were discussed in these books are in tune with modern Astronomical findings and at many instances they excel the present day knowledge.

To perceive astronomical facts, one requires certain special instruments. What were the instruments that were used by ancient Indian Astronomers? If they had used instruments, what happened to them today? Do they exist today? If they had disappeared with the passage of Time, do we, atleast have suitable references about their usage?

Jantar Mantar, Delhi, built by Raja JaiSingh

Most of the Indian Astronomical Instruments might have been destroyed during various foreign invasions on India. Today, we get the glimpses of their usage from the ancient astronomical texts. For example, Āryabhatta, the renowned Astronomer lived near Kusumapura during the Fifth century AD. He was monitoring heavens from an observatory called *"Khagola"* kha means space, gola means spherical instrument. Some believe that Indian astronomy got its name khagola-śāstra from the observatory of Āryabhatta.

Lalla, a famous Astronomer wrote a text called *"śiśyādhivridhida"*. In that text, he explains twelve kinds of astronomical instruments called yantras. They are

(1) Gola yantra (2) Bhagan yantra (3) Chakra yantra (4) Dhanus yantra (5) Gatiyantra (6) Sanku yantra (7) Shataka yantra (8) Karthari yanthra (9) Pita yantra (10) Kapala yantra (11) Shalaka yantra (12) Yasthi yantra.

Bhaskaracharya's text Siddhānta-śiromaṇi describes about Nadivalaya yantra and other yantras, which were used to calculate planetary motions and determine time.

In recent times, the person who had revived the lost knowledge about our Indian Astronomy and re-constructed the Astronomical yantras or instruments was none other than the Raja of Jaipur, Sawai Jaisingh-II.

Raja Jaisingh was a vassal king of Moghul Empire. During 1724-1727, he established Astronomical observatories called, "Jantar-Mantar" and hoisted the Flag of Indian talent. He founded them in five cites namely Delhi, Jaipur, Mathura, Ujjain and Varanasi. Among them except Mathura all the remaining four observatories exist today.

These observatories exhibit not only astronomical excellence but also architectural splendour and Engineering Ingenuity. The Sundial of Jaipur is the biggest exisisting Sundial of the world today. It observes various movements of Sun and the angles of other celestial objects.

"Sasthamsa yantra" can easily calculate the diameter of sun *"Jayaprakash yantra"* can study the nightsky and stars. *"Kapala yantra"* a bowl shaped instrument had been used to determine the latitudes and longitude and thus enabled astronomers to depict the picture of celestial space. *"Ramayantra"* had been constructed in cylindrical shape to record the movements of Astronomical objects.

Sun Dial at Jantar mantar

A few modern historians are of the view, that Jaisingh was influenced by Arabic and Persian Astronomy. But the instruments that were built by Jaisingh in his observatories had been mentioned in ancient Indian astronomical texts. Alburni, the Arab historian says, Indian Astronomy, Chemistry, Mathematics and Medicine influenced Arabia and Persia in many ways.

9 Comets

A train of light rarely appears in the sky. It is called as "Dhuma-ketu" by ancient Indians. Today we call it, Comet. The word "Comet" in Latin means the one that has long hairs. The Western world never had knowledge about these comets till Edmond Halley in the year 1759 pioneered the study about the comets. He propounded that once in 95 years, these comets visit us. One of the comets had been named after Halley.

The ancient Indian Astronomical texts dealt with the knowledge of comets very extensively. They are (1) *Bhṛhat vimana śāstra* written by *Bharadwaj* (2) *Agastya's śakti tantra* (3) *Jaimini's keta sarvasva*

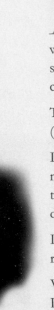

In *"Vimana Sastra"* in the chapter *"Kriya Sara Tantra"* we find mention of Dhuma-ketus. It had been mentioned in that text, that there are 3,07,30,221 Comets in the space. Among them around eight thousand are empowered with electrical currents. Twelve of them are very fierce, powerful and dangerous.

In Agastya's *śakti tantra,* the names of Twelve Comets are given. It had been mentioned that during rainy season the potency of comets would be very high.

Vimana Sastra says that the Comets are formed because of Sun burning certain objects in its vicinity. Please do not forget the word "Dhuma" in Saṁskṛta means smoke or gases. The modern knowledge about the comets also concurs with that. Modern science explains that because of the proximity of certain celestial objects to the sun, the gases in them get combusted and become a stream, which appears as a tail or train of Light.

Medical Talents
Ārogya Pratibhā

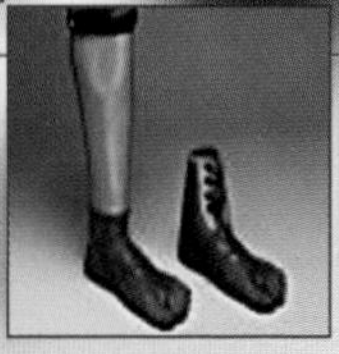

10 Pioneering the Surgery – World's First Surgeons

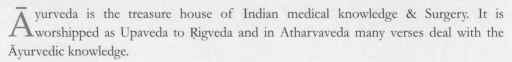

Āyurveda is the treasure house of Indian medical knowledge & Surgery. It is worshipped as Upaveda to Ṛigveda and in Atharvaveda many verses deal with the Āyurvedic knowledge.

This "knowledge-chest" is a gift to world from the great seers of yore like *Bharadwaj, Atreya, Agnikaya, Charaka, Dhanvantari, Suśruta* and many others. In fact, it is an eternal gift of India to the world.

In Ṛigveda the verses (1.116.14 & 15), mention that, a woman warrior called "Vischala" the queen of king Khela, had been fitted with an artificial Iron leg by the Aśvini physicians, when she lost her leg in a war. These physicians were adored for eye transplantation in the next verse.

Indians pioneered surgery ages ago, Suśruta (500B.C) was the World's earliest Surgeon. He learnt the skills of surgery from Dhanvantari (considered to be God Viṣṇu) and wrote a treatise on surgery and Āyurveda called "Suśruta Samhitā" which had stood the test of time and is even now being followed.

In his text he had divided the methods of surgery into eight parts :

1. *Chedya* –cutting
2. *Lekhya*- separating
3. *Vedhya*- removing the toxic objects from the body.
4. *Ishya*- probing the blood capillaries for finding the cause of disease.
5. *Aharya kriya*- eliminating the production of harmful elements in the body.

6. *Visradavya-* removing water from the body

7. *Civya-* suturing

8. *Bedhya kriya-* making holes and performing surgery

We find the mention of advanced level of surgery, the plastic surgery mostly Rhenoplastary in Suśruta Samhitā. These surgeries were performed to reconstruct the noses and ears. He performed many eye surgeries. There are many references about Caesarean operations. Indians not only performed surgeries, but also studied the human Anatomy by dissecting dead bodies. In Suśruta Samhitā, we find many methods of preserving dead bodies for dissection. Suśruta had mentioned about 125 surgical instruments in his treatise.

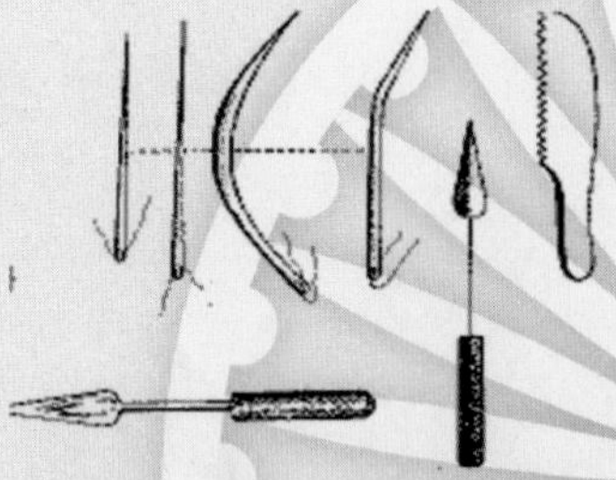

Surgical instruments-Sushruta samhita

In Bhoja Prabandha (927AD), it had been mentioned that king Bhoja had undergone a surgical treatment, for getting a tumor removed from the brain. The King had been administered Anesthesia called "Sammohini" while the surgery was being performed.

Gauthama Buddha's physician called Devaka had performed many surgeries. Buddhistic texts mention about them. "Vinaya Piṭika" a buddhistic text reveals that germs in the brain were removed by performing a surgery.

The photograph of a person on whom, the plastic surgery was performed. Photograph was taken during the British rule of India.

Āyurvedic knowledge adopts surgery as a last measure in treatment, but it focuses mostly on prevention than cure. It laid stress on bio-medical remedies though aware of chemical pharmacology and surgical interventions. All the books like *"Charaka Samhita"*, *"Aṣṭāṅga Hṛidaya"*, and *"Bhavaprakasa"* including *"Suśruta Samhitā"* mention about medicinal plants. Today, Western world had understood its potentiality and has become crazy after medicinal plants. Madhava's *"Nidana Sāstra"* contains diagnosis of various diseases by observing human gestures and smells that emitted from the body.

11 Āyurveda – A Therapeutical Treasure

Knowledge of Ayurveda had descended from Lord Brahma to Prajapati, from Prajapati to Ashwini kumars, from them to Indra, from Indra to Bharadwaj, from him to Atreya, and to his disciples Agnivesha, Khela, Harita and others. Over a period of time it got divided into two schools of thought 1. Atreya Parampara 2. Dhanvantari Parampara.

In Atreya parampara, kaya-chikitsa (medicine/bodily treatment) is given prime importance. The famous text of this school of thought is Charaka Samhita, named after the famous physician, Charaka.

In Dhanvantari parampara salya-chikitsa (Surgery) also had been dealt with. In the line of surgery Sushruta is considered to be an authority and the famous treatise is Sushruta Samhita, written by him.

Apart from the above two schools of thought, Siddha medicine founded by sage Agastya is famous, even today in South India. In the yogic text *Yoga Vashishta,* it has been said that diseases first orginate in mental plane, slowly they descend to pranic plane and then affect various nerves, arteries and veins, which in turn result in the bodily aliments etc.

Indian medical science had linked human thoughts to human health and evolved the therapeutical knowledge ages ago. The purer and positive the thoughts, the better the health.

Today, modern medicine is slowly accepting the psychosomatic reasons for the advent of diseases. For this reason Yoga, Ayurveda and Naturopathy are becoming popular as alternative medicine to Allopathy. Our seers who had bequeathed us this knowledge deserve to be thanked, adored and worshipped.

Charaka Samhita, talks about a healthy person in the following lines

samadoṣaḥ samāgniśca samadhātu malakriyaḥ
prasannātmendriya manāḥ svastha ityabhidhīyate।

In whom there is a balance of three doshas like vata, pita, kapha; seven dhathus like lymph, blood, flesh, fatty tissue, bone, bonemarrow and semen and malakriya (proper balance excretion of fasces, urine and sweat) and who has self control of sense organs and mind, such a person has been defined as a healthy person.

Even from Vedic times the knowledge of Ayurveda had been divided into eight parts

1. *Kaya chikitsa* - General medicine & therapeutics
2. *Kaumara-bhritya*- Paediatrics & obsterics
3. *Shalya tantra*- Surgery
4. *Shalakyatantra* –ENT, ophthalmology
5. *Bhutavidya*-Psychiatary & Para psychic studies
6. *Vishatantra*- Toxicology
7. *Rasayana*-Rejuvenation therapy
8. *Vajikarana*- Virilification therapy

Medicinal plants:

"Nature is bestowed with suitable and necessary medicines for all kind of diseases," says Charaka. In his Charaka Samhita, around 582 kinds of medicinal plants have been mentioned. Similarly in Sushruta Samhita, around 496 medicinal plants have been described. From them, many medicinal preparations like powders, tonics and distillations are prepared.

Alchemy & Medicine:

Acharya Nagarjuna and Vagbatta had used many chemical preparations including metals and alloys as medicines. Many of the Alchemy's methods were adopted by Arabs and from the Europeans.

Today, modern medicine is slowly accepting the psychosomatic reasons for the advent of diseases. For this reason Yoga, Ayurveda and Naturopathy are becoming popular as alternative medicine to Allopathy.

Pañcakarma treatment: (Methods of Internal Cleansing)

Charaka Samhitā -sūtrasthāna (chapter 16- verses 17-21) describes Pañca karma treatment. The concept of Pañca karma is to keep the stomach clean from toxicities and impurities (Tridoṣas). If the stomach (the internal furnace within the body for all metabolic reactions) is clean, the person would be free from many kinds of diseases.

1. *Vaman*- Emesis (through vomiting, doṣas are cured)
2. *Viraychanam*- Purgation
3. *Basti*-enema
4. *Nasya*-administrating medicines through nose
5. *Raktamokshan*-Bloodletting

After Pañchakarma treatment, the sense organs work efficiently. Colour of the skin becomes bright. Person obtains enough strength and would not appear aged. In Raktamokṣa therapy usage of leeches is popular. Today it is being called as Leech therapy. Suśruta Samhitā "Sūtrasthāna" (13 &19 paras) clearly describes the usage of leeches in the therapy. Kudos! To knowledge that has used mother's milk for therapeutical usage in 70 diseases. For example it is said, that milk of women of black colour can cure many eye diseases.

Famous Āyurvedic Texts Available today

1. *Ṛig veda & Atharva veda*
2. *Charaka Samhitā (600 BC)*
3. *Suśruta Samhitā (500 BC)*
4. *Aṣṭāṅga Hṛidaya (vāgbhatta-600AD)*
5. *Sarangadhara Samhitā (1200AD)*
6. *Bhava Prakaśaka (1600AD)*
7. *Madhava's Nidāna Śāstra (700AD)*

12 Hṛdayam – for Healthy Heart Beats

William Harvey, (1628AD) a British scientist, had found that heart is essential for blood circulation, but could not describe how blood reaches the heart and flows from it. In the year 1669 a scientist named Marcello Malphigi clearly described how blood flows into Heart and comes out of it.

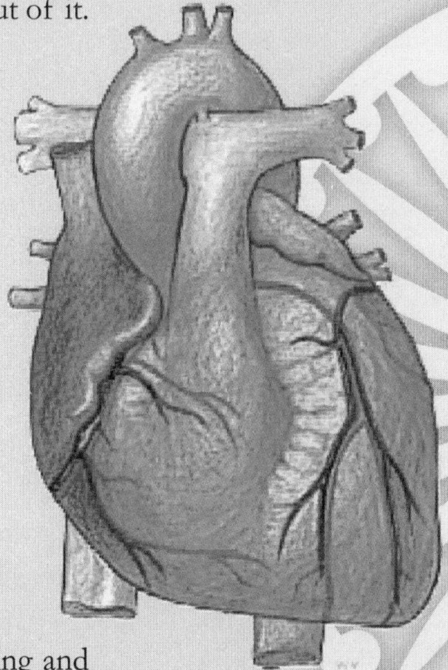

Now, let us hear the echoes of ancient Indian heartbeats and its hearty revelations.

Satapatha Brahmana of Yajur Veda, had defined Hṛdayam (the heart) as under,

"Hru" means *"harinay"* (that receives)

"Da" means *"daanay"* (that gives)

"Ya" means *"enngathow"* (that circulates)

That which receives (blood), gives and circulates is called Hṛdayam.

Nirukṭha śāstra had defined Hṛdayam as follows

harāterdadāterayaterhṛdayaśabdaḥ *(Niruktam)*

Suśruta says:

kapha pittāvaruddhastu māruto rasa mūrcitaḥ
hṛdisthaḥ kurute śulam uccvāsārodhakaṁ param

"Heart diseases are caused because of "kapha" and "Pita" doṣas (defects) and thus thickening and narrowing of coronary arteries resulting in acute pain in the chest and difficulty in breathing."

Charaka says:

tanmahattā mahāmūlāh taccaujaḥ parirakṣatā
parihāryā viśeṣena manaso duḥkhahetavaḥ *(Charaka Samhitā Sūtrasthānam 30/13)*

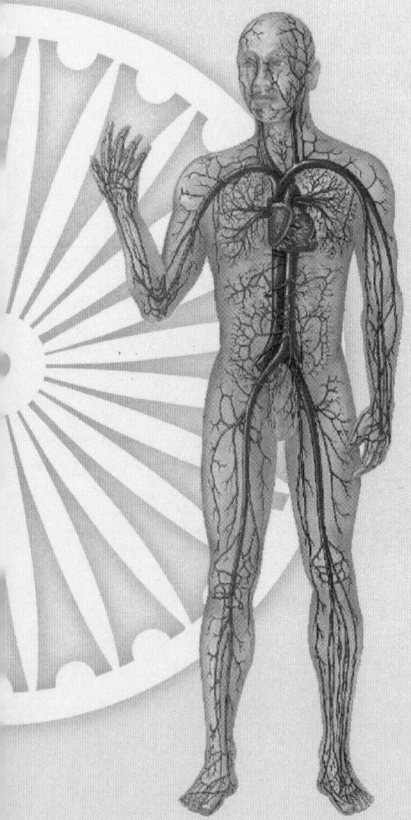

hṛdyam yat syādyadaujasyaṁ srotasām yat prasādanam
tattat sevyaṁ prayatnena praśamo jñānameva ca

(Charaka Samhitā Sūtrasthānam 30/14)

"Those who want to preserve "Ojas" and maintain heart in good condition should be away from mental worries and should exhibit self-restraint in diet and should consume the medicines that increase vital priniciple (ojas) and blood circulation. For healthy Heartbeats, meticulous efforts are to be made to obtain tranquility with awareness & wisdom.

Indian traditional medical knowledge had rightly recognized the preventive measures for the Heart diseases ages ago and advised suitably to exercise self-restraint and adopt moderate food habits and a composed mindset. If these suggestions are followed today, one can avoid heart surgeries and expenditure.

The Rasa is the energy produced from well-digested food. It is stored in the Heart. From the heart entering through the 24 arteries, 10 going upward, 10 going downward and four horizontal, it satisfies, grows and maintains the entire body every day by an invisible force or cause. Blood is carried from heart to the entire body through them. (Ref: Suśruta Samhitā, Sutrasthānam, adhyāyaḥ 14 para -3)

It has been mentioned in the book, "Nighantu Ratnākara, that "vrinda" medicinal plant Terminalia Arjuna (Arjuna tree) is used to cure heart diseases.

13 Test Tube Babies

In the year 1978-80, modern medical knowledge had claimed that it had achieved a miracle in the history of human race. Female ovum and male semen had been fertilized in a test tube and was transferred into uterus. Thus, the first test tube baby was born.

Is this for the first time in the history of mankind such miracles have happenend? No, ages ago, many such instances had occurred on Indian soil.

Let us first refer to Ṛig Veda. Sage Agastaya's birth is not from the mother's womb. He had been fertilized in a pot. (Refer Ṛig Veda 7.33.13)

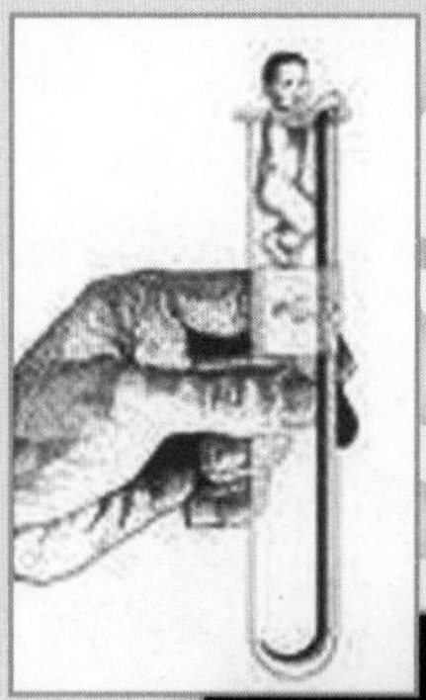

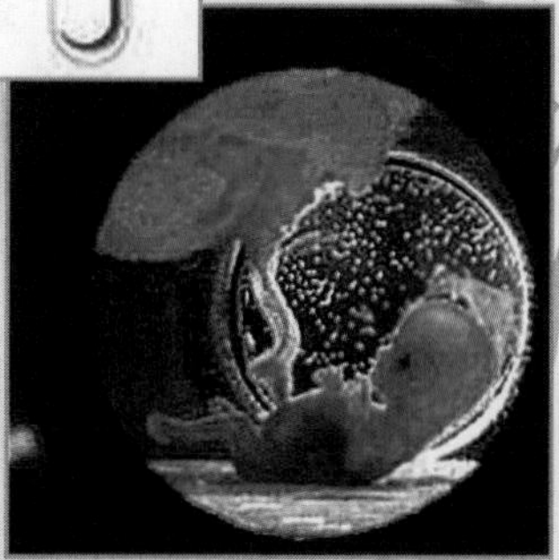

In Mahābhārata, there are a few instances of childbirth similar to today's test tube babies:

- Let us look into the episode of Droṇa, the guru of Pāṇḍavas and Kauravas. He is said to have been born only from the sperm of male, without the female ovum in a vessel called "Droṇi" under the technical guidance and supervision of sage Bharadwāj. Hence he had is famous by the name Droṇācārya.
- King Drupada had performed a yajña to bring forth Draupadi and her brother Drushtadyumna. The methodology referred therein, resembles the cloning concepts of today.
- Sage Gautama had created twins Kripa and Kripi by using certain vessels, rather instruments. Hence they became famous by those names resembling the shape of the vessels.
- We are all aware of the famous episode of the birth of Kauravas. When Kauvara Queen Gāndhāri had undergone self-abortion, sage Vyāsa collected the foetus and preserved it in one hundred and one pots and thus could produce 100 Kaurava Brothers and one sister Dussala.

All these frequent references are not figments of imagination, but are the instances of the then prevailing knowledge about the birth of babies, that are not from the mother's womb.

14 Benefiting from the Cow

On June 2003, American patent office had given patent to "Go-Mūtram" (cow-urine) as an antibiotic in curing diseases like tuberculosis and cancer. This product had been patented by Nagpur NGO "Go-vijñāna Ansundhāna Kendram".

This news had created sensation among medical community worldwide and debate, discussion and research got initiated in many medical universities throughout the world. Today a new science called "Cowpathy" is evolving.

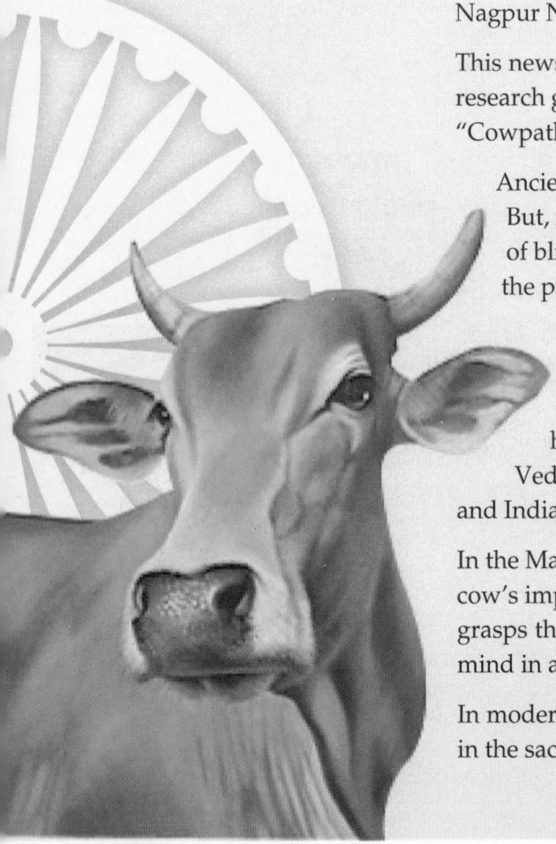

Ancient Indians had indepth knowledge of "Pañchagavya chikitsā" including cow urine therapy. But, for centuries modern medicine had considered the cow urine therapy as a primitive practice of blind beliefs. Medical fraternity had woken up recently to the reality and started recognizing the potential therapeutic value of Cow products.

Indians worship cow as holy mother. Indian Cow is respected as the embodiment of all divine forces. Gifting a cow is considered to be the greatest of all charities. During the performance of yagnas and yajñas, Cow & Cow products are very essential. Indian culture has placed cow in the sacred position of "Kāmadhenu" (the wish-fulfilling holy Deity). Vedas, Purāṇas and Itihāsas, all adore the sanctity and utility of cow in many ways. Holy cow and Indian life have a sacred bondage. Ṛgveda says that killing a cow is the greatest of all crimes.

In the Mahābhārata, Anuśasanaparva, Bhiṣma reveals about the greatness of Goumati yaga and holy cow's importance. He further says, if anyone studies (any kind of subject) by staying near a cow, one grasps the essence of that study in no time, as cow always emits positive vibrations which keep the mind in a composed state.

In modern times, the first Indian war of Independence (Sepoy mutiny) in the year 1857 had its roots in the sacrilege made to Cow.

In India, Brāhmaṇas, Kṣatriyas, Vaiśyas and Sūdras all worship and benefit from the cow in many ways. From giving milk, ploughing fields, performing yajñas and up to curing many diseases, Cow helps Indians; Cow protects them and nourishes them in every way. Lord Kṛṣṇshna being a cowherd is dear to millions and millions of devoted hearts.

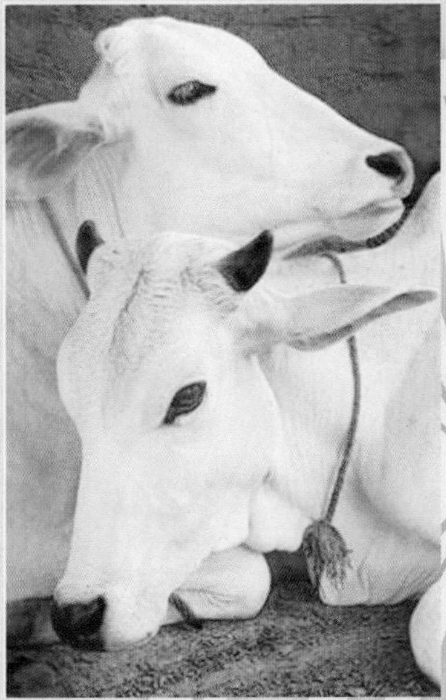

Pañcagavya Chikitsā

In preparation of Āyurvedic medicines, the Pañca Gavyas (Five cow products) are used very extensively. The Pañcagavyas are (1) Cow Milk (2) Curd (3) Ghee (4) Urine (5) Cow Dung.

In the famous Ayurvedic texts like Charaka, Sushruta and Vāgbhatta Samhitās, Pancha Gavyas are used to cure skin diseases, urinary problems, kneejoint pains and ulcers.

In Indian agriculture, Cow's role can never be de-linked or belittled. Cow dung is natural manure, being used by Indians since ancient times. Cow urine and neem leaves are mixed together and used as a pesticide. Many NGOs are working in furtherance of research in this regard.

Treatment with Pañca Gavyas had obtained prominence and importance after WHO started recognizing the traditional health remedies worldwide. In America and Africa, Pañca gavya is being used and tested for curing AIDS and clinical results seem to be encouraging.

Modern medicine is accepting these cow products as anti-biotics and bio-enhancers.

Normally environmentalists raise their voice about adverse green effects and pollution of burning firewood. Interestingly, the fire obtained by burning cowdung cakes had cleaned the atmosphere instead of polluting it. The holy process of Agnihotra is becoming popular throughout the world for its miraculous cleaning effects.

When Bhopal gas tragedy struck, a household, where there was regular practice of the ritual of Agnihotra, was not affected; whereas the neighboring households had to run amuck in fear of poisonous hazards that the gas leak had created. The research findings point to the Agnihotra Fire, which was created by burning cowdung cakes, that fire had protected that small family by cleaning the atmosphere that night.

It is our duty to protect Cow. Today, many Gow-Rakṣaṇa Samitis had been formed at many places to protect cows. In these cow-protection movements Gujaratis, Marwaris and some voluntary & spiritual organizations had taken a lead role and are doing their best to spread the awareness.

Indian agriculture and Indian lifestyle are
intimately linked to the cow.
As we protect the cow,
so does the cow protect us.

15 Tulasi – The Wonder Herb

Tulasi redeems us from all sins. Tulasi provides us with all the wealth. Tulasi and Indian families have symbiotic relationship. A house without Tulasi plant is like a temple without deity.

Since ancient times, in every Indian household, Tulasi occupies a prominent place. Every backyard of the Indian house is adorned with Tulasi Fort. (Structure that is built around Tulasi). Indians believe Tulasi as an incarnation of goddess Lakshmi. Indians worship the holy Basil (Tulasi) every day at a prescribed time.

There are many varieties of Tulasi. The popularly adopted Tulasi plants are (1) Kṛṣṇa Tulasi (2) Rāma Tulasi (3) Lakshmi Tulasi.

- Kṛṣṇa Tulasi is widely used in preparing medicines. Tulasi and pepper powder are used to cure malarial fever. Tulasi and Ginger are made into juice and are used to alleviate the knee joint pains.
- Vomitings can be avoided by consuming curd or honey mixed with Tulasi seeds.
- For curing asthmatic problems, the essence of Kṛṣṇa tulasi leaf and black pepper combination works wonders.
- For skin disorders, paste made of Tulasi and Lemon can be applied externally.
- For soar throat, water is boiled along with Tulasi leaves and is consumed. Tulasi rasa reduces Kapha doṣa and re-energizes the body.

Modern research

1. It reduces glucose levels and is being used to cure Diabeties
2. It reduces cholestral levels

3. As a Cox-2 Inhibitor, it is being used as a pain reliever in cancer treatment

4. To store food grains

Certain Viṣu devotees do not use Tulasi as a medicinal herb and consider it as a sacred plant. They consume Tulasi water (Tirtha) for purification of sins.

Tulasi beads are used in Japa and Meditation. Garlands of fresh Tulasi leaves are offered to deities in temples every day. In Hindu temples, holy Tulasi water is given to devotees as Tirtha.

Tulasi is worshipped as the incarnation of Goddess Lakshmi.

During the month of Kārtika, Tulasi Vivaha (Wedding of Tulasi) is grandly celebrated. Hindus consider that day as a very auspicious day.

In *Agastya Samhita* it is said that, by planting Tulasi, watering Tulasi, worshipping Tulasi, rather touching Tulasi, one obtains mokṣa, the enlightenment.

Hindus believe that Tulasi plant contains all the holy rivers, all the Vedas and all the deities. Persons on the deathbed are watered with *"Tulasi Tīrtha"* by pouring a few drops into the mouth. It is believed that, Tulasi purifies them from sins and gives them better positions (circumstances) in the next life.

Tulasi, the holy plant, the wonder herb, the sin redeemer is always with us from our birth to death, as an eternal companion.

16 Long drawn battles for Turmeric and Neem

Beware! Applying Turmeric paste on the wounds is a Punishable offence!! If one gets Chickenpox and Measles, then to use Neem products in their treatment, we require permission from multi-national companies. Otherwise one has to face court cases.

This is the situation, we Indians are forced into. A few European and American based multi-national companies claim that they own the knowledge about Turmeric and Neem as medicinal products, as they have patented them.

During the decade (1995-2005), Indian voluntary organizations, Indian Governmental institutions and a few intellectuals of Indian origin had waged fierce intellectual battles with US patent offices and multi-national companies.

It became a Herculean task to convince them that usage of Neem and Turmeric as medicinal herbs is known to Indians since ancient times and had been mentioned extensively in Āyurvedic texts. Not only Neem & Turmeric but also Lemon, Gauva, Āmlā and many such Āyurvedic medicines are being subjected to similar destiny.

Once we (Indians) were ridiculed, belittled and disparaged as charm-healers of blind faith for using Neem leaves and Turmeric. Today after understanding their potential medicinal value, these Western companies, patent them and bar us from using them. Does it not appear foul, funny, visicous, scornful, brutal and deceitful?

Before getting dragged into this controversy, let us understand the greatness of these wonder drugs.

Neem

In every Indian village, in front of every household, there appears a neem tree. Cattle are sheltered under its shade. During summer nights, people sleep under the Neem's breezy shade. Even today 50% of Indians use Neem sticks as toothbrush. Neem paste is applied over body while taking bath. Preparing toilet soap from Neem oil & Neem seeds is known to Indians for ages. Vaginal application of neem oil by the women prevents pregnancy. Indian monks use Neem as a medicine to subside their carnal passions. Neem oil is used for lighting lamps. Lamps lit by Neem oil act as good Mosquito repellents.

The traditional agricultural text *"Upavanavinodī"* had elucidated the usage of neem in agriculture. It has been described as an effective pesticide. The text mentions the names of about 200 insects that neem can effectively eliminate. Every part of neem tree, enhances the fertility of the soil multifold.

In Āyurvedic classical texts like Charaka & Suśruta Samhitas, Neem's medicinal value had been greatly described. During the last 50 years many Indian voluntary organizations, Āyurvedic experts had done extensive research and had enhanced the knowledge of Neem's medicinal, cosmetic and pesticidal usage and value.

Efforts of Indian Agricultural Research Institute, Malarial Research Institute, Tata Energy Research Centre, and Khadi Gramodyog are laudable.

Now let us get into patent battle and see what exactly had happened,

- 1995- European patent office in Munich (Germany) had given patent to American Agricultural Institute and to a company called W.R.Grace for usage of Neem.
- 2000- India raises objection against this patent right. After effective legal battles, the patent

had been revoked by a court order. The role of Indian environmentalist Vandana Shiva in this crusade is admirable.

- 2001- Multinational company W.R.Grace opted for an appeal to cancel the revocation.
- 2005- Appeal was set-aside by declaring Neem as traditional medicine since many people know the knowledge of its usage. Finally the Patent that was issued had been cancelled.

Turmeric

Traditional Indian women's beautiful face shines brightly with Turmeric's lustre. Without applying Turmeric paste to face, hands and legs, Indian women never take bath. This is applied just not only to beautify the skin, but also used as medicinal protection and for auspiciousness.

Kumkum or Red Tilak that adorns the face of every Hindu is made by powdering Turmeric and drying it after mixing it with Lime. The yogic spot on the fore head is protected with this Kumkum and considered sacred by Indian women.

Every Indian threshold shines brightly with Turmeric paste and Kumkum, a product obtained from Turmeric.

Turmeric is used in Indian rituals and worship. Turmeric is used in cooking, not just for adding colour but also for preparing a healthy dish.

In many of the Indian households, it is a practice to consume Turmeric along with milk for effective control of cough, cold and sorethroat. Turmeric vapours are inhaled to clear the Phlem in the lungs.

Turmeric is used very extensively for dying the clothes. Many Āyurvedic medicines are prepared by using Turmeric as an important ingredient. Turmeric is applied on the wounds to heal injuries.

This practice confirms Indian knowledge about the anti-septic nature of this great herb.

According to an article published in the *Hindu* dated 25 April 2005, Turmeric is being used in treating the Alzheimer's disease. It is even applied as a preventive medicine in its treatment. Dr. Cinthapalli Rao and his collegues, at American Health Foundation, New York, have succeeded in using Turmeric in cancer ailments.

In the year 1995 American patent office had granted patent to Mississippi Medical Centre (5401504). With this, the age-old knowledge of applying Turmeric, as a medicine became the intellectual property of that Institute.

Dr Mashelkar, renowned environmental activist , had filed objection to the above patent. His untiring "knowledge crusade" during the last decade had ultimately yielded the results. Recently the patent issued to the above said institute had been revoked.

How longer have we to fight these kinds of Knowledge battles? The traditional Indian medical texts are replete with the knowledge of using more than 1,50,000 medicinal herbs. How to save them from being patented? One of the effective solutions is to digitalize the knowledge that is latent in our Āyurvedic texts. Preparing the effective database of medicinal plants is a gigantic task that requires untiring efforts and huge funds. Many patriotic citizens of India have taken up this challenge. It is believed that more than 5000 Indian Herbs have been already patented. It is time that we have to build up a great movement to protect our traditional medicinal knowledge. Let us be united in our efforts and move forward effectively for the glory of Motherland.

17 Copper shields our Health

Today, we prefer bottled mineral water, of course! cleaned and purified. We often purchase purified, potable water and drink it. We take this precaution to protect ourselves from ill health, which is often caused by contaminated water or impure water. This health tip is not just modern, but known to Indians ages ago. They knew the technique of purifying water and preserving it.

Ancient Indians used copper and brass vessels to purify and store water. They used to drink water in the copper pots and tumblers. This practice had drawn attention of many modern researchers. They wanted to find the rationale behind the age-old usage of copper and brass vessels for drinking and storing water.

Today, after indepth investigations, it has been found that, the sunlight that falls on the copper vessels instantly eliminates microbes present in the water by a chemical reaction. Thus, water is protected from contamination.

Rob Reed, a London-based Micro-Biologist had verified this fact by filling the copper, plastic and earthen vessels with Escherichia coli bacteria which causes diseases like dysentery etc. After 24 hrs bacteria in copper vessels got dramatically reduced and at the end of 48 hours there were no traces of bacteria in copper vessels. On the other hand, the bacteria in the plastic and earthen vessels got increased substantially.

(Source: The Hindu dt 20.4.2005)

Today, Indian star hotels serve rich delicacies and doubly purified water in copper vessels.

18 Successful Jai – "Poor" Foot

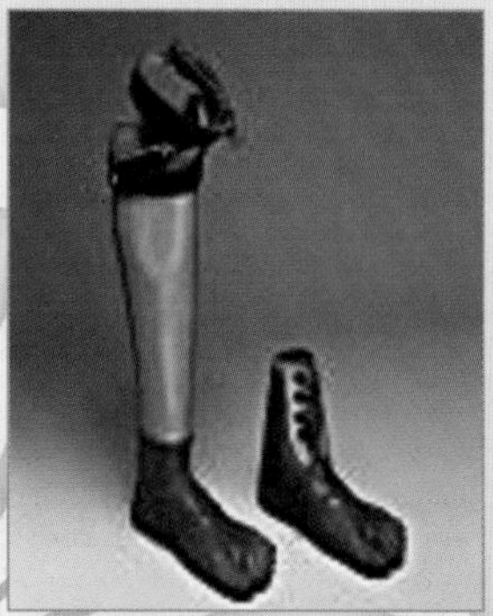

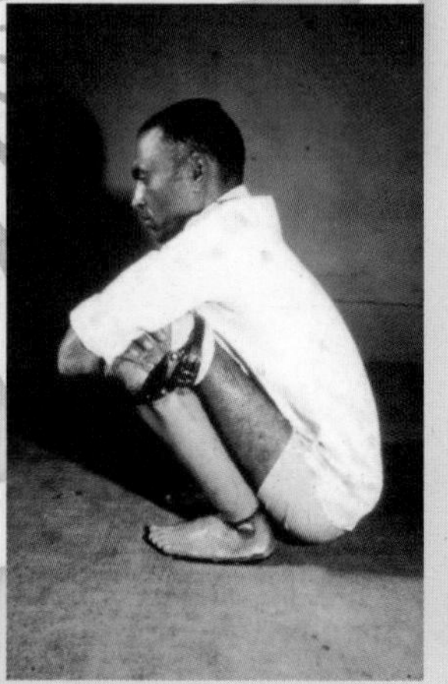

In Ṛigveda there is a reference that an artificial leg made of Iron had been fitted to a woman warrior called Vischala, the wife of King Khela, by the eminent divine surgeons Aśvin Kumars. (Ref 1.116.14& 15)

This Vedic reference substantiates the fact that the ancient Indians knew the skill of making artificial limbs.

Twenty years ago, a film called "Nache Mayuri" was a big and sensational hit. The heroine of that movie Sudha Chandran did not have a leg and danced with an artificial leg designed and fitted at Jaipur. For the past thirty-five years this Jaipur-foot had created, senasation & history and served millons of poor by providing them, "the joyful ride of life journey".

So let us get into the saga of successful Jaipur foot.

In the year 1968, a team of doctors from SMS College, Jaipur and a traditional sculptor had come together to design this world famous Jaipur-foot. The team was headed by an orthopaediac professor Dr P.K.Sethi. The other members of the team were Dr S.C.Kasliwal, Dr Mahesh Vidhawat and master sculptor Sri Ramachandra Sharma.

The reasons for the popularity of Jaipur-foot or leg

1. It is a very low cost artificial limb.
2. It is a very effective artificial leg, with which one can perform all the activities, as one having a natural leg.
3. It is very easy to fit it and use it.

Till today around 10 Lakh, people had been fitted with artificial limbs by this institute. People from all over the world come all the way to Jaipur to get this fitted.

Bhagvan Mahavir Vikalang Sahayak Samiti (BMVSS) is the organization behind this miraculous feat. Since 1975, this organization had helped many a physically challenged persons, especially the poor to take giant strides in their life journey.

In the year 2005-2006, around seventy thousand people were helped and fitted with artificial limbs.

In India an artificial limb is being fitted for Rs 1200, when it costs Rs 40-50,000 in Western countries, thanks to the efforts of BMVSS. Poor people can pedal cycle Rikshaws, can perform all the agricultural activities etc with this artificial leg.

The service hearted Ramchandra Sharma's personal supervision and meticulous attention are a living example of dedication and commitment in offering this noble service

This Indian success story is unique in the world.

It stands as a testimony to Indian genius, Indian resolve and Indian spirit of service.

"

Three-quarters of the wealth of the world has come out of India, and does even now. The commerce of India has been the turning point, the pivot of the history of the world. Whatever nation got it, became powerful and civilized. The Greeks got it and became the mighty Greeks; the Romans got it and became the mighty Romans.

India has been the one country to which every nation that has become strong wants to go and conquer - it being reputed to be very rich. The wealth of the people had become a fable, even in the most ancient history. [Many foreign invaders] rushed to become wealthy in India and conquered the country."

- Swami Vivekananda

"

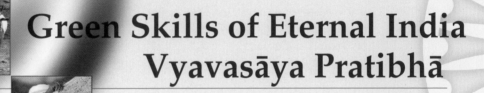

Green Skills of Eternal India
Vyavasāya Pratibhā

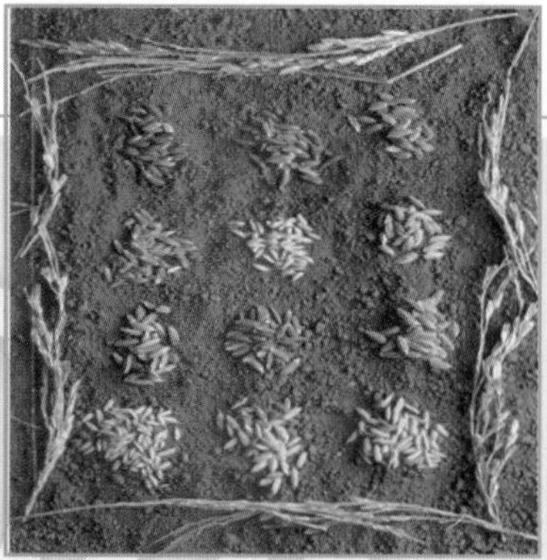

Variety of Rice Seeds

Some Interesting Agri Facts of India

- The Tank irrigated area has come down from 16.51% (1952-53) to 5.18 % (1999-2000). The Ground water tapping has increased from 30.17% (1952-53) to 55.36% (1999-2000). This shows we are depleting ground water potential of the country.
- As early as 300 B.C. Megasthenes, the Greek ambassador in the court of Chandragupta Maurya, mentioned in his memoirs - "the whole country is under tank based irrigation systems and is very prosperous because of the double harvests which they are able to reap each year."
- According to the late Dr. Richharia, the well-known rice scientist, there are over 200,000 varieties of rice in India alone. The so-called green revolution has resulted in a massive loss of on-farm biodiversity.
- India has 2% of the world's land and 16% of the world's population and 68% of live stock population.
- The immense commercialisation of agriculture has also had a very negative effect on the environment. The use of pesticides has led to enormous levels of chemical buildup in our environment, in soil, water, air, in animals and even in our own bodies.
- Fertilisers have a short-term effect on productivity but a longer-term negative effect on the environment where they remain for years after leaching and running off, contaminating ground water and water-bodies. The use of hybrid seeds and the practice of monoculture has led to a severe threat to local and indigenous varieties, whose germplasm can be lost for ever. All this for "productivity".

Traditional organic farming is the only solution.
Let us together bring new organic green revolution.

A Typical Tank of Vijayanagar Period

19 Traditional Agricultural Expertise

India is the cradle for Agriculture. Knowledge of Agriculture and its evolution as Agricultural Science can be traced from Ṛig Veda. It reveals , how one has to prepare oneself for ploughing the fields and the rituals involved there in.

Ṛig Veda extols Sun not only as God, but also recognizes Sun as the source of light, for all the living beings. It explains the water cycle, how water evaporates because of sunlight and how these vapors become clouds and reach the earth as rains.

At various instances, ṚigVeda gives us the knowledge of Green skills and Cattle Science that are required by a farmer.

Measuring the Rainfall:

Kauṭilya or Cāṇakya in his treatise "Artha Śāstra" (written during 4th century B.C.) had explained the methods of measuring the Rainfall. In this legendary book we can find the rainfall recorded at various places during those times.

Varahamihira in his encyclopedic work, *"Bhṛhat-samhithā"* (written during 6th Century A.D) had explained about the instruments that are required for measuring the Rainfall. "Ādika" is the vessel like instrument that collects the rainfall, which was 20 inches in diameter and 8 inches in depth. The Adika was also a unit of measure for recording rainfall. Four Adikas were equal to one Droni.

Varahāmihira had explained that the rainfall accompanied by thunders, clouds, sunlight and heavy winds would scatter around 400sq miles of area. On the other hand the rainfall accompanied by clouds and heavy winds, limits itself to smaller area.

Fertility of the soils

Sage Kashyapa in his text *"Kṛṣi-Sūkta"* had described about the soil that is most suitable for producing Rice. He had even classified the crops that can be produced on fertile lands and dry lands. In the Saṁskṛta text *"Amarakośa"* (written during 4th century BC) twelve varieties of soil that are suitable for agriculture had been explained. Surapala in his famous text *"Vṛkṣa Āyurveda"* (written during 10th century AD) explains three types of soils and their utilities.

Seed cultivation:

Parāsara in his book *"Kṛṣi Parāsara"* reveals the methods of producing seeds and methods of preserving the quality of the seeds. Kauṭilya's Arthaśāstra discloses the methodology of purifying the seeds through cowdung, milk, fish, bones etc.

Water storage & Irrigation:

Traditional Indian Texts are replete with ways and means of storing water for Agriculture. Kauṭilya and Kashyapa had recorded in their books how kings of their times had constructed reservoirs for the wellbeing of farmers.

The dams and reservoirs in India existed as early as 4th century B.C. The *'Sudarshana'* reservoir of Gujarat and Kallanai dam in Tamilnadu stand as the testimonials (even today) for Indian irrigational expertise. Various texts of Buddhism written centuries before the birth of Christ make reference to the existence of reservoirs and other water storage mechanism. Chakrapāṇi in his book "Viśvavallabha" explains the methods of detecting the under ground water sources. Varahāmihira in his book "Bṛhat-samhitā" explains the tracing of underground water, based on the nature of trees, herbs, anthills that exist on the ground.

Methods of yield preservation & storage

Parāsara describes about the methods of storing the grains and other agricultural produce. He even explains the precautions one has to take while preserving the crop yield. According to him, the month of February (Phālguna) is best suited for storing the grains.

Famous Indian Agricultural science Texts:

Many ancient Indian texts had described various methods of agriculture, ploughing, seed cultivation, water storage, varieties of soil, measurement of rainfall, storage of crop yield etc. The famous texts are being listed below:

S.No.	Text	Author	Time
1.	*Ṛgveda*	-	Vedic times
2.	*Artha Śāstra*	Kauṭilya	4th century B.C
3.	*Kṛṣi parāsara*	Parāśara	1st century B.C
4.	*Agni Purāṇa*	Vyāsa	
5.	*Bhṛhat-samhitā*	Varahāmihira	5 th century A.D
6.	*Kṛṣisūkta*	Kashyapa	9th century A.D
7.	*Vṛkṣa Ayurveda*	Surapala	10th century A.D
8.	*Manasonullasa*	Someswara	11th century A.D
9.	*Upavana vinoda*	Sarangadhara	13th century A.D

Artha Śāstra discusses the organic manures, crop rotation, crop intervals etc.

"Parasara in his book Krishi Parasara reveals the methods of producing seeds and methods of preserving the quality of the seeds."

Animal Husbandry:

Since Vedic times, we lived with cattle, we reared them and we loved them and even worshipped them. Cattle wealth was considered to be a sign of prosperity in ancient India.

Vedas, Āyurvedic texts of *Charaka, Suśruta and Salihotra, Manusmṛti, Bhṛhat-samhitā, Agni Purāṇa and Vishnu Dharmothara purāṇas* had discussed extensively cattle science and animal husbandry.

Artificial Rains:

According to modern knowledge sprinkling of Sodium Chloride and Silver Iodide over clouds in the sky produces rain. Clouds are very essential for creating artificial rains. The success rate is only 30%.

During ancient times, Indians attracted clouds through yajñas and rains poured in. The ingredients used in yajñas for attracting clouds have certain special properties. The mantras that are chanted during these yajñas stimulated necessary vibrations in the sky along with the Agnihotra fire. Above all, the pure resolve and prayers of our elders had convinced the mother nature, to shower her grace through rains.

Lord Kṛṣṇa in the Gītā says:

"All beings are born from the Anna (Nourishing food). This nourishment takes place because of rains. Rains are obtained through yajñas. Yajñas are possible because of sacrificing endeavours (karma) of human efforts."

20 Father of Botany – Sage Parāśara

In the year 1665 AD, Robert Koch, a Botanist with the help of his microscope, explained to the world about the Plant cell and its structure. One thousand and six hundred years ago prior to that date, sage Parāsara in 1st century A.D had clearly explained the structure of a Plant cell in the Saṁskṛta work *"Vṛkṣa Āyurveda"*.

Parāsara had even explained the phenomenon of the Photosynthesis (process of self-nourishment in the plants) in the fourth chapter (Vṛkṣa śarīra dharma śāstram) of the same book.

In the year 1894 AD, a scientist called Dixcona Joli had proved that plants take food and water through their roots. Ancient Indians were aware of this fact. In the Indian epic Mahabharatha, plants had been described as "padapa" which take water through their roots. (Ref Shanti parva,184 chapter,18 sloka)

In the text *Vṛkṣa Āyurveda*, Parasara clearly explains that plants prepare food through their leaves, for which they take water from their roots. He called this process as "syandhana".

He had categorised plants according to the various types of fruits, flowers, leaves and roots. Many other ancient Indian scientists like Varahamihira, Charaka, and Suśruta had also classified the plant kingdom.

Varahamihira in his book *Bhṛhat-samhitā* had discussed four important plant diseases.

Since Vedic times, India had the in-depth knowledge about plant kingdom and its varieties.

Every classical Indian text, starting from Upaniṣads, The Rāmāyaṇa, The Mahābhārata and The Srimad Bhāgavata deal with science of plants as a passing reference in many instances.

Indians considered plants as the gift of Nature. Plants had been used very extensively and intimately by our elders in the fields of medicine, art, agriculture, food (fruits & vegetables) and in the daily rituals and worship.

"Vṛkṣo Rakṣati Rakṣitaḥa" "Protect the plants, plants in turn protect you", was the philosophy that guided our ancestors who lived in tune with nature.

AtharvaVeda had classified plants into eight categories based on their growth.

"Charaka Samhita" describes four catergories of plants based on fruits and flowers.

"Sushruta Samhita" classifies plants into ten categories based on the plant utility.

Parasara had classified the seeds into two varieties namely Eka-dala-bīja (mono cotyledons) and dvi-dala-bīja (di-cotyledons). He had classified flowers into various categories. His classification resembles the modern classification in many ways.

"Upa-vana-vinodhi" is a classical text that deals with Horticulture.

Another text *"Pridhivi Niraaparyam"* describes various responses of plants, including sleeping, happiness, sorrow, etc. In modern times, the great Indian scientist JC Bose had proved about the various plant responses through his experiments and instruments.

21 Indian Cattle Science

Ancient Indians lived in tune with nature. Plants, animals and of course all living beings were considered sacred by them. Cattle were the part of their lives. Cows were worshipped with all sanctity. They were cared well and their wellbeing was given the top priority. Kings considered Horses, Cows and Elephants as wealth.

Purānas and Cattle Science

- King Nala had the title "Ashva-vith". It means the person who had complete knowledge about Horses.
- Pāṇḍava Kings Nakula and Sahadeva were experts in cattle science. Nakula wrote a book called *"Ashva Chikitsa"* (Treatment of Horses). Sahadeva had expert knowledge about cows.
- King Dasaratha of the Ramayana had a contemporary who was a master in Gajāyurveda.

Indian Medical Sciences and Cattle

Āyurvedic texts deal with treatment of cattle. Charaka, Sushruta & Harita Samhitas deal with various animal diseases and their treatments.

Father of Veterinary Science

Salihotra, who lived in 8th century B.C, is considered to be the Father of Veterinary science. He wrote a famous text called *"Haya –Ayurveda"*. It consists of 12,000 verses and had been divided into eight parts. Complete text is not available today.

- First chapter of the book deals with horses, their types, their characteristic features, and methods of finding a Horse's age, their anatomy and the horses that the kings alone should ride.

- Second chapter of the book deals with diseases of the cattle, fevers, eye problems, snakebites, wounds and their treatment.
- Third chapter deals with Gynecological problems of horses, pregnancy and other venereal diseases in horses.
- Fourth chapter deals with food to be given to horses, their rearing, oral diseases, dysentry and its treatment.
- Fifth and sixth chapters deal with planetary influence on horses.
- Seventh chapter deals with the impediments that a veterinary physician had to face.
- Eighth chapter deals with the Physical marks & signs on horses and their interpretation. It also deals with training of horses and making of various chariots.

- Agni, Garuda and Matsya puranas refer to the book *Haya-ayurveda.* This book was translated into various foreign languages, like Persian, Arabic, English etc.

Even today, in certain places of North Western India and Central Asia, veterinary physician is often called as "Salotri" an eternal tribute to this great Indian physician.

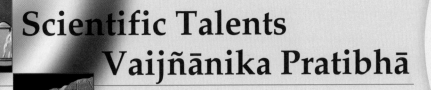

Scientific Talents
Vaijñānika Pratibhā

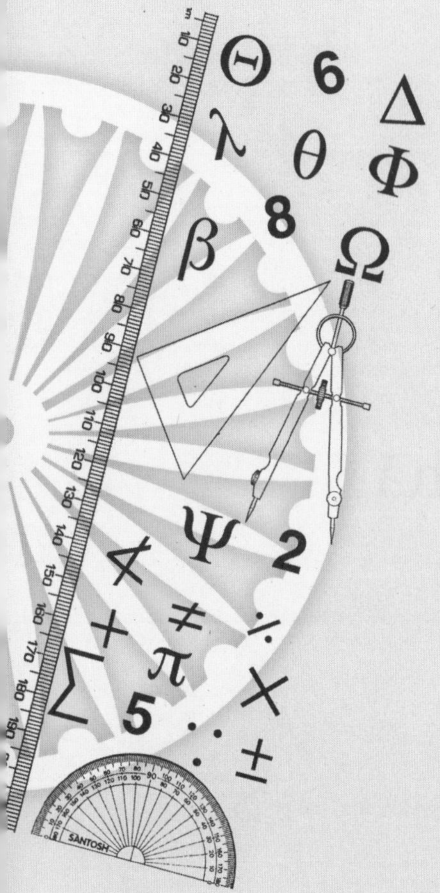

22 Genius of Indian Mathematical Brains

Mathematical knowledge that exists today is a gift from ancient India. Believe it or not, it is true.

One of the Twentieth century's greatest brains, **Albert Einstein** had said about India's contribution in the following words,

"We owe a lot to the Indians, who taught us how to count through decimal system, without which no worthwhile scientific discovery could have been made".

1. Decimal system: Nine numbers and a zero can be combined to form infinite mathematical expressions and measurements. This knowledge is said to be the unique contribution of ancient Indian genius to world's progress.

During Vedic times, this decimal system was very much in vogue in India. Yujur Veda Samhita 17th chapter, 2nd mantra describes the numerical values in a sequence like

Eka, dasa, sata, sahasra, ayuta, laksha, niyuta, koti, arbud, vrinda, kharav, nikharav, Shankha, Padma, sagar, antya, Madhya, parardha etc. Parardha's value is equal to $\mathbf{10^{12}}$

A Buddhistic text called "Lalita Vistara" (1st century BC) describes upto$\mathbf{10^{53}}$ and called that numerical value as *"Talakshna"*. Another Jain text (Anuyogadwara) describes numbers up to $\mathbf{10^{140}}$.

During the ancient period, Greeks gave the biggest numerical value called myriad, which is equal to $\mathbf{10^4}$, ie.10000 only.

Biggest Roman numericals were $\mathbf{10^3}$.ie 1000 only. It was called as "milli".

The numbers from zero to nine were first adopted by Arabs from India and had spread to Europe. Today we call these numericals as Indo-Arab numericals

2. Zero's Glory: Without India's richest "zero", the whole of mathematical knowledge becomes zero. Indians used zero not only as the mathematical expression but also as philosophical concept.

Vedas, Upanishads, Puranas and many Indian classical texts had dealt with zero in various ways.

Pingala (2nd century BC) in his Vedagana text "Chandas Sastra" (A guide to study Vedic prosody), while explaining Gayatri Chandas mentions zero.

Gayatre sadsamkhyamardhes panite dvyanke avasista srayastesu
Rupamapaniya dvyankashah sunyam sthapyam!!

In the domain of Mathematics, usage of negative numbers came into existence because of zero's invention.

In Īśāvāsya Upaniṣat, in the Shanti mantra, there is a verse, which describes the philosophy of zero

pūrṇa madaḥ pūrṇa midaṁ pūrṇāt pūrṇa mudacyate
purṇasya pūrṇamādaya pūrṇameva vaśiśyate

"From zero or completeness everything came and into zero or completeness everything merges, zero or completeness alone exists". In Sanskrit, "pūrṇam" is used to denote "zero" or "completeness."

Brahma Gupta in his mathematical text *"Brahma sputa siddhānta"* (written during 620 AD) proves that any number divided by zero becomes infinity.

० - 0 - shununyá
१ - 1 - ekaḥ
२ - 2 - dvau
३ - 3 - tryaḥ
४ - 4 - catvāraḥ
५ - 5 - pañca
६ - 6 - ṣaṭ
७ - 7 - sapta
८ - 8 - aṣṭa
९ - 9 - nava

> Geometry, an important branch of mathamatics had originated in India. The word Geometry is a Sanskrit word means measuring the earth. Jya in Sanskrit means earth, miti means measurement. Jyamiti or geometry means measuring the earth.

"Suryapragnapti" (400 BC), a Jain text had classified the numbers into three varieties. It describes five kinds of infinites.

Addtions, subtractions, multiplications and divisions; squares, square roots and cube roots were known to Indians and can be found in most of the mathematical texts of India.

Bhaskaracharya (11 century AD) had said, all kinds of mathematical expressions can be said in two processes. They are (1) Process of Increase (2) Process of Decrease. From them all the other mathematical concepts evolved.

In the text *Ganitasarasangraha* (850 AD), *Sridharacharya* explains LCM, zero, finding square roots and solving quadratic equations etc.

Sridharacharya in his text *Pathi-Ganitam* describes concepts of calculating simple interest, compound interest, problems on time and distance, time taken for filling the water etc.

In Jain manuscripts of *Bhakshali,* we can find about negative numbers, fractions, sequences of Arithmetic progression and geometric progression etc.

Geometry: Geometry, an important branch of Mathamatics had originated in India. The word Geometry is a Sanskrit word which means measuring the earth. "Jya" in Sanskrit means earth, "miti" means measurement. "Jyamiti" or geometry means measuring the earth.

Kalpa Sastra, a part of Vedangas contains "Sulba Sutras", which explains the techniques of constructing yajña vedicas (vedic sacrificial altars and platforms). From these verses, the branch of Geometry evolved.

Today, what we call **Pythagoras Theorem** is a mere repetition of what had been said in *Baudhayana "Sulba Sutras"*, written five to six hundread years before Pythagoras.

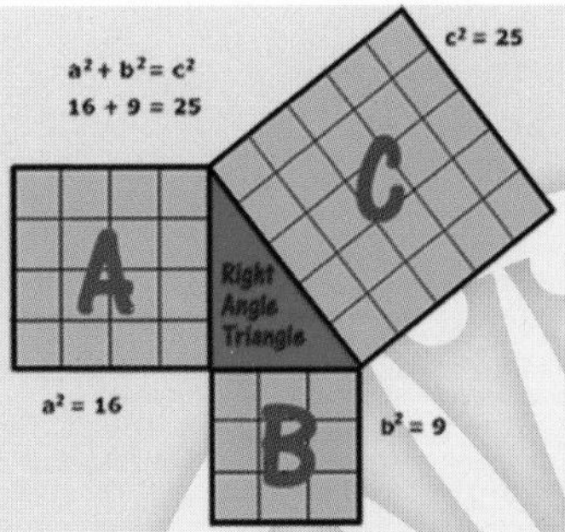

> **dīrgha caturasasyākṣṇyā rajjuḥ pārśvamānī tiryak mānī ca**
> **yatpṛthagbhū te kurutah tadubhayaṁ karoti**

In a right-angled triangle, the square of the diagonal on the hypotenuse is equal to the sum of squares of other two sides.

(Baudhayana sulba sutras ch 1-12 sloka)

Pi value: The value of pi had attracted the attention of every Mathematician whether Indian or Western, ancient or modern. The pi is constant value of the ratio between the circumfurance and diameter in a circle.

Great Indian Astronomer Aryabhatta (5th century AD) had calculated the value of Pi as 3.1416, which is accurate upto four decimals. (Aryabhattiyam-ganitapada-chapter 2- 10 verse)

Apart from *Aryabhatta, Mahaviracharya, Bhaskaracharya, Nilakanta Somayaje, Ramanujam* also had calculated the value of pi.

Circling a square and rectangle, which are equal in areas, can be found in Indian Mathematical texts.

Brahmagupta in his text *Brahma Sputa Siddanta* (12th chapter, 28th verse) describes the mathematical methods for finding the lengths of diagonals of rectangle that is embedded in a circle.

Bhaskaracharya in his book *"Leelavati"* describes cyclic quadrilateral, cyclic pentagon, cyclic hexagon and cyclic octogen, and further postulates that sides of quadrilaterals and the diameter of circle that is circumscribing them shall be in a constant ratio.

"Today, what we call Pythagoras Theorem is a mere repetition of what had been said in Baudhayana Sulba Sutras, written five to six hundread years before Pythagoras"

Aryabhatta in his text Aryabhattiyam gives the formula for calculation of area of triangle as 1/2BH where "B" is the base of triangle and "H" is the height of the triangle.

tribhujasya phala śarīram samadalakoṭi bhujārthā samvargaḥ।

Trignometry: Trignometry is a gift of ancient India to the mathematical world. The concepts of sign and cosign had been evolved by Indian Mathematicians.

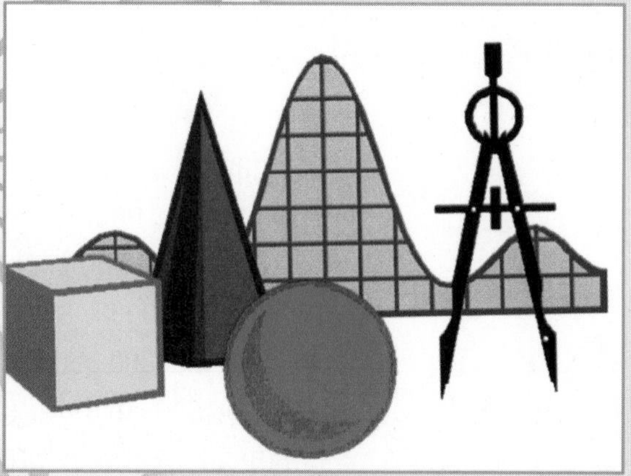

Aryabhatta had tabulated the several values of sign from 00 to 900 in his famous mathematical work Aryabhattiyam.

Bhaskaracharya had postulated various trigonometric principles and equations in his text Leelavati.

Varahamihira, Brahmagupta, Lalla and other Indian Mathematicians had given various Trigonometric formulae.

Kerala Mathematician Madhava (1340-1425) in his book "karana paddathi" dealt extensively with Trigonometric formulae & functions.

Calculus: What we call today, "Calculus" was called by ancient Indians as "Kalana Ganana sastra". Ages before Newton had made use of it, Aryabhatta and Bhaskaracharya had dealt with this branch of Mathamatics in their Astronomical calculations.

Bhaskaracharya in his work "Siddhanta Siromani" (4th chapter, Graha Ganita) deals with the concept of differentiation and its application by considering the temporal positions of various planets.

Aryabhatta had pioneered this method of calculating the temporal positions of various planets and had introduced to the world the knowledge of Calculus.

Brahmagupta and Madhava had developed this branch of Mathematics by introducing Integral Calculus.

Algebra: This branch of Mathematics is also an Indian invention. During 9th century AD, Arabs adopted it and from them it has spread to the other parts of the world.

Indian seers of yore like Apasthambha, Baudhayana, and Katsyayana in his Kalpa Sutras had introduced the "unknown" value in their Mathematical expressions. Afterwards, Aryabhatta, Brahmagupta, Bhaskaracharya, Madhava and others developed various Algebric formulae, equations and functions.

Bhaskaracharya calls Algebra as ***Ayakta Gaṇita or Bīja Gaṇita.*** He had said that Vyaktha Ganita leads to Ayakthaganita. In his book Leelavati he deals with vyathaganita (Arithmetic) before dealing with Ayaktha Ganita.

Indian Mathematical genius is evident from seers of Vedic times to Twentieth century Ramanujam. Today, what we call as computer language (Bakus Normal form) is a replication of Panini's grammar rules.

Indian Mathematical crown has ever-shinning gems to its credit.

"Bhaskaracharya calls Algebra as Ayaktha Ganita or Beeja Ganita. He had said that Vyaktha Ganita leads to Ayakthaganita. In his book Leelavati he deals with vyathaganita (Arithmetic) before dealing with Ayaktha Ganita."

23 Indian Chemistry through Ages

The Science of Chemistry flourished since 1500 BC in India. There are many evidences to substantiate this fact. Indians called Chemistry as "Rasa Vidya".

Even texts like *Vatsyayana Kama Sutra*, mention about Chemical processes like "Suvarna Rasa Pariksha" (A chemical test to find the purity of gold).

From making pots out of the mud to melting of metals and other products and vapourizing them, distilling them, solidifying them and the other Chemical processes were known to Indians since the dawn of History.

Ancient Indians had the knowledge of making plain Glass and coloured glass. This fact can be supported by Historical references in Indian literature and Archeological evidences. The books that support the existence of Glass and Glass products in India are the Ramayana, *Bhṛhat-samhitā* and Kautilya's *Artha Sastra.*

The Harappan people of Indus valley civilization had the knowledge of utilizing the metals like Gold, Silver and other alloys. In Vedas there are ample references to the ornaments that are made of various alloys of some metals. (*Rig Veda 1-122-14, Shukla Yajurveda 8-13).*

Advanced knowledge of Chemistry is required to make metals into alloys and turn them into products of utility like idols, ornaments, vessels, instruments & artifacts etc. The text *Rasarnavam-* (11.213.17) deals with this process.

The period between 600 BC to 800 AD can be called as The Golden period of Indian Chemistry. The Science of Indian Chemistry is rooted not only in the classical texts written exclusively on Chemistry, but also in various Ayurvedic texts like Charaka & Sushruta Samhitas, encyclopedic works like *Bhṛhat-samhitā* and Kautilya's Artha Sastra.

S.No	Important classical Chemistry texts of India	Authors
1.	*Rasaratnakaram, Kakshaputa Tantram, Arogya Manjari, Yogasaram & Yogashatakam*	Nagarjuna
2.	*Rasaratna Samuchayam*	Vagbhatta
3.	*Rasarnavam*	Govindacharya
4.	*Rasa Prakasha Sudhakaram*	Yasodhara
5	*Rasendra Chintamani*	Ramachandra
6	*Rasendra Chudamani*	Soma deva

The knowledge of basic building blocks of universe as "Paramāṇus" (atomic particles) of "Padarthas" (Matter), can be found in *Vaisheshika Sutras* of *Kanaad*(6th century BC). The basic five elements(Pañca bhūtas) and their intermingling properties were clearly mentioned in many Indian books of varied branches of science.

Process of Distillation

Ayurvedic texts had revealed various chemical processes that take place within the Human body, centuries before the birth of Christ. Kautilya's Artha shastra had reference to the availability of various metallic ores at various places, the methods of purification, the utility of various metals & alloys, layouts of chemical laboratories (Rasaśālās). The gold plating of copper also has a special mention in this book Ref- (2-12-30). In books of Sanskrit, Telugu, Tamil & Marathi, we find the preparation of gunpowder and fireworks. The Sanskrit references of Gunpowder can be found in *Sukra Niti* & *Rasa-Upanishad.* In Rigveda, we find the mention of cotton dyeing & leather tanning and the chemicals used in the processes.

Making of Soaps, Toiletries, Perfumes & other drugs require highly advanced knowledge of Chemistry (Reference: Manusmriti, Yagnavalkya smṛti)

Indian Textiles were dyed using vegetable colour and by making suitable chemical treatment, which had attracted Europeans to come to India. The finest clothes of world are produced in India; the skills of dyeing them require advanced chemical knowledge.

Indians used mercury as divine medicine. It was used in many Ayurvedic preparations. Mercury was subjected to 18 types of chemical purification processes, before it was used as medicine. In a text called *"Rasaratna Samucya"* (7th chapter), there is a description about the Chemical laboratory, the various instruments used therein and the orderly placement of various instruments that process the chemical reactions. Thirty-two instruments had been mentioned therein. The names of a few instruments are (1) Dola Yantra (2) Swadhini Yantra (3) Patana Yantra (4) Adhaspadhana Yantra (5) Daki Yantra (6) Balak Yantra (7) Tiryaka patina Yantra (8) Vidhyadhar Yantra (9) Dhupa Yantra (10) Koshti Yantra (11) Kachappa Yantra (12) Damaraka Yantra.

A Pancha loha idol of Divine Mother Parvati

Indian Chemical knowledge had grown with the Knowledge of "Tantra" (Indian mystical practice) and deteriorated with it. Tāntric knowledge of India had followed two systems of practice to attain "siddhi" (enlightenment). They are Deha siddhi and Loha siddhi. In the method of Deha Siddhi, mercury is mostly used to eliminate body Toxicities and protect the body from decay, old age and delay the process of death. Deha in Saṁskṛta means, "body". In the method of Loha siddhi, metals & alloys of Iron & Copper were converted into gold & silver and were used as medicines. Through Loha siddhi, they aimed at deha siddhi. Loha in Saṁskṛt means (metal).

Iron Pillar at Delhi stands tall as a testimonial for Indian metallurgical marvel and superiority of chemical Knowledge.

The father of modern Indian Chemistry, Sri Prafulla Chandra Ray, had done an extensive research in the History and evolution of Indian Chemical knowledge. His book "History of Hindu Chemistry" speaks volumes about chemical ingenuity of Indians through ages.

24 Ship Building Skills

The English word "Navigation" had been derived from the Saṁskṛta word "Navagati" meaning sea voyage. India has 5,000 years of navigational history. Our navigational skills date back to the times of Indus valley civilization.

There is evidence to substantiate that India for the past 30 centuries was as central commercial hub. It had trade links not only with Greeks, Romans, Egyptians, Portuguese, Dutch, French and British but also with Asian countries like China, Japan, Indonesia, Burma, Java and Singapore through Navigation.

In a treatise written by King Bhoja by name *Yuthakalpatharu,* it was described how ships are to be constructed, their varieties and their nomenclature.

Ships, which were built in India, were of two categories namely Soumya (simple) and Vishesha (Complex). They were built in different shapes. Most of the ships are multistoried and compartmentalized.

Indian ships were mostly built of teak wood; hence their quality was of superior nature.

The persons involved in building the Ships were highly skilled artisans. For this reason, Indian ships were in great demand. Further, the longetivity of ships built in India was for half a century, in comparison with occidentally built ships, which had only ten to twelve years of longevity and were subjected to frequent repairs.

Because of usage of lighter wood in construction, Indian ships had the capacity to bear greater loads. There are enough evidences to substantiate that nearly 275 ships were built in Hoogly harbour from 1781 AD to 1821 AD.

The total transport capacity of these ships was nearly 1,22 lakh tonnes. In Mumbai, between 1736AD to 1863 AD, nearly 300 ships were built and British exploited the ship building skills of Indians during that period.

It was mentioned in a book called "Le-hindus" published in 1811 AD, wriiten by Francoius Balazar Solvyans, a French navigator, that Englanders had learnt ship-building skills and allied techniques from Indians.

Here is a recent reference to India's superior ship building skills. The Wall Street journal dt; 28.05.2003 had published a news item regarding America's war on Iraq. It says "A ship built based on the technology mentioned in old Indian literature, proved extremely successful in the war. This ship travels faster than many other ships. It transported more number of tanks than other ships and had capacity to convey nearly 5000 Soldiers. Further, it used to cover 2,500kms in 48 hours" --(report based on www.hindu.com , www.tribunal.com).

Marcopolo, a famous navigator reported that Indian ships had the capacity to transport nearly 300 persons. Marcopolo graphically described Indian ports and harbours. (Reference: India through ages by G.Kuppuram page 521-529)

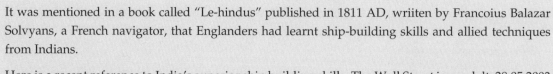

Even today, it is believed that Japan is the first Asian country, which had defeated European ships on a sea battle in the year 1905. But in the year 1742, king Marthanda Varma of Travancore deafeated the Dutch Naval Cavalry. Consequently, the Dutch Navy was completely humiliated and its naval commander surrendered to Marthanda Varma and served him loyally for more than two & half decades. This may be called as the first Asian naval victory of modern times.

Most of the ancient Indian exports were made to Roman and Eygptian empires. Most of the merchandise was cotton and Silk Textiles, Gems, Perfumes etc. Roman women were crazy about the superior quality of Indian cloth. They exchanged gold for cloth. (Enclycopedia Britanica 11 chapter -459 page)

Kautilya's Artha sastra describes the various governing principles and administration procedures of ancient times. In that famous book, we find mention about the port management system prevailing in those days. He describes the hierarchy of port administration; accordingly, the port commissioner and harbour manager and other officials assist the minister for navigation

Ancient Indian navigation made it possible to establish Indian settlements in Indonesia, Sumitra, Java, Malaysia, and South America etc.

From Gulf of Kutch to Bay of Bengal, the entire Indian coast was once radiantly vibrating with seaports and harbours. Various Kingdoms along the Indian seacoast constructed ships, established ports and traded with Europe and Asian countries.

The Indian skill of building ships was viewed with awe and wonder and of course with envy & fear as well.

British Government, that ruled India had brought a legislation in the year 1814 AD, which had destabilized the Indian shipbuilding Industry. It had banned the entry of Indian made ships into European ports. By the year 1863, Indian ship building artisans were jobless and were completely rooted out.

Sir William Deigo sarcastically comments that with the law in force, British queen had eliminated the Indian naval queen.

25 Machine Science of India

Modern world is all mechanical. Without machines, nothing moves in the modern man's life. Machine and Man have become symbiotic in existence. Industrial revolution had bonded the man with the machine wheels. They rather bounded him within their automatic chains.

If machine is so important, what was ancient India's perception about machines and machine science? What was the level of advancement of Indian mechanical knowledge?

Indian seers had extensively described utility of machines and its limits too. Machines were called "Yantras" in Sanskrit. Yantra in Sanskrit means, "that which controls". The word Yantra is a very broad term, its scope in Indian context is just not limited to mere mechanical device. The term had wide usage in various fields of Indian sciences like Āyurveda (medicine), Rasasastra (Chemistry), Khagola (Astronomy), Jyotish (Science of light, popularly called Astrology), Yuddhashastra (warfare), and in rituals of worship like Tantrashastra.

Bharadwaj's *"Yantrasarvaswam"* is considered to be an authoritative text on Indian mechanical science. It contains the description of various machines and their utility.

In Balakanda of the Ramayana, while describing Ayodhya, Sage Valmiki refers to the separate zone within the city, where machines and weapons were kept; something like secured Industrial Estates of today (refer Balkanda-sarga 5.sloka10). In Ayodhya Kanda, Rama advises Bharata on techniques of Governance. In that context Rama asks Bharata about the safety of machines that are placed in various forts. (Ayodhaya kanda-sarga 100-Sloka53).

In the Mahabharata, Arjuna hitting the "Matsya yantra" and marrying Draupadi is a well-known fact to most of the Indians. The description of Matsya yantra reveals to us that it was an automated marine device and often compared with today's marine compass.

Kautilya's Artha Sastra mentions various machines that were used in warfare and civil works. "Yantra-varnavam" a mechanical science text in Sanskrit defines machine in the following manner.

daṇḍaiścakraiśca dantaiśca saraṇi bhramaṇadibhiḥ
śakterutpādanaṁ kiṁ vā cālanaṁ yantramucyate

Yantra (Machine) contains the following parts such as a Danda –lever; Chakra-pulley, danta -toothed wheel, sarani -inclined plane; and bhramana -screw; which is used to produce force or used to divert force.

Raja Bhoja in his work *"Samaranganasutradhara"* describes twenty characteristics of an efficient machine. They include effective coordination between various parts of the machine, accuracy, fine-tuning, and noiseless functioning of various parts. He had also described the utility of various machines. In the 31st chapter of *"Samaranganasutradhara"* hydraulics had been discussed. In the Astronomical text "Surya Siddhanta" in the chapter Yantradhyaya, there is clear description of the water wheel (Slokas 53 -56). Bharadwaj in his text "Yantrasarvasva" in the chapters on "Vaimanika Sastra" explains 31 types of machines used in an Aircraft. Viswakriya Darpanam, Disadarsi, Vakraprasarana yantra, were a few devices, which guide a pilot to monitor the surroundings, to trace movements of enemy aircraft and to mislead an enemy Aircraft.

GR Joyser in his book "Diamonds, mechanisms, weapons of war and Yoga sutras", describes various machines that were used by ancient Indians by using fuel as power. Some of the machines described therein resemble "Artificial Elephant machine" similar to the one described in famous Sanskrit historical drama "Swapna Vasavadatta" written by Basa.

Sage Kanaad in his text *Vaiśeṣika Darśana* describes five types of actions/motions. These laws relate to the modern laws of mechanics. Prasistapada, in his commentary on *Vaiśeṣika Darśana* describes the "Gati-sutras" (the laws of motion which resemble in every way Newton's "Laws of Motion").

Almost one thousand years before Newton's Laws of Motion, India's Mechanical knowledge flourished. It remains a mystery, why Indian mechanical devices and the knowledge related to it withered away. Perhaps seers of wisdom understood the dangerous effects of industrialization on human life.

> "Sage Kanaada in his text Vaisheshika Darshana describes five types of actions/motions. These laws relate to the modern laws of mechanics."

26 Hijacked Indian Aeronautics

On Dec 17th 1903, an aircraft thrust into the skies and became the (so called) first aircraft in the human history. Wright Brothers became its inventors. We all greatly adore them today and we teach this fact to our children in schools. But to our surprise the truth seems to be different.

> "Eight years before Wright brothers aerial show - in India, in the year 1895, at the Chowpaty beach, in Bombay, an aircraft flew in the skies upto 1,500 ft, when large Indian audience watched this feat."

Eight years before Wright brother's aerial show, in India in the year 1895, at the Chowpaty beach in Bombay, an aircraft flew in the skies upto 1,500 ft, when large Indian audience watched this feat. And this performance happened in the august presence of His Highness Maharaja of Baroda, Sri Sayaji Rao Gaikwad and honorable Judge Mahadev Govind Ranade. This event was covered and published by the then popular newspaper "Kesari" which was published from Pune.

The inventor of that aircraft was an ordinary Sanskrit scholar, named **"Siva Kumar Bapuji Talapade"**

The name of this aircraft was "Maruti Shakti ". This aircraft had been built based on the technology mentioned in the Sanskrit Text written by Bharadwaj called *"yantra Sarvasvam"*. Talapade adopted the technology from the chapters of *"Vaimanika sastra"* of Bharadwaja's book. The then British Government, after strictly warning the Baroda Maharaja not to fund the project, stalled this experiment. It seems that the experimental remnants of the plane and various working plans had been taken over by the British Government. (Source: Deccan Herald, Tuesday Dec 16, 2003)

Did our ancestors have much advanced knowledge about aircrafts? If so, what happened to all that? Why such an advanced knowledge had been kept as a secret? What is this Vaimanika Sastra of Bharadwaj? What are its contents? Whether modern scientists did any research on its contents? If so, what are their findings in this regard?

For almost twenty years, many scientists at Aeronautical society of India, NASA, Professors and students of many prominent universities of the world were doing research in their own way on this Vaimanaki Sastra of Bharadwaj. They were able to appreciate the advanced level of knowledge about

Aeronautics in this book. But much of their research findings are not being revealed to public.

Bodhananda, a scholar had written a commentary on and explanations to Vaimanika sastra of Bharadwaj.

Another scholor called "Subbaraya Sharma" of Mysore had composed a text on aeronautics on *Bharadwaj's Vaimanika Sastra.* This book was translated and published by Sir R.S.Jyoser in English. The English version of this book is available today on the website www.sacred-texts.com.

Bharadwaj's vimana sastra contains,

Eight main chapters-100 Adhikarnas (sub chapters),

500 sutras (aphorisms), 3000 slokas and 32 aeronautical secrets.

In this text, there are references to about 25 existing texts related to Aeronautics (Vimana sastra).

Drawings done in1923 from vimana texts

Among the referred books we find *"Sakti Sutram"* of Agasthya, *"Saudhamini kala"* written by a scholar named Eswara, *"Vayu Tatwa Prakarana"* of Sakataayana, *"Vysanala Tantra"* and *"Dhuma Prakarnam"* written by Narada, *"Vasraayaana Tantra"* of Saunaka, *"Vimana Chandrika"* written by Narayana Maharshi, Garga's *"Yantrakalpa"* and *"Yanabindu"* written by Vachaspati etc.

The above texts were referred to by Bharadwaj to define Vimanas, types of Vimanas that are available in various Yugas, qualifications of pilots, dress code of pilots and travellers, food to be consumed while flying, various machines of Vimanas, fuels that are suitable to fly Vimanas, metals and their treatment for building a Vimana, the situations that a pilot had to encounter in the air on flight and the ways and means of overcoming them etc.

According to Narayana Maharshi, the Vimana had been defined as a vehicle that travels on the land

Sage Bharadwaj the Author of Vimaāna śāstra

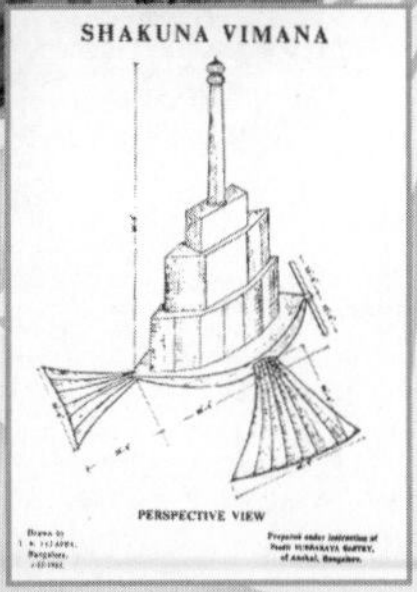

Drawings done in 1923 from Vimana texts

and water and can fly like a bird in the sky.

Referring to Paunaka Mahamuni, sage Bharadwaj says "A vehicle that travels in the sky from one place to another is called a Vimana".

Bharadwaj had dealt about four types of fuels that can be used by vimanas. They are:

1. Vanaspati Oil.
2. Mercury Gas
3. Solar Energy
4. Directly consuming power from the air.

The modern aircrafts are run by burning the hot gases. But recently scientists at NASA had experimented with the techniques of using mercury as mentioned in vimana sastra texts of India and designed mercury vortex engines successfully.

They adopted the technology mentioned in "Samaranganasutradhara " written by King Bhoja and translated by William Chlorundon into English.

Machines mentioned in Vimana sastra:

There are 31 types of machines mentioned in this text

1. Viswa kriya darpanam: This is an effective mirror device, which shows to the pilot the surroundings around the aircraft. Mercury and Mica are used in its preparation.

2. Parivasha Kriya Yantram: It is a self-propelling device that operates the aircraft.

3. Tamogarbha yantra: During aerial fights, this device hides the aircraft from being viewed, a kind of stealth technology. A special alloy called "Tamo garbha" was used in this device.

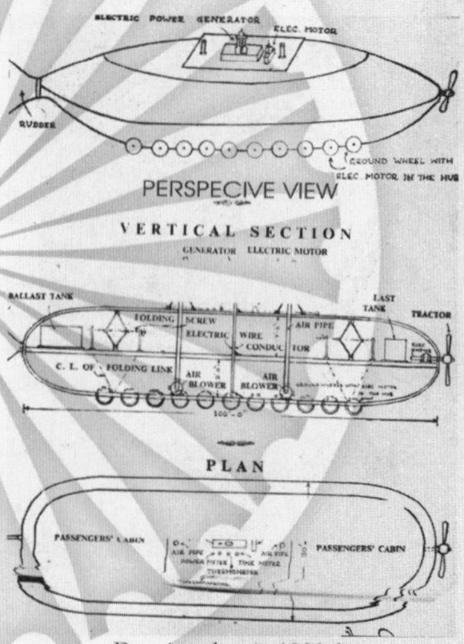

Drawings done in 1923 from Vimana texts

Scientists at Birla science centre, Hyderabad and IIT Bombay had done research on the metals mentioned in Vimana Texts and could decipher their utility and techniques of making alloys suitable for building aircrafts.

The Vimana text mentions the 32 secrets that a pilot should know. The pilot should have expert knowledge. They are like - propelling the flight into the sky, halting the flight in the sky, making suitable somersaults and driving the flight in jig jag way, suddenly increasing the speed and reducing the speed within the shortest possible time, techniques of protecting the flight when attacked by enemy aircrafts during aerial fights.

Bharadwaj refers to Sage Saunaka, who had classified the situations that a pilot faces during the flight into five categories.

Types of Vimanas: During the Satya and Tretha Yuga, vimanas were called & classified as "Mantrika-vimanas". They were of twenty-five types. They used to work with physical and mystical powers.

During Dwapara Yuga, Vimanas were categorized as "Tantrika Type". There are 56 varieties of this kind. During Kali Yuga, Vimanas have been named as "Kritika" type. There are 25 varieties of this kind, which are run by machines.

The above classification confirms that, the views expressed in Puranas cannot be brushed aside as figs of imagination.

Indian Puranas have many references to vimanas, Rakshasas called "Tripurasuras" had aerial cities, which used to fly in air and travel on earth and water. When they were torturing people, Lord Siva eliminated them.

In the Ramayana, Sage Valmiki had wonderfully described the "Pushpaka Vimana". The description resembles an aerial city that can move. Ravana captured this Vimana from Kubera.

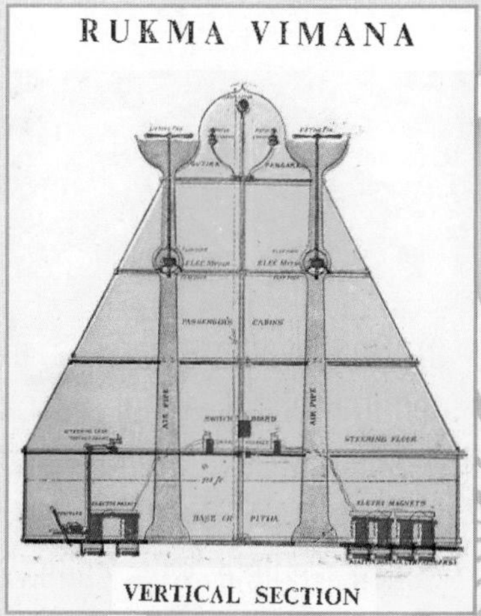

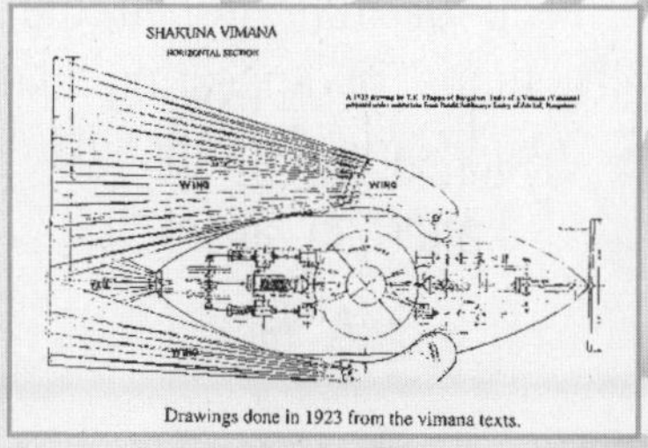

Drawings done in 1923 from Vimana texts

> "In Bhagavatam there is a mention about aerial attack by Shishupala's friend Salva on Krishna's Dwaraka. His space vehicle was called as "Soubha" and was made of Iron. It had the technique of appearing and disappearing in the sky after an attack."

In Bhagavatam there is a mention about aerial attack by Shishupala's friend Salva on Krishna's Dwaraka. His space vehicle was called as Soubha and was made of Iron. It had the technique of appearing and disappearing in the sky after an attack. It can thrust out many aircrafts from itself. It was not just an aircraft or Vimana. It can be called as an aerial city. Lord Krishna after waging a fierce battle destroyed that space vehicle. Vyasa, the writer of Bhagvatam goes at length to explain the power & functions of this space vehicle used by Salva against Krishna.

In the same text Bhagavatham, Kapila's parents, sage Kapartha and Devahuthi go for inter-stellar travel in a Vimana.

While discussing administrative principles, Kautilya's Artha sastra refers to the importance, due recognition and respect that had to be given to pilots by the Government. Kautilya called the pilots as "Saubhikas" and persons who were involved in aerial battles as "Aakasa Yodhas".

Recently Chinese Government had handed over the Sanskrit manuscripts that were discovered in Tibetian region to professor Rutherana of Chandigarh University to decipher the contents. These manuscripts contain the information about inter-stellar travel and anti-gravitational flights (laghima). This only confirms the height of Indian Aeronautical excellence achieved ages ago.

27 Sound Secrets

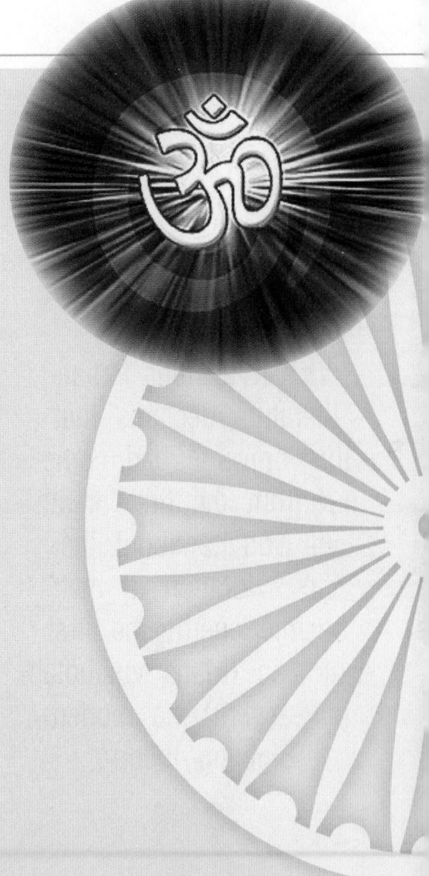

Ancient Indians duly recognized the importance of sound & sound energies.

During the 17th century, Galileo had postulated that sound travels in waves. Afterwards, many scientists have done extensive research on the properties of sound waves. They had found many utilities by using sound vibrations. Ultra Sonics, Echo-graphy, Radio etc., are the modern applications of the sound waves.

Ancient Indians had also utilized sound energy in various ways. Indians knew the secrets of sound and made extensive use of them in many day-to-day activities.

If sound waves are the vibrations, conversely, vibrations should produce sound. It means that every vibration has sound associated with it. Albert Einstein and other modern scientists had described this universe as an embodiment of energy. We normally recognize energy through vibrations. It means energy is manifested through vibrations and vibrations in turn manifest sound.

When ancient Indian literature declares that this universe had come out from the first breath of God, it's about the first vibration of that cosmic energy, the first explosion (Maha Visphotam in Sanskrit), the modern Big bang theory.

The vibrations of Sound are eternal, so are the Vedas. These sound vibrations never vanish; they would remain latent in space. Suitable stimulations manifest sound energy. Ancient Indian seers through their efforts of penance produced the necessary vibrations. They virtually tapped these eternal sound energies after visualizing them. They systematized the knowledge and had bequeathed the same to posterity, as Veda mantras with each sukta (a group of mantras) revealing each aspect of cosmic function. (Devata).

Hence, Vedas are eternal and are without beginning. They are not man-made sound vibrations. They

> When ancient Indian literature declares that this universe had come out from the first breath of God, its about the first vibration of that cosmic energy, the first explosion (Maha visphotam in Sanskrit), the modern Bigbang theory.

exist in the cosmos eternally. The person often taps them by making necessary stimulations within through a precise sound pattern. They are often called "Srutis".

Now, coming to the aspect of producing the sound within, Panini, the world's first grammarian had given the science of it, the phonetics through his treatise *"Astadhyayi"*. Sage Patanjali had written wonderful commentary, (Maha bhashya) on Panini's Book.

He explains the origin of sound within the human body in four stages called ***(1) Para (2) Pashyanti (3) Madhyama (4) Vykari*** Human soul or the Atman is the ultimate. The sound manifests from the Atman. This stage is called "Para Vakhu ". Then this assumes a pattern through the mind. This stage is called "Pashyanti ". Then it gathers the required energy and reaches the throat region. This stage is called "Madhyama". Afterwards, it finds expression through mouth, with the help of upper jaw, lower jaw, tongue and lips. Final expression is called "vykari" which is what we hear.

Indian alphabets have been divided between the letters "A" to "ksha" ("Aksha"). They have been categorized into various varieties based on the pronunciation.

Some of them are (1) Kanthyas (Gutturals) (2) Talavyas (Palatals) (3) Murdhanyas (linguals) (4) Dantyas (Dentals) (5) Osthyas (Labials) etc.

The pitch of the sound is also divided into three parts (1) Udata (High pitch) (2) Anudata (low pitch) (3) Swarita (Balance between the high & the low)

As explained earlier, Vedas are called Srutis. Since Vedas are infinite sound vibrations, our seers have commanded us only to utter or hear Vedas and not to write them. Seers had given them to us for our wellbeing. Vedic hyms connect human soul with cosmic vibrations. It is for this reason; Indians had given great importance to sound.

Before chanting the Veda mantras, a person should obtain proficiency in the following six subjects. They are called "Vedangas".

1. *Siksha Sastram:* It is about ways and means pronouncing Veda mantras.
2. *Vyakaranam:* The grammar involved in Vedas and structured expression of language.
3. *Niruktam:* Etymology of Vedic verses and their contextual meanings.
4. *Kalpa sastra:* The ways and means of performing Vedic rites and rituals.
5. *Chandas:* It reveals the metre of the Vedic verses and prosody.
6. *Jyotisham:* Knowledge of time for timely performance of Vedic rituals.

For human wellbeing, our seers had discovered the cosmic laws and secrets and have transmitted them to us through the Vedas. Infinite are Vedic vibes. The essence of Vedas is in Pranava, the Omkar. Sri Krishna says in Geeta "Pranavaha Sarva Vedeshu". Cosmos and sound originated together. The sound of the first cosmic explosion (Big bang) and the eternal sound of minutest vibration is "Omkar". It is called "Nada Brahma". Omkar is the key to unlock immense cosmic potential. Omkar is the engine for every activity, whether cosmic or mundane. Omkar is the sound that exists in the past, present and the future. Omkar is not just a letter or a symbol; it is the very essence of cosmic vibrations. It is the sound of sounds and the sound of silence.

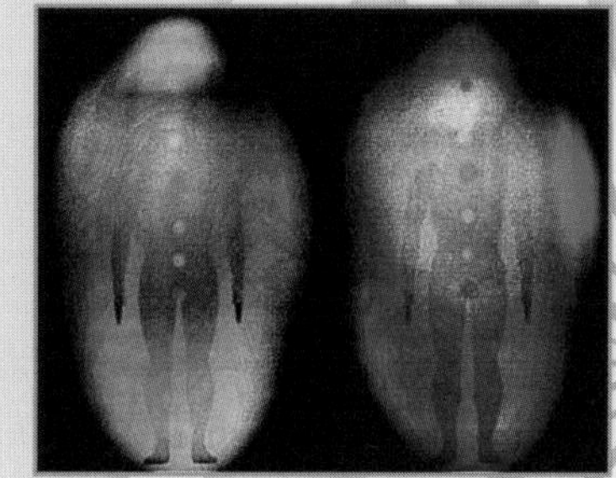

Before After

The Aura of person before chanting Mantras & After.

(Blue colour indicates positive and serene vibrations)

Indians used the sound energy in many ways; Indian classical music is nothing but an applied science of sound energy. Melodious music charms snakes; Wild animals get tamed; Cows give excess milk; Plants blossom with flowers; Trees bear fruits; Rains pour out; Nature responds with joy. Lamps can be lit just by the melody of the music; many a disease can be cured through the science of music; it is all but an application of sound vibrations. The knowledge of mantras is again an applied aspect of sound. Ancient Indians played with sound, enjoyed sound and protected themselves with sound vibrations. Kudos! To them, for their knowledge about Sound Secrets.

28 Hidden Knowledge in Naṭarāja's Cosmic Dance

Indians worship Siva in the form of Linga (Parabolic sacred stone) and at the same time adore him in the form of Nataraja (the dancing Siva), as divine personification of the entire domain of arts.

The Idol of Nataraja has ubiquitous presence in all the houses, throughout the world, both in Indian and Western Homes.

Behind this dancing pose of Siva, there seems to be a hidden cosmic secret. These words are not said by an ordinary person, but by a world-renowned professor of Nuclear physics, Fritj of Capra. He had explained the philosophy behind Nataraja's cosmic dance in his popular book "The Tao of Physics".

"Behind this dancing pose of Siva, there seems to be a hidden cosmic secret. These words are not said by an ordinary person, but by a world-renowned professor of Nuclear Physics, Fritj of Capra."

For a modern scientist of Physics, Siva's dance appears to be the dance of Atomic particles. The ancient Indian perspective about the world is nothing but the eternal cosmic dance of creation, sustenance and dissolution that happen with a rhythm. This is the root cause for everything.

According to Quantum theory of Physics, creation is full of Atomic particles. Each particle has enormous energy latent in it. These particles are very dynamic in nature and change their form within split seconds.

Sub-Atomic particles have dual nature, some times they appear as particles, sometimes they become continuous stream of energy. They often change from wave to particle and *vice versa* in a rhythm and eternally lose their existence.

Matter is nothing but a group of atomic particles. Particles move within it in a structured rhythm. Because of that, forms get created, forms get dissolved, forms grow and decay in a continuous way. In every change or move there is a rhythm in life, there is a beauty and harmony in this subtle change.

It is a dance of cosmic life; forms appear, disappear and reappear; from the minutest particle to a gigantic star all are changing and are in a flux; dancing to the symphony of cosmic breath of life; dancing to the tunes of cosmic rhythm;

Fritj of Capra could see Siva's cosmic dance as the secret of creation. The description of this experience was given on the opening page of " The Tao of Physics"

"I was siting by the ocean one late summer afternoon,watching the waves rolling in and feeling the rhy thm of my breathing, when I suddenly became aware of my whole environment as being engaged in a gigantic cosmic dance. Being a physicist, I knew that the sand,rocks,water and air around me were made of vibrating molecules and atoms, and that these consisted of particles which interacted with one another by creating and destroying other particles. I knew also that the earth's atmosphere was continually bombarded by showers of ' cosmic rays', particles of high energy undergoing multiple collisions as they penetrated the air. All this was familiar to me from my research in high energy physics,but until that moment i had only experienced it through graphs,diagrams and mathematical thl theories. As I sat in that

The philosophy of Siva's dance is the congruence of Science, Arts and Religion, the hidden knowledge about cosmos.

29 Finding the Basic Building Blocks of the Universe–Atomic Theory

What are the basic building blocks of this universe? Even today, Modern scientists are not in a position to answer this question. Many theories are being propounded and are being amended subsequently. Finally scientists of Particle Physics (a branch of Physics) are accepting the oriental views and trying to understand the ancient Indian perception about the universe.

> "Finally scientists of Particle Physics (a branch of Physics) are accepting the oriental views and trying to understand the ancient Indian perception about the universe."

Let us now look into perceptional changes that happened over centuries among the so-called modern scientific community influenced by Western outlook.

450 BC: Preliminary Atomic theory, propounded by Democritus says that atoms are indivisible particles of matter.

300 BC: Aristotle had postulated that Universe is made up of four elements earth, air, water and fire. (Similar to the already exisiting oriental view)

17th century AD:

a) Dalton's atomic theory: Dalton is the first person to propound atomic theory that the Smallest particles of matter are atoms, but each atom of different element differs in size and shape from the other element. Atoms combine in definite ratio of weights to form molecules without Atoms getting broken down.

b) Newton proposed a mechanical Universe that consists of smallest indivisible particles of matter. According to Newton, Time is absolute and uni-dimensional. Space is three- dimensional (Length, Breadth and Height). Time and space are not related to each other.

19th century AD:

1840 AD: Micheal Faraday had proved with his experiments about Electro–Magnetism. He had explained the charged fields around a particle; both negatively charged and positively charged fields.

1895 AD: Wilhelm Roentgen discovered X-Rays.

1897 AD: JJ Thomson discovered the negatively charged particles of an atom called electrons.

20th Century A D:

1905 AD; Albert Einstein had proposed the special theory of relativity. Accordingly

a) He had given famous equation $E= mc^2$ through which he had postulated that the matter is the manifestation of energy; energy and matter are inter convertible.

b) Time and Space are inter-related and are relative to each other.

c) Light has dual nature; Light rays are waves as well as energy particles. Scientists of later years have found photons (particles of light) as predicted by Einstein.

Einstein's special theory of relativity had changed the domain of physical science. A new branch of physical science evolved called "Atomic Physics" or "Nuclear Physics" or "Particle physics" or "Quantum Physics".

1911-1913: Neil Bohr and Ruther Ford had postulated the orbital structure of atom.

Accordingly

- In every atom there shall be a nucleus.
- Around the nucleus, there shall be negatively charged particles called electrons moving in a structured orbit.
- In the nucleus, there shall be positively charged particles called protons and neutrally charged particles called neutrons.

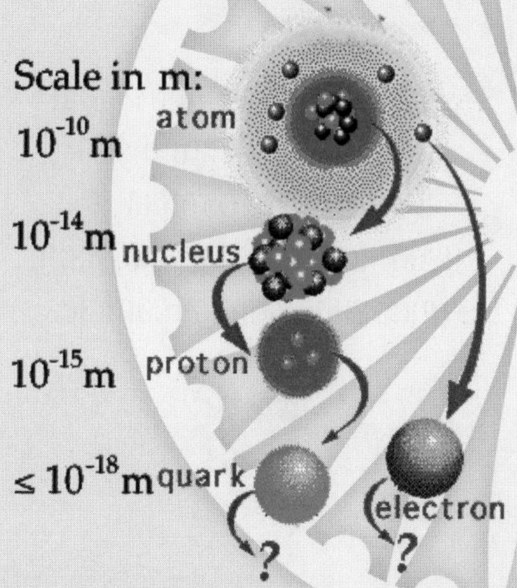

> The words "Anu and Parmaanu" are the Sanskrit words that are used to describe the atom and sub atomic particles

- If electrons orbit around the nucleus in a structured way, atoms remain stable. In an excited state, if electrons jump from one orbit to another orbit, they gain in strength or lose in strength changing the structure of atom.

1927- Warner Heisenburg proved through his "theory of Uncertainty" that the electron is not a particle and its structure cannot be determined easily as it continuously changes its position.

The journey of investigation of finding the fundamental building blocks of universe continued within the atom and today we have around 200 sub-atomic particles.

These particles are divided into two basic categories namely "Quark" particles and "Lepton" particles.

The quark particles are the minutest particles. They remain at the very subtle level of existence. They lose stability within no time. The very identification of these particles depends upon the perception of the observer. This means, each observer sees them in a different way. In other wards, quark particles exist according to the subjective perception of the observer. So with the advent of particle physics, the observer of the experiment is becoming the participator in the process. The universe at the subtle level is becoming completely subjective.

At the subtle level within an atom, there are many interactions that are happening between these particles of energy. The stability of an atom depends upon these interactions of various energy particles.

Every interaction depends upon the charged fields that surround a particle. Four basic forces influence these charged fields and interactions.

1. Gravitational force
2. Electro-magnetic forces
3. Strong nuclear forces
4. Weak nuclear forces

Unified field theory visualizes the grand unification of these forces. This has pushed physics into another domain of study that is finding the basic building blocks of Nature in a holistic way.

Today, universe is being studied as unified- interconnected stream of energy particles.

During the last years of twentieth century, a new theory came into existence called string theory. According to string theory, quarks and leptons are not particles but vibrating strings and loops. The whole universe is interconnected through a super-string of vibrating strings.

Kanaad Maharshi

What are the basic Building Blocks of universe- Indian perception?

Vedas, Upanishads, Puranas, Shad-Darshanas, (among them Sankhya, Vaisheṣika, Nyaya Darshanas) had postulated many theories about Universe and its atomic structure in their own perspective.

In the sixth century BC, Kanaad Maharshi had written Vaisheshika sastra and had postulated verses about structure of Universe from the atomic point of view.

The words *"Aṇu"* and *"Parmaanu"* are the Sanskrit words that are used to describe the atom and sub-atomic particles.

Vaisheshika Darshana has 373 verses spread over twelve chapters.

Vaisheshika Darshana had described the universe as the interplay of seven aspects or states of material things. They are (1) Dravyam (Matter) (2) Guna (Quality) (3) Karma (Action) (4) Samanya (Generic species) (5) Vishesha (unique trait) (6) Samavaya (inherence or intergrated part of the whole) (7) Abhava (Non-exisistence).

dravya guṇa karma sāmānya viśeṣa samavāyānāṁ padārthānāṁ

Vaisheshika Darshana-Verse;(1.4)

> "In the sixth century BC, Kanaada Maharshi had written Vaisheshika sastra and had postulated verses about structure of Universe from the atomic point of view. Vaisheshika Darshana has 373 verses spread over twelve chapters."

Dravyam (Matter) is again subdivided into nine aspects; they are: (1) Prithvi (Earth) (2) Jala (Water) (3) Teja (Light) (4) Vayu (Gas) (5) Akasa (Ether) (6) Dik (Direction -space dimension) (7) Kala (Time) (8) Manas (Mind) (9) Atma (Soul)

"pṛthivyāpastejo vāyurākāśaṁ kālodigātma mana iti dravyāṇi "

Vaisheshika Darshana -Verse;(1.5)

As described by Kanaad maharshi, the mind and atman were also considered as the aspects of matter. Today modern science is also considering the perception of mind in atomic structural analysis.

vibhavānmahanākaśastathā ca ātmā – *Verse (7-1-22)*

Parmaanus get influenced by Atman (person)

"nityam parimaṇḍalaṁ"– *Verse (7-1-20)*

Parmaanu is always in continuous state of motion.

There are two states of matter. One is "anu sthiti" (micro level state) another is "mahat sthiti" (macro-level state). – *Verse (7-1-11)*

When matter is continuously divided into sub-atomic particles (parmaanus) it reaches a state, wherein divided further, the particle looses its basic nature and identity. –*Verse (7-1-12-14)*

Ancient Indians perceived the relativity of time and space. For this reason, Maharshi Kanaad had categorized both of them as aspects of matter and included them in Dravyas.

According to Prasistapada, who had written commentary on the *"vaisheshika darshanam- padartha artha sanghraham"* (Ref:2.2.9)- a particle's creation, sustenance and destruction can only be expressed in terms of time .

Vaisheshika Darshana had wonderfully proposed the interactions among various particles of the matter. The same can be expressed, as a combination and interplay of three factors namely matter, quality and action.

Two atomic/sub-atomic particles come together to form a particle called "dwi-anukam" three – "triyaanukam" four- "Caturanukam".

Because of heating of atoms or exciting of energy particles, called "Pilapaka kriya" the process of creation is happening.

Many scholars had commented Kanaad's Vaisheshika Darshana. Among them works of Prasistapada, Vyomasiva and Chandramati are considered to be authoritative commentaries. These commentaries are attracting the modern nuclear scientists in many ways. Apart from Kanaad, Kapila through his Saankhya Sastra had described about 24 aspects of Universe and its components.

Vedas, Upanishads, Brahmasutras, Bhagavad Gita and other classical texts of India considered this universe as one unit, pervaded by Paramatma (cosmic soul). Indians perceive that whatever is in micro-cosm is also in the macro-cosm and are intimately connected. The modern string theory also reveals the same about the Universal truth.

"Indians perceive that wghatever is in micro-cosm is also in the macro-cosm and are intimately connected."

30 String Theory

Modern science is yet to conclude that subatomic particles like quark particles and lepton particles are basic building blocks of the universe.

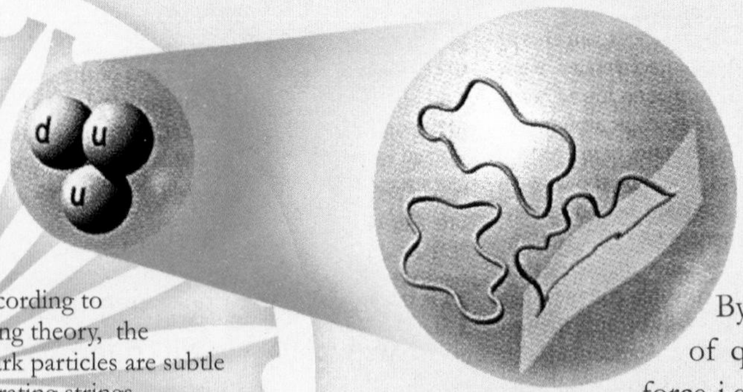

According to string theory, the quark particles are subtle vibrating strings

Reason for this is that scientists could unite three of the four fundamental forces of interaction among subatomic particles, they are: -

1. Electro-Magnetic Forces
2. Strong Nuclear Forces
3. Weak Nuclear Forces

By uniting the three forces, scientists could study the behaviour and properties of quark and lepton particles. Yet they could not unite the fourth fundamental force i.e Gravitational force with the other three forces in studying the behaviour pattern of subatomic particles.

During the last years of the 20th century, scientists have proposed a new theory called string theory. According to that, quarks and leptons are not particles. They are the subtle vibrating strings with closed and open loops. The gigantic star and minutest quark string are connected through a super-string. Hence the whole universe is being considered to be one unit by the most modern concepts of science. This theory facilitates the study of all the four fundamental forces of interactions.

> "In Vedas in Sata Pata Brahmana (8.7.3.10) it is said that sun and the entire universe are connected in a string"

Indian perceptive:

In Vedas in Sata Pata Brahmana (8.7.3.10), it is said that sun and the entire universe are connected in a string. That string is Vayu. Please note that Vayu is not gas or air according to Vedic meaning. Veda

Nirukta defines Vayu as one that pervades everything.

In Bhagvad Geeta in the sloka (7.7) Sri Krishna says to Arjuna,

mattaḥ parataraṁ nānyat kincidasti dhananjaya
mayi sarvamidaṁ protaṁ sūtre maṇigaṇā iva

"Like pearls strung in a string, the whole cosmos is strung within me"

As revealed by Lord Krishna, the whole cosmos from the gigantic star to the minutest particle, everything is stringed. (Together). Today our modern scientists call it as super-string.

The influence of stars on the minutest particle or on an event on the earth had been studied by Indian Jyotish Sastra (the Indian science of light, popularly called as Astrology).

Ancient Indian knowledge recognized everything in the universe as one consciousness and cultured our minds in that direction. There is huge literature to support this fact. Modern science is also arriving at the same conclusions.

Super-string as revealed by Lord Krishna in Gita

31 Time-Space & Relativity – Einstein Vs India's Perspective

In the year 1916, Einstein had proposed his general theory of relativity after postulating special theory of relativity in the year 1905.

According to the General theory of relativity

1. Time & Space are relative to each other.
2. Rate of flow of time changes according to the size and shape of planets. In the vicinity of larger planets, the rate of flow of time shall be slow. In the vicinity of smaller planets, the rate of flow of time shall be fast. It means various planets shall have different rates of flow of Time.
3. If a person after travelling at the speed of light in space and returns to the earth, the changes that happened on the earth shall be many times more than the changes that happened to him. Many centuries would have elapsed on the earth during that interval.

Before Einestein's theory of Relativity, Western world never considered the view that Time and space are relative to each other. But, in India every "thing" is described with reference to Time. Prasistapada in his commentary on Vaisheshika Sastra of Kanaad says, a thing (matter's) of creation, sustenance and destruction can only be described in terms of time. (Ref: Padartha Artha Sangraha-2-2-9).

Indian culture had assimilated this scientific fact into its daily life. Hence Indians valued Time and related every thing and every event in terms of Time.

Jyotish sastra (Indian science of light, popularly called as astrology) considers the movements of various planets and relates them to the human behavior. It means, it is co-relating various rates of flow of time of various planets on the human behaviour on the earth's surface.

For example, while preparing a Jyotish chart (Horoscope) or kundali of a new born, the time of birth and place of birth were taken together and are compared with various planetary positions (which vary according to the respective rates of flow of time). Different life pictures would evolve for the babies born at the same time, but at different places. The birth chart of a baby born at Delhi at 8.30 am would be different from the birth chart of a baby born at Madras at the same time.

The reason for this variation is due to Time & Space relativity.

Aryabhatta in his famous text Aryabhattiyam explains this concept of relativity differently with a wonderful example. He says for a person who is travelling in a boat sees the tree on the bank travelling in the opposite direction. Similarly if a person stands at the centre of equator and observes the galaxies, they appear to him that they are moving in the western direction. He means that our observation of Universe is relative to our presence on the earth and is a factor of our rate of observation.

An Artist's imagination about man travelling at the speed of light

To substantiate the fact that our seers of yore understood this time-space relativity, there is an episode in Maha Bhagvatam, which can precisely be related to Einstein's example of a person travelling in space shuttle with a speed of light for a few hours and returning to the earth and finding to his surprise that many centuries had passed by during his journey away from the earth.

The story goes like this.

Once upon a "time", there was a King called Raivataka. He had a son called Kukudmi. And Kukudmi in turn had a daughter called Revati, who was very tall. He could not find a suitable groom for his daughter, because of her height. Then, King Kukudmi with his power of penance goes to the Brahma loka along with his daughter. When he reaches Brahma loka, he finds lord Brahma listening to a music recital. The king waits till the end of the recital and approaches Brahma and asks him why he had created his daughter, so tall a person.

> Our seers of yore understood this time space relativity, there is an episode in Maha Bhagvatam, which can precisely be related to Einstein's example of a person travelling in space shuttle with a speed of light for few hours and returning to the earth.

After, listening to the king's plight, Brahmā laughs loudly and reminds him that during the period of recital of 15 minutes at Brahma loka, 27 chathuryugas had elapsed on the earth (4320000 years X 27). He further advises that on the earth, in the 28th chatyur Yuga, Dwapara Yuga is running and the king should go back and marry his daughter to Krishna's brother Balrama. As a concluding remark he says, that the king had done the good thing of bringing his daughter along with him to Brahmā loka. (Bhagavatam -9th chapter-36 sloka)

The above story may be called a fiction, but the essence of the story says that there are different rates of time flow at different celestial regions, which the author wanted to convey. Please do not forget that ancient Indian Astronomers and Mathematicians had contributed Calculus, Trigonometry, Algebra, Geometry to world thought. We are yet to unravel the many advanced concepts mentioned in our ancient literature.

In books like "Yogavashishtha", there are concepts like going beyond Time and Space. These concepts were thoroughly debated in Indian philosophy and Indian schools of logic like Saankhya, Nyaya, Mimamsa and Vaisheshika Darshanas.

In Bhagavad Geeta, Krishna says to Arjuna ;

bahūni me vyatītāni janmāni tava carjuna
tānyahaṁ veda sarvāni na tvaṁ vettha parantapah *(4 Ch -5 Sloka)*

"Oh! Parantapa, for you and for me, many births and deaths had taken place. I know them all, you don't know them at all."

Here Krishna was explaining to Arjuna the concepts of knowing things beyond time & space. In the Indian context, we come across many an Indian yogi, who remains in a state of going beyond the concepts of Time & Space.

32 Evolution theory – Animal-Human-God or reverse, Which is true?

Life in the creation began from the minutest uni-cellular organisms, which evolved into multi-cellular organisms, then into flora and fauna and finally from monkeys human beings evolved. This is the story of evolution; we read in our textbooks.

Modern theory of evolution is called Darwin's theory of evolution. According to it

1. There is variety in every species of life.
2. All the living beings compete with each other, to utilize the limited available resources.
3. The species capacitated to reproduce more alone shall thrive.
4. In a species, genetic features get transmitted from one generation to another.
5. Natural selection and survival of the fittest are the main reasons for evolution of one species to another.

This theory was propounded by Darwin in the year 1850, through his famous book "The origin of species". It had created sensation and became popular instantly. It had changed the face of "science of Biology". The words "Natural selection", "Survival of the fittest" and "struggle for existence" became the words of Mantra.

But there were many criticisms against this theory. During 1930, a new theory called Neo-Darwinism came into being. With the discovery of DNA, in 1970, the biological science had taken a new turn and a new branch called Molecular Biology evolved. Study of Genes and Genetic code became its main function. Between 2000 -2004, the Genomes had been classified and experiments such as cloning are being conducted. In the context of 21st century Biological knowledge of genomes and genetic engineering, the concepts of natural selection, survival of the fittest have become redundant and outdated.

Even from the ethical point of view, Darwin's theory was critised by none other than the world-renowned behavioral scientist Bertrand Russell, 'From evolution, as far as our present knowledge shows, no ultimately optimistic philosophy can be validly inferred.'

Modern evolution theory confines itself to physical and biological aspects. Whereas Knowledge of ancient India, not only considers, physical aspects of evolution, but also takes into account physical, mental and spiritual dimensions of evolution.

> "Modern evolution theory confines itself to physical and biological aspects. Whereas Knowledge of ancient India, not only considers, physical aspects of evolution, but also takes into account physical, mental and spiritual dimensions of evolution."

Indian perspective about evolution:

"From perfection every thing manifested and everything merges again into perfection and perfection alone remains." this is the central theme of Indian evolution.

From the lowest protoplasm to the perfect human being, there is really but one life. Just as in one life we have so many various phases of expression, the protoplasm developing into the baby, the child, the young man, the old man, so also, from that protoplasm upto the most perfect man we get one continuous life, one chain. This is evolution, but we have seen that each evolution presupposes an involution. The whole of this life, which slowly manifests itself, evolves itself from the protoplasm to the perfected human being---the Incarnation of God on earth the whole of this series is but one life, and the whole of this manifestation must have been involved in that very protoplasm.

Yet Indians classified various species of life and had complete knowledge of each species. Many ancient Indian sages, scholars or scientists had classified the species according to generic characterstic basis. The famous among them are Charaka, Sushruta, Prasistapada, Panini, Varahamihira, Parasara and Patanjali.

The *Bhṛhat-Viṣṇu Purāṇa* states that there are around 84, 00,000 species in the creation

- *Sthavara* - 20, 00,000 species of non-mobile plants
- *Jalachara* - 9, 00,000 species of aquatic creatures
- *Kurmas* - 9, 00,000 species of amphibian and reptiles
- *Pakshi* - 10, 00,000 species of birds
- *Pashu* - 30, 00,000 species of other creatures such as animals etc.
- *Vanaras* - 4,00,000 species of anthropoids (Vanaras)
- *Manushya* - 2,00,000 varieties of human beings come into being

The modern concepts of Genetic Engineering, cloning, do find a place in Indian literature, like puranas and yoga sutras of Patanjali.

Swami Vivekananda's views on Darwin's theory are as under-

"In the animal kingdom we really see such laws as struggle for existence, survival of the fittest, etc., evidently at work. Therefore, Darwin's theory seems true to a certain extent. But in the human kingdom, where there is the manifestation of rationality, we find just the reverse of those laws . . . The highest evolution of man is effected through sacrifice alone. A man is great among his fellow beings in proportion as he can sacrifice for the sake of others, while in the lower strata of the animal kingdom, that animal is the strongest which can kill the greatest number of animals. Hence the struggle theory is not equally applicable to both kingdoms. Man's struggle is in the mental sphere. A man is greater in proportion, if he can control his mind. When the mind's activities are perfectly at rest, the Atman manifests itself. (Complete Works of Swami Vivekananda, Vol. VII, p. 154-55)

Patanjali in his Yoga Sutras reveals what is meant by evolution

"jātyantara pariṇāmaḥ prakṛtyā pūrāt" *(Patanjali Yoga sutras-Ch4-sloka2)*

Internal nature is the main reason for evolution from one species to another.

Patanjali declares in the next sutra that,

"The change of the body from one species to another is caused by the inflowing of the jiva's nature. Good and bad deeds are not the direct causes of its transformation. They act as breakers of obstacles to the inflow of nature, just as a farmer breaks down obstacles in a water course to let water flow of itself."

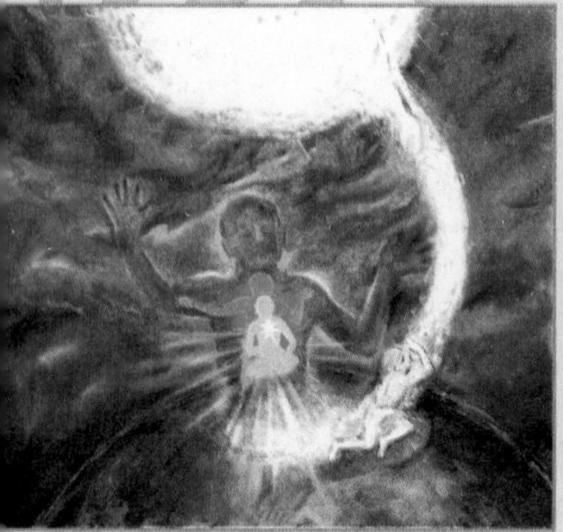

Expanding on this declaration of Patanjali, Swami Vivekananda has written commentary in his book Raja yoga regarding evolution,

"Perfection is man's nature, only it is barred in and prevented from taking its proper course. If anyone can take the bar off, in rushes "nature". Then the man attains the powers, which are his already.... It is "nature" that is driving us towards perfection, and eventually she will bring everyone there.... which is our birthright, our "nature".

Today, the evolution theory of the ancient Yogis will be better understood in the light of modern research. Yet the theory of the Yogis is a better explanation. The two causes of evolution advanced by the moderns, viz sexual selection and survival of the fittest, are inadequate. Suppose human knowledge to have advanced so much as to eliminate competition, both from the function of acquiring physical sustenance and of acquiring a mate. Then, according to the moderns, human progress will stop and the race will die. . .

Swami Vivekananda further says...

"But the great ancient evolutionist, Patanjali, declares that the true secret of evolution is the manifestation of the perfection which is already in every being; that this perfection has been barred and the infinite tide behind is struggling to express itself. These struggles and competitions are but the results of our ignorance, because we do not know the proper way to unlock the gate and let the water in. This infinite tide behind must express itself, it is the cause of all manifestation. Competitions for life or self-gratification are only momentary, unnecessary, extraneous efforts, caused by ignorance. Even when all competition has ceased, this perfect nature behind will make us go forward until everyone has become perfect. Therefore, there is no reason to believe that competition is necessary to progress." (Complete Works of Swami Vivekananda, Vol. I, p. 292-93)

In Bhagavatam there is a verse describing human evolution lucidly,

> **sṛṣṭyā purāni vividhānyajayātma śaktyāvṛkṣāṇ**
> **sarīsṛpān paśūn khagadamśa matsyaṁ**
> **tasmai atuṣṭaḥ hṛdayah puruśaṁ vidhāya**
> **brahmā valokādhiśaṇaṁ mudaṁ māpa devah**

"Cosmic Being manifests itself as creation. Trees, acquatic beings, insects, reptiles, animals, birds, germs and all the species of living beings manifest. But the consciousness never manifests in full in all of the above species. Hence Human being is created. Through Human being there is an opportunity to manifest that perfection"

Vedanta always talks about the divinity of Human being. This concept of divinity is indicative of three factors:

a) The feeling of oneness,
b) Recognizing the infinite power within,
c) The perennial urge to evolve and outgrow the limitations by the removal of obstacles through the greater manifestation of the divinity within.

Then "Tat twam asi–thou art that" becomes the watchward to manifest perfection.

> "Today, the evolution theory of the ancient Yogis will be better understood in the light of modern research. Yet the theory of the Yogis is a better explanation. The two causes of evolution advanced by the moderns, viz sexual selection and survival of the fittest, are inadequate
>
> - Swami Vivekananda"

"Oneness amongst men, the advancement of unity in diversity – this has been the core religion of India."

Rabindranath Tagore
Poet and writer of India's national anthem and Nobel Prize for Literature in 1913, (1861-1941)

"The Indian way of life provides the vision of the natural, real way of life. We veil ourselves with unnatural masks. On the face of India are the tender expressions which carry the mark of the Creator's hand."

George Bernard Shaw
Irish dramatist, literary critic, socialist spokesman
(1856-1950)

Technological Talents
Sānketika Pratibhā

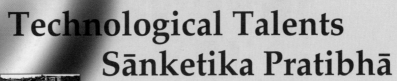

An Engineering Marvel of Ancient India

Meenakshi Temple Tank
With Two Floors Madurai,
Tamil Nadu.

33 Sage Agastya's way of Generating Electricity

In a Sanskrit treatise called, Agastya Samhita, sage Agastya had reavealed the method of generating electricity in a simple way. Modern battery cell resembles Agastya's method of generating electricity.

For generating electricity, Sage Agastya had used the following material :

1. One earthen pot
2. Copper plate
3. Copper sulphate
4. Wet saw dust
5. Zinc amalgam

saṁsthāpya mṛṇmayaṁ pātraṁ tāmrapatraṁ susaṁskṛtam
cādayet śikhigrīvena cārdrābhiḥ kāṣṭhapāṁsubhih
dastāloṣṭo nidhātatvaḥ pāradaccāditastataḥ
utpādayati tanmitraṁ saṁyogastāmradastayoḥ

(*Verse from – Agastya Samhita - Shilpa Sastra Sara.*)

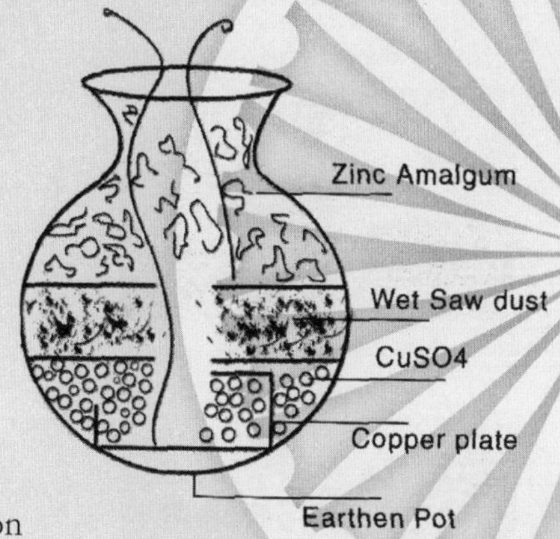

Agastya had further explained that if electricity generated from one hundred pots is thrown on water, then water splits into Hydrogen and Oxygen. He had also stated that this hydrogen (Udajani vayu) can be used as fuel in aircrafts.

In the same text many utilities of electricity, thus, generated had been mentioned. Techniques of electroplating of various metals and alloys with gold silver and copper were also mentioned.

34 Building Technology of India

Brick walls of Mohen-jo-daro – strong & ever lasting Indian Building products

800 year Chandragiri fort near Tirupati, (Andhra Pradesh)
No steel or wood had been used; in this multi storied building, only lime stone mortar

Indian Building technology dates back to Indus valley civilization. The existing archeological re-m-nants of Mohen-jo-daro and Harrappa stood ages, to testify the Indian building skills.

Ancient Indian edifices are known by their everlasting building products used therein. Dwelling places, Temples, Forts and other utility buildings were built in different forms and styles of architecture.

Building materials like bricks were manufactured in a scientific way. Klined bricks were used in con-structions. There are many evidences to support it.

The then British Government used the 5,000-year-old bricks found near Harrappan sites while laying railway line to Lahore in place of metal bed. They found them in fifteen standard sizes. (Ref: Lost Discoveries by Dick – Teresi Page 60)

"Mayamatha- kalamula Sastra", written by Kapila Vatsyayana, mentions about methods of making bricks and products used in brick making. (slokas 114-120)

catuṣpañcaṣaḍaṣṭābhiḥ mātraistaddhidviguṇāyatāḥ
vyāsārthārtha tribhāgaika tīvrā madhye paraśpare
iṣṭakā bahuśaḥ śaṣyah samdagdhaḥ punaśca taḥ

(Mayamatha- kalamula Sastra)

The book "Mayamatha- kalamula Sastra" also mentions methods of preparation of lime mortar and products that are used in making it. It also mentions about the solidifying strengtçh of that lime mortar.

35 Indian Town Planning Skills

When buildings of ancient India displayed beauty, towns of ancient India enhanced the beauty multifold. Five thousand years ago towns and cities of ancient India flourished with majesty and grandeur.

Broad roadways, streets running from North to South or East to West, with well-planned sectors of residential zones, underground drainage systems, centrally located temple square are typical of Indian style of town planning.

Kushinagar was the city of ninth century BC. Buildings of this city had the cylindrical structures erected on its top to allow free flow of air and light. These structures stand today to the astonishment of world.

Great bath, drainage systems, well-planned dwelling places of Mohan-jo-daro create awe and wonder within us. Mortar coating appears on the ruined walls of this ancient city. The quality and sizes of bricks used for construction are visible to us even today. They reflect the height of engineering excellence of our ancestors.

Valmiki Ramayana describes the three cities namely Ayodhya, Kishkindha and Lanka. Each of the three cites was described in a unique way; yet multi-storied buildings, broad roads, Industrial zones and business clusters were typical of each city.

Every book of Indian literature describes the city and its civilization related to the context before getting into the main theme of the book. The splendour of cities described in these books only reflects the advanced urban civilization of ancient India.

There are many technical texts like Vaastu Sastra in Sanskrit that describe the methods of planning and building towns and cities.

"Sukraniti", describes how to construct roads. It describes the ratio of products that are used in the lime stone mixture applied on the roads. The roads of ancient India appeared as hard and as smooth as tortoise's

Ruins of world's oldest city - Mohen-jo-daroa

Drainage system of mohan-jo-daro

Under ground drainage Tunnel at mohan-jo-daro

City of Madurai, Tamilnadu, with Meenakshi Temple at the centre (Brahma sthana)

shell. Ancient Indian Kings gave importance for construction of drains and culverts by the side of main roadways. *(Surkraniti ch-1-sloka165 & 166)*

Kautilya in his treatise Artha Sastra describes various types of roads prevailing during those times. According to this book, there were separate roads for pedestrians and chariots. There were separate roads for national transport and for royal vehicles.

Viswa karma in his vaastu sastra mentions about the techniques of constructing ghat roads, culverts and plain roads. *(Viswa karma vaastu sastra- 68-ch- marga lakshna 4-7)*

In the treatise called Mayamatam- Kalamula sastram (verses 60-61) describes the swastik pattern of town planning, grid pattern of town planning and radial pattern of town planning.

Most of the Indian towns were built in the form of perfect squares or concentric circles with a temple being located at the central position, along with formation of royal roads on the four sides of the temple. Creating a special functional zone for every activity is typical Indian town planning style.

kūrmapṛṣṭhā mārgabhūmaḥ kāryagrāmyaiḥ susetukā
kuryāṇmārgaṇ pārṣvakhātāṇ nirgamārthe jalasya ca

svastikamuditaṁ grāme yathā tathā svastikam vidyāt
prāguttaramukhamārgāḥ ṣaṭ ṣaḍabhīṣṭāstu tadbāhye

City of Tiruvannamalai, Tamilnadu, that exists around the famous Siva temple

36 World's First Constructed Dam

World's first dam was constructed in India. Even today, this dam is able to store water and regulate water. This dam remains today as a testimony for our ancient engineering expertise.

The name of this ancient dam is called "kallanai dam". It was built in 1st century AD across the river Cauvery in Tamilnadu of South India. This dam is located 48 kms away from the temple town Tanjavur.

The height of the dam is 320 meters and width is 60 metres. The important feature of this dam is that no binding materials like limestone or cement were used. It was constructed by the method of interlocking the granite stones.

Karikala Chola, who ruled the province during the 1st century AD, built this dam. He seems to be a great conqueror.

Even today, water stored and collected at this dam is being used for agriculture.

Sudarshan Jalasayam, the oldest man-made reservoir built during 4th BC, in the region of today's Gujarat, reminds us of the ancient Indian expertise in civil works.

1st Centrury AD, Kallani Dam built by Karikala Chola

37 "Paper" made in India-first

It is believed that a person called Tshai-lun of China, invented paper and gifted that to Chinese emperor in 105 AD. The art of making paper was kept a secret till the eighth century and Arabs had learnt that art from Chinese and from Arabs it spread to the world and was introduced into India in 10th century and 11th century.

But there are many evidences to show that paper was an Indian invention. It was made from cotton rags. Later it got migrated to China along with Buddhists.

- *Yajnavalkya Smriti* was composed around fourth century BC. In chapter 1:319 the word "pata' is used for writing material made from cotton rags. Making of paper from cotton rags is known to the Indians ages before Chinese claim of inventing paper. *(Eapat 1912, p-104)*
- Itsing, a chinese traveller visited India during 671A.D to 695A.D. He saw that paper was known even to laymen in India and Indians also used paper for impressing the images of dieties for worship, also with silk.
- In Jain books "Manavijya's Commentary" part-1 page 167 the word "kagad" or kadgal occurs as equivalent word used for writing material.
- Even Max Müller in the book " History of Ancient Sanskrit Literature", 1860 page 517 had said that Nearchus, the ambassador of Alexander who was in the Punjab for some years had stated that Indians used to make paper by beating cotton fabrics.
- Magasthenes, the Greek historian who accompainied Selucus in Chandra Gupta's court reported that Indians used durable paper for writing horoscopes and almanacs which necessiated long preservation. (Source GS OZA, the palaeography of India p-144)
- Sir M.A Stein, British archaeologist traces the wide usage of paper evidencing many manuscripts of second century A.D, written in "kharoshiti" & "paishachi " scripts which were colloquiial languages of Sind, Turkisthan and Central Asia, once the hinterland of

ancient India. (Source: L.P Barnett, antiquities of India 1913, p-227) These papers were made of cotton rags and are naturally sized.

- David Hunter in his book "The paper making- history and technique of ancient craft" had published a photograph of ancient paper, which is available in British muesum, London. It clearly shows the script "Taxshila", the once famous Indian centre of learning.
- French book "L"INDE CLASSIQUE, written by Manuel Dos, (etudes Indiannes), on page no 685 mentioned that origin of paper around 45 BC. pointing to script "Takit- I-BA" indicating Taxshila of Ancient India.
- Encyclopedia Britanica indicates the origin of paper to second century B.C (Volume xv11, p-229). "There is no definite evidence to show where and when the paper was invented". This stament appears in many books like Bristish Paper Maker Association book called "Paper making", London page-3: Colliner encyclopedia Vol xvi, 1957 p -460, Book called "paper" by H. A Meddox, 1939, p-3;
- Kashmir paper was made from pulp of rags and hemp with lime and soda added to whiten paper. The Kashmir paper even aquired the staus of being presented as an important article to the kings. By fourteenth centrury A.D there were many paper-producing centres in India (Sialkot) Punjab, Oudh (Zafarabad), Bihar (Bihar town and Atwal) Bengal (Murshidabad and Hoogly) Gujarat (Ahmadabad), Aurangabad and Mysore (during Tippu's period). Indian paper was exported to many countries of central Asia and elsewhere by fourteenth century. When Chinese paper was made from Bamboo-pulp, Indian paper was made from cotton rags and other material like jute etc. the style of making of paper was unique to India and it was common throughout India. If Indians learnt paper making from other countries, how could Indians excel in making paper within such a short time?

"Yajnavalkya smriti was composed around fourth century BC. In chapter 1:319 the word pata is used for writing material made from cotton rags. Making of paper from cotton rags is known to the Indians ages before Chinese claim of inventing paper."

38 Technique of predicting Earth Quakes

Can 21st century's scientists predict Earthquakes? Not surely. They are making sincere attempts to forecast the forthcoming catastrophes.

An American Scientist of Chinese origin, who lives in California, Mr Zhonghao Shou had been doing experiments to predict earthquakes for the past fifteen years.

He had found the technique of identifying the clouds in the sky before the advent of earthquakes. Clouds in the sky appear in mysterious shapes. So far he had predicted 39 earthquakes.

The rationale behind formation of clouds is that before the advent of earthquake at its epicenter, there would be generation of enormous amount of heat. The heat escapes into air and results in the formation of thick and fancy clouds, 50 days before the actual disaster.

Then what are Indians to do with it?

In the 6th century AD, Varahamihira, an ancient Indian Astronomer and Mathematician had mentioned the above fact in his famous encyclopedic work,

"Bhṛhat-samhitā ". The Thirty-second chapter of this book deals with various ways of predicting earthquakes.

According to Varahamihira, there would be fanciful clouds in the sky, seven days before the earthquake. He had even classified the various types of earthquakes and the related cloud formations.

He had analyzed the planetary influence and underground water's disappearance before the advent of earthquake. He had even analyzed the abnormal behaviour of birds and domestic animals days before the earthquake. The information and knowledge about the earthquakes that lie latent in that book shall save the lives of millions, if an earthquake is predicted in time.

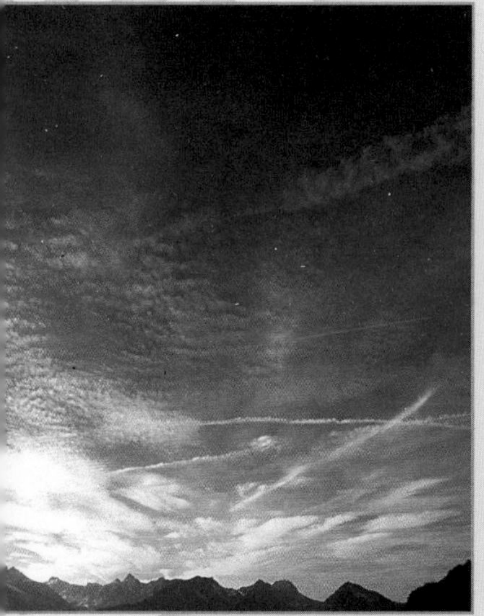

Interesting Cloud Formations

Source: *Times of India 28th April 2001 & Bhṛhat-samhitā -32nd chapter written by Varahamihira*

39 Finding the underground Water Resources

Varahamihira (6th century AD), the great Astronomer has a great encyclopedic work to his credit *"Bhṛhat-samhitā "*. The *Fifty Fourth Chapter* of this great book deals with the technique of exploring the underground water potential. Following are the few techniques mentioned therein: -

Rainwater falling from the sky possesses no colour and taste. But it acquires various colours and tastes when it reaches the earth owing to the differences in the nature of the soil. Hence water should be examined in relation to its environment.

Just as there are veins in the human body, there are veins inside the earth carrying water; some close to the surface and some others at a deeper level. These flow in eight directions and are named after the presiding deities. There is also a ninth vein known as Mahashira. Hundreds of smaller veins branch off from these main veins.

If there is an anthill covered by the holy grass to the north east of a mountain ebony tree, there will be inexahaustible water at a depth of twenty-two and a half cubits between the tree and the anthill.

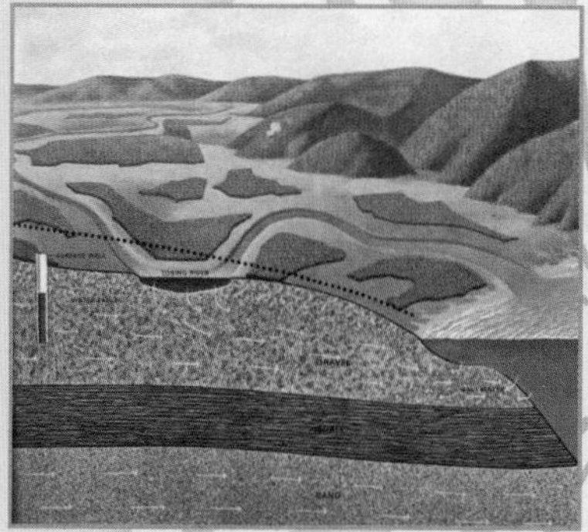

Water Stream below the Earth

The appearance of a snake of the colour of lotus calyx at a depth of five cubits from the surface level, followed by layers of red earth and coryndon stone indicates the presence of water.

The trees, which are short and widespread, with long hanging branches and glossy leaves, indicate the presence of underground water nearby, whereas trees, which are hollow and dry with pale leaves, indicate non-existence of underground water nearby.

> Just as there are veins in the human body, there are veins inside the earth carrying water; some close to the surface and some others at a deeper level. These flow in eight directions.

If there were an anthill to the east of a Jambutree, there would be sweet water at distance of three cubits to the north of the tree and at a depth of ten cubits under the ground.

If fish is found from the surface level, at a depth of two and a half cubits followed by layers of stone in the colour of a dove and blue clay, then under these layers there will be inexhaustible source of water.

If a Rotang tree is seen flourishing in a waterless tract, it indicates the presence of water at a distance of three cubits to the West of the tree and at a depth of seven and half cubits under the ground.

At a depth of two and a half cubits from the surface level, if a pale white frog is seen followed by layers of yellow clay and hard stone, water will be found underneath these layers.

According to the geologist, Dr. EAV Prasad, in the year 1981 ISRO and Venketeshwara University, Tirupati had successfully undertaken a project of digging borewells according to the water tracing methods of Varahamihira. Even today these borewells are flourishing with water.

40 A metallurgical marvel – Delhi Iron pillar

Iron pillar located in the compound of Kutubminar, Delhi, is a metallurgical marvel and stands today as the tallest evidence of Indian talents and Indian genius.

There is no parallel to this iron pillar, anywhere in the world.

Standing firm on the ground to the test of time for past 1,500 years, taking heat, storm, thunder into its stride, the Iron pillar never rusted an inch in its marathon innings.

The height of this Iron pillar is 7.5 metres, and 40 cm in diameter, six tonnes in weight. This marvel seems to have been manufactured during the time of Gupta Kings.

Recently, students and professors of metallurgical department, IIT, Kanpur made an intensive study on this Iron pillar and concluded that the *"Misawite coating"* that exists on the Iron pillar had protected it from rusting. The Misawite is a compound made of Iron, Oxygen and Hydrogen. The iron used in this pillar contains Phosphorus in major proportion.

Buddha's bronze statue found in Bihar, never rusted an inch and stood the test of time for more than 2500 years.

The two metallic monumental remnants that appear before us today, speak volumes about the advanced metallurgical knowledge prevailing in ancient India. Great chemical legends like Nagarjuna and others had contributed immensely to this science of metals. Alchemy of Arabs was inspired by the Indian skills of converting ordinary metals into gold.

(Ref: The Hindu 29.8.2002)

Iron Pilllar –An existing testimoninal for India's Matellurgical expertise

41 Origin of Lens

Modern knowledge pronounces that Bacon Roger 1214 AD - 1286 AD had invented lens. Does this imply that ancient world was ignorant of usage of lens?

Indians pioneered in surgery. Sushruta (800 BC) was considered the earliest surgeon. His famous treatise *"Sushruta Samhita"* declares that he had performed many eye surgeries and removed cataract. Ancient doctors who performed eye surgeries and eye transplants could not be unaware of utility of lens.

Gautama had written a textbook of Logic called Nyaya sastra, wherein he refers to the usage of lens

"aprāpya grahaṇam kācābhra paṭala sphaṭikāntarito palabdheḥ"

(Nyaya darshana chapter -3-46)

"That which cannot be viewed by the naked eye, can be viewed with the help of Kacha –Glass/lens, Abrapatala- Mica and Spatika- Crystal."

There would be many such references in our Sanskrit literature, we are yet to discover them. Our search into antiquity may require a special type of lens.

42 Art of Brightening Diamonds

India for eternity is a diamond mine. India was called ***"Ratna Garbha"***. Diamonds are mined here. Diamonds are cut here. Diamonds are polished here. These Indian Diamonds shine everywhere, in all ages. Indian diamond history dates back to 3000 BC.

Vedas speak of Diamonds. Among the Nine gems, Diamond stands glowing with importance. Indian science of light-Jyotish Sastra (popularly called as astrology), Ayurveda, (Indian medical knowledge), Alankara Sastra (Indian knowledge of beautification & jewellery), speaks volumes about diamond usage.

Raw Diamond

In Ayurveda there is a process called *"Agada Tantra"*, which removes the toxic elements from the body. Diamonds are used in medicinal preparations for removing toxic substances, along with lead and mercury. Indian Medical texts like Charaka, Sushruta and Aṣṭāṅgahṛidaya, mention the above process.

Diamond being cut

Indian medical texts had mentioned eight kinds of diamonds. Only diamond ash is used in medicines. Powdered diamond or liquefied diamond is harmful to health. The person who consumes them dies immediately. Diamond ash is used to cure diseases like paralysis, psychic and other neurotic problems.

Tips to identify a pure diamond…

1. Pure diamonds always remain flawless without any scratches.
2. When a diamond is placed in a glass of warm milk (having room temperature), the milk becomes chill.
3. When diamond is dropped in a cup of buttermilk or ghee, they freeze out.

Cut and Polished Diamond

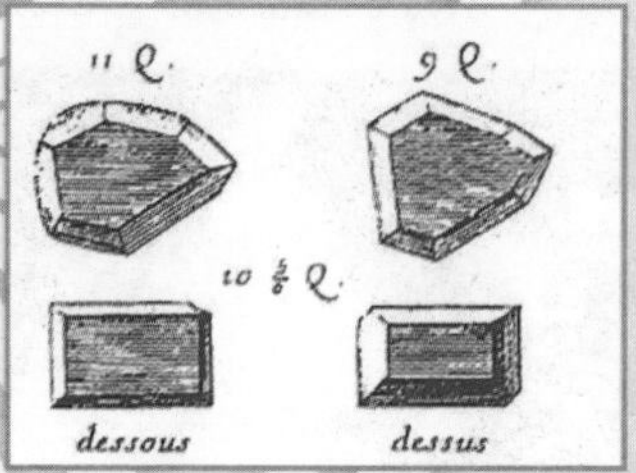

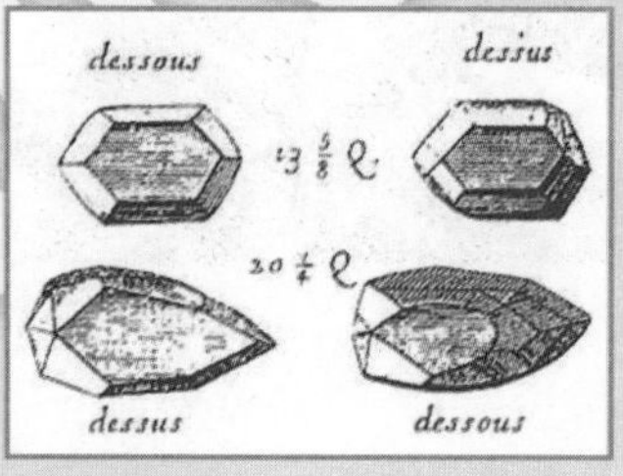

Jyotish Sastra mentions nine gems. Each gem is ascribed to a planet. Among them, Diamond is assigned to "Sukra Graha" (venus). If Venus is not properly placed in a person's birth chart (Jyotish kundali), then that person may be dull without creativity, without sexual vigour, without comforts, without vehicles. Etc.

If such a person wears diamond, then that person shall receive positive vibrations of planet Venus and may get relieved from the maladies mentioned above.

India was the home of diamonds up to the 18th century. Even Kautilya had mentioned diamond exports in his book Artha Sastra.

Since 1870, the Diamond scenario of the world changed with the discovery of diamond quarries in South America and Brazil. Yet India maintains its superiority in Diamond cutting and polishing.

India had been robbed of its wealth in many ways. Diamonds are no exception. The costliest diamond called "Kohinoor" (found in India) is now shining radiantly on the British crown. Diamond studded Peacock throne had been looted from India, by Nadir Shah.

In the year 2004 AD, the Diamond trade in India was around 10.3 Billion Dollars. Eight of ten diamonds that are produced in world come to India for cutting and polishing. Diamonds shine forever, so do India's talents of brightening diamonds shine forever.

43 Magnet & Its Varieties

Natural magnets are abundantly found in a place called Magnesia. It attracts Iron, deflects to north. Magnets can be either natural or artificial.

Ancient Indian books on Chemical science reveal an extensive knowledge about Magnets. In the book called *Rasarnavatantra,* Ninty kinds of magnets have been mentioned. (Ref. Rasarnava tantra-six patala). Among them there are five major varieties:

1. *Bramakam.*
2. *Chumbukam*
3. *Karshakam*
4. *Dravakam*
5. *Romakam*

Each of these five varieties had been further divided into six sub-categories based on its side or surface like Ekamukha (single surface), Dwimukha (two sided), Trimukha (three sided), total coming to thirty types of magnets. Each of the above combinations is available in three colours like Yellow, Red and Black. All the varieties including colour and facet combination are ninety in number.

Horse shoe Magnet

Utilities of Magnets as mentioned in Indian Texts

Yellow coloured magnets are of thirty varieties and normally used to convert ordinary metal into gold.

Black coloured magnets are also of thirty varieties and used in medicinal preparations for curing various diseases.

Red coloured magnets are again of thirty types, mainly used to solidify Mercury.

Grades of Magnets

Bramakam type of magnets is of low grade.

Chumbhukam type of magnets is of medium grade.

Karshakam type of magnets is good.

Dravakam type is the best.

Magnetic properties:

Bramakam can only move the Iron

Chumbukam attracts the iron and can hold it

Karshakam attracts all kinds of materials

Dravakam acts as a catalyst while melting gold and platinum at low temperature

Romakam causes attraction in metals

> **bhrāmayellohajātam tu tatkāntam bhrāmakam priye**
> **cumbaye ccumbakam kāntam karṣayet karśakam priye**
> **yatsākṣāddrāvayelloham tatkāntam drāvakam bhavet**
> **tadromakantamsphuṭitāt yatharomādgamo bhavet!!**

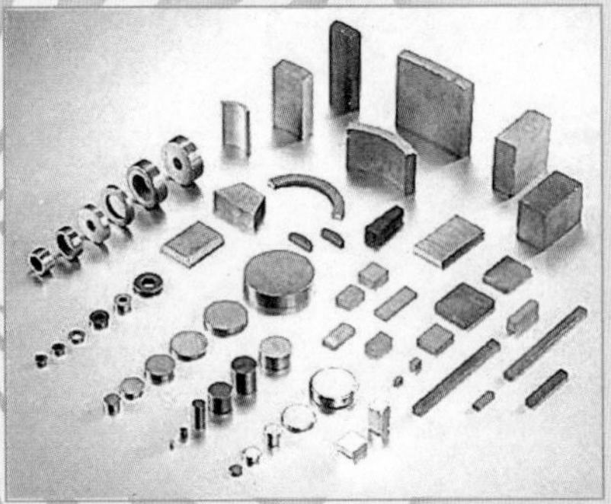

Various Kinds of Magnets

Indian books that give us the knowledge of magnets:

1. Rasarnavam
2. Rasavaghbatta
3. Rasendra chudamani
4. Rasaratna samuchhaya
5. Rasa khamadhenu
6. Loha padhati
7. Loha tantra

44 Marconi's wire "Less" values

Twenty first century is a "wireless" Century. Radios, TVs, Cell phones, satellite communications and most recent blue tooth technologies are all the technological marvels that are working on the "Wireless Technology".

Our schoolbooks portray Marconi as the hero and the inventor of "Wireless Technology" or Radio. We are told that in the year 1901, Marconi had transmitted the Morse code without using wires for the first time. He had transmitted them across the continents between England and Canada and became its Inventor.

But truth seems to be different. A brilliant child of mother India, Jagadish Chandra Bose, the then professor of Physics, Presidency College, Calcutta, was its inventor. India is deprived of taking into its stride this greatest technological achievement of Modern world. Today, we remember him for his achievements in Botany alone.

As early as 1895, JC Bose had demonstrated to the public of Calcutta about this technology. He had blasted the gunpowder and made the bell ring, which was one mile away from the place of demonstration. "Wireless" communication era was born in Calcutta from that Moment. This demonstration had been reported in an international Magazine called "Electrician" during that time. Important British dignitaries also watched the JC Bose demonstrations at Calcutta.

On September 21st 1896, JC Bose delivered a lecture cum demonstration at Royal Institute, London on wireless transmission. Eminent scientists including Marconi were present in that session.

JC Bose, demonstrated before the scientific community at London, his instruments, mainly the instrument called Co –Herer by using Mercury as the conducting material and a telephone. Bose gave number of demonstrations in Europe and America regarding wireless technology.

JC Bose – First Inventor of Wireless Technology

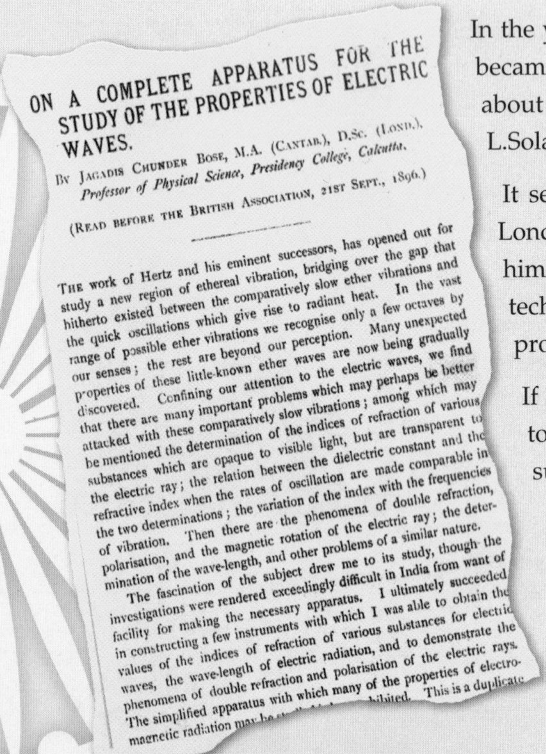

ON A COMPLETE APPARATUS FOR THE STUDY OF THE PROPERTIES OF ELECTRIC WAVES.

By Jagadis Chunder Bose, M.A. (Cantab.), D.Sc. (Lond.), *Professor of Physical Science, Presidency College, Calcutta.*

(Read before the British Association, 21st Sept., 1896.)

The work of Hertz and his eminent successors, has opened out for study a new region of ethereal vibration, bridging over the gap that hitherto existed between the comparatively slow ether vibrations and the quick oscillations which give rise to radiant heat. In the vast range of possible ether vibrations we recognise only a few octaves by our senses; the rest are beyond our perception. Many unexpected properties of these little-known ether waves are now being gradually discovered. Confining our attention to the electric waves, we find that there are many important problems which may perhaps be better attacked with these comparatively slow vibrations; among which may be mentioned the determination of the indices of refraction of various substances which are opaque to visible light, but are transparent to the electric ray; the relation between the dielectric constant and the refractive index when the rates of oscillation are made comparable in the two determinations; the variation of the index with the frequencies of vibration. Then there are the phenomena of double refraction, polarisation, and the magnetic rotation of the electric ray; the determination of the wave-length, and other problems of a similar nature.

The fascination of the subject drew me to its study, though the investigations were rendered exceedingly difficult in India from want of facility for making the necessary apparatus. I ultimately succeeded in constructing a few instruments with which I was able to obtain the values of the indices of refraction of various substances for electric waves, the wave-length of electric radiation, and to demonstrate the phenomena of double refraction and polarisation of the electric rays. The simplified apparatus with which many of the properties of electro-magnetic radiation may be ... hibited. This is a duplicate

Paper submitted By JC Bose at British association

In the year 1901, Marconi had patented the technology, used and demonstrated by JC Bose and became its inventor and owner. Many scientists had raised objections to this and asked Marconi about its important part called "Co-herer". He told the world community that a friend called L.Solar gave it.

It seems that JC Bose had written a letter to Ravindranath Tagore, on May 17th 1901 from London. He wrote that a millionaire, who was the owner of a Telegraph company, approached him and begged him to sell the "wireless technology" for 50% profit rights, by patenting the technology. At that instance, JC Bose was about to give a lecture in London and denied the proposal.

If JC Bose had patented the technology, he would have become the source of inspiration to many young Indian scientists of that time. And Indians would have patented many of subsequent inventions that are mostly claimed and patented as Western inventions.

Instruments used for Demonstration
Photo Courtesy: JC Bose Institute, Calcutta.

45 Textile technology of India

Since time immemorial, Indians had the knowledge of growing cotton, weaving it into clothes and tailoring them into dress material.

Greek Historian " Herodatus", (400 BC), describing India's greatness, had said that in India there are plants that produce the sheep's wool. (Referring to cotton plant).

During the Gupta's reign (200BC), Indians were exporting cotton to China, Greece, Egypt, Rome and Arabian countries with an expensive price tag.

If a commoner in India wore a cotton cloth, the richest of the western countries wore the same Indian cotton cloth as a luxury item.

Cotton is one of the major attractions that made Europeans throng to India.

Vedas mention about the cotton weaving and cotton growing. Vedas refer to a seer called "Grusthayudha ", who had grown cotton plants and made the cotton thread from them. The seer had obtained 10 measures of cotton from that plant.

Vedic terminology describes raw thread as "Tantu" and remnant cotton as Othu "

From the Vedic beginning, Indian cotton story had come a long way, as Indians became experts in cotton growing and achieved the height of excellence in textile technology.

Indians had the skill of weaving a wafer thin cloth that could be packed in a small matchbox sized golden box. A French traveller called Tavernier (17th century) had recorded the above fact in his writings.

Best-woven cotton cloth was tested at Dacca (now in Bangladesh), by piercing that cloth through a diamond ring and cloth would go through that small hole smoothly.

> Indians had the skill of weaving a wrapper thin cloth that could be packed in a small matchbox sized golden box. A French traveller called Tavernier (17th century) had recorded the above fact in his writings.

Indians offer new clothes in their worship to Gods and Goddesses. Indian deities are often decorated with splendid Indian fabrics. Culturally India's rich art is inter-woven with Indian textiles and Indian lifestyle.

American Historian Will Durant says in his famous book "The Story of civilization or oriental heritage: "Textiles were woven with an artistry never since excelled; from the days of Caesar to our own the fabrics of India have been prized by all the world. From homespun khaddar to complex brocades flaming with gold, from picturesque pyjamas to the invisibly-seamed shawls of Kashmir, every garment woven in India has a beauty that comes only of a very ancient, and now almost instinctive art." *(Source: Story of Civilization: Our Oriental Heritage - By Will Durant MJF Books. 1935 p. 585).*

Indian handwoven clothes or Indian dyed handlooms are called chiniz. Natural Coloured Dyes, Colour Mix, Cloth's texture, the artistic expression on the cloth, all remain as mystery and puzzle to the Europeans even today.

A famous historian " Andre Dubus" had said, "at the beginning of 17th century India was a very big commercial centre for textile trade".

Ahmedabad and Surat were the biggest textile centers of medieval India. From costliest fabric to cheapest cloth, from silk to cotton every variety of cloth was available in these textile centres of India.

During the sixteenth century for the first time in world, dyed cotton fabrics were exported. These dyed fabrics had created huge demand in European markets. The craze towards Indian clothes was very high among European women. They had even resisted the ban imposed by various European Governments on Indian textiles.

In the year 1658, Hollanders attempted to make dyed clothes imitating Indian dyes. These fabrics resulted in unnatural colours and unbearable smell; and so they remained as unwearable grotesque. It took seventy years for them to attain a level of refinement in dyeing technology.

In certain European libraries, we find many manuscripts of letters written between 1742 & 1747. These letters speak about the greatness of Indian textile talents.(Ref: Decolonizing History, technology and culture in India, China and the west from 1492 to present day- Clande Alvares p55-67)

Till 1850, India remained an undisputable queen in textile business. With the advent of Industrial revolution, British began producing the machine made cloth and simultaneously created many black laws against Indian hand-made textiles.

Many of Indian weavers were thrown out of jobs. Many traders in Indian textiles became insolvent in their trade due to economic sanctions imposed by the British.

Inspite of hurdles created by the British laws and heavy competition from machine made textiles, Indian textiles created their own brand image and survived bad times.

Kashmir shawls, Benaras, Dharmavaram, Kanchi, Kalankari, Palampur, Dongri, Paisley and Bengal fabrics earned their own brand image throughout the world and re-established Indian textile's supremacy.

Today, India has become the largest producer & exporter of textiles and dress material. The best, the cheapest and the costliest fabrics of the world are available only in India today.

The infinite cultural heritage of India had absorbed the Textile industry's temporary setbacks during the period of lull. Now the wave of Indian textile talents has taken an upward surge in its eternal flow, gushing ahead with all vigour.

"India is the Land of religions, cradle of human race, birthplace of human speech, grandmother of legend, great grandmother of tradition."

Mark Twain
American Author (1835-1910)

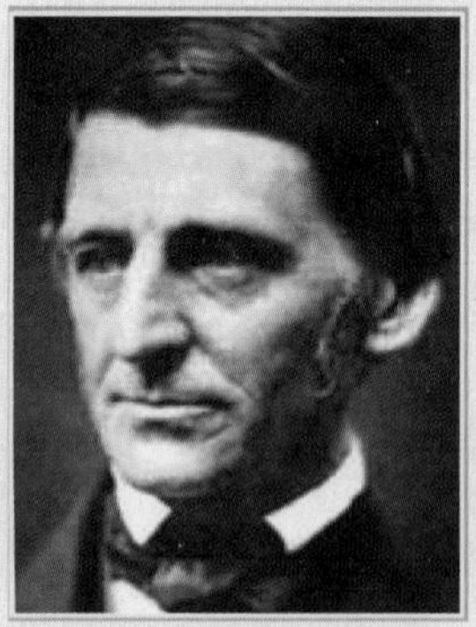

Ralph Waldo Emerson
American Philosopher
(1803-1882)

"I owed a magnificent day to the Bhagavad-Gita. It was the first of books; it was as if an empire spoke to us, nothing small or unworthy, but large, serene, consistent, the voice of an old intelligence which in another age and climate had pondered and thus disposed of the same questions which exercise us."

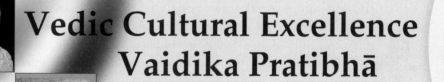

Vedic Cultural Excellence
Vaidika Pratibhā

46 Vedas – The Creator's Manual

"vedo'khilaṁ dharma mūlam "- ***Manu Smṛti.***

All the Dharmic laws are ever rooted in Vedas

Cosmic laws of nature, human laws of nature, animal laws of nature, and all the laws of nature, including man-made laws are rooted in Vedas. The word Veda means knowledge. Etymological root "vid" of the word Veda means 'to know'.

To create anything we require knowledge of making it; to create a pot, we should have the knowledge of making a pot; to cook food we require the knowledge of cooking; similarly to create this cosmos, the knowledge that the Creator had applied is Veda.

Human being is an intellectual being, who has freedom of will and action. Other living beings do not need any intellectual exhortations; animals do not require intellectual inputs and lectures; because they float with nature's rhythm and cadence; Animal's life is a sensual experience; where as Human's life alone is an attitudinal expression. The independent intellectual expression of human being requires certain guiding principles, which govern this creation. They are Vedas. So human actions are to be performed according to the guidance of Vedic precincts, then and then alone, Human excellence and human wellbeing manifest as the best possible expressions. Such is the importance of Vedic knowledge to human beings.

Indian culture is rooted in Vedas. Dharma Sastras, Puranas, Music, Literature, Sculpture, Dance etc, various branches of sciences, Mathematics, Ayurveda, Astronomy, Chemistry, Botany and all the oriental knowledge had evolved from Vedas.

Vedas are not any textbooks to teach knowledge. They are not even the ethics that are usually taught by any religious texts. Sound is given prime importance in Vedas. For this reason, Vedas are called Shrutis. (That can only be heard or uttered)

Today, modern science considers this universe to be a big pack of energy. Energy is identified or recognized by its vibrations. Every vibration is accompanied by a sound. Conversely through sound, vibrations can be created. That sound repository is Veda. But Vedas are not the man-made sounds. They exist in creation as cosmic vibrations. Vedas are called "Apaurusheyam" meaning that they are not created by man. They are hymns, which were perceived or seen by the seers of yore. Hence Vedic seers were called as "Mantra Draṣṭās".

Through penance and austerity, the seers had controlled the senses and had perceived the truth that is beyond the grasp of senses. For the human wellbeing they had conveyed these truths known as Vedas.

The facts of the creation and life in it are called "Truth" (Satyam). Surya (the sun), Chandra (the moon), Pancha bhuthas (earth, water, fire, air and space) are all the parts of creation and are considered "Satyas" (Truths). "Ṛtam" is the ultimate cause for these truths. "Ṛtam" reveals the ultimate truth. "Ṛtam" is the cause of all causes.

Branches, leaves, flowers and fruits of a tree are visible to us; then we perceive the trunk of the tree; but roots are far below them and are not visible to us. Because they are not visible to us, can we say that they do not exist? Similarly, it is our foolishness to deny the truths that are the roots and seeds for the tree of creation.

Without roots there is no tree. Without the truths of Vedas, there is no creation. These truths that are being called as "Ṛtam" are the roots. One has to get hold of these roots. If we can catch hold of them (the truths or roots) we will understand the relationship between the creation and the "Ṛtam".

The health & strength of a tree depends on its roots. So does the creation's wellbeing or harmony depend upon the Vedas. To understand the creation, one has to understand the Vedas. We therefore , have to nourish the minds with the water of Vedic wisdom, the "Ṛtam".

"To create anything we require knowledge of making it; to create a pot, we should have the knowledge of making a pot; to cook food we require the knowledge of cooking; similarly to create this cosmos, the knowledge that the creator had applied is Vedas."

The state of mind that links the mind with Ṛtam is "Ṛtambharā Prajñā". The person who earns that or perceives that truth is a "Rishi". That knowledge discovered & shared by him with us is Vedic knowledge. These seers had neither created anything afresh nor told us out of their vivid imagination. They visualized the facts with intuition and conveyed them to us for our wellbeing.

Vedas got mingled in the Indian blood for ages. Indians were cultured and refined by Vedas. Vedic culture became the culture of India. Vedas are not hidden in the books or confined to bookish learning. They have become the very life-breath of Indian society. Indian-ness means Vedic culture; Indian society is a Vedic society.

Varied ethnic groups, varied customs, varied, languages, varied lifestyles of Indians, have common Vedic background. Kingdoms, boundaries or politics can neither become the cause for it nor can influence it. Indians are rooted in Vedas. For ages, the Vedic culture is being protected by the Indian society and Indian seers by adhering to strict austerities of penance and self-discipline.

"Learning Vedas" means acquiring mastery over the fourteen branches of Vedic studies.

They include

A) Four Vedas- Ṛg Veda, Yajur Veda, Sāma Veda & Atharva Veda.

B) Six Vedangas-Siksha, Vyakarana, Chandas, Niruktha, Jyotisya & Kalpa Sastras

C) Four Upaangas: Mimamsa, Nyaya, Purana & Dharma Sastra

Vedas

Ṛg Veda	It contains various hymns about the deities for obtaining their grace. It contains the knowledge about Creation and celestial bodies. "Rukh" means vedic mantra. Āyurveda is being considered as an Upaveda of Rigveda.
Yajur Veda	For the mantras of Ṛg-Veda, it describes the methodology of performing yagnas and Karmic rites. The upa-Veda is Dhanur Vedaa) Shukla Yajur Veda: Mostly followed in North India.b) Krishna Yajur Veda: Mostly followed In south India.
Sāma Veda	Sāmaveda is a collection of hymns or mantras with melody of music, rhythm, and precise svaras (musical pitch) in praise of deities. The seven notes of music (sa-ri -ga-ma- pa-dh-ni) originated from Sāmaveda. The Upaveda for Sāmaveda is Gandharva veda.
Atharva Veda	Atharvaveda has the hymns, which protect us from evil forces, and also contains the knowledge about our health and various Technologies useful for day-to-today living. The upaveda for Atharva veda is Artha sastra.

Each of the four Vedas is divided into four parts	1. Samhita	*Mantra part of worshipping the deities.*
	2. Brahmanam	*Explains the mantras and karmic rites*
	3. Arnyakam	*Talks about the philosophical meanings of mantras*
	4. Upanishads	*Para vidya- explains the intricacies in obtaining Liberation (Mokhsa) and knowledge of cosmic secrets.*

"Without roots there is no tree. Without the truths of Vedas, there is no creation. These truths that are being called as Ruthum are the roots. One has to get hold of these roots. If we can catch hold of them (the truths or roots) we will understand the relationshi p between the creation and the Ruthum."

Vedangas

Sikṣā Śāstram — It is like the nose to the Veda Purusha. It is the science of phonetics. It deals with ways and means of pronouncing a word. The pitch, the mode, the cadence, the timing, the strength, with which the words are to be uttered are discussed in Siksha sastram

Vyākaraṇam — It is like the mouth of Veda purusha. The science of Grammar. Sanskrit is a structured language. Vedic nouns, adjectives and prepositions require accurate placement and pronunciation; hence the grammar rules. The most famous grammar rules of Sanskrit were written by Panini called *"Ashtadhyayi"*. Patanjali had written a commentary on it called *" Maha bhasyam"*.

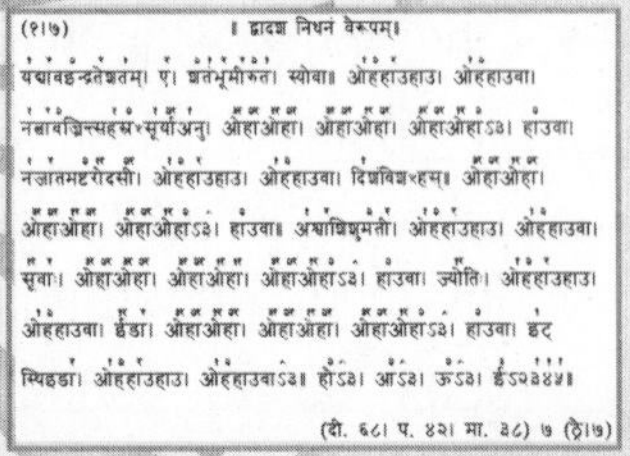

(१।७) ॥ द्वादश निधनं वैरूपम्॥

यथावछन्दतेशतम्। ए। शतंभूमीरुत। स्योवा॥ ओहहाउहाउ। ओहहाउवा।
नत्वावज्रिन्सहस्र॰सूर्याअनु। ओहाओहा। ओहाओहा। ओहाओहाऽ३। हाउवा।
नजातमष्टरोदसी। ओहहाउहाउ। ओहहाउवा। दिव्यविश्व॰हम्॥ ओहाओहा।
ओहाओहा। ओहाओहाऽ३। हाउवा॥ अश्वाश्रिशुमती। ओहहाउहाउ। ओहहाउवा।
सूवा। ओहाओहा। ओहाओहा। ओहाओहाऽ३। हाउवा। ज्योति। ओहहाउहाउ।
ओहहाउवा। इडा। ओहाओहा। ओहाओहा। ओहाओहाऽ३। हाउवा। इट
म्यिहडा। ओहहाउहाउ। ओहहाउवाऽ३॥ होऽ३। आऽ३। ऊऽ३। ईऽ२३४५॥

(दी. ६८। प. ४२। मा. ३८) ७ (ठै।७)

Chandas — It is like the feet of Veda Purusha. It reveals Prosody and meter of vedic verses. Precise number of letters, that, the vedic verse should contain etc, are dealt in Chandas Sastra. *Pingla's* work *Chandas Sastra* is the famous work in this branch of study.

Niruktam — It is like the ear of the Veda purusha. It gives the etymology of vedic words. Meanings of Vedas are contextual and cryptic. They differ from the meanings of ordinary usage.

Jyotiṣya — It is like the eyes of the Veda Purusha. It reveals the time for performing the Vedic yagnas. It contains the Mathematical and Astronomical calculations. It is the science of light that co-relates the Planetary influences on the earthly events and individual.

Kalpa Sutras

It is like the hands of Veda Pursha. It reveals to us how a Vedic Act has to be performed in the form of sutras. (Aphorisms). Kalpa Sutras are divided into two types *1. Gruhya Sutras 2. Srota Sutras.* Srota Sutras deal with measurements, methods of constructing the vedic altars, platforms for perfoming sacrifices etc. the methods of performing yagnas etc. Sulbha sutras are a part of srota sutras. Sulbha sutras contain the knowledge of mathematics in general and geometry and trigonometry in particular.

Gruhya Sutras deal with various purification ceremonies that a householder has to perform like, *Seemantham, Namakaranam, Annaprasana, Upanayanam. Vivaaham, Sashtipoorti, Dahana samskaram and Sraadha* Karmas.

Baudhayana, Apasthamba, Mannava, Maitrivaruna had written both Srota and Gruhya Sutras. Where as *Katsyayana, Drahyayana* and others had written Gruhya Sutras.

> "Vedas are not hidden in the books or confined to bookish learning. They have become the very life breath of Indian society. Indian-ness means Vedic culture; Indian society is a Vedic society;"

Veda Bhashyas: According to Niruktha, it is sinful if a person utters Veda without knowing its meaning. The persons who perform the Vedic sacrifices are called Rithviks. They should be well-versed in the meanings of Vedic performances.

Hence there are many who had written commentaries on Vedic verses. Sri Madhvacharya had written commentary on 40 suktas of Ṛg-veda. Batta Bhaskara had written commentary for Krishna Yajur Veda. Mahidhara had written commentary for Shukla Yajurveda.

Sāyanācārya had written commentaries for the four Vedas. They became very popular. Foreigners had this Bhashya as authority and learned the Vedas. Swami Dayananda Sarswati had also written commentaries on selected Vedic Suktas.

pra kṣodasā dhāyasā sasra
eṣā sarasvatī dharuṇamāyasī pūḥ
prabābadhānā rathyeva yāti
viśvā apo mahinā sindhuranyāḥ
Rig Veda 07.095.01.1-2

Upaangas

Mimamsa

Mimamsa had been divided into two parts as follows:

1. Purva Mimamsa: It contains karma kanda. It describes the purpose of the mantra & Yagnas; their importance, their performance and benefits. Jaimini sutras are an authoritative text of Purva Mimamsa school of thought

2. Uttara mimamsa: It contains Upanishads, Brahmasutras, and the related commentaries. It is called Jñana Kanda.

Nyaya

Nyaya is the school of logic and reasoning. It builds the Chain of logic and brings out the rational perspectives of the vedic principles. It evolves a system of questioning and leads to final conclusions.It has two branches 1. Nyaya 2. Vaisheshika Nyaya Darshana was written by Gauthama. Vaisheshika Darshana was written by Kanaad. It also deals with many aspects of Physics, Chemistry and Cosmology.

Purana

Puranam means past. Puranas teach us the Veda dharmas based on life incidents of people who lived in the past. Veda Vyasa had compiled eighteen puranas. Apart from puranas we have two famous epics called Itihasas, the factual history. They are 1. Ramayana 2. Mahabharata

Dharma sastras

Dharma sastras are Smritis. They deal with the ethics and Human behaviour for obtaining the liberation, which is the ultimate goal of human life. They reveal the qualifications of vedic performers and related aspects. They deal with the expected ethical behaviour from a person for the over all human wellbeing. Important Smritis are Manu Smriti, Parasara Smriti, Yagnavalkya Smriti, Gautama Smriti and Yama Smriti.

For the past one thousand years, there were colossal attacks on Indian culture from various fronts. The attacks on Indian Culture can be classified into two major aspects

1. Physical attacks 2. Intellectual attacks

Physically, Temples, the living symbols of Indian culture were looted, destroyed and the idols were smashed. Our Libraries were ransacked, and books of knowledge were burnt.

Intellectually, they attacked the educational system, by introducing Western thought and culture. They debased Vedas by writing improper commentaries of wrong interpretations. They started interpreting Veda without obtaining the minimum proficiency in Vedangas. The major blow came when they decided the time of eternal Vedas, which were never created by any human being.

> "Varied ethnic groups, varied customs, varied, languages, varied lifestyles of Indians, have common Vedic background. Kingdoms, boundaries or politics can neither become the cause for it nor can influence it. Indians are rooted in Vedas"

Vedas and human wellbeing:

The secular knowledge is also rooted in Vedas. Many branches of science and technology like Mathematics, Astronomy, Medicine, Surgery, Metallurgy, Agriculture, Animal Husbandry, Aeronautics, Warfare, Building Technology, and Literature were inherited from Vedas. (These aspects are being dicussed in the other parts of this text).

Let us dwell upon the aspects of human wellbeing mentioned in the Vedas; Vedas are replete with feelings of human wellbeing; Vedas have revealed to us how to look at the world with the Vedic eyes? *"Mitrasya chakshusa samiksha mahay"* let us see the world with the eyes of friendliness" *"Mitrasya"* means with a feeling of friendliness; *"Chakshusa"*, *"Samiksha Mahay"* means seeing with the eyes or developing a vision of friendliness ; The above Vedic verse reveals the kind of approach that we should have towards the world ; Vedas contain many such sublime thoughts of Human wellbeing; Let us see the world with friendly eyes, not with a feeling of hate; Your world of creation depends upon your mind's vision; As is your vision, so is your creation; If you see the world with friendly eyes, world becomes friendly to you; When you initiate a conversation with others, you see a friend in him and if you talk to him in a Positive way, then there are chances of even the cruelest person becoming a friend.

Let us live together; Sam-gacchatwam (let us travel together): Sam-vadatwam (let us speak with one voice); similarly let us all have one mind; let us eat together; let us live together;

samānī va ākūtiḥ samānā hṛdayāni vaḥ
samāna mastu vo mano yathā vaḥ susahāsati (Atharva veda 6.64.4)
These feelings express the feeling of unity and oneness in every aspect of life; when Vedas are replete with such exhortations; what more can be said about human wellbeing; The primary objective and wish of the Vedas is that all should live together; share together and evolve; Vedas never accept the grabbing mindset of an individual. The whole world is the manifestation of God. Therefore, a friendly relationship should exist from individual to the world and from the world to the individual for mutual prosperity. This is the Vedic perspective about society's growth and development.

In Vedas one can find the inter-human relationship very clearly depicted; these revelations pertain to a period of immomerial time. See the expansiveness and vision of these eternal Vedas; According to historians, normally it takes many thousands of years for a civilization to evolve. The pristine and refined Vedic thoughts are surely not man-made aphorisms but existed since the advent of creation and is the very basis of it.

47 Great bluff of Aryan Invasion Theory

Our schoolbooks are stuffing our minds from our childhood with many distorted facts. One such great bluff is Aryan Invasion theory, the brainchild of our imperial invaders, the British. It is Sixty years since they left us free, yet we carry those sham & concocted versions with us, more in our history books and stuff our future Indians with slavish mindsets.

Let us try to understand, what this theory is all about; how it originated, how it is a fake story of malice and falsehood, evolved with an intention of "Divide India to rule India"

Racially, the Aryans had been projected as the white coloured race, migrated from middle Asia, or from Black Sea into India on horsebacks and had driven out the local Dravidians into South India and established superior culture and civilization in Northern part of India. There are many allied stories that are added to flavour the main fictitious theory.

This theory had done great harm to Indians. It ripped apart Indians into Aryan and Dravidian. North Indians were projected as Aryans. South Indians were branded as Dravidians. Further the upper classes (Brahmins, Kshatriyas and Vaisyas) of India were depicted as Aryans in orgin. The Sudras were termed Dravidian in origin.

This theory had not only torched the Indian minds, but also influenced the German dictator Adolf Hitler with Aryan superiority complex, that had resulted in Second World War, the greatest human tragedy of the modern times.

Aryan race story is a creation of the British. Let us analyze this theory from different perceptives to understand the malicious intentions of the people who concocted it

1. Vedas do not mention anywhere that Aryans migrated from any far-off Lands.

"One such great bluff is Aryan Invasion theory, the brainchild of our imperial invaders, the British. It is Sixty years since they left us free, yet we carry those sham & concocted versions with us, more in our history books and stuff our future Indians with slavish mindsets."

Great Bath of Indus valley Ruin

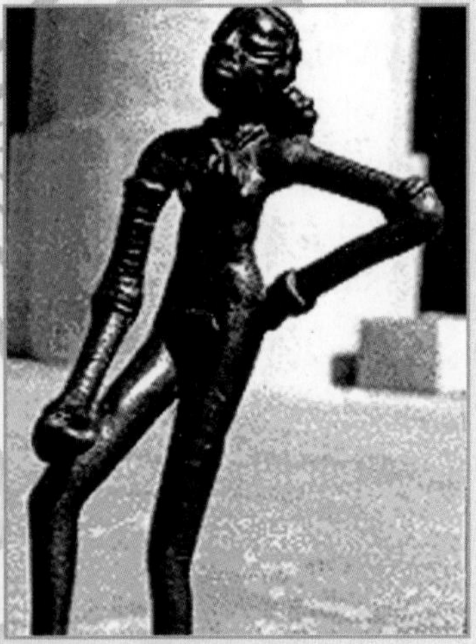

Dancing Girl of Indus ruins

2. According to the Vedic meaning, the word "Arya" is the qualitative pronunciation uttered with respect to denote the exemplary behaviour of a person. The word was never used in Vedas to signify a racial meaning. The word Arya means "noble", "cultured","revered" etc.

3. The word- "dasyu" means the person who has no control on oneself, or one who is under the influence of senses. It was used to describe the character of a person. The word was never used in the racial or ethnic context in the entire gamut of Vedas.

4. Arya Varta and Dravida Pradesha are the locations in India. Vedas, Puranas and other literatures of India describe them so.

5. The Aryan invasion Theory's birthday seems to be April 10th, 1866, at a secret meeting held in England by Royal Asiatic society.

This was "to induct the theory of the Aryan invasion of India, so that no Indian may say that English are foreigners...India was ruled all along by outsiders and so the country must remain a slave under the benign Christian rule." *(Ref: Proof of Vedic Culture's Global Existence - By Stephen Knapp p. 39).*

6. Two European intellectuals had widely popularized the word "Arya". They were Sir William Jones and Prof. Max Muller.

Sir William Jones (1746-1794) was the honorable Judge of Calcutta's Supreme Court. He was the first person who had found the connectivity between Sanskrit and other European languages. Max Muller, the German Linguist on the other hand had translated the Vedas into English.

7. In the year 1784, William Jones wrote a letter to the then Governor General Warren hastings, how to spread "our pure faith" as "no mission from the Church of Rome will ever be able to convert the

Hindus." He wrote about translating Bible into Sanskrit and "then quietly to disperse the work among the well-educated natives."
(Source: West Asian languages derived from Indus script - By Bhikhu Patel)

8. Muller did his scholarly work with certain ulterior motives. When writing to his wife in 1866 about his translation of the Ṛg Veda, he observed: "This edition of mine and the translation of the Veda will hereafter tell to a great extent... the fate of India, and on the growth of millions of souls in that country. It is the root of their religion, and to show them what the root is, I feel sure, the only way of uprooting all that has sprung from it during the last 3000 years."
(Source: The Life and Letters of the Rt. Hon. Fredrich Max Muller, edited by his wife. Longmans, London, 1902, Volume I, p. 328)

9. In 1946, Dr. Ambedkar wrote a book titled, "Who were Sudras?" In it, he pooh-poohs the Aryan invasion myth. He says "That the theory of the Aryan race set up by the Western writers fail to the ground at every point, goes without saying....Anyone who comes to scrutinize the theory will find that it suffers from a 'double infection.' In the first place, the theory is based on nothing but pleasing assumptions and the inferences based on such assumptions. In the second place, the theory is a perversion of scientific investigation. It is not allowed to evolve out of facts. On the contrary, the theory is preconceived and facts are selected to prove it". He had completely devoted one chapter, "Sudras Vs Aryans" and discussed at length the malafide intentions of propunders of this theory.

10. Swami Dayananda (1824-1883) was perhaps the first Indian to dispute the Aryan myth: "In none of the Sanskrit history textbooks" he wrote, "has it been stated that the Aryans came from Iran, vanquished the aborigines...and became rulers". He stressed that the word Arya referred in the Veda to a moral or inner quality, not to any race or people, and insisted that India was Aryavarta, the home of the Aryans- a word he used purely in its original sense of "Vedic Indians."

Dr.Ambedkar-who saw the evil designs of this Theroy

"That the theory of the Aryan race set up by the Western writers fails to the ground at every point, goes without saying. Anyone who comes to scrutinize the theory will find that it suffers from a double infection.
-Dr.Ambedkar

11. Swami Vivekananda (1863-1902) was the one who was quick to see through the gaps in the Aryan theroy. In a lecture in the U.S.A., he remarked scornfully: "And what your European Pandits say about the Aryans swooping down from some foreign lands snatching away the land of aborigines and settling in India by exterminating them, is pure nonsense, foolish talk. Strange, that our Indian scholars too say "Amen" to them".

12. In his Secret of the Veda, Sri Aurobindo (1872-1950) called on Indians not to be "haunted by the unfortunate misconstruction of the Veda which European scholarship has imposed on the modern mind". "The indications in the Veda on which this theory of a recent Aryan invasion is built, are very scanty in quantity and uncertain in their significance. There is no actual mention of such an invasion..."

13. Bluff of the great Aryan theory got mitigated with excavations of Indus valley civilizations at Mohen-jo-daro & Harappan sites in the year 1920. Later Archeological evidences like Lothal port and other Harappan sites had substantiated the existence of superior civilization in India, ages ago. It appears to be ridiculous to fabricate a story of Aryans coming on horsebacks to conquer this highly advanced cities and civilizations of India.

14. The Vedas mention about a mighty river called the Saraswati, where Indian communities flourished on its riverbanks. In the early 1980's, proponents of the Aryan Invasion Theory got a terrible shock. The Satellite photos had identified the dry bed of an enormous river and its paleio channel. All these days, Western scholars were projecting River Saraswati, as a Vedic myth, to falsely fabricate the Aryan invasion myth.

15. Voltaire Francois Marie Arouet (1694-1774) France's greatest writer and philosopher wrote: **"I am convinced that everything has come down to us from the banks of the Ganges, - Astronomy,**

Astrology, Metapsychosis, etc." ....."It is very important to note that some 2,500 years ago, at the least, Pythagoras went from Samos to the Ganges to learn Geometry...But he would certainly not have undertaken such a strange journey had the reputation of the Brahmins' science not been long established in Europe..."

16. In recent years many intellectuals had demolished the intellectual edifice of Aryan theories. To detoxify ourselves from the noxious Eurocentric notions injected by the "standard" history textbooks on India's cultural heritage, we have to read the following books:

- *In Search of the Cradle of Civilization by Georg Feuesrstein, Subhash Kak, & David Frawley*
- *The Myth of the Aryan Invasion of India by David Frawley*
- *The Politics of History: Aryan Invasion Theory and the Subversion of Scholarship by Navaratna Rajaram*
- *Return of the Aryans by Bhagwan S. Gidwan*
- *The Invasion, that never was by Michel Danino.*

Fredrich Max Muller,

48 Saraswati River & once Glorious Civilisation

"ambitame nadītame devitame sarasvati" *(Ṛgveda 2.41.16)*

Oh! Mother Saraswati,

You are the best among Mothers,

You are the best among Rivers,

You are the best among Gods & Goddesses.

"sarasvatī saptāti sindhūmātā" *(Ṛgveda 7.36.6)*

Holy River Saraswati had been referred to in Ṛgveda, more than 72 times.

Today, we don't find this river flowing anywhere in India. Western scholars misinterpreted the above fact and concluded that the Saraswati River mentioned in Vedas is a myth. Thereby they have belittled Vedas as mere poetic emotions and figurative literature. Some of these scholars went to the extent of calling the River Sindhu, as the river Saraswati.

River Saraswati is not a Small River. Vedas refer to it as a mighty river. It had cultural links with Indians. Great civilizations might have flourished along its riverbanks. To know about this river is, to know about India's ancient life-style, culture and glory and of course its history.

For decades, many patriotic Historians and scientists had made untiring efforts in

Identifying its palieo channel, its hinterland, its origin and the way it had become the underground river etc.

River Saraswati might have originated in the Himalayas and would have flown in the states of the Punjab, Sindh, Rajasthan and Gujarat and might have merged into the sea at Rann of Kutch.

To substantiate its presence as a river, one can consider the Vedic & Purāṇic references, Historic indications and modern research findings etc.

8,000 to 10,000 years ago, it was a mighty river. As mentioned in Rigveda it was one among the Sapta Sindhus. River Saraswati is not just one among the seven rivers, but the mother of all.

The seven sindhus mentioned in Vedas are (1) Saraswati (2) Satadu (Sutlej) (3) Vipasa (Beas) (4) Askini (Chinab) (5) Aeroshini (Rabi) (6) Vitastha (Jhelum) and (7) Sindhu (Indus). Among these seven rivers, Saraswati and Sindhu are the mighty rivers that flow from mountains to sea.

Hydrological evidences:

Saraswati River is often called the river of "saras" (river of pools). In the states of the Punjab, Sindh Rajasthan and Gujarat, we find its palieo channel & hinterland. Even today one can trace many lakes, as evidence to its flow. Normally, in lakes no deposits of alluvial soil are found. The alluvial soil is found only at the riverbeds. But the lakes of these states, where its palieo channel had been identified, we find the alluvial soil deposits. This indicates that the River Saraswati still exists as under ground current.

Institutions like Rajasthan Water Works Department, Bhabha Atomic Research Institute (BARC), Physical Research Laboratory, Ahmedabad (ISRO's sister organization) have identified the River Ghaggar as part of the river Saraswati in the year 1983.

This Gaggar River flows into Thar Desert and becomes the underground current. The objective of these institutions is to tap and utilize the under-water current of this river for the benefit of the people living in these desert areas.

> "River Saraswati is not a Small River. Vedas refer to it as a mighty river. It had cultural links with Indians. Great civilizations might have flourished along its riverbanks. To know about this river is, to know about India's ancient life style, culture and glory and ofcourse its history."

Satellite's Pictures

The pictures taken from space through the "Land set" satellites had clearly exposed the palieo channel of the river Saraswati. Originating from the Himalayas, flowing westwards and northwest and then becoming river Gaggar, it merges with the sea at Rann of Kutch in Gujarat.

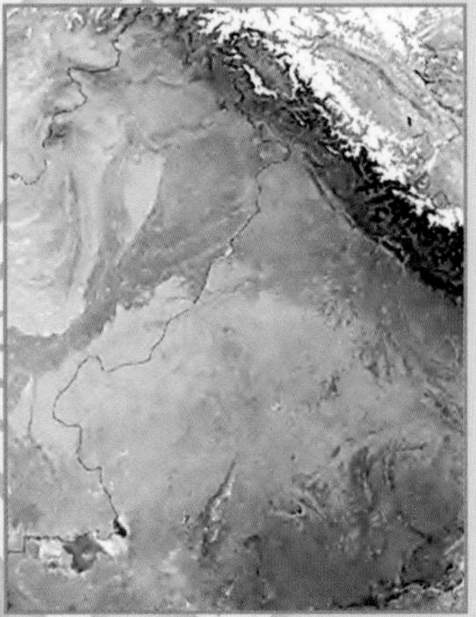

Satellite's Pictures of River Sindhu & Palieo Channel of River Saraswathi

These pictures clearly indicate that the river Sindhu and river Saraswati as two independent rivers.

Archeological evidences

Excavations along the river flow had unearthed the many ruins to indicate the existence of residential settlements and urban life along its valleys in the states of UP, Rajasthan and the Punjab. These ruins had many similarities with Harrappan sites. Many of excavations indicate them to Pre-Harappan in their existence.

Puranic references

We find many a reference in the Mahabharata about the river Saraswati. Balarama, the brother of Krishna, goes on pilgrimage to the various pilgrim centres located along the banks of Saraswati (Mahabharata 3-80-118, 9-36-1, 3-130-4) In Anushasaka Parva of Mahabharata, we find that Kurukeshtra, (the battlefield) was located to South of River Saraswati. (Ref: MB-AP-134-15)

In Manusmriti, we find a reference to the river Saraswati. The region west of Saraswati had been described as "Arya varta" and the region east of Saraswati had been described as "Brahma varta". (Ref: MS-11-17-18) Skanda Purana and other Puranas do have reference to the river Saraswati.

Knowledge of the River Saraswati is very essential to every Indian, as it links us with our ancestral roots. As it bonds us to the Vedic culture, the cradle of human civilization.

River Saraswati eternally flows within the minds of Indians, as an underground current of talents and skills. We bow to the stream of knowledge and learning that ever drenches the Indian soil to vivify the Indian minds.

49 Underwater City of Lord Kṛṣṇa

Dwaraka, the once fabulous city built and dwelt in by Lord *Krishna* exists today. It is visible to us now, as underwater ruins.

In the *Mahabharata, Musala-parva, Arjuna* describes the drowning of the city in the following words,

"Gushing waves of the sea, suddenly stormed Dwaraka. Water flashed into the streets, dashing beautiful buildings. Every mighty mansion of that wonderful city was razed to ground like a falling pack of cards, the devastation was total, I have seen with my eyes, the complete submergence of everything into the sea; Today Dwaraka exists only in name; as a sweet memory in our minds"

After Krishna's departure to the holy abode of Vaikuntha, the city perished. Then the domain of Kali-yuga began". *Vishnu Purana* says so.

Lord Krishna and his clan lived here. This city was built on the seashore, on the banks of the river Gomati. It was a well-planned city of various sectors consisting of residential, commercial, professional workshops and other utility establishments.

Underwater excavations of Dwaraka

The roads were very broad and they criss-crossed the city in a grid design. The whole of the city was well-fortified. There was a big and centrally located community auditorium called "sudharma". Dwaraka had a wonderfully built fort.

Dwaraka is one among the four Divya Dhamas, a devout Hindu should visit. The remaining three are Puri, Badrinath and Rameswaram. Today, one can locate Dwaraka, the city of Krishna in the state of Gujarat, on the banks of Gomati river, on its confluence with sea.

Under sea excavations conducted between the years 1983 and 1990 had brought forth various hidden facts into light. The Archeologists had discovered an underwater city hidden deep in the sea, from a distance of half a kilometer from the sea.

The underwater ruins had revealed that the city was divided into six sectors. The boundary wall seems to be well-fortified and was built on the reclaimed land from the sea.

According to the excavations conducted so far, on the northern side of the present temple town Dwaraka, there exists underwater ruins called "Bet dwaraka" (otherwise called sokodhara); On the southern side ruins are found upto a place called "Okamadi". On the Eastern side, the extensive ruins are visible at "Bindra". Archeologists and historians had found many similarities between the present ruins of the underwater city and the Ciy of Dwaraka described in our epics;

The Existing Dwaraka Temple

The reclaimed archeological artifacts from the sea were subjected to carbon dating. Most of the remnants were dated to be 10,000 years of age. Prof. S.R. Rao, under sea water archeologist, is the man behind these greatest excavations; after his intensive research and untiring efforts, he had written a book called, "The Lost city of Dwaraka"; in his book, Prof S.R.Rao discussed many unknown facts about Lord Krishna's city.

For the past two decades, the Gujarat, Government is making its best efforts to establish the underwater museum. This will enable the visitors to go into the sea and to get a glimpse of the then city of Lord Krishna, who walked on this great land ages ago.

An artist's impression of the then Dwaraka- city of Lord Krishna

50 Landmarks of Rama's Bridge on Indian Ocean

"There was neither Rama nor the Ramayana. It was all a myth and imagination", some people say so. What can we say to them? How can we convince them otherwise? The so-called rationalists do not believe what Ramayana says; At least would they believe the revelations of modern technology?

The NASA (American space research organization) had released a few satellite photographs of a huge man-made construction (Bridge of 48 kms in length) that connected India and Srilanka that is lying submerged on the surface of Indian Ocean.

As per Hindusthan Times report dated 10.10.2002 (PTI Washington, quoting NASA's findings) "the bridge's unique curvature and composition by age reveals that it is a man-made structure".

This bridge extends from Dhanuskoti of Rameswaram to Thalimannar in SriLanka. The gulf between these two places is called "Palk strait".

The Ramayana says that Lord Rama constructed the bridge with the help of Vanaras (monkey brigade) to cross the ocean to reach Lanka. Viswakarma's son Nala (Divine Architect) had guided the construction of the bridge.

According to Archeological findings and calculations, the age of this man-made structure had been estimated to be of seventeen lakh and fifty thousand years. Does thes findings, match with the time scale mentioned for Treta Yuga of Ramayana?

According to Dr Badri Narayan, Former Director of Geological Survey of India and Sri Kalyana Raman, reputed Historian and archeologist, Ram setu is a "man-made structure".

"As per Hindusthan Times report dated 10.10.2002 (PTI Washington, quoting NASA's findings) "the bridge's unique curvature and composition by age reveals that it is a man made structure.""

Researchers from the Bharthidasan University, Trichy, had estimated this bridge to be of 3500 years old. Subsequently even NASA distanced from its claim of declaring it as man-made structure (as revealed by Chairman of Tuticorin Port Trust in the press conference dated 28th July 2007)

Varied calculations, estimations, arguments, counter arguments, controversies do happen always, when we deal with a "Timeless Truth". The Ultimate Truth is that, there exists a man-made structure (though disputed recently) between Rameswaram and Srilanka as mentioned in The Ramayana. Millions of Indians believe that Rama constructed it.

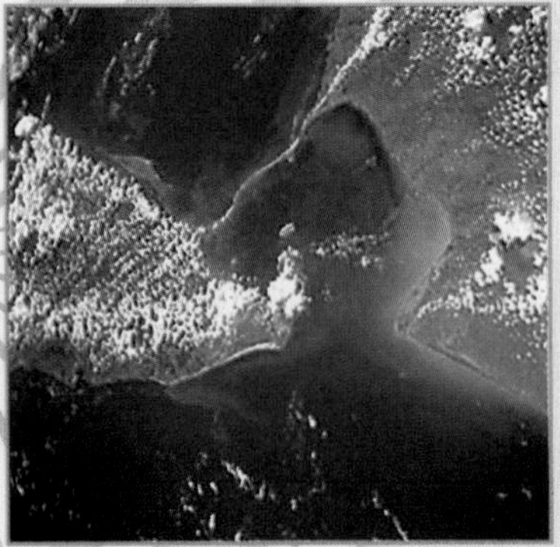

Satellite Picture of RamaSethu pictured by NASA

Today, the Indian government terming this bridge as obstruction for the ships to reach the other side of the coast, is planning to demolish a part of the bridge for constructing a shipping channel. The name of the project is called Sethusamudram project.

Indians should feel proud of this ancient Engineering feat. It is a subject matter of eternal Indian talents. The piling and inter linking the huge boulders across the ocean is not an ordinary fact. Instead of assimilating the technology adopted by the ancient genius, our rulers are trying to demolish the existing symbol of Indian culture and Indian talents.

Our rulers should understand that this issue pertains to the Indian psyche and Indian sentiments. Secular governments should value them. Ram is not just God, but the beloved king of Indian History.

Let us hope that our rulers protect this unique heritage monument, which represents the Indian ethos, Indian knowledge, Indian talents, Indian faith, and Indian culture.

51 World's Oldest Port – Lothal

The Oldest port city has been found in India. The port city is called Lothal Port. Today it is situated in Dolka Taluka of Ahamedabad district in Gujarat state.

During the year 1954, the ruins of this port city were excavated. The archeological studies reveal that this ancient port city was once a part and parcel of Indus valley civilization, which flourished 4500 years ago. (Around 2400 BC).

World's Oldest Port -Lothal – an impression-Design stands unique

This port city flourished with the trade and commerce. From here, beads, jewellery, textiles and mineral ores were exported.

Lothal engineers accorded high priority to the creation of a dockyard and a warehouse to serve the purposes of naval trade. The dock was built on the eastern flank of the town, and is regarded by archaeologists as an engineering feat of the highest order.

It was located away from the main current of the river to avoid silting, but provided access to ships in high tide as well. The warehouse was built close to the acropolis on a 3.5-metre-high (10.5 ft) podium of mud bricks. The rulers could thus supervise the activity on the dock and warehouse simultaneously. Facilitating the movement of cargo was a mud-brick wharf, 220 metres (720 ft) long, built on the Western arm of the dock, with a ramp leading to the warehouse. There was an important public building opposite to the warehouse, whose superstructure has completely disappeared

Lothal was a planned city with radial streets and divided sectors. Householders possessed a sump, or collection chamber to deposit solid waste in order to prevent the clogging of city drains. Drains, manholes and cesspools kept the city astonishingly clean, and deposited the waste in the river, which was washed out during the high tide.

"During the year 1954, the ruins of this port city were excavated. The archeological studies reveal that this ancient port city was once a part and parcel of Indus valley civilization, which flourished 4500 years ago. (Around 2400 BC)."

Many artifacts, tools, terracotta materials and metallic utensils, that were found during excavations reveal the advanced civilization and culture of Lothal.

Instruments like shell compass and various weights and measures only confirm the scientific knowledge of this maritime city.

Ruins stand today to testify the exsistence of a major port, where ships were not just docked, but were repaired and fabricated.

"The Lothal", a book written by SR Rao, published by Archeological Survey of India, 1985 gives a detailed account of Lothal's glory and greatness.

The site of Lothal Port-as exists today

52 The Eighteen Purāṇas

The Puranas were written to popularise the doctrine of the Vedas. They contain the essence of the Vedas. The aim of the Puranas is to impress on the minds of the masses the teachings of the Vedas and to generate in them devotion to God, through concrete examples, myths, stories, legends, lives of saints, kings and great men, allegories and chronicles of great historical events. The sages made use of them all things to illustrate the eternal principles of religion. The Puranas are meant not for the scholars, but for the ordinary people who cannot understand high philosophy and who cannot study the Vedas.

All the Puranas belong to the class of *Suhrit-Samhitas*, or the Friendly Treatises, while the Vedas are called the *Prabhu-Samhitas* or the Commanding Treatises with great authority.

The Puranas are of the same class as the *Itihāsas* (the Ramayana, the Mahabharata, etc.). They have five characteristics (Pancha Lakshana), viz., history, cosmology (with various symbolical illustrations of philosophical principles), secondary creation, genealogy of kings, and of Manvantaras (the period of Manu's rule consisting of 72 celestial Yugas.

Veda Vyasa is the compiler of the Puranas, which are eighteen in number and are very popular.

Sage Vyasa- the compiler of Puranas

1) Vishnu Purana - 23,000 verses.

Told by sage Parāsara to his disciple; It contains stories of various devotees of Lord Vishnu. A description of Varṇāśrama; the six Aṅgas of the Veda; a description of the age of Kali; description of SvetaVaraha Kalpa, Vishnu dharmotara. It also preaches the oneness of Siva and Vishnu.

2) Naradiya Purana - 25,000 verses.

Told by sage Narada to the four sons of Brahmā.This Purana contains a synopsis of everything; it describes Jagannatha Puri, Dwaraka, Badrinath, etc.

The aim of the Puranas is to impress on the minds of the masses the teachings of the Vedas and to generate in them devotion to God, through concrete examples, myths, stories, legends, lives of saints, kings and great men, allegories and chronicles of great historical events.

3) Padma Purana - 55,000 verses.

It preaches dharmas, and rituals. It also contains the glory of Srimad-Bhāgavatam the stories of Rama, Jagannatha, Matsya, Ekadasi, Bhṛgu, etc.

4) Garuḍa Purana - 19,000 verses.

Told by Lord Vishnu to his beloved bird Garuḍa, contains mainly about matters pertaining to birth, death, after death, reincarnation, merits and evil effects, heaven and hell etc. .

5) Varaha Purana - 24,000 verses.

Describes different Vratas (ritual performances) Lord Vishnu's glories etc.

6) Bhāgavata Purana - 18,000 verses.

The most popular among all the eighteen puranas; It contains glories and stories of Lord Vishnu and his incarnation as Lord Krishna. Vyasa reveals this purana to his son Suka and Suka in turn had told this to king Parikshit.

7) Brahmāṇḍa Purana - 12,000 verses.

It tells about various celestial regions; Indian geogrophical location (Bharatavarsha); Most popular hymns about divine mother, Sri Lailita Sahasra Namam, are described in it. It Describes the Vedangas and the Ādi Kalpa.

8) Brahmavaivarta Purana - 18,000 verses.

It describes the creator, creation and the link between the two; it contains exhortations about human behaviour and mostly about the hospitality to be provided to the guests. It contains the glories and pastimes of Radha and Krishna.

9) Markandeya Purana - 9,000 verses.

Preached by Markandeya Maharshi, it contains glories of Siva and Vishnu and included in it is the very popular "Chandi Homa".

10) Bhavishya Purana - 14,500 verses.

It was revealed by Lord Surya (Sun God) to Manu. It contains various dharmas to be adhered to by the fourfold castes. Mostly, it tells about the future happenings.

11) Vamana Purana - 10,000 verses.

Lord Narada told it to sage Pulastya. It contains the story of Lord Trivikrama. It explains the worship of Siva and Vishnu. It gives us the knowledge about earth and formation of seasons and its effects etc.

12) Brahma Purana - 10,000 verses.

It describes the benefits of protecting dharma (the righteouness). The kings are benefited by longevity, fame, heavenly abode and liberation, if they protect Dharma.

13) Matsya Purana - 14,000 verses.

Revealed by Lord Vishnu in the form of Matsya (fish) to sage Manu; It describes the benefits of performing funeral rites, Shraadha ceremonies to departed elders; Temple construction. The description about Vamana and Varaha Kalpas are also found in it.

14) Kūrma Purana - 17,000 verses.

Revealed by Lord Vishnu during his Kurma Avatara (tortoise incarnation); It mentions the holy places; Unity of Siva and Vishnu and their worship etc;

15) Linga Purana - 10,000 verses.

Various stories about Siva, Siva's preachings; Glories of Siva; knowledge of the earth, celestial regions, Astrology and Astronomy etc.

16) Siva Purana - 24,000 verses.

Told by Vayu deva. It contains the knowledge of time; and Solar region, glories of Siva etc;

17) Skanda Purana - 81,000 verses.

Told by Kumara Swamy (Son of Siva). It contains various aspects of knowledge about celestial regions etc; dharmas; glories about Siva and Vishnu; the famous Satyanarayana ritual is available in this purana.

18) Agni Purana - 15,400 verses.

Revealed by Lord Agni (fire) to sage Vasiṣṭha; It contains grammar, prosody, medical knowledge; Astronomy, Astrology and Dharmas (Laws of Righteousness). It contains the description of Shaligrama.

53 Vedic Chandas & its Excellence

Indian Dharmic edifice stands on the Vedic foundation. Indian culture is eternally rooted in the Vedas.

Vedas are again based on the Hymns or mantras –vibrations of sound. Hence Vedas are called Shrutis. (That can only be heard or uttered). Vedic meanings change with the change in the way of mantras being pronounced. Hence utmost importance is to be given for the chanting of the Vedic mantras.

Mastery in six Vedāngas is very important while chanting the Veda-mantras.

Vedic Chandas is one among them. Vedic Chandas deals with Vedic metre or prosody.

The letters in the Vedic mantras are systematically arranged. There is an order and harmony between the letters. Pingala's *Chandas Sutra* is the authoritative text on Vedic Chandas. It deals with Mathematical concepts also. The letters in Vedic mantras have mathematical significance.

The Sanskrit root *"Chad"* means Happiness. The word Chandas means that which gives happiness while uttering. Vedic utterance has a rhythm inbuilt in it. Our sages have assimilated the rhythm of Veda mantras and evolved the science of Chandas or prosody with strong Mathematical and logical foundation.

Rhythmic mix or combination of Laghus and Gurus gives systematic march of words. Hence Chandas is called the feet of Veda Purusha.

When a letter or syllable is uttered within one "Mātrā" 's time, then it is called "Laghu". If it is uttered within two "Matra" 's time, it is called "Guru".

A Vedic mantra or stanza contains fixed number of "Padas" or lines, and each line contains fixed number of letters or syllables. The metre or "Chandas" depends upon the number of letters in each "pada" and the total number of "padas" in a "mantra".

"The letters in the Vedic mantras are systematically arranged. There is an order and harmony between the letters. Pingalas Chandas Sutra is the authoritative text on Vedic chandas. It deals with Mathematical concepts also."

Normally each mantra has four Padas except *Gayatri Chandas*, which has only three padas; in each Pada the syllables may vary between 1 and 26. The Chandas of a hymn is determined, based on the number of syllables in a Pada.

There are four varities of Chandas:

1. **Anadhista Chandas:** (Between one and five syallables): Ukta, Atyukta, Madhya, Prathista, Su-prathista.

2. **Bruhat Chandas:** (between six and twelve syallables):

   - *Gayatri (eight syallables in a pada and three padas in total)*
   - *Anustubh (eigtht syallables in a pada and four padas in total)*
   - *Brihati (nine syallables in a pada and four padas in total)*
   - *Pankti (ten syallables in a pada and four padas in total)*
   - *Tristubh (eleven syallables in a pada and four padas in total)*
   - *Jagati (tweleve syallables in a pada and four padas in total)*

3. **Ati Chandas** (between thirteen to nineteen): Ati Jagati, Sakvari, Ati Sakvari, Asti, Atyasti, Druti, and Atidruti.

4. **Kriti Chandas** (between twenty to twentysix) Kriti, Prakruti, Akruti, Vikruti, Abhikriti, Utkruti.

   Purshasukta in Rigveda reveals the origin of Chandas (10.90.9).

   Gayatri with its three padas was considered to be the earliest among Chandas, revealed or discovered by sage Yadhachanta.

Sage Valmiki had written the Ramayana in "Anustubh Chanda"s (Eight letters of Four padas-total 32 letters)

Pingala had introduced various techniques of maintaining the Vedic metre. If there is excess of one letter it is called "Bharik"; if there is excess of two letters than the prescribed order, it is called "Swarat". If there is shortage of one letter, it is called "Nibrath". If there is shortage of two letters it is called "Virat".

Sages discovered Vedic mantras. From these mantras various types of Chandas were identified and science of Chanda Sastra evolved. These metrical forms had taken the form of various Sanskrit poetic works.

The poetic literature of various Indian languages is based on Vedic Chandas. Dance dramas, devotional songs, verses and all aspects of poetic literature have their roots in Vedic chandas.

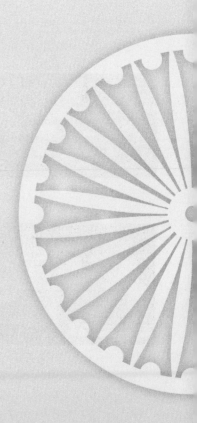

54 Transport System During Vedic Times

Modern systems of transport, do find a mention in the Vedic literature. They have been explained in clear terms. Logical conclusion of those descriptions drives us to the splendour of awe and wonder about the advanced technological knowledge possessed by the ancient Indians during Vedic times.

Artifacts found at Indus valley Excavations

ye te panthāno bahavo janāyanā rathasya vartmānasaśca yātave

yaiḥ sañcarantyubhaye bhadrapāpāstaṁ
panthānaṁ jayemāna mitramataskaraṁ
yaccivaṁ tena nomṛḍa !! *(Atharva Veda 12-1-47)*

Roads of cities as mentioned in Vedas were segregated for three services,

For pedestrians, for bullock carts and vehicles (rathas) that run at different speeds;

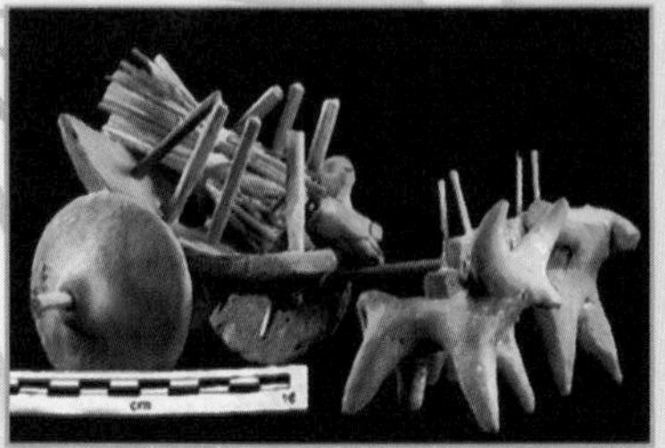

Artifacts of Indus valley civilization

In a verse of Yajur Veda (9-8), there is a description about the vehicle that uses a machine and runs with the jet speed.

In a mantra of Rig Veda (1-37-1) we find a mention of a sports car.

There were also mass transport systems prevailing at that time. In *Atharva Veda* verse (20-76-2) mentions a sort of public transport system resembling bus or train.

triśokaḥ rathaḥ kutsenaśataḥ nṛṛn āvahat

In *Rig Veda* (6-62-6) mantra, there is a description of vimanas. (Aircrafts).

The words like "Steam generating" vehicle, "Magnetic powered" vehicle, "Solar Energy fuelled" vehicle mentioned in Vedas cannot be ignored. Please note that the modern inventions of machine-run vehicles are of recent origin (say only 200 years old).

55 Ancient Scientific Texts of India

The wisdom of Vedas had evolved into various systems of knowledge. Each system of knowledge is called a Sastra. The sages of yore systematically organized that knowledge into Granthas. (Texts). Even the fine arts of India were studied systematically and the science of arts had been developed in India. Hence we call knowledge of dance as Nāṭya Śāstra. The knowledge of sculpture is called Shilpa sastra. The knowledge of culinary skills is called Pāka or Supa Sastra; knowledge of prosody is called Chanda Sastra etc.

Given below are a few Sanskrit texts, which reveal the knowledge of various applied sciences and arts;

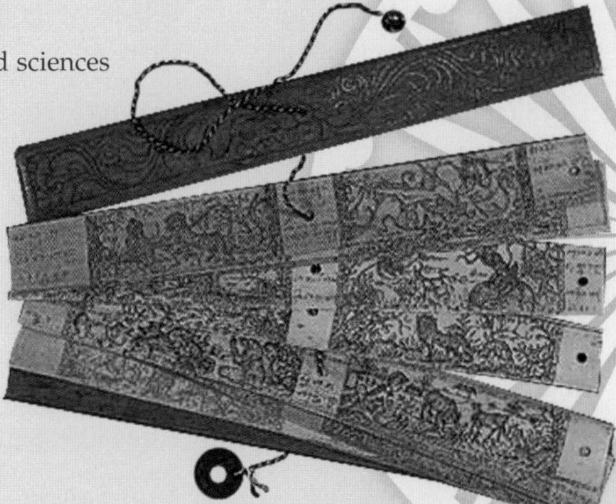

Akṣara-Lakṣa:

Akshara-Laksha is the first encyclopedic Sastra, which goes by the name of Akshara-Laksha. The authorship of this science is attributed to Sage Valmiki. All kinds (325 to be exact) of Mathematics including modern Geometry, Algebra, Trigonometry, Physics or Applied Mathematics; Minerology, Hydels; the method of measuring Air, Heat and even Electricity; Geography etc., are said to have been discussed. This work comprehends earlier discoveries by Sage Kashyapa, Ganapati, Soorya, Brihaspati, Jaimini, Hanuman and others.

Sabda Sastra:

The science of sound is called Sabda Sastra, written by Kandika Rishi. It deals with sounds, echoes of moving and non-moving objects in creation. It also deals in five chapters, with capturing or mechanically reproducing sounds, measuring their pitch, velocity, etc.

> Even the fine arts of India were studied systematically and the science of arts had been developed in India. Hence we call knowledge about dance as Natya Sastra. The knowledge about sculpture is called Shilpa sastra.

Lakshana Sastra:

Sage Sakatayana is the author of Lakshana Sastra, or the science of determining the sex in animate and inanimate creation.

Kanya-Lakshana Sastra:

Babhru Muni has written about Kanya-Lakshana in which 32 marks are indicated for chastity of women etc.

Sakuna Sastra:

Sage Garga has written on Sakuna Sastra, the determination of good and bad effects from the sounds of birds, words of human beings etc. (in other words, omens).

Shilpa Sastra:

Shilpa Sastra is said to have been written by Sage Kashyapa and it consists of 22 chapters. 307 varieties of Shilpas including 11 types of constructions like temples, palaces, halls etc. are detailed. Earlier writers on this subject are Vishwakarma, Maya, Maruti, Chayapurasha, etc. whose thoughts have been incorporated in the above.

Supa-Sastra:

Supa-Sastra deals with the science of cooking. Sukesa is the first author of this science. 108 varieties of preparations, from condiments and pickles to sweetmeats, cakes, puddings, and 3032 kinds of dishes meant for people living in different parts of the world are mentioned.

Malinee Sastra:

Sage Rishyasringa is credited with writing a comprehensive treatise on the science called Malinee Sastra which consists of flower arrangements, making garlands, bouquets, hair-do's in various styles for women, writing love messages on flower petals to convey to beloveds in codes. This work consists of 16 chapters.

Kala Sastra:

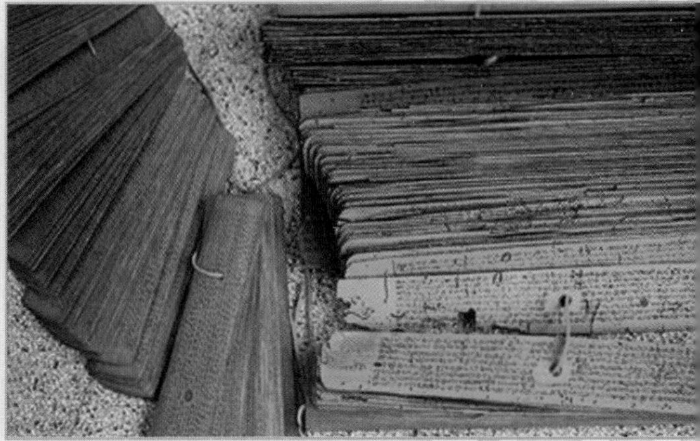

Lord Karttikeya wrote the science of Kala or Time. Its time divisions into definite periods, their classification into auspicious and inauspicious moments, and the deities that preside over each are dealt with in this work.

Samudrika Sastra:

Samudra Raja, or the Lord of the Ocean is the original author of Samudrika Sastra. He noted down the auspicious marks on the body of Lord Vishnu while the latter was resting on Adisesha in the ocean. Sages like Narada, Varaha and Mandavya and Lord Kartikeya later developed this science. Palmistry belongs to this sastra.

Dhatu Sastra:

Ashwini Kumaras are credited with writing the science of Dhatuvada, which in 7 chapters treats with natural as well as artificial Dhatus or primary substances, their combinations and transmutations. Alchemy or converting copper into gold etc., is dealt with in this work.

Visha Sastra:

The science of poisons or Visha Sastra is said to have been exhaustively written by Ashwini Kumaras. This deals with 32 kinds of poisons, their properties, preparations, effects and antidotes.

Chitra Karma Sastra:

Bhima is credited with having composed the science of fine arts called Chitrakarma Sastra. It consists of 12 chapters and expounds nearly 200 kinds of drawings. There is a section in which students are taught to redraw the figure of a person after seeing a single hair or nail or a bone of that person.

Malla sastra:

Malla is said to have composed a comprehensive work on Malla Sastra, which deals with 82 kinds of gymnastics and sports necessary for preservation of health and athletic activities and 24 kinds of infantry warfare where hand-to-hand combat is involved. This work consists of 3 parts.

Parakaya Pravesha:

The revered Valakhilyas are credited with writing the science on Parakaya Pravesha i.e. entering into one body from another body, and it teaches 32 kinds of Yogas and the eight-fold Siddhis (super-human capabilities), Aṇimā, Mahima etc.

Aśva Sastra:

Agnivarma has written exhaustively on the science of horses, their auspicious marks, their physiology, breeding, training etc.

Gaja Sastra:

Similarly, Kumaraswamy has written exhaustively on Gaja Sastra (about elephants). He has given 16 methods to test various marks on the bodies of elephants.

Ratna Pariksha:

Sage Vatsyayana has composed a work on Ratna Pariksha or testing of gems (precious stones). His analysis shows 24 characteristics of gems or precious stones, natural and artificial ones; their forms, weights etc are discussed and classified into categories. 32 methods of testing them for genuineness are also described.

Mahendrajala Sastra:

Veerabahu, the lieutenant of Lord Subrahmanya, is the author of a work on Mahendrajala or the science of magic. It teaches how illusions, like walking on the water, riding in the air etc. are made.

Shakti Tantra:

Sage Agastya is the composer of Shakti Tantra consisting of eight chapters in which Mulaprakriti, Māyā etc., and 64 kinds of external Shaktis of bodies like those of the Sun, Moon, Air & Fire etc. are explained; their particular applications are also described. Atomic fission or nuclear science appears to form a part of this science.

Soudamini Kala:

Sage Matanga is credited with composing a science called Soudamini Kala by which all phenomena could be attracted through shadows and even ideas. He has also taught the science of photographing interiors of mountains, earth etc.

"Sage Agastya is credited with the composing of Shakti Tantra consisting of eight chapters.... Atomic fission or nuclear science appears to form part of this science."

Megha Sastra:

Authorship of the science, which deals with the clouds, is attributed to Sage Atri. This work deals with 12 kinds of clouds, their characteristics; 12 kinds of rains, 64 kinds of lightnings, 32 varieties of thunderbolts etc.

Yantra Sastra:

In a work on Yantras by Bharadwaja, he explains 339 types of vehicles useful for travelling on land, 783 kinds of boats and ships to be used on water and 101 varieties of airshipsusing the Mantra, Tantra, and artificial means; and those used by semi-divine beings like Gandharvas etc., are also explained.

Sthapatya Vidya:

It is a science of engineering knowledge dealing with construction and planning of civil works; Architecture, Vaastu, town planning and other engineering design & related subjects form part of this branch of knowledge.

Other technological treatise:

The four Upavedas are (1) Ayurveda (2) Dhanur Veda (3) Gandharva Veda (4) Artha Sastra.

Ayurveda:

Ayurveda, as the name suggests, is the science of life and health, including medicine & surgery. It is considered to be Upaveda of Rigveda; Even in Atharva Veda many mantras are about health.

Brahma, the Ashvini Devatas, Dhanvantari, Indra, and Rishis like Bharadwaja, Atri, Agnivesha and others have composed treatises on the above subject. Subsequently Charaka collected this knowledge in his book, known as Charaka Samhita. Later, Sushruta followed him. Still later Vagbhatta composed a work on the subject. Besides medicine, surgery and even injections appear to have been known to them. Ayurveda treats the whole man under eight principal heads of treatment. Pharmacology, too, is included in this category. Sushruta has written a work on rejuvenation.

Dhanur Veda:

Dhanur Veda is considered to be an Upaveda of Yajurveda.The authorship of Dhanur Veda or the science of Archery is attributed to Sage Vishwamitra. This work, comprehending earlier works of Brahma and others, consists of four chapters, dealing with Diksha, Sangraha, Siddhanta, and Prayoga. Both the offensive and defensive modes are described. Missiles like Chakra, sword, and propelled forms of weapons, form part of it. Brahmastra, Vaishnavastra, Pashupatastra, Agneyastra are some of the missiles described in this work. The deities to be invoked, the spells to be uttered, the description of weapons and mock warfare are all dealt with.

Gandharva Veda:

Gandharva Veda is considered to be an Upaveda of Samaveda. Gandharva Veda deals with the science of music and dance. It is said to have been composed by Sage Bharata comprehending earlier works by Nandikeshwara, Narada and Hanuman. Vocal and instrumental music and dances constitute this science. The object of this science appears to be spiritual i.e. to rise in ecstasy in the worship of God.

"There are many ancient Indian manuscripts, which are still lying undiscovered. There are many more manuscripts, which are preserved in various libraries of the world; knowledge of these texts is lying dormant and is yet to be made known to the world."

Artha Sastra:

Artha Sastra is considered tobe an Upaveda of Atharva Veda. Sage Vyasa is believed to have composed a work on Artha Sastra consisting of three chapters, in which he teaches 82 ways of earning money, even while leading a righteous life.

Under this head, there are Nitisastra, Shilpasastra, the sixty-four Kalas and also other physical and metaphysical subjects. The famous Artha sastra texts are Kauṭilya's Artha sastra and Sukraniti.

There are many ancient Indian scientific texts, which have been mentioned at other places in this book. There are many ancient Indian manuscripts, which are still lying undiscovered. There are many more manuscripts, which are preserved in various libraries of the world; knowledge of these texts is lying dormant and is yet to be made known to the world. There were many manuscripts of knowledge that were destroyed during foreign invasions on India, for the past one thousand years.

Modern Indian Talents
Navīna Bhāratīya Pratibhā

56 Indian Elephant Dancing its way to become an Economic Super Power

"Angus Maddison, a Cambridge historian, has estimated that in 1700, India and China, each had a share of world income of about 23%, about the same as Europe's. By 1950, Europe's had increased to around 30%, China's had fallen to around 5%, and India's had collapsed to just 3.8%. This decline is now beginning to be reversed. Rapid growth -- witnessed first in China 25 years ago and more recently in India -- suggests that both countries are on the way to reclaiming their rightful places in the world economy"

- Dr.Manmohan Singh, Prime minister of India

(In an article published by Wall Street Journal-Jan 27, 2006- www. ibef.org)

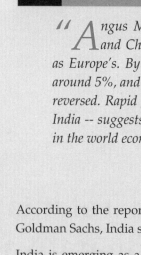

According to the reports and analysis prepared by world's reputed financial analysts Mckinsey & Goldman Sachs, India shall be a major economic force in the world by the years 2020-50.

India is emerging as a strong outfit in every sector of the world Economy; From Iron to IT, from Pharma to Pan masala; from entertainment to spirituality; from milk to mineral water; from food grains to packed foods; from knowledge workers to manual labour, from stock market investments to infrastructure enterprises, India is becoming an attractive poor for riches. Indian multinationals have emerged at last and are in a buying spree of foreign companies. Indian Diaspora' have become first-rate wealth creators everywhere, be it an American nation or an African nation.

Mighty Indian Elephant is on his majestic march, dancing its way to become an economic superpower. Let us watch its gigantic gait as it dances to economic tunes, to the peaks of global glory.*(Inspite of global recession and economic meltdown during 2008-2009, India continues to march ahead, undaunted by the engrossed gloom and despair)*

Indian National Income

- Gross Domestic product (2008-09) is US$ 982.83 billion (Rs 49,14,150 Crores).

- GDP growth rate: (2008-09) is 6.7% (This growth rate is despite of economic recession through out the World.But for the past ten years India is achieving a growth rate of 7% plus, which is again a world record.).

- Fourth largest economy in the world according to purchasing power parity estimations. (A FOUR TRILLION DOLLAR ECONOMY, as per IMF tabulation)

- Per capita income (2008-09) US$ 750.13 per annum (Rs 37,507 per annum- Rs 3125 per month)

- Foreign exchange reserves as on May2009 the foreign exchange reserves 255.9 billion dollars

(Exchange Rate has been considered @US$= Rs 50/-)

Exports

For the first eleven months of 2008-09 India exported USD 144.27 billons; there is a 20% increase in the growth of exports this year, when global trade has shrunk drastically.

- Fastest export growth rate of 24% is being maintained by India for the past three years.

- Today we are exporting to 175 countries.

Stock market

- Bombay stock exchange (BSE) is the second biggest stock exchange of the world.
- India has 23 stock exchanges in various cities.
- More than 10,000 companies are quoted here.Second Important Investment destination.
- BSE Index crossing 20,000 points is a world record (Dec-11,2007). After making a roller coaster ride BSE Index is getting stabilised around 12500 to 14000 points.

Bank Deposits

- Largest banking system of the world with 70,000 branches
- Bank deposits are to the tune of 32% of GDP

Indian Middle Class

- Middle class growing stronger day by day
- World's largest middle class.
  - ★ 52 million high income-middle class families.
  - ★ 500 million middle class consumers
- Average annual income varies from USD1800 to USD 20,900 (Rs 81000 to Rs 940500)
- The average age of 54% of Indians is less than 25 years. So India is a very youthful country.

- In India on an average 30 lakh graduates pass out every year.
- Around five lakh engineers graduate every year.
- Yet in India, the literacy rate is only 64% .

Agriculture

- India has produced 230.67 million tons of food grains during the year 2007-08
- India stands today as a country of largest cultivable area.
- India stands first in production of rice & wheat. (In the year 2007-2008: rice 96.4 million tons; wheat 78.4 million tons;)
- India is the largest exporter of Basmati rice.
- As per the economic survey Feb.06, buffers stocks of food grains- 23.6 million tons.
- Share of Agriculture in GDP is 20% but 60% of people are depending on Agriculture.
- Share of Agricultural sector in exports is around 13%

Fruits

- India is the largest producer of fruits in the world with the production of 47.5million tons.
- 10% of world's fruit production is from India.
- India occupies the second position in the export of fruits.
- India occupies the first position in the export of mango and banana fruits.

Vegetables

- India occupies the second rank in vegetable production, next to China.
- Annually, India could produce 100 million tons of vegetables.

Milk-Eggs

- India occupies the first position in the production of milk.
- Annually, India produces around 110 million tons of milk.
- India stands 5th in rank in the production of eggs.
- Eggs produced during 2003. is 40.4 millon tons.

Fish –Meat

- India stands sixth in rank in the production of fish.
- Yearly production of 6.2 millon tons.
- India occupies seventh position in meat production.
- Yearly production of six millon tons.

Commericial crops

- India occupies first position in the production of commercial crops like sugarcane, cotton, jute etc.
- In the production of Coconut, pie, turmeric, spices, India occupies the first position.
- World largest producer of Tobacco is India

Tea

- India stands first in the production of and Tea first in the with consumption.

  India produced around one billion kgs of Tea during 2008-2009.
- 31% of world's Tea comes from Indian Tea estates.
- The turnover of Indian Tea is estimated to be 2.2 billion Dollars.
- After independence, India has achieved a growth rate of 25%.
- Indian Tea is considered to be of superior variety.
- Among many Darjeeling, Assam and Niligiri varieties of Tea are famous.
- Two crore of Indian population earn their livelihood from Tea industry.

INDUSTRY

Indian Industry has achieved higher growth rate in recent years and had become sluggish during the current reccession of world Economy.

Automobile

- India stands first in the production of motorcycles.
- India, occupies second position in the production of tractors and two wheelers.
- In the production of commercial vehicles India stands fourth in world ranking.
- In car sales India occupies the fourth position In 2008-2009, 18.38 lakhs were produced in India and 3.31 lakh cars had been exported.(Source: Society of Indian Automobile manufactures-www.siamindia.com)
- India occupies the first position in the manufacture of automobile spares.

Pharma

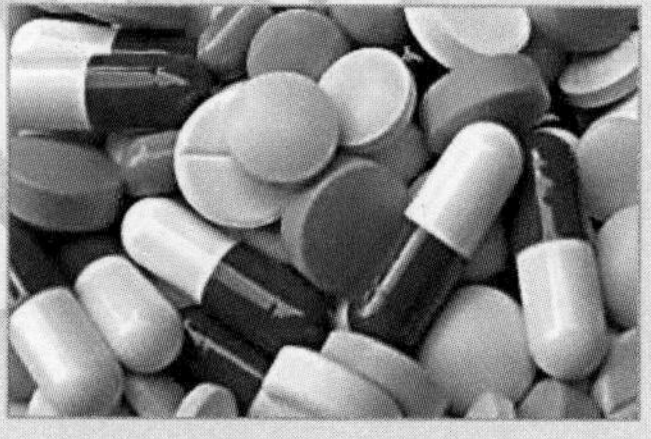

- Indian pharma industry occupies the fourth position in terms of production.
- Thirteenth position in terms of value.
- 2008-2009 Indian Pharma Industry did exports of 7.2 billion dollars. and has a 10 billion dollars domestic market.

- India occupies a special position for producing low cost and high quality formulations and bulk drugs.
- 61 USFDA permitted Pharma manufacturing outlets are located in India. India is the only country to have so many USFDA permitted manufacturing outlets outside USA
- Ranbaxy laboratory is considered to be one of the top ten Pharma companies of the world. It has manufacturing locations in seven countries.(Daiichi Sankyo, a Japan's pharma major acquried this company in 2008).Recently Dr. Reddy Labs had purchased world's fourth biggest pharma company.Indian research & development capability is considered to be one of the best in the world.Indian pharma companies are in a buying spree and are acquiring many foreign companies abroad.
- India is emerging focal point in Biotechnology Trade & Industry. India is emerging as the third country after Australia and China in Biotechnology trade.

Telephone

- From mere 22.8 million consumers in 1999, India today (December 2008) has more than 385 million mobile & Land line consumers. Among them cell phone consumers occupy the major part.
- One of every third Indian has a cellphone connection.India cell phone consumers are growing at the rate of sixty percent.
- Every month Indians are purchasing around 80 lakh Cell Phones.

Electricity and other basic Infrastructure

- In power generation India occupies the fifth position in the world.
- On an average, India is producing 600 billion kilowatt hours during a year.
- Inspite of such a massive generation of electricity, thousands of Indian villages are without electricity.
- Indian roads extend to 3.32 billion kilometers; largest road network in world.
- World's biggest railway network with 63000 kms of rail route
- India occupies the second position in cement production with 170 millon tons of cement production (2007-2008). India is the fifth largest poducer of Steel around 53 millons tons annually

Textile Industry

- Indian textile industry occupies the 7th position in Textile Trade, 2nd in Cotton, 1st in jute, 5th in Man made fabrics, 2nd in Silk production etc.

Cinema

- India is the only country that produces maximum number of films every year.
- No other country in the world has as many cinema halls as India has today.
- During the year 2004, Indian cinema had accounted for a trade of 4.5 billion Dollars.

Diamonds

- India stands first in cutting and polishing of diamonds.
- 90% of diamonds unearthed in the world come to India for cutting & polishing.
- Diamond trade occupies 29% share of export earnings, with exports being USD14.18 billion Dollars.
- Gold consumption in India is highest in the world- 800 tons-20% of World Consumption.

Millionaires & Billionaires

- During the year 2006-2007, 36 Billonaires from India had been listed in Forbes magazine: annual, top Billionaires list of the world. (Persons whose official net worth is above Rs 4500 crores).
- Around 2 Crores of non-resident Indians have remitted USD 21 billion dollars to India (Rs 94,500 crores).

Debt

- India's external debt burden is below 15.8% of GDP.
- India has repaid most of its debt and waived the debts of several countries.

IT facts

- India is becoming the number one IT HUB of the world.
- India earned USD 47.3 billion dollars (Rs 2,18,500 crores) from software (IT & BPO) exports during the year 2008-09.(Source: Nasscom)
- India has earned USD 10.9 billion dollars from BPO services during the year 2007-2008 .
- There is a growth of 25% to 30% every year in this industry.
- As on 31st March 2005, IT industry has 10,40,000 skilled manpower working for India's prosperity.
- Many "fortune five hundred" companies have development facilities in India.
- Today, India occupies the first position in BPO (Business process outsourcing) services.

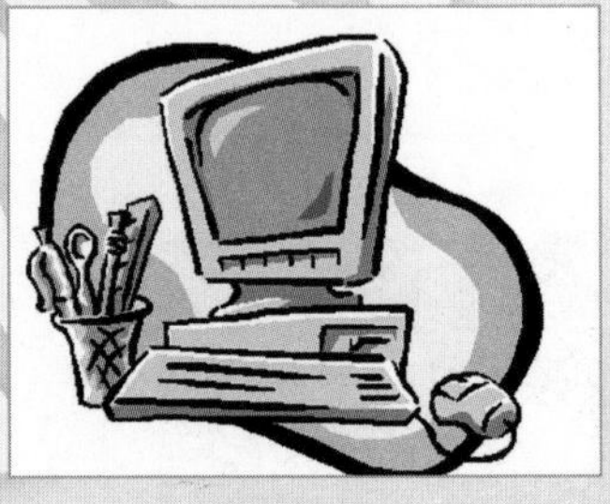

The Moot Question

But India's success story is not without a blot. With suicides of farmers, migration from villages to cities, illiteracy, lack of minimum health facilities, infrastructure deficiency, unabating terrorism, corruption etc, can we call ourselves a rich country? Can these be considered to be India's economic growth indicators?

According to Human development index evolved by UNO, India occupies the 127 position among 180 nations of the world. This Index is prepared based on the factors of education, health, infrastructure, pollution and basic (minimum) facilities. Of course don't be surprised to know that this human devlepment index had been contributed by an Indian, who is a noble laureate & reputed economist, Sri Amartya Sen.

For the past one thousand years, India's wealth had been plundered in many ways. But India ever remained an attractive destination of trade and commerce in every millennium of known history. Today, after gaining independence, its wealthy stroll is impressive and is on the verge of reaching its summit position that it occupied for ages. India today is occupying the first or second positions in many sectors of wealth-creation and is re-emerging itself as an economic superpower. India was never a superpower of arrogance and hegemony, but remained a sublime power of prosperity, peace and knowledge.

Be Positive about India

To rejuvenate India, all that we have to do is to purify politics, eradicate corruption and to strike a balance between urban lifestyle and rural lifestyle. Then new and strong India is bound to emerge. Let us rebuild India with traditional values. Its heartbeat is in its culture. Let us fill India with wealth of high-end Indian values.

Then, the future India shall retain its past glory and leadership of human excellence.

57 Modern Indian Scientists

Today India is a scientific superpower. Nowhere in the world, in any of the countries, there are as many scientists as in India. Many Indian scientists who have settled abroad have contributed immensely to the modern scientific knowledge. But Indian scientists were not given due recognition for their contributions & courtesy – due to racial reasons.

But there are many scientists, whose achievements make us feel proud about Indian genius and dedication. Let us remember a few of them, who had laid strong foundations for Indian scientific edifice.

Prafulla Chandra Ray (1861-1944)

In Modern India he is known to be the Father of Chemistry. He was born in the year 1861, in today's Bangladesh. In the year 1887, he became a graduate in Chemistry and returned from England to join as lecturer in the Presidency College Calcutta.

His research work:

He found a chemical compound called Mercurous Nitrate.

He discoveredthe easiest method to produce Nitrogen gas, which is even now popularly used in the field of Agriculture.

He authored a research book called "The History of Hindu Chemistry –Volume 1 & 2" between the years (1902-1909). The whole world came to know the greatness of ancient Indian Chemical & Metallurgical knowledge through his book.

In the year 1901, he started the first Chemical factory of modern India at Calcutta called "The Bengal Chemicals & Pharmaceutical Works".

He encouraged many young entrepreneurs to start Chemical institutions and factories.

1. Bengal Technical Institute (Now Jadhavpur University).
2. Bengal Potteries.
3. Bengal Canning & Condiments.
4. Bengal Paper
5. Bengal Enamel works.

He spent his earnings in helping poor students and in encouraging the freedom movement. His greatest contribution is in moulding his students into world-renowned scientists. Let us list out his student's contributions,

1. Jnana Gosh- the laws of dilution.
2. Dhar- invented Nitrogen fertilizers.
3. Sasir Kumar Misra – a world-renowned scientist in radio communications & electronics.
4. Prof Saha: Astronomical scientist
5. Satyendra Bose: a famous scientist in Physics who worked with Einstein.

One of the greatest scientists of India, Jagadish Chandra Bose was his colleague at Presidency College. Ray inspired Bose in many ways.

He had submitted 142 research papers in the field of Chemistry. They stand to be the most valuable documents.

He participated in the freedom movement very actively and ended his noble life in the year 1944.

> "Today India is a scientific super power. Nowhere in the world, in any of the countries, there are as many scientists as in India. Many Indian scientists who have settled abroad have contributed immensely to the modern scientific knowledge."

JC BOSE (1858-1937)

Plants respond to stimulus; they weep; they laugh; they become angry. This was proved scientifically by one of the greatest scientists of modern India Jagdish Chandra Bose. He is a modern Rush. A scientist in Physics but did many inventions in the domain of Botany. He had for the first time in the modern science, removed the barriers between Physical sciences and Natural sciences.

He invented an instrument called Resonate recorder. It records the subtlest responses in the plant. He published a book called plant physiological investigations. He submitted 150 research papers throughout the world.

He had built his own equipments to undertake research. The most popular equipment invented by him is "Cresograph". It magnifies a thing 10 million times. His equipment called "wave guide", determines the structure of matter with the help of microwaves. It is most popularly used in the investigation of particle Physics.

Today we are living in a world of wireless communication. The technology was first invented by J.C.BOSE. He demonstrated it in the world forums and seminars; but Marconi had patented the technology first and became the owner of its applications. The credit of this greatest achievement should go to J.C.BOSE not to Marconi.

P.C. Ray & J.C. Bose together worked in Presidency College and inspired many youngsters to become scientists.

Ramanujam

Ramanujam shines as a star of the twentieth century's Mathematical Genius. He is considered to be a phenomenon in the modern mathematical world.

He was born at Kumbakonam in Tamilnadu and was working as a clerk in Madras Port Trust.

He had immense interest in Mathamatics from his childhood days and was rather crazy about it. His teacher, his friend, his God, his playmate was Maths.

In the year 1911, he had written an article on "Bernoullis Number" in the magazine called "The Journal of Indian Mathematical Society".

In the year 1913 he had even obtainted research fellowship from the Madras University.

In the year 1917, Professor Hardy of Cambridge University invited Ramanujam to England to undertake further research in Mathematics.

Ramanujam had postulated many Mathematical principles and theorems on the numbers and their combinations. Any number can be split into various combinations of number using his formulae.

His ill health forced him to return to India. He was the first Indian to obtain the fellowship of Trinity College. He had been nominated to the membership of Royal Society of England.

Today, Tata Foundation had brought out Ramanujam's Mathematical theorems in the form of a book. This book is considered to be one of the important books in Mathematical domain.

During 1920, Professor Hardy came all the way to India, to visit the ailing Ramanujam. Professor Hardy casually told Ramanujam about the taxi number "1729", in which he travelled. Ramanujam immediately responded by saying that 1729 is a peculiar number, which can be split into cubes of two numbers in two ways. (1729= 13 +123 =93+103). Hardy was struck with wonder at Ramanujam's Mathematical genius.

CV Raman (1888-1970)

India's first Nobel Laureate in the field of Physics and the world famous scientist was C.V. Raman.

He was awarded Nobel Prize for his investigation, caled, "Raman effect". 'Raman effect 'means, when a light ray travels through a transparent thing, it reveals the impact of diffusion of light in various ways. With the help of his investigation, the structures of more than 2000 chemical compounds were analyzed. The popularity of Raman effect grew many times with the invention of laser technology. He was the director of Indian Institute of Sciences, Bangalore for a period of ten years and shaped that organization to grow into world-class scientific research institute. He was awarded " Bharata Ratna", India's highest civilian award.

M. Visweswaraiah (1861-1962)

The modern India's foremost engineering genius. He hailed from a Telugu family settled in Kolar of Karnataka. (Today). His ancestors belong to a village called Mokshagundam in Andhra Pradesh. He had graduated from Madras University and completed his degree in engineering from Pune Science College.

He started his career by joining in public works department, Bombay and later became a member in Indian Water Commission. He had designed the wonderful water canal system for Deccan region. He had designed automatic water gates for regulating water in dams and reservoirs. In the year 1903, the water gates were first erected at khadakvasla near Pune. Afterwards, the same kinds of water gates were erected at Gwalior and Mysore's Krishnaraj Sagar.

He was instrumental in desiging the water flowage system for the city of Hyderabad and saved that city from the disaster of floods. He had designed many buildings in Hyderabad. He played an important role in the construction of Vishakapatnam Port.

In the year 1908, he joined as Diwan at Mysore Royal State and had created wonderful architectural marvels in Bangalore and Mysore. He was instrumental in establishing Bangalore Engineering College in the year 1917.

British Government honored him with the title "Sir". In the year 1955, Indian Government honored him with "Bharata Ratna".

Yallapragada Subba Rao (1895-1948)

In the field of medicine he was one of the Modern India's greatest scientists. After graduating from Harvard school of Tropical Medicine, he joined a research laboratory called "Ledralay".

His contributions to the world of Medicine;

1. Invention of the drug "Hetrazon" which is used to cure elephantiasis;

2. Under the guidance of Subbarao, in the year 1945, Benjeman Duggar had invented, Tetracyclin antibiotic ' Aueroyomycin".

One of his colleagues named "Pesca", had treacherously spoiled the research work of Subba Rao, because of which, it took many years to isolate the medical virus called "Nucleayo tidean" by other scientists.

"Under the guidance of Subbarao, in the year 1945, Benjeman Duggar had invented, Tetracyclin-antibiotic Aueroyomycin ."

> In the year 1966, Homi Baba died in a plane crash. Our scientists walked the way Dr Bhabha had envisaged for us and conducted its first Nuclear blasts in the year 1974. India became the sixth country in the world to conduct nuclear tests. Today we are using fast breeder technology to produce electricity, thanks to Homi Bhabha's vision.

As a mark of respect, medical community named a particular fungus in his name; and it is called "Subba Rao myces splendens"

In the year 1947, America awarded him the citizenship which he politely rejected and retained his Indian identity.

Homi Bhabha (1909-1966)

Homi Bhabha is the Father of modern India's atomic programme. Homi Bhabha was born in the year 1901 at Bombay; went to Cambridge, London for higher studies; returned to India and joined the Tata Institute of Fundamental Research in the year 1945. In the year 1937, he had intensively researched on the subject cosmic radiation and found the particles called "Misons". He became world famous with that Discovery.

He had been nominated to Atomic commission in the year 1948 and he had visualized the Indian atomic research programme. Kudos to his exemplarily vision, India achieved self-reliance within the shortest possible time and developed its Nuclear Technology.

During the year 1963, India established its first Nuclear Reactor; this is because of Bhabha's leadership abilities. Within two years, India had surprised the world with the establishment of Plutonium plant.

In the year 1966, Homi Bhabha died in a plane crash. But to the World 's surprise of all, all over the world Indian Atomic programme was not deterred with the demise of Homi Bhabha. Our scientists walked the way Dr Bhabha had envisaged for us and conducted its first Nuclear blasts in the year 1974. India became the sixth country in the world to conduct nuclear tests. Today we are using fast breeder technology to produce electricity, thanks to Homi Bhabha's vision.

It was he who designed India's three-phased nuclear programme. In India the fuel like Uranium which required for nuclear plants is not available. So he visualized the alternative fuel as "Thorium" and designed the nuclear technology for India. This decision had pushed India into advanced research and advanced Nuclear capability.

Modern India cannot forget the contributions of the architect of India's nuclear programme.

Vikram Sarabhai (1919-1971)

Dr.Vikram Ambalal Sarabhai has become synonym for India's success in Space Research Programme.

From small rockets to mighty rocket launching vehicles & space satellites, India's journey into space was piloted and pioneered by this visionary scientist. Be it a satellite or launch vehicle, India developed every bit of space technology, indigenously and achieved the heights of excellence. As world looks at India with awe & wonder, India is thrusting zealously into many ambitious space missions. Thanks to Vikram Sarabhai's efforts, resolve & vision for chiselling the ISRO- Indian Space Research Organization into a mighty institution.

Technology required for Space Research, Communications, Remote sensing data in the fields of Defence, environment etc were visualized by Vikram Sarabhai.

Though India launched its first satelliete in the year 1975, Vikram Sarabhai passed away in the year 1971. India continued the space research programme on the lines envisaged by Vikram Sarabhai and achieved success. His vision inspires our scientists eternally to carry the space mission successfully.

> Meghnath Saha's isonation forumula is considered as the milestone achievement in the domain of Astro-Phyiscs. It helps the Astronomers to calculate the temperature of the various celestial bodies like sun, planets and stars.

Sasir Kumar Mitra (1890-1963)

Sasir Kumar Mitra is responsible for establishing India's Radio Transmitting Station in the year 1923. From 1927 India started transmiting radio programmes. His efforts in Radio Physics & Electronics had earned him high reputation among the scientists of the entire world.

He had undertaken extensive studies about "Ionosphere", the atmospheric layer. The waves transmitted by the radio station or the TV station reaches the ionosphere and gets reflected back to the earth. He had even established an institution called Radio Physics & Electronics. He had been awarded Padma Bhushan in the year 1962.

Meghnath Saha (1893-1956)

He is one of the great Astronomical scientists of India. His isonation forumula is considered as the milestone achievement in the domain of Astro-Phyiscs. It helps the Astronomers to calculate the temperature of the various celestial bodies like sun, planets and stars.

He had proposed a theory called thermal ionization of atoms. The principles of this theory help the astronomers to estimate the physical features of stars. He had published two great books. First one was, "A Textbook of Heat". Even today this is considered to be the authority for physical science students. Another book called "The Principle of Relativity', he co-authored with another scientist Satyendranath Bose. This book is a classical Physics' textbook. He started a magazine called "Science and Culture". He was a Member of Parliament during the years 1952-1956.

Shanti Swarup Bhatnagar

He is instrumental in streamlining various scientific research organizations under one banner. He brought effective coordination mechanisms between scientific research and industry. He was the first Chairman of the University Grants Commission. He encouraged many young scientists to become entrepreneurs and adventure in the domain of research.

Satyendranath Bose

Today there are sub atomic particles named after him they are called "Bosons". He is India's greatest nuclear Physicist. He wrote an article called "Plank's Law and Light Quantum Hypothesis". He had sent this article to many scientists, yet nobody responded. In the year 1924, he had sent this article to Albert Einstein. The great scientist Einstein not only appreciated this article, but also personally translated this article into German and even said that this article is the milestone achievement in the field of research.

Photons and alpha particles emit a kind of radiation .The factors that reveal the behaviour pattern of this radiation are called as "Bose statistics". He and another scientist Meghanath Saha had translated Einstein's papers on 'Relativity' into English. Bose even worked with Einstein on certain scientific projects.

Many Indian scientists of world repute like Satish Dhawan, Abdul Kalam, Swaminathan, Hari Narayana and many others remain to us today as the legends of Modern Indian science era.

Sri Abdul Kalam
Scientist, Humanist, and Ex-President of India

Indians are eternally talented. Modern or ancient, the name India is synonymous with knowledge both material and spiritual. The contribution of Indian scientists for world's progress is like silent dew, subtle and sublime. Long live, the world's largest scientific community, ie India. Long live, the Indian scientific communities, who are staying in various countries and are contributing immensely for scientific growth.

58 Indian Industrial Giants

India got Independence, when its industrial scenario was at its nadir. Indian small-time workmen, artisans, traders, young entrepreneurs were tossed between the siphoned-out Indian resources by foreign rulers on the one side and the adverse impact of Western Industrial revolution on the other side.

Budding Industries of the then independent India required a protective environment from multi-national giants. Capital deficiency and resource crunch was evident when Indian industry took its first steps in the post-independence era.

In spite of many bottlenecks and hurdles; six decade long Indian industrial journey was a roller coaster ride towards aspired goals of self-reliance & Global competitiveness.

The World recognizes today, India's Industrial achievements with awe and wonder. Captains of Indian Industry are venturing into foreign lands and are adding many colourful feathers to their caps of success. God bless their entrepreneurship.

The then sapling of Indian industry had grown into a mighty tree today- courtesy Indian public sector. One should not forget that Indian Public sector stood as a strong hedge around the tender sapling, as it matured into a strong industrial tree. We built our own rail engines, railway coaches, aeroplanes, ships, telephones, iron & steel plants, mega pharma units, spinning mills, machine tools, oil and gas wells, power plants, mines etc in public sector and continued our winning stroll. For the grown-up industrial tree, public sector protection is not required as it is strong enough to handle itself.

Among the top 2000 companies of world today there are around 34 Indian Corporates according to the recent ranking list relased by the Forbes magazine for the year 2006-07. ONGC (239 rank), Reliance (258), SBI (326) are the best three Indian corporates according to the magazine.

"Among the top 2000 companies of world today there are around 34 Indian Corporates according to recent ranking list relased by the Forbes magazine for the year 2006-07. ONGC (239 rank), Reliance (258), SBI (326) are the best three Indian corporates according to the magazine."

Indian success stories stand tall to substantiate the above fact. The heroes of these success stories are industrial legends, whose vision and leadership had paved the way for such a splendid performance. Let us inspire ourselves by learning about a few of them.

Tata Group

Modern India's Industrial history is linked with Tata Group's evolution into an industrial giant.

During the year 2005-06, Tata group achieved a turnover of Rs 96,722.9 crores.

This constitutes the 2.8% of India's GDP. Tata group has establishments in all the six continents, 40 countries. Under its banner, there are 96 major companies.

The luminary who had founded the Tata industrial empire is Jamshedji Tata, (1839-1904). He became an entrepreneur at the age of 29 and Tata's history began with that.

Jamshedji Tata, (1839-1904)

1874 - Spinning mills were established

1902 - Taj Mahal- First luxury hotel of India.

1907 - Tata Iron & Steel was founded

1910 - Tata Electric Company went into steam, first hydroelectric company.

1911 - Indian Institute of Science was established. Today it is one of the world's premier institutions.

1912 - First time in the history of the world, standard of working eight hours in a day had been implemented in Tata institutions.

1917 - Factories to produce Soap, oils and household utensils factories were established.

JRD Tata- who brought many laurels to Indian Industry

1932 - Tata Airlines was founded and this institution later became Air India.

1939 - Tata Chemicals

1945 - Tata Locomotive came into existence. Today this institution has changed into famous Tata Motors.

1952 - Lakme – cosmetic company

1954 - Voltas- Air Conditioning Company

1962 - Tata Tea today is one of the largest tea producing companies in the world.

1968 - India's first software company & today's highly reputed TCS (Tataconsultancy services) was founded- during the year 2002- this company's turnover stood at Rs 4500 crores.

1970 - Book Publishing Company was established

1984 - Titan Watch Company was founded

1996 - Tata Teleservices was established

1998 - Indian-designed first car- Indica rolled out.

2000 - Purchased Tetly-Great Britan's tea producing major. This is the first time in the industrial history of our country that an MNC is being purchased by an Indian company.

2001 - Insurance Company – TATA –AIG came into being

2002 - Purchased majority stake in VSNL.

2004 - Created history by purchasing 'Dawee motors', one of biggest Korean car manufacturing company.

2005 - Tyco global network and a steel company were purchased.

2007 - Feb 1st-created history by purchasing British Iron & steel major –CORUS with this takeover Tata Iron & Steel had become the fifth largest steel producing company in the world.

After Jamshedji Tata, the Tata group was expanded and consolidated by its illustrious chairman late JRD TATA (1904-1993). He was instrumental in establishing Air India, BARC, Tata Motors etc. JRD was awarded Bharat Ratna in the year 1992. He passed away in the year-1993- He was also a reputed pilot.

Ratan Tata is the present chairman of the Tata Group of companies. He had taken the chairmanship from JRD Tata in the year 1991. He had established a voluntary organization called Tata Foundation and had undertaken many service activities. Government of India has awarded him "Padma Bhushan" in the year 2002.

He has set his ambitions of producing an Indian-made car for one Lakh rupees. He is on the board of many world-class reputed organizations.

GD Birla (1894-1983)

Ghanshyam Das Birla wanted to be innovative in his trade pursuits; hence he got into jute business at Calcutta, when his father was doing cotton business. He faced tough competitions from the British and Scottish traders and could withstand them with resolve. Second World War had given him enough opportunities to establish himself and he never looked back afterwards.

GDBirla with Gandhiji

BITS, Pilani, Engineering College established by Birla at Pilani is one of country's premier institutions.

In the year 1957, Indian Government had honoured him with Padma Bhushan.

Birla group got divided into three family business groups. Among them Aditya Birla group and his son Kumar Mangalam Birla's business establishments flourished. CK Birla was instrumental in establishing Hindustan Motors, country's premier car manufacturing company. The famous Ambassador car was once, all pervading on Indian roads.

The Aditya Birla Group is one of India's largest business houses. It owns companies like Hindalco, Grasim and Indian Rayon. The Group's operations span 40 companies over 18 countries, which include - Thailand, Malaysia, Indonesia, Egypt, Canada, Australia and China. Its revenues are in excess of US$ 6 billion

The Aditya Birla Group is a dominant player in all its areas of operations:

Aluminum, Copper, Cement, Viscose Staple Fibre, Carbon Black, Viscose Filament Yarn, Fertilizers, Insulators, Sponge Iron, Chemicals, Branded Apparels, gas, palm oil, Insurance and Asset Management, Software and Telecom

Birlas have undertaken many philanthropic activities and have established famous temples in many parts of the country.

GD Birla was a close follower of Mahatma Gandhi and was funding the freedom struggle.

59 Indian Multinational Companies

The year 1992, that was when India opened up its Economy and invited foreign investments. Many feared that, Indian companies would be taken over by foreign Multinationals, and would wipe out the budding Indian Entrepreneurial talent. It is fifteen years since, Indian economic reforms started rolling over; Indian industrial flag zoomed high and is fluttering with pride in the international skies; Today many business houses of India are in the acquiring spree of multinational companies world-wide; Indian multinational companies are born. During the year 2005-06, FDI inflows in India was 10 billion US dollars, Indian Companies have invested 20 billion dollars outside India and the trend continues. In the year 2006-07, Indian companies had invested estimated amount of 35 billion dollars.

- Indian car "Tata indica" is penetrating into European market, by establishing strategic marketing arrangement with Rover.
- Tatas have purchased the Korean company "Daewoo motors" and is consolidating its position in Korea and China.
- Tata Iron & Steel has become 5th largest steel company of the world by acquirng the European major "Corus" for a premium prize.
- Lakshmi Mittal, world's fourth richest person and NRI had acquired a multinational steel giant "Arcelor", last year.
- Ranbaxy Labs, India's top pharmaceutical company, earns 76% of its revenues from outside India. It is rated the ninth biggest generic company of the world with manufacturing locations situated across the globe.**(Today, Ranbaxy is not an Indian Multinational, as it has been purchased by a Japanese Pharma Major)**

Indian Made Tata Indica Car Penetrating International Markets

- Videocon, the TV manufacturing company of India, had bought the world famous TV Company Thompson in the countries of China, Italy, Poland, Mexico etc.
- The Reddy Labs is the first Indian company to be listed in NYSE. (New York stock exchange)
- Reddy Labs, Aurobindo pharma, Sun Pharma, and other pharmaceutical companies are acquiring many pharma units worldwide.
- ONGC & IOC have purchased oil wells in the countries of Africa & Dubai.
- Asian Paints have manufacturing plants in 24 countries. Asian Paints is considered as the leader in segment of selling paints.
- Bharat Forge had purchased a German forging company Carl Dan Peddinghouse. With the purchase of this German company Bharat Forge has become the second largest producer of forgings in the world.
- ESSEL Propack makes lamitubes- packing tubes for toothpastes and other cosmetics. It has 17 factories in eleven countries and is the industry leader in that sector.

Many Indian software giants are opening software development centers across the globe and are acquiring stakes in many reputed companies worldwide. TCS, Wipro, Infosys are pioneers in establishing businesses worldwide.

Many Industrialists of India today are moving ahead with broader vision and perspective and are able to take into their stride the competition and are making India feel proud by their achievements worldwide.

> "Indian Industrial flag zoomed high and is fluttering with pride in the international skies; Today many business houses of India are in the acquiring spree of multinational companies world wide; Indian multinational companies are born."

60 Massive Indian Railways

On April 16th 1853, at Mumbai (then Bombay), Indian Railways, began its humble journey with 14 coaches and 400 Guests. Today it has become the largest Railway network and one of the efficiently run railway systems of the world.

63,940 kilometers of railway line; one million railway passengers; 650 million tonnes of cargo; biggest employer in the world with 16 lakh employees on its rolls; around two crore people depending on Indian railways for their livehood; Indian railways shines brightly with grandeur and splendour;

As per 2005 statistics, Indian Railways has 2,16,717 wagons, 39,936 passenger bogies, 17,339 engines and 14,244 trains crisscross the country among them 8002 trains carry passengers;

Fairy Queen world's oldest working Engine

India started building railway engines in the year 1895 and immediately built a Rail Engine for Uganda in the next year. India has been manufacturing all the required machinery and tools for its railways. The advanced technology and quality of goods used in Indian rail systems stands on par with most of the developed countries of the world.

In the year 1950, "Chittaranjan Locomotive Works" had been established to manufacture coal-powered steam engines; today it has grown into world's largest manufacturer of electric locomotives. The Diesel Engine manufacturing unit in Varanasi not only fabricates engines for Indian Railways alone, but it also exports engines to countries like Bangladesh, Srilanka, Vietnam, and Tanzania etc. Integral coach factory situated at Perambur, exports railway coaches to many foreign countries after meeting the internal demand.

IRCON, another subsidiary of Indian Railways, constructs railway routes in many countries and undertakes many railway projects. It could complete ninety projects in 21 countries. A separate budget of Railways is always presented in the parliament every year. This indicates its size of operations and massiveness. Over a period of 150 years, Indian Railways had grown in strength, proved its efficiency and has become a force to reckon with.

61 Success Story of Indian Space Technology

The Indian space effort was started in the sixties with the establishment of Thumba Equatorial Rocket Launching Station near Thiruvananthapuram for the investigation of ionosphere using sounding rockets. Thanks to the efforts of visonary Vikram Sarabahai, Satish Dhavan, Abdul Kalam and other eminent scientists.

Today, India is among the top five countries, which have the capacity to build satellites, launch space vehicles, explore space and send unmanned missions to moon and other planets. The greatness of Indian scientists is that, they entered the race very late in sixties and within three decades they became world class and even became pioneers in certain areas of space research by developing self-reliant technologies for its ambitious space programmes.

The Indian Space Research Organisation (ISRO), the institution responsible for India's gigantic strides in space technology, was established in 1969 working under the Department of Atomic Energy. In June 1972, ISRO was also brought under Department of Space and Space Commission of Government of India.

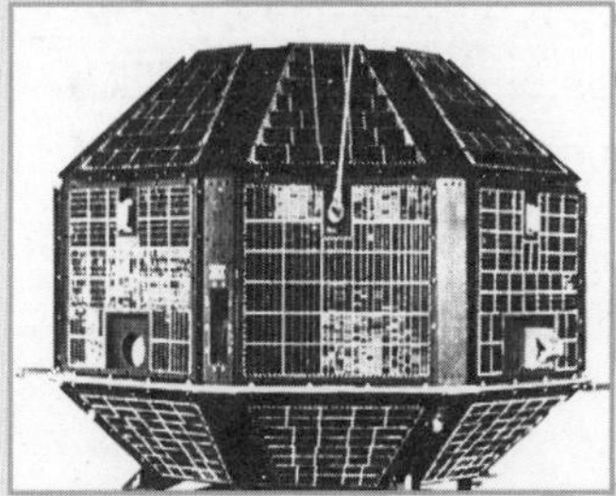

India's first satellite-Aryabhatta

India has achieved an enviable progress in the design, development and operation of space systems, as well as in the use of the systems for vital services like Telecommunication, Television broadcasting, Meteorology, Disaster warning and Natural resources survey and management.

Between 1963 and 1975, scientists acquired familiarity with elementary rocket-launching operations. Towards the mid-1970s, the space programme focussed mainly on experimental projects that allowed scientists to gain experience in the construction and operation of satellites and launch vehicles like Satellite Instructional Television Experiment (SITE conducted in the year 1975-1976),

Satellite Telecommunication Experiments Project (STEP carried out in 1977) and APPLE Experiments.

Today, India is among the top five countries, which have the capacity to build satellites, launch space vehicles, explore space and send unmanned missions to moon and other planets

The entire space research story can be broadly classified as :

a) Building of varieties of satellite series like Aryabhatta, Bhaskara, Rohini, INSAT, IRS etc

b) Building Launch vehicles that send the satellites into orbit like SLV series, ASLV Series, PSLV Series, GSLV Series etc.

Indian made Satellites:

S. No.	Satellites	Types	Launch dates	Special features
1.	Aryabhatta	The first Indian satellites.	April 19, 1975	Indian made Aryabhatta Launched from the erstwhile USSR through Inter cosmos rocket into a near -earth orbit.
2	Bhaskara-I & II	Earth observation satellites.	June 7, 1979 and November 20, 1981	Indian made Bhaskara I & II launched by the erstwhile USSR via Inter cosmos rocket
3.	Rohini Series	Scientific purposes	1979,1980 Onwards	These satellites were launched by SLV-3, ASLV-3 etc; (Indian made launch vehicles) famous experiments conducted like Gamma rays bursting
4.	INSAT Series	Communication Purpose	From1980 Onwards	● INSA T Series is being used for telecommunication, TV broadcasting and meteorological services, ·

				• INSAT is one of the largest domestic communication satellite systems in the world with five satellites, INSAT-2C, INSAT-2DT, INSAT-2E, INSAT-3B and INSAT-3C. • Seven satellites are proposed in the INSAT-4 series
5.	IRS series	Remote sensing purpose	From 1988 onwards	• We have surpassed many developed nations in putting into use the satellite based remote sensing data • The data from IRS satellites is used for soil mapping, grassland mapping, forest survey, land use/land cover mapping, locating underground water resources, estimation of snow cover and snow melt/run-off, monitoring water level in reservoirs, environment monitoring, etc

> "The greatness of Indian scientists is that, they entered the race very late in sixties and within three decades they became world class and even became pioneers in certain areas of space research by developing self-reliant technologies for its ambitious space programmes"

Satellites Launch Vehicles (SLV)

1. **SLV series** India's capability in the Launch Vehicle Technology was first demonstrated through the successful launch of SLV-3 in July 1980, which placed a 40 kg Rohini satellite into a near-earth orbit. Two more launches of SLV-3 were conducted in May 1981 and April 1983 with the Rohini satellites.

		The SLV-3 — for instance, was modified to have a range of 2,000 km and one tonne payload IRBM called Agni, the missiles for military purpose.
2.	**ASLV series**	The Augmented Satellite Launch Vehicle (ASLV) was successfully launched twice from Sriharikota Range (SHAR) on May 20, 1992 and May 4, 1994, respectively. These were the third and fourth developmental launches (ASLV-D3 and ASLV-D4). They injected the SROSS-C and SROSS-C2 (Stretched Rohini Satellite Series) satellite, respectively into a near-earth orbit.
3.	**PSLV series**	• Polar Satellite Launch Vehicle, PSLV, is capable of putting 1,000 kg class remote sensing satellite into 900 km polar sun-synchronous orbit. The second launch of PSLV-D2 on October 15, 1994 was a total success. • The PSLV could form the base of a more powerful IRBM Agni-2 with an extended range of 5,000 km. • Successful launch of PSLV-C3 (October 22, 2001) placing three satellites India's TES, Belgian PROBA and German BIRD, into Polar sunsynchronous orbit.
4	**GSLV series**	• India's Geo-Stationary Satellite Launch Vehicle enables it to launch heavy communications satellites at a height of 36,000 km above the earth and, at the same time, confers on India an Inter-Continental Ballistic Missile capability. Similarly, the Technology Experiment Satellite, besides being used for civilian purposes, provides India military reconnaissance (investigation) capability.

- Successful flight test of Geosynchronous Satellite Launch Vehicle (GSLV), (April 18, 2001) with an experimental satellite GSAT-1 on board.
- Geo-Stationary Satellite Launch Vehicle, which was successfully used to place Edusat, India's first dedicated educational satellite, into orbit in September 2004. Edusat is mainly intended to meet India's domestic demand for an interactive satellite-based distance education system.

Other Highlights:

- India today is in the "satellite launching" business in a very big way, The Antrix Corporation established in the year 1992 could obtain orders for launching foreign satellites into orbits and successfully launched them.
- Remote sensing data collected through satellites is being sold to many countries.
- Could supply hardware and spares to various countries related to space technology.
- Assisting UN in various ways.
- Rakesh Sharma First Indian Astronomer was sent to space.
- **Chandrayaan- Successful unmanned Space Mission to the Moon**

India's latest achievement on 10th Jan 2007, is a remarkable milestone in its space odyssey; through its PSLV, India has not only placed a satellite (SRI-1) into orbit but got retrieved it back to Earth with ease, accuracy and precision making it fall in the Bay of Bengal on 22nd January 2007. With this India has joined the elite club of six countries of space research innovativeness and efficiency.

62 Largest Postal Network of the World

The Indian postal network is among the largest networks in the world in terms of area covered and population served, and it constitutes an important mechanism of communication.

As on March 31, 2004, there were 1,55,669 post offices or outlets, of which roughly 89 per cent were outside the cities. On an average, one Post Office serves an area of 21.13 square km, and a population of 6,602

With 5,66.000 employees, handling a mail traffic of 736 crore letters per annum with 1.25 lakh post offices located in rural areas and the network having 5.83 lakh post boxes, 460 railway mail services, India's postal service is unique in the world.

The Indian Postal System currently provides 38 services, which can broadly be divided into four categories:

- *Communication services (Letters, Postcards etc.),*
- *Transportation services (Parcel),*
- *Financial services (Savings Bank, Money Order, Postal Life Insurance), and*
- *Premium Value Added Services (Like Speed Post, Business Post).*

The Post Office Savings Bank is the largest bank in India in terms of network, accounts and annual deposits. (As on 31.03.2005 there are 14 crore account holders and deposits worth more than Rs 1,00,000 crores.)

	Country	No of Post Offices	Population Served Per Post Office	Average Area Served Per Post Office
1.	India	155618	6602	21.13 sq km
2.	China	76358	16851	125.68 sq km
3.	UK	17243	3460	14.16 sq km
4.	USA	37683	7657	248.72 sq km

Fig pertain to 2003, drawn from dept of posts, UPU publication on statistics Dec 2003 website: http:/Indiabudget.nic.in, Economic Survey 2004-2005

User charges in the postal system cover only 78.3 per cent of costs. There is a significant subsidy element.

The advent of computers and communications has had profound implications for the postal system. In some countries, more letters are sent by e-mail than by post. The postal systems world over, including India Post, have been able to respond to these changes by redefining their roles. Presently, there are 839 Head Post Offices and 1,448 other Departmental Sub-Post Offices, which are computerised for both counter and back office works.

The Department of Posts has undertaken projects for computerizing Post Office Counters at General Post Offices in Bangladesh, Myanmar and Nepal with funds being provided by the Universal Postal Union.

A VSAT network with 150 High Speed VSAT stations which are further connected to 1,327 Extended Satellite Money Order (ESMO) stations located in the Post Offices have been set up for quick

> "The Indian postal network is among the largest networks in the world in terms of area covered and population served, and it constitutes an important mechanism of communication."

transmission of money orders across the country. The Department is transmitting about 60,000 money orders every day through this VSAT network.

A strategic alliance with Western Union Financial Services has helped to strengthen the payment business by providing facilities for the processing of in-bound international money transfers. Indian Post commands 30 per cent of the market share of the international money transfers undertaken through Western Union Financial Services. In the year 2004-2005, it could bring 170 million US dollars as remittances.

The world's first stamps were called the Penny Blacks. They were issued in Great Britain by Sir Rowland Hill in 1840. The first stamps of India issued just before 1854 came to be known as "Scinde Dawks", as they were issued in the Province of Sindh. "Scinde" was how the British spelt the province of Sindh and "Dawk" is the anglicized spelling of the Hindustani word "Dak" or Post. And so, to this day, India's first stamps are referred to simply as The Scinde Dawks.

The year 2004 marked the 150th anniversary of the Indian Postal department. October 1854 saw the formation of a centralized control of the subcontinent's post offices under the first Director General. That year also saw the establishment of a Railway Mail Service across India – with a skeletal network of 701 post offices across the subcontinent -- and a new Sea Mail Service from India to Great Britain and China. In February 1911, a French pilot, named Henri Pequet, flew with 6,500 pieces of mail in a Biplane from Allahabad to Naini (a distance of six miles). This flight was the first official Air Mail in the world!

The Indian postal system also boasts of postal code area "172114" in Sikkim, which – at 15,500 feet (more than 4700 meters approx.) – is the highest post office in the world.

63 Ingenious Tank Irrigation System in India

India is gifted with eternal waters. The veneration people have towards water is evident in their ways of conserving water, preserving water and protecting it.

The ingenuity of ancient India is reflected in the ways of harnessing the water into pools, lakes and tanks and utilizing it judiciously for irrigation.

The tanks remained at central point of Indian agrarian life. Wealthy individuals patronized them as a pious act. Village communities owned tanks and maintained them with highest regard.

Keri, Eri, Cheruvu, Kulams, Kuntas,Kattas, Kunds, Tankas, Naadis, Jheels, Johads, Talabs, Pokhar, Pushkar, Jhil, Beel, Sagar are the names given to these tanks at various parts of India . In every region rainwater or river water was creatively harvested without harming the eco system and utilized for agriculture.

They are the testimony to the Hydraulic Engineering Genius of India.

Ingenious Tank methodology

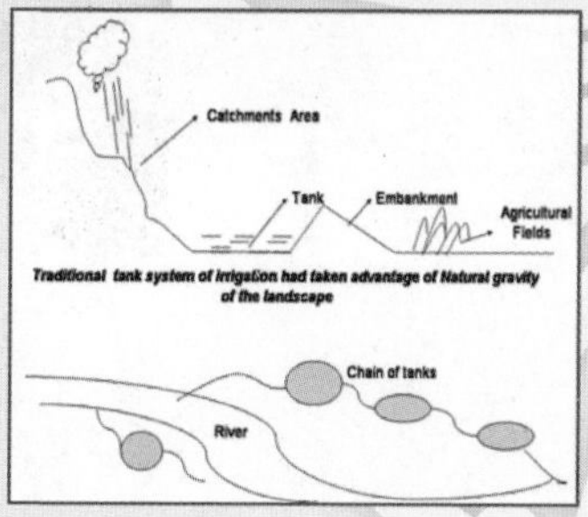

Traditional tank system of irrigation had taken advantage of Natural gravity of the landscape

Chain tanks are interlinked and create an integrated design. A series of tanks having common upper catchments area are called chain tanks. The tank at higher level releases its surplus water as runoff to a tank at lower level. This in turn may release its supply to another located further down slope.

A gravity irrigation tank with independent catchments is called an isolate tank.

When tanks are fed by canals taking water from a river they are called system tanks.

Ancient Indian legacy of Tank Irrigation

River Saraswathi-River of lakes : The Vedic river Saraswati meant a river of pools. Though this mighty river is nonexistent today, one can trace many lakes underground through the satellite.

In the *Ramayana*, Rama advises Bharata on the importance of protecting water bodies.

The *Mahabharata* narrates that while advising Yudhisthira on administrative principles sage Narada laid particular stress on excavation of large and swelling lakes so that cultivation should remain independent of rainwater.

Kautilaya's Arthasastra marks tanks as state property. Punishment was prescribed for a person who failed to cooperate in the building of an irrigation work. Similarly fines were imposed for damage to embankments or misuse of water from the dams and failure to repair them.

Several ancient Indian texts and numerous inscriptions of different periods mentioned in almost every part of the country a wide range of information about tanks, embankments, their upkeep and management.

Indus Valley Civilization: Dholavira excavation of Indus Valley Civilization dating back to third millennium BC reveals a series of water reservoirs which almost entirely surround the city. Stone bunds were raised across them at suitable points in order to divert the flow of water through inlet channels into a series of reservoirs.

The intricate Harappa drainage system at Dholavira achieved an unusual degree of engineering sophistication.

Lake Sudarsana at Junagadh , Gujarat, was constructed during the reign of Chandra Guptha Maurya.

The stone inscriptions of 150 AD provide information about restoration of Lake Sudarsana.

World's Oldest working dam of Tamilnadu: Karikala, the Chola king of south India (AD190) built a number of irrigation tanks. The 320 m long grand anicut on Kaveri river is considered to be oldest hydraulic dam still working intact. Engineers still wonder how the foundation was secured in the permeable soil of unlimited depth.

World famous Allahabad Chain of Tanks : Archaeological excavations near Allahabad have brought to light an extraordinary example of early Indian hydraulic engineering dating back to end of 1stcentury BC. The tank was designed to use flood waters of Ganga. A series of tanks ensured desilting and filtering and a waste weir and seven spill chambers ensured that overflow was properly channeled back to water.

Bhopal Lake- India's Central Point- Water Body: The location of the famous lake of Bhopal known as "Bada Talab" [1010AD] has been chosen to perfection, where a minimum effort would have given the maximum benefits. The dam is a circular/cylindrical structure which has been created using dry masonry of huge boulders.

Some other ancient dams are **Kashmir Tank**, [referred in the 12th century account of Kashmir, "Rajatarangini" by Kalhana describing a well maintained irrigation system with canals, embankments aqueducts, barrages wells and water wheels], **Ananta Raja Sagar** in Andhra Pradesh with a reservoir area of 41 square kilometers and the **Kundis of Rajasthan**. Rajasthan has been at the forefront of constructing large lakes such as Lakes Pichhola, Jaisamand, Fatehsagar, Umaidsagar and Lake Mansagar.

South India had been a great citadel for tank irrigation. In Karnataka, about 39000 tanks were there, varying in size from small ponds to extensive lakes, like the lake in Sulekera was 64 kms in circumference.

Telangana is known as "The land of a thousand tanks" as dams were constructed in series by bunding the same valley at several points. The surplus water of upper area fed the tank lower down. Surplus irrigation water from the fields under upper tanks also seeped through the subsoil and flowed into lower tank. In this way, the benefits of irrigation were distributed over the entire watershed.

Mahanandi Temple tank is a marvel. The inlets and outlets of the tank are so arranged that the depth of the water is constantly kept at five feet, thus enabling all pilgrims to have a plunge. The source of supply of water to this tank has not been traced until now. The outlet of the water feeds 2,000 acres (8.1 km^2) of fertile land surrounding the Mahanandi village.

The Palar water system in Tamilnadu had one thousand tanks in the valley. Especially the Ramnad district of Tamilnadu was abundant with tank irrigation.

British Regime:

In the British regime, tanks were neglected because of radical changes in revenue administration by introduction of Zamindari and Ryotwari systems. These systems greatly undermined collective responsibility of maintaining the tank. The village communities lost control over them and gradually villagers lost interest in maintaining them.

Present Situation & Remedies:

The Water Tank of India is a special manmade structure created for irrigation without harming the ecosystem. The very purpose of a tank is to supply water for irrigation purpose, when there is a scanty rainfall.

Tank irrigation is a basic requirement for rain fed agriculture. It saves ground water over exploitation and recharges the soil.

Regular de-silting of tanks, creating proper inlets and outlets into the tank, strengthening the embankments are required for restoration of tanks.

Instead of providing subsidies on chemical fertilizers, government of India should allocate more funds for restoration of village tanks. Government should involve NGOs and village communities in reviving tank irrigation system in India. Most of India's rainfall is being wasted without being harvested for agriculture.

Our ancestors have shown us the way of obtaining riches through agriculture. The traditional wisdom holds the key for future India's prosperity. Restoration of Tank culture holds the key for golden watershed in future, if we and our rulers act wise today.

Let that sense of wisdom prevail and vivify our elected representatives' intellect to guide us into future.

Spiritual Excellence
Adhyātmika Pratibhā

64 Ṛṣis - Great Seers of India

One lamp lights another lamp.
That lamp consecutively lights
many lamps; and the transmission
continues;

Darkness vanishes as luminance
grows; Ignorance disappears as
wisdom glows; and the radiance of
knowledge flows- from the teacher to
the disciple forever.

The first teacher –Ādi Guru is the
God himself; the eternally beaming
lamp. Light of wisdom is brought
to us from that ever-shinning lamp
of divinity through a medium.
That channel of transmission is Ṛṣi
Paramparā the lineage of seers;

India ever remains as a temple of learning; the abode of seers and sages; India retains its place forever as the world's teacher-*Viśva Guru.*

Knowledge and culture flourished in India, when the other parts of the world remained dormant and asleep in the lap of Mother Nature. India was shining bright as beacon of wisdom and knowledge, guiding humanity eternally.

The very word "Bhārat" means love of knowledge; "Bhā", means knowledge or light; "ratham", means interest or love;

The word Ṛṣi means the person who is travelling towards "Ṛtam"- the ultimate truth. Ṛṣis are always in search of Truth -the researchers of cosmic Truth. The toils, efforts, penances, researches and austerities of the Ṛṣis are to unfold the ultimate truth. The knowledge obtained in that process, is conveyed to the humanity at large for its well-being & happiness. Indian Sciences, Arts and every branch of Indian learning owe their allegiance to these great souls-Ṛṣis.

Modern researchers limit themselves to physical and material aspects of this creation. They perceive what their senses permit. But our ancient seers perceived the truths that were beyond the grasp of senses and dived deep into the subtler aspects of creation and the spiritual aspects.

The spiritual domain begins, as one transcends the physical or material domain. Going beyond the sensual plane, is growing beyond the senses. To grow beyond senses, one has to control the senses, by turning these outgoing senses inwards.

Journey inwards is the journey into our inner realms; into our spiritual being that is beyond body & mind.

> The toils, efforts, penances, researches and austerities of the Rishis are to unfold the ultimate truth. The knowledge obtained in that process, is conveyed to the humanity at large for its well-being & happiness. Indian Sciences, Arts and every branch of Indian learning owe their allegiance to these great souls-Rishis.

Our seers taught everyone about, one's own real nature (spiritual being) after knowing and experiencing the truth for themselves; these truths remain as the invaluable treasure of spiritual wealth.

India had been robbed of its materialistic and intellectual wealth but spiritual wealth cannot be robbed and can only be transmitted since it remains transcendental.

So our Rishis remain with us in their spiritual form to convey that spiritual wealth to the right recipients. Hence Indians trace their lineage to these Rishis, the seers of yore. Indians respect and worship them every day.

Sapta Rishis are prominent among them; even today they appear to us as the brilliant stars in the sky. People with spiritual eyes alone can perceive them and communicate with them and get benefited by the transmission of Self-knowledge.

The Sapta Rishis are

1. Agastya 2. Atri 3. Aṅgiras 4. Kashyapa 5. Bhṛgu 6. Vasiṣṭha 7. Viśvamitra.

There are various lists of Sapta Rishis mentioned in various Indian texts. They vary according to the times. Let us know about the above-mentioned seven revered sages.

Agastya

Agastya is one among the *Sapta Rishis.* He is a brother of Sage Vashistha. He was born from a Pot. (Not from mother' womb... concepts like Test Tube babies prevailed during those times);

Legend says that he had stopped the growth of *Vindhya Mountains.* On the request of Devatās, he had swallowed the ocean; he had suitably instructed Rama on spiritual things and asked him to stay at Pañcavaṭi by giving certain weapons charmed and charged by mantras.

At the battlefield, he taught *Rama*, the famous mantra *"Aditiya Hṛdaya"*. The hymns of this mantra appear to us, as the praises offered to Sun God. But it's in depth spiritual meaning reveals the power of the ever-glowing Ātmā- the Self-or the real nature of the soul.

"Lalita Sahasra Nama", the 1000 names extolling the divine mother of universe had been conveyed to him through Devatas and he in turn conveyed it to the world. Even today millions and millions of Hindus chant this mantra and perform Pūjās (rituals).

In Southern India, he is considered to be the founding father of the medical science called Siddha Medicine.

In the name of *Agastya* there are many Sanskrit texts, which discuss the utilization of power, and power generation (today's electricity etc). They are *"Shakti Tantra & Shakti Samhita"*.

During the month of Bhadrapada, Agastya appears as a bright star in the night sky.

Atri Maharṣi

Atri was one among the seven seers of yore. Atri's wife was *Anusuya.* He was the brainchild of Brahmā, the creator. This sage had assisted Brahmā in creating life on the planets.

Atri's wife *Anusuya* was also a spiritual powerhouse. Legend says the Tri-mūrtis were transformed into small babies and were fed by her.

Atri had given hospitality to *Sri Rama, Sita* and *Lakshmana,* during their stay in the forests.

In *Rig Veda*, there are hymns called *Atri Samhita,* which were perceived by him.

Atreya Dharma sastra or Atreya Smriti is a famous Dharma sastra text. Even today many Hindus follow his code of Ethics.

Aṅgirasa

Angirasa was also a brainchild of Brahma, the creator aspect of divine function. Like sage Atri, he also had assisted Brahma in building this creation. He had married shraddha the daughter of Prajapati Kardama. Angirasa lineage had multiplied and his descendents became famous.

He had contributed Angirisa Smriti, a Dharma sastra text. Angirasa had compiled many mantras in *Atharva Veda.* In Upanishads, we find the reference of sage Angirasa. He had revealed the secrets of *Omkar Mantra.* He glows as one of the celestial star in the night sky.

Bhṛgu Maharṣi

Sage *Bhrigu* was a brainchild of Brahmā. He is also considered to be one among the Nine Brahmas. He was the founding father of Bhrigu lineage.

He married Khyati a daughter of Kardama Prajapati. When Rishis of yore performed a yajña and wanted to convey the fruits of yagna to the best among Brahmā, Vishnu and Siva; they deputed Sage Bhrigu to find the best among the Trimūrtis.

There is an astrological text in the name of Bhrigu. He had taught sage Bharadwaj, the cosmic principles. He had instructed Parasurama to perform penance on Lord Siva for obtaining "Bhargva Astra" (a mighty weapon similar to of present day nuclear device).

He had revealed many subtle aspects of righteousness to many of his disciples.

Kaśyapa Mahariṣi

He is the son of Marichi, one of the ten Brahma Manasa Putras (sons progenarated through Brahmā's Mental Resolve). The Prajapati Dakṣa gave his thirteen daughters (Aditi, Diti, Kadru, Danu, etc.) in marriage to Kashyapa. In the family line of Kasyapa, along with him there are two more discoverers of Mantras, namely, his sons Avatsara and Asita. Two sons of Avatsara, namely, Nidhruva and Rebha, are also Mantra-seers. Asita had a son named Shandilya, from whom the famous Shandilya family line started. Garuda and Aruna are also the sons of Kashyapa.

The twelve Adityas are sons of Aditi and Kashyapa. He was the father of the Devas, Asuras, Nagas, Apsaras, Gandharvas, Rahu and all of humanity. He is married to Aditi, who gave birth to Agni and the Adityas. His second wife, Diti, begot the Daityas. Diti and Aditi were daughters of King Daksha and sisters of Sati, Shiva's consort.

He had composed Kashyapa Samhita, a vāstu śātra text, which reveals the techniques of engineering skills of building kings' palaces, temples, auditoriums etc.

Vasiṣṭha

Vasiṣṭha, was the chief of the seven venerated sages or Sapta Rishis and the Rajaguru of the Suryavamsha or Solar Dynasty, the lineage of Lord Rama . He was the mānasaputra of Brahmā (Brain child). He had in his possession the divine cow Kamadhenu and Nandini her child, who could grant anything to their owners, worshippers and devotees.

Arundhati is the wife of Vashishtha and appears as the small star of the stellar constellation Ursa Major (Sapta Rishi mandala) beside the big star Vashishtha. At the Hindu marriage ceremony, newly wedded couple are shown the star Arundhati, as the symbol of sacredness, nobility chastity and auspiciousness.

Vashishtha is credited as the chief seer of Mandala 7 of the Rigveda. Vashishtha and his family are glorified in RigVeda 7.33, extolling their role in the Battle of the Ten Kings, making him the only mortal besides Bhavayavya to have a Rigvedic hymn dedicated to him. Another immortal treatise dedicated by him to the humanity is "Vashishtha Samhita" - a book on Vedic system of Astrology (Muhūrta/ Muhūrt)- based on which theory & principles of Electional Astrology have emanated & followed through millenniums & which have withstood the test of time.

"Yoga Vashishtha", is an ancient scripture narrated by sage Vashishtha to Rama. A unique and an extremely profound discourse, it provides innumerable insights into the inner world of consciousness. This extremely huge scripture covers all the topics that are related to the spiritual study of a seeker.

This scripture is a must for anyone trying to understand the concepts of consciousness, creation of the world, the multiple universes in this world, our perception of world, dissolution of the world and the liberation of this soul.

"Vashishtha Smriti" is a Dharma Sastra Text and is as famous as Manu Smriti. He was instrumental in the evolution of Vishwamitra an ordinary king into great sage Brahmarshi Vishwamitra.

Viśvamitra

Brahmarshi Vishwamitra is one of the most venerated rishis or sages of ancient India. He is also the exponent of most of the Mandala 3 of the Rigveda, including the *Gayatri Mantra*. This mantra is chanted by millions and millions of Hindus every day during twilight, noon, dawn & dusk.

The ordinary *King Kaushika,* after having a quarrel with sage Vashishtha, for owning the divine cow, realized that the power obtained by penances was far greater than mere physical might. He renounced his kingdom and began his quest to become a greater rishi than Vashishtha. He took on the name Vishwamitra. It is very interesting to see all the challenges that Vishwamitra faced in his life to become a Brahmarshi.

In the process of becoming Brahmarshi, he had even created a new universe (heaven) called Triśaṅku Svarga.

Vishwamitra trains Young Rama & Lakshmana. He gives them the knowledge of the Devāstras or celestial weaponry, and teaches them advanced religion and guides them to kill powerful demons like Tataka, Maricha and Subahu. He also leads them to the Svayamvara ceremony of princess Sita, who becomes the wife of Rama.

There were many sages who had contributed immensely to the spiritual wealth of India. The knowledge bequeathed by them cannot be termed as mere spiritual or religious exhortations. It includes most advanced principles of material sciences, which the modern science is yet to reveal.

In addition to Sapta Rishis, Vyasa and Valmiki have contributed immensely to the Sanskrit Literature and strengthened Indian Culture.

- *Valmiki* is called *Adikavi* and his work *"Ramayan"* remains as the eternal treasure house of inspiration.
- *Vyasa* not only wrote *Mahabharata*, the greatest record of history on the face of earth, but also had classified Vedas into four parts and compiled eighteen puranas.
- His disciple Paila compiled Rigveda. Vysampayana- Yajur Veda; Jaimini Sāmaveda; Sumanthu -Atharva Veda.
- Apart from imparting spiritual knowledge our Rishis had even given us the secular knowledge.
- Bharadwaj learnt Ayurveda from Lord Indra and taught it to his disciples. He had even

"Bharadwaj learnt Ayurveda from Lord Indra and taught it to his disciples. He had even written a treatise on Mechanics and Machine science Yantra sarvaswa , which contains the subject of Aeronautics as well."

written a treatise on Mechanics and Machine science "Yantra sarvaswa", which contains the subject of Aeronautics as well.

- Panini has given the science of sound and grammar rules- called Aṣṭādhyāyī.
- Patanjali lives eternally with his greatest contribution of science of yoga, "Yoga sutras". He had also written a commentary called Mahabhashya on the Panini's work.
- The science of medicine had been contributed by Ashwini devatas, Bharadwaj, Atri, Agnivesha, Charaka, Sushruta, Vagbhatta and many others.
- Nandikeshwara, Narada and Hanuman had contributed immensenly to the Science of music, the Gandharwa Veda. Bhakti sutras of Narada contain the knowledge of devotion.
- Bharata Muni evolved the Science of Dance and Drama.
- Kapila's Shankhya Sastra, Kanaad's Vaiśeṣika Sastra and Gautama's Nyaya Sastra contain doctrines of general & Atomic Physics, Logic and Reasoning.
- Parāśara wrote Dharma Sastra and Jyotish Sastra. One of the descendents of Parasara had contributed immensely to the science of agriculture (Vṛkṣa Ayurveda by Parasara).
- Jabali, Nachiketa, Skanda, Sanatkumara, Vatsyayana, Boudhayana, Apasthamba, Kaundinya, Markendeya, Yajñavalkya, Romasa, Sanka, Maricha, Kanwa, Rishysringa, Garga, Jaimini, Dhadhichi and many other seers had gifted us with spiritual powerhouse of knowledge.

In ancient India, the great sages had developed every branch of secular knowledge from the spiritual perspective. We are yet to comprehend the truths endowed to us by our ancestors – the Ṛṣis of yore.

"In ancient India, the great sages had developed every branch of secular knowledge from the spiritual perspective. We are yet to comprehend the truths endowed to us by our ancestors the Rishis of yore."

65 Global Influence of Indian Spiritual Gurus

As is a Prayer room in a House – so is India, the sacred place for the whole universe.

From times immemorial, the spiritual spring of India is eternally surging up. From the times of Vedic lore to the present day, many a great soul had been born in India and had quenched the thirst of many people within India & abroad with their peerless power of penance and wisdom. Directly or indirectly each of them had influenced the millions across the globe.

For the past two thousand five hundred years, Gautama the Buddha, Mahāvīra, Adi Sankara, Gurunanak, Ramakrishna Paramahamsa, Shirdi Sai Baba, Ramana Maharshi and many others and today's Mata Amritanandamayi, Sri Sri Ravi Shankar, Ramdev Baba had descended on this land and blessed this world with showers of spirituality. They are our Vishwa gurus – world teachers, who made India the "Vishwa Guru Pīṭham", the seat of spiritual learning.

There are innumerable gurus, who are born in this holy land. They come and go unnoticed; yet they would have worked wonders for the spiritual awakening of millions, the real unsung & unknown Heroes. Here let us discuss a few great personalities in brief to inspire ourselves.

Gautama Buddha

Gautama Buddha (5th Century B.C) : Buddha, the ever-shinning lamp of India whose effulgence has spread throughout the world, is a personification of peace, compassion and wisdom. He strolled on the sacred soil of India 2500 years ago, preaching the gospel of salvation and social rising up.

Born amidst pleasures in a royal family. The Siddhartha accidentally hit upon the human sufferings. He came out from his golden cage, straight into Human agony. His quest took him to every ascetic person, but could not find the answer for his quest. At last at Gaya (in today's Bihar), under a Bodhi tree, he realized his self and found the cause for the human sufferings. Henceforth he became the

> At last at Gaya (in todays Bihar), under a Bodhi tree, he realized his self and found the cause for the human sufferings. Henceforth he became the Buddha and delivered the greatest solutions for human sufferings in most systematic and scientific way.

Buddha and delivered the greatest solutions for human sufferings in most systematic and scientific way.

At Sarnath near Banaras he gave his first discourse "Dharma Chakra Pravartana" the four noble truths

- **Existence of sufferings:** Birth, decay, disease to be united with unpleasentness etc.
- **Causes of Sufferings:** Craving for sensual pleasure, possessions, ambitions, clinging to life and relations.
- **Cessation of sufferings:** Complete separation from cravings, rather becoming free from desires is the only solution to cessation of sufferings.
- Ways or methods that lead to cessation of sufferings. He had exhorted eightfold path in this regard, they are:
    - Right understanding
    - Right thought
    - Right speech
    - Right action
    - Right livelihood
    - Right effort
    - Right mindfulness
    - Right concentration.

Buddhism had spread to many parts of the world and mostly influenced China and other parts of Asia. With the spread of Buddhism, the Indian culture had also spread into the world.

He spoke to people in their languages and touched their hearts. Human beings and animals enjoyed the state of bliss and peace of mind when they were around Buddha. He was one with the world and world was one with him.

Mahāvīr (B.C.599- 527) : The Founder of the Jain religion. In his thirties he left his family and became a wandering monk in search of reality. He attained 'Jnana' and wandered spreading and explaining the truth, to all people alike, that was revealed to him. Ahimsa, Satya, Asatya-Tyaga (avoiding untruth), Asteya, (nonstealing), Aparigraha & Brahmacharya are the principles he taught. He said all people are one and the same in their path to liberation and he rejected the differences due to the religion, caste, community and language.

AdiSankaracharya

Adi Sankaracharya (1st Century B.C) : Today "Modern Science" has recognized the universe to be undivided single stream of consciousness. But two thousand years ago the same knowledge was made known to the world by Adi Sankara, through his doctrine of Advaita Vedanta. Because of sincere & enduring penance the sacred couple Aryamba and Sivaguru could beget such a brilliant child "Sankara". He was born in a village called Kaladi in Kerala. This boy wrote his first book at the age of six. At his young age, many Kings & great personalities used to consult him to seek knowledge and get their doubts cleared on subtler aspects of religion. At the age of eight he sought the permission from his mother to take up Sannyāsa and attained it after great difficulty. Afterwards, without caring what to eat and where to go, he wandered from Kerala to Madhya Pradesh on foot and met his Guru 'Govindapada' on the bank of Narmada River.

After completing his education, Sankara with the blessings of his guru started writing commentaries (Bhāṣyas) on Upaniṣads. He wrote commentaries for Bhagawad Gita, Upanishads and Brahmasūtras, which are known as PrasthanTraya and were praised even by great pandits. After that he authored his own compositions like SoundaryaLahari, Sivanandalahari, Bhaja Govindam, Atmabodha, Tattva-bodha, Dakshinamurthy Stotra, Vivekachudamani etc. All of them are great spiritual books, useful to quench the thirst of those who pursue liberation. Adi Sankara established 4 mutts in the four corners of our country and re-established Sanatana Dharma: Sringeri, Puri, Dwaraka and Badrinath are the four Mutts. It is believed that he had left his body at Kanchi.

Many kings, intellectuals, scholars and traders became his followers. Within the Lifespan of 32 years, he had completely revitalized the decaying Sanatana Dharma and revived its past glory. The 72 aspects of Hinduism and various schools of thought were wonderfully converged by Adisankara into his doctrine of Advaita siddhanta, the non-dual philosophy. Today, he is not remembered as a person, but as a phenomenon. (A few Western Historians relate AdiSankara to 8th Century AD, which is rejected by many Indian Scholars.)

Thiruvalluvar:

Thiruvalluvar : He wrote "Tirukkural"- the sacred book in Tamil.This is also known as "Muppural" which means that it has "Three Vargas". This book describes and explains the three aspects called Dharma, Artha and Kama, hence the name. Correct Data about "Thiruvalluvar" could not be secured. Some believe that he was the king of Kanya Kumari and sacrificed everything like Buddha and some others believe that he was born in a weaver's family. 'Kural' means a small stanza. Such 10 slokas are grouped into a chapter and there are 133 chapters in this book.

In this great book of life, love, luck, family relationships, truth, knowledge, wife, good habits, chance, karma and such many day-to-day problems are discussed. For example a Gentleman is known by his qualities like smile, charity, impartiality & good words" –says Thiruvalluvar.

Ramanujacharya (1017-1137) : Ramanujacharya was born in 1017 at Sriperumbur. From childhood he was an intelligent student. He used to correct the mistakes in the teachers. Unable to put up with his wife's ignorant behavior he had taken 'Sannyāsa'. After that he became the head of a Vaishnava mutt at Srirangam. As per the orders of his Guru, he wrote Bhashyam (Commentary) on "Viśiṣṭādvaita". He also wrote some great books like 'Vedanta Sara', 'Vedanta Sangraha', 'Vedanta Deepam'.

After great scrutiny 'Swami Nambi' instilled in Ramanuja the great Mantra, 'Om Namo Narayanaya' and asked him to keep it as a secret. But Ramanuja assembled all the people near the temple without making any difference between the religion, caste and creed. He climbed up the temple tower and openly announced the holy mantra for all people. He was not ashamed of his act. He said he was prepared to face Naraka (Hell) for his announcement if that mantra was going to give benefit and Swarga (Heaven) to all the people. He kept open the temple entrance to all the outcasts who were present there. He lived for 125 years. The well-established good traditions and discipline followed in performing pūjās and temple rites, what we see today in Vaishnava temples, goes to his credit.

Ramanujacharya

Basaveswara (1131-1167) : He is the chief guru for 'Lingayat Sect' of Saivas. He was a great scholar in Kannada literature, a Jnani, whom the people believe to be an avatar of Nandi (Bull) of Parama Siva. His guru was Sangameswar. He underwent very hard training under his guru for nearly twelve years. He believed all religions and all gods to be one. He said man is the temple of God and practically showed serving man is serving God. (Manavaseva Īswaraseva).

Madhvacharya (1238 – 1317) : One day a Sannyāsī was crossing the river Ganges with his group of disciples. There was a Muslim Kingdom on the other side. When the army of that side tried to attack the group of Sannyāsīs, the head swamiji told them, that they are going to meet the king and had not come to confront with their army. When the king had heard this, he exclaimed, how he dared to enter

Shree Madhvacharya

Namdev

Sant Gyaneswar

into his kingdom. Then the sannyāsī calmly gave a reply saying, "O king, the Lord who is protecting all of us is above us. If he is 'Allah' for you, He is 'Narayana' for us." That man is Madhvacharya.

Madhvacharya propagated the "Dwaita" philosophy. To the nation which was deteriorating with caste junk, he said that all are equal in God's creation; everyone should seek God according to their capabilities. "The real work is doing service to others", said Madhvacharya.

Born in 1238, he took sannyāsa at the age of 12. He toiled all along his life for the spreading of VedaVijñā. He wrote commentaries on BhagawadGita, Ten Upanishads and Brahma sutras. Madhvacharya was not seen after 1317, when he took leave of his people and journeyed towards Badri.

Sant Gyaneswar (1275 – 1296) : Gyaneswar was born in Maharashtra in the 13th Century. He combined devotion and literary ability and paved a path of liberation with an attitude of self-analysis. He exhorted all to make sincere efforts in eliminating crooked tendencies within oneself and to cultivate the trait of having love towards every being. His "Jnaneshwari" commentary on Bhagawad Gita is very famous in Maharashtra, which he sang with melody and purity.

Namdev (13th Century) : He is a contempory of Gyaneswar. He spent most of his childhood days, by singing devotional songs in the temple of Lord Vitthala. Honeybee never rests and always aspires for honey. Similarly my mind always aspires to be in the company of God, says Namdev. One day he sees a dog stealthily carrying a piece of bread (roti). He ran after it with a pot of ghee shouting loudly "Narayana" to wait till he butters it. He could see God even in the stealing dog. He is a source of inspiration to millions of devotees in central India, even today.

Potana (1400-1470) : A Telugu saint, who wrote Bhāgvatam in Telugu. He wrote that book with high devotional fervour. Some times, Lord Rama himself used to fill the verses kept incomplete by

Potana. Even today, people in Andhra Pradesh worship that book and offer puja. He told people that in Kaliyuga many diseases would haunt mankind, and these diseases can be cured only with the devotion towards God and saintly company. He also said one has to conquer oneself, not the world. One's enemies are one's own anger, ego, hatred, jealousy and greed.

Annamacharya

Annamacharya (1408-1503) : One of the greatest poet saint of south India, who wrote 32,000, devotional songs in Telugu on Lord Venkteswara of Tirupati.

He condemned untouchability; propagated universal oneness and the presence of Lord Vishnu in every being. Even today, his songs inspire millions of devotees in Andhra Pradesh and else where.

Kabir Das

Kabir Das (1440-1518) : In the medieval ages, India was gifted with many great souls who had drenched this land with gigantic tides of devotion and spirituality. One such crown jewel is "Kabir". He was a devotee of Ram, though born in a Muslim family. He advocated the impersonal aspect of God and wrote several books full of "Saakis" (devotional songs of spiritual wisdom). He stood as the symbol of confluence of Sufi (Muslim philosophy and Bhakti tradition of Hinduism). He propagated that God is one.

Guru Nanak

Guru Nanak (1400-1539) : The founder of Sikh religious thought. He strongly believed that the whole universe is God's creation and all beings are his children. God is the only reality and is the omnipresent creator, protector and assimilator. "One should never hurt others" is the central theme of his philosophy. Today, Gurunanak's followers are spread throughout the world.

Vallabhacharya

Vallabhacharya (1472-1531) : He was a child prodigy, who acquired mastery over Vedas at the age of six and went round many holy places. He advocated the Krishna marga of pure Dwaita tradition and propogated that devotion to Krishna alone is the path. He wrote Bhāgavatapurāṇa, which became famous. He had scholastic discussions with the elders of the court of Krishnadeva Raya on the matters of devotional philosophy. There are many followers of his tradition of thought.

Suradas

Suradas (1479-1589) : Suradas was blind by birth. He could see everything with his mind's eye. Once his parents had lost two Gold coins, he pointed them, where they lay inspite of his blindness. He was a child prodigy. He propagated Bhakti marga and wrote many devotional songs. Suradas practiced the "Pushti marga", which is filled with devotion, compassion and contentment. He wrote about one lakh devotional songs called "Sura Sagar", but today only 8000 songs are available. He lived on the banks of the Ganga.

Chaitanya Maha Prabhu

Chaitanya Maha Prabhu (1485-1533) : He is the Adi Guru who pronounced the Krishna Tattva to the world. Krishna Chaitanya or Chaitanya Maha Prabhu hails from Bengal. His travel to Gaya had brought within him great transformation. Days together he used to spend in constant meditation, without food and sleep. Among his writings only eight slokas are available (Siksa Ashtakas). Chaitnaya's devotional eulogies about Lord Krishna remain as eternal inspration to many.

Sankara Deva

Sankara Deva (1486-1568) : He is a great teacher of Assam and North East, a highly revered personality for the people of Assam. Without confusing the people's minds with new schools of thought, he tried to propagate the existing schools of spiritual glory. He had chosen the path of Bhakti and propagated its essence through songs and stories. He wrote many translations. He translated most part of Bhagavatam into Assamee folklore (language) known as "kamaroopi". He wrote "Bhakti-Ratna" spreading Bhakti-Tattva. He wrote six playlets in the name of "Ankai-nat". He composed svaras to many songs. His songs are very popular and very familiar among Assamese in the name of "Bar-gits". (Great songs)

Sant Tulasi Das (1532-1623) : When we hear the name, "Rama Charita Manas", we remember Tulasi Das. Rama Charita Manas is also known as, "Tulasi Ramayan". Goswami is the other name of Tulsidas. Every Indian household, whether in South or North of India recite Ramacharitamanas with devotion and sacredness. Along with Lord Rama, Tulasi's eternal words remain in the hearts of millions of Indians. Though he was a Sanskrit scholar, he wrote many books in colloquial languages of Awadhi & Vraja. His books are Vinaya patrika, Krishna Geetavali and Dohavali and Kavitavali.

Tulsidas gives the essence of all scriptures in the following words: "Kindness is at the root of dharma and egotism is at the root of hell. Oh Tulasi, the five great qualities in the world are association with great souls, chanting the name of Hari, compassion to all, and humility and helping others".

Sant Eknath (1533-1606) : "A student feels immensely happy, if he could find one mistake in his text book, so also how much bliss a man would feel, if he could find out the defects in his own daily life?" This question has changed the vision of Eknath and a spiritual beacon was born. Eknath is personification of love and devotion. His scripture "Eknath Bhāgavata" in Marathi not only inspires maharashtrians but also instills devotion in the hearts of millions of Indians. According to him "money and desires are the two obstacles that hinder the spiritual unfoldment of a person.

Meera Bai (1547-1614) : Meerabai is India's eternal symbol for devotion. Her songs on Lord Krishna, the Giridhara Gopala, still echo in every Indian heart. Her strong belief is that one could only get God's grace by having immense love and unshakable faith in him. She sang, "O mind! Practise devotion; sing bhajans, only then the Lord shall reveal unto us".

Raghavendra Swamy (1581-1671) : Sri Raghavendra Swamy is a highly revered saint, a embodiment of truth and righteousness, propagator of Dwaita siddhanta.

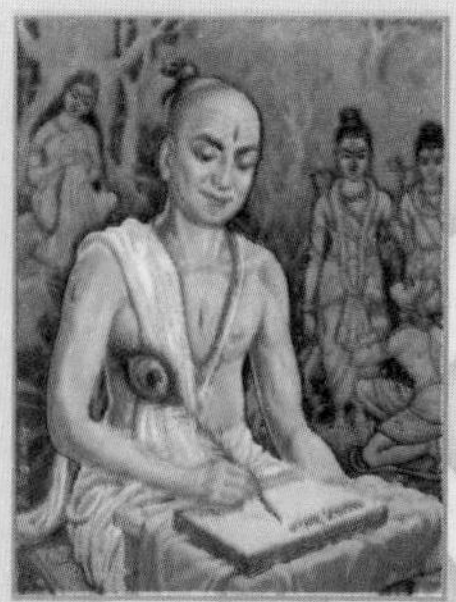

Sant Tulasi Das

Meera Bai

Raghavendra Swamy

Sant Tukaram

Samartha Rama Das

He wrote philosophical books like "Chandrika", "Nyaya Sudha", "Tantra Deepika" and "Nyaya Mukthavali". Even today he has a very large following in South India, mostly the people of Madhwa tradition. He is considered to be Sri Hanuman's Avatar. "Those who are devoid of family bondage, desires, greediness, cravings for name & fame only would progress in the way of liberation" said Raghavendra swamy.

Sant Tukaram (1598-1650) : The poet saint was a great devotee of Lord Panduranga. He was born in Maharashtra. From his childhood he used to worship God with melodious voice and devotional heart. He did not care much for the material benefits in the day–to-day life. This virtuous man had even attracted the emperor Shivaji by his devotional attitude towards God. He propagated dharma (righteousness), Devotion and love by means of songs called "Abhangas". By chanting the Lord's name with devotion, one can obtain His grace. According to him repeating Lord's name in silence is the best way of attaining His ever-blissful abode.

Samartha Rama Das (1608-1682) : Samartha Rama Das is famous among Indian saints. He meditated not for his enlightenment but for re-establishing the Sanatana Dharma and glory of his country. Chhatrapati Shivaji established one of the strongest Hindu empires under his guidance, inspiration and tutelage. His book "Dasa bodha" is famous in Maharashtra. It is believed that, he stayed in Andhra Pradesh for a very long time and wrote many books in Telugu, which are not available to us today. He established a tradition called "Darakari" tradition. He exhorted every body to chant "Ram nam" for eradication of all evils and sins.

Bhadhrachala Ramadas (1620-1680) : One of the greatest poetic legends of South India; an ardent devotee of Rama, who had built the famous Bhadrachalam temple on the banks of the river Godavari. Nawab of Golkonda imprisoned him for constructing this temple. It is said that eventually Lord Rama came to the rescue and freed him from the prison. His devotion to Rama lives through his songs. The songs written by him on Rama are considered to be classical wealth for carnatic Music and can be heard in many parts of Telangana and Andhrapradesh and South India.

Saint Thyagaraja (1767-1847) : Saint Thyagaraja is considered to be the pillar of Carnatic music. Being a devotee of Lord Rama, Thyagaraja showed the world that devotion is the best way to obtain liberation. He had written thousands of Kirtanas, each composed in specific melody or raga. His songs remain to us as the treasure house of caranatic music. He had also written musical works like Nauka Charitham and Prahalada Bhakti Vijayam. Thyagaraja is considered to be a personification of Narada, Paraasara, Pundareeka and Prahlada. He had the darshan of Lord Rama and obtained samadhi. Indian music is eternal so is the name of Thyagaraja.

Thyagaraja

Swami Narayan (1781-1830) : As Ramanuja of South, Swami Narayana of Gujarat belongs to broad-minded Vaishnava tradition. Countless followers from all walks of life flocked around him. He continued his mission of transporting and transforming the man from material realm to spiritual domain. At the age of seven, he had mastered, Vedas, Puranas and Upanishads by heart. At the age of eleven, he renounced the world. He said Mukti (liberation) means not becoming one with absolute but is exclusive service of God by assuming a divine body. He enriched the land with the legacy of two scriptures, "Vachanamritam" & "Shikshapatri". Today Swami Narayan temples throughout the world reflect the grandeur and splendour of devotion & God's love.

Swami Narayan

Swami Dayananda Saraswati (1824-1883) : The founder of Arya Samaj. He dedicated his entire life to re-establish the Vedic truths and Vedic dharma; by shunning idolatry. His childhood name was Moola Shankar. He left home in search of truth after an incident on Shivratri day. In 1860, he became a disciple of Virajananda, at Mathura in Uttar Pradesh. In 1875, he started Arya samaj and wrote his

Swami Dayananda Saraswati

eternally powerful book "Satyartha Prakash (Light of truth). He travelled length and breadth of the country holding discussions with scholars, initiating followers into Arya samaj by inducing them to adhere to Yajñas. He wrote interpretations to Vedas and tried his best to revive the Vedic knowledge. The greatest contribution of Arya samaj is it could stop unabated and treacherous conversions into Islam and Christianity for a period of time.

Shirdi Saibaba

Shirdi Saibaba (1836-1918) : Today millions and millions of people in India worship Shirdi Saibaba, as the greatest Satguru, who appears to them, in the form of their Ishta devata (adoring Godhood like Rama, Krishna, Siva Ganesha, Durga, etc). Nobody knows the background of Saibaba. But he was brought up as a Sufi Fakir and later Venkusha became his guru. He appeared at Shirdi in the year 1854 and stayed there in a dilapidated mosque, the rest of his life. His life was filled with miracles and he had transformed many materialistic persons into spiritual seekers. He had Muslim and Hindu followers. He used to exhort that God is one, in whatever form you worship (sab ka malik ek). He advised devotees to cultivate "Shraddha" (sincere devotion) & "Saburi" (patience with faith), which shall take them to the ultimate destination, 'God'. With every passing day, more and more people are becoming his devotees through out the world.

Sri Ramakrishna Paramahamsa (1836-1886) : *Sri Rama had been an embodiment of Dharma. Sri Krishna had been a redeemer of Dharma. Sri Ramakrishna Paramahamsa had been the personification of all Dharmas. He had been adored as the best among Avataras by none else than his prime disciple Swami Vivekananda.*

He lived as an ordinary priest; but manifested the extraordinary devotion towards Mother Kali. He propagated that truth is one but scholars say it differently. He had found the point of convergence of various religious paths in Sanatana Dharma, the Universal Religion. Today, in his name stands the

Ramakrishna Mission, which is rendering spiritual, cultural and social service to the mankind. The branches of Ramakrishna mission are present worldwide.

His companion was Sri Sarada Devi, who had been the embodiment of purity and motherhood. She had become the real mother of many spiritual seekers. Sri Ramakrishna Paramahamsa looked upon every woman as manifestation of Divine Mother including his wife.

Narayana Guru (1854-1928) : During the 19th century, in Kerala state, many changes and reforms took place. These changes happened at various fronts like social, economic, political & intellectual. Narayana Guru expounded that all are equal before the God. Narayana Guru felt that social awareness is an important path of devotion. To show his resentment against the practice of untouchablity, he himself had built Siva temple and had invited everybody to worship there, irrespective of caste & creed.

Sri Ramakrishna Paramhamsa

Swami Vivekananda (1863-1902) : The young Indian rebel monk criss-crossed the world and proudly proclaimed the greatness of India. To the world, he thundered "India never dies nor did it die". It only went into a temporary slumber and bound to wake up surely with rejuvenating vigour very soon.

Such was his prophecy that India obtained within a short time the independence and is now marching ahead to become a superpower of the 21st century.

Sri Sarada Mata

He was a man of words and action too. He awakened the nation, trained the young sanyasins to work for the poor & downtrodden. He established Ramakrishna Math. He invited foreigners to come and work for India. He only asked them to love his country (India) as a reciprocatory gesture (Guru Dakṣiṇā) for teaching them Vedānta.

Swami Vivekananda

His childhood name was Narendranath Dutt and was a youth of reasoning nature. He wanted to meet a person who had seen God and that search took him to a divine incarnation Sri Ramakrishna Paramahamsa. The first meeting ended in an ever-lasting bondage between them. He was chiselled, moulded and was prepared for the great task by the noble master Sri Ramakrishna Paramahamsa. Naren became the leader of a core group of disciples after the demise of Sri Ramakrishna. He took sannyāsa and wandered the length and breadth of the country feeling for the plight of Indians, meeting Maharajas and explaining to them about their duty towards the Motherland.

He travelled to the West with a mission of helping the West spiritually and taking the help from the West materially to rouse India. He became instantly popular at the world Parliament of Religions and his first address and his first words, "Brothers & sisters of America", stirred the hearts of millions. A wave of spiritual awakening drenched the land of opportunities (America) and India became a land of sacredness to Westerners who heard him. From 1893 to 1897, he went round America and Europe and returned to India. In his last two years of life, he moulded many young sannyāsins of Ramakrishna order and finally left the body to become a voice without form in the year 1902.

He lives today in spirit and inspires many about India and Spirituality. Netaji, Gandhiji, Nehru, Aurobindo, Tilak, Dr.Hedgewar, Guru Golwalkar, Jamshedji Tata, Mysore Maharaja, Rajas of Khetri, Ramnad etc were all inspired by his teaching and became the Architects of National Independence movement. He had even inspired Westerners like Rockfeller, Henry Ford, Leo Tolstoy, Margaret Nobel, Romain Rolland and many reputed singers, artists, millionaires and even commoners about spiritual living and social service.

Even today, many youngsters get attracted towards his teachings; he lived young and died young. He wanted everybody to be young in spirit and bold in nature and lovely in life. He is the voice that guides us to eternity & bliss.

Aurobindo (1872-1950) : Aurobindo was a great revolutionary turned spiritual guru, who had influenced Westerners into Yogic way of living. Born at Calcutta in the year 1872, he had his education at Cambridge, passed his Civil Service Examination and returned to India in 1893. After working as professor and administrator for some time at Baroda, he went to Bengal and joined active politics and started a revolutionary paper called "Bande Mataram". He was jailed for his anti-government activities in Alipur. He suddenly realized his spiritual mission and arrived at Pondichery and stayed there for the rest of his life, teaching many spiritual seekers the Yogic way of life.

The greatest classics written by Aurobindo are "The Life Divine", "Synthesis of Yoga" and the famous epic "Savitri". His famous disciple is a French lady called Mirra, whom the world calls as Holy Mother.

Ramana Maharshi

Ramaṇa Maharṣi (1879-1950) : Venkata Ramana was born on 30th December 1879 at Tiruchuli village near Madurai of Tamil Nadu. At the age of 16, he experienced the death and transcended the body and realized the real 'I".

The soul started yearning for solitude & silence. This yearning pulled him to Arunachala Siva of Tiruvannamalai. He stayed the rest of his life at Tiruvannamalai, the abode of Arunachala Siva, teaching the method of self-enquiry.

His method of enquiry into "oneself" starts with the question "Who am I"? This practice, withdraws the wavering mind into the real self. As each thought arises, one must be watchful and ask to whom this thought is occurring. The answer will be "to me". Then if it is further enquired, "Who am I"? The mind then will return to the source from where it sprang up and Peace, the real nature of Self shines eternally.

Many intellectuals, commoners, even foreigners were attracted to his ashram and took his guidance for spiritual progress. His answer to questions was "look within and find out who wants the answer". His exhortations are now available in many books. He wrote "Upadesa Saram" and "Sat-dharshnam" Etc. Luminaries like Kavya Ganta Ganapati Muni, Paul Brunton, and Radhakrishnan went to Sri Ramana Maharshi for spiritual advice.

Even today, many a foreigner visits his ashram and seeks the serene inspiration from the abode of Arunachala. On the day of full moon of every month, millions go round the hill of Arunachala, where Ramana did his penance of self-enquiry.

Papa Ramdas

Papa Ramdas (1884-1963) : Vitthal Rao from Karnataka manifested the greatest quality of devotion and became Papa Ramdas. He chanted the name of Rama and made the whole world chant the divine "Ramnam". He established Ananda Ashram in Kerala and went round the world spreading the inherent potential of "Ramnam" for spiritual progress. "The worldly pleasures are of no value before salvation. One who gets immersed in the meditation of God even without a second's rest is sure to attain salvation", was his message.

Malayala Swami (1885-1962) : Swami Asangananda popularly known as "Malayala Swami" was a great saint who lived in and around Tirupati (Andhra Pradesh). He established a spiritual institution called Vyasa Ashram, with an objective of training spiritual seekers, who after training, expound the scriptures and give spiritual guidance to ordinary people. Today this institution is rendering solemn service to the mankind. He did penance on top of seven hills of Tirumala and obtained the grace of Lord. He used to say, "A tank full of water gets emptied through a small sluice. Similarly your soul-force (Atma sakti) will diminish with one foul word. There is no greater Tapas than integrating one's heart and word."

Swami Sivananda (1887-1963) : Swami Sivananda wore clothes to cover his body; he ate food to live and lived to serve mankind. His childhood name was Kuppuswamy and he exhibited the attitude of service within him. Having qualified from Tanjore medical school in 1913, he left for Malayasia to work in a hospital. As a doctor, he showed exemplary skill in curing diseases. He had a compassionate heart while dealing with the patients. One day a Siddha gave a book called "Jiva Brahmanyam". That book has increased his spiritual quest in him. He returned to India, took sannyāsa and became Swami Sivananda. He did penance at Rishikesh and then started a great organization called "Divine Life Society". Today Divine life Society has branches worldwide and is serving mankind with varied services like orphanages, hospitals, schools and many spiritual seekers go to Sivananada Ashram for their spiritual progress and sādhanā. His words are but a mantra to spiritual seekers. They are very simple; Serve, Love, Meditate and Realize.

Paramahamsa Yogananda

Paramahamsa Yogananda (1893-1952) : Mukundalal Ghosh was born in 1893. After completing his education; he met his master "Sri Yukteswara Giri" in 1910 and became a sannyāsin in 1917 and was called Swami Yogananda. His small effort of making the kriyā yoga popular had become the gigantic spiritual institution of "Yogada satsang". In 1920 he left to America to propagate the Indian Yogic way of life and 'Kriya Yoga' among Westerners. He became popular and was very much sought after. In 1946, he published his book named "An autobiography of a yogi" It is the international bestseller and had sold more than 20 million copies after being translated into many Indian and foreign languages. He passed away in the year 1952 in America. His body remained fresh & pure for twenty days after his demise. This was a wonder to the medical community and the above fact is clearly mentioned in the postmortem report of this great Yogi.

Brahma Baba (1876-1869) : Brahma Baba is the founder of Brahmakumari's World's Spiritual University Movement, which propagates the core values of human life like Patience, Tolerance, Sacrifice, Kindness and Love. These values become the foundation of spiritual progress, human relations and better living. Today this spiritual institution has become a global phenomenon with its branch centres spread all over the world.

Brahma Baba's childhood name was Lekhraj Kripalini. He was a successful jewellery merchant. At the age of sixty he had continuous spiritual visions, which guided his spiritual mission. Since then he moulded many young people with the core spiritual values of life. In October 1937, Brahma Baba formed a Managing Committee of eight young women and in February 1938, he surrendered all his property and assets to a Trust administered by them.

At Mount Abu as its headquarters (Madhuban), guided by spiritual luminaries who were chiseled by Brahma Baba, the institution is doing wonderful service to Humanity by re-establishing the core spiritual values.

Dadi Prakashmani, Dadi Janaki and Dadi Hridaya Mohini and many spiritual giants guide that institution firmly establishing the legacy of Brahma Baba.

ChandraSekhar Saraswati

Chandra Sekhar Saraswati Swami (1894-1994) : His holiness Sri Chandra Sekhar Saraswati was the source of inspiration and guidance in the matters of Hindu Dharma or Veda Dharma. He had been worshipped as the walking God. He travelled the length and breadth of country bare footed and never used any vehicle. He is famous for his austerity and holiness. A scholar in many languages, he expounded the Vedic truths with all rationality and had given scientific explanations. He was the 69th Pontiff of Kanchi Kamakoti Peetam of

Sankarācaryā tradition. His followers include many Prime ministers, Presidents, Scientists, Industrialists, scholars of not only India, but from many countries of the world. He is certainly a Viswa Guru, the world teacher.

Mahesh Yogi (1917-) : Maharshi Mahesh Yogi's, institutions are visible to us throughout the world. Millions and millions of foreigners are practising Mahesh Yogi's method of transcendental meditation. He hails from Jabalpur of North India. A graduate in Physics from Allahabad University, he became the secretary to Sri Brahmananda Saraswati of Joshi Math, Badrinath and served from 1940 to 1953. He did severe penance at Uttarkashi before he became the Maharshi Mahesh Yogi. In 1957 he started a movement called Spiritual Regeneration Movement. That small sapling is today's gigantic banyan tree of Mahesh yogi's International Universities and Institutions spread across the world with spirituality being its underspread.

Mata Amritanandamayi (1953-) : Mother gives us birth. Mother protects us. Mother nourishes us; Mother teaches us; Mother loves us; Mother patiently withstands our faults and absolves us; Mother scolds us and corrects us; Mother wants her children to be happy and progressive. Today world is gifted with such a spiritual mother, who wanted her children to be happy and to progress in the domain of spirituality. "Amma" or "Ammachi" or Mata Amirtanandamayi is our spiritual mother, who embraces the millions every day to give them spiritual awakening and spiritual warmth. Millions of spiritual seekers from all parts of the world rush to her and pour out their hearts; millions of devotees are attracted towards her and confess their material difficulties; Scholar, Saint, President, Peon, Rich person, Poor person, Sinner and Sick patient, all are loved equally by her. Once she sat continuously for twenty hours and had embraced fifty five thousand people; she sings devotional songs in 30 languages; she has initiated many service activities like establishing schools, colleges, hospitals, rural development Programmes etc. She cleans the wounds of leprosy patients personally and even embraces them. She supported Tsunami victims with 100 crore rupees recently. She had supported American hurricane victims with one lakh Dollars. She had even addressed United Nations General Assembly. The saga

Mata Amritanandamayi

of transformation of the little girl Sudhamani from a remote fishing hamlet of Kerala to the Universal Mother is replete with hurdles, difficulties, slanders and even brickbats. She accepted every situation in life and completely surrendered herself to the divine power by eternally manifesting, her heart of nectar "Amrita hridayam". Modern India is fortunate to have such a divine dynamo in its midst.

A wave rises after a wave, guru comes after a guru, and sometimes we see the mighty waves in an ocean, of course great gurus of spiritual might also. But they all form part of one divine ocean of consciousness. Forms of waves disappear fast. Ocean remains the same. So does the spiritual ocean. Behind every little bubble and the mighty wave, there is infinite background of ocean of divine consciousness. Bubble becomes a wave and wave becomes a bubble. Names & forms vanish, but eternal truth remains.

Jai guru dev

66 The Grandeur of Indian Spiritual Excellence

World has come closer and has become one global village...but as individuals, we are drifting apart. We are very much connected in this info-age, yet are its remote citizens.

We are the lonely beasts of this electronic jungle of the 21st century; Bio-machines of ensuing cloning age. Career and colleague come in between husband & wife conflict ensues; In-laws trouble the in-laws and their hearts are broken; kids grow up in "TV –Duniyās" and "Internet Ecstasies"; virtually children become living toys in ego games played by elders; bequeathing the future citizens, the legacy of stressful future, strained relations and promising world of competition and envy;

Science is not concerned about attitudinal excellence in human behaviour for that matter with spiritual aspects. Commercial viability supercedes the artistic abilities and talents; Human distress gets a corporate hospitality and concern. Even medical attention is a package. Concrete jungles continue to hamper the eco-balance and bio-unity. Religious fundamentalism terrorizes the harmonious living. Family tensions, neighbourly indifference & frustration with momentary pleasures continue.... relationships are managed, not lived.

OM Parvath-Himalayas

There is a deep crisis within the human being of modern age... and he continues to suffer from a dreadful disease called "selfish-isolation" combined with his ignorance of totality.

Our Ancient Indian seers had an answer to this problem. Their search was inwards. The seers went deep into the core of our being and discovered the ultimate spiritual reality, which brings the joy of oneness into our living. That knowledge is beyond the perception of our senses and is completely spiritual. It is an experience of awareness of ultimate reality- the oneness. Indians called it as "Brahma Vidyā or Ātma Vidyā- the Science of Self". The Upaniṣads are replete with the knowledge of Self. Indian spiritual excellence is the grandeur of Upaniṣads.

The Upanishads are called Vedanta, meaning culmination of Vedas. The teacher expounds the truths of Upanishads to the deserving spiritual aspirants. The students learn the knowledge by living with the teacher, by sitting at his feet, hence the name Upanishad. The word Upanishad means, "sitting nearby". It is not bookish Knowledge. It is an experience of "oneness", which the inquisitive student obtains after enquiring the path from the master. There are around 108 Upanishads or even more. Adi-Sankara wrote commentaries for ten of them. They became the core of Self-knowledge.

Among Upanishads, India's greatest philosophical contribution to the mankind is "Srimad Bhagvad Gita". It is a conversation between Lord Krishna and Arjuna in the battlefield of Kurukshetra. This Song Celestial remains as the crest Jewel of Self-Knowledge. The great Western Philosophers and Modern Scientists were baffled by its "in-depth" exposure of the ultimate reality, which is the core of the every Human being. The various paths (yogas) are revealed to humanity to experience that yogic bliss in the midst of day-to-day struggles of life. The beauty of it lies in the synchronisation of various paths of yogic knowledge. Adi -Sankara had also written wonderful commentary on Gita. Millions of Indians chant Gita everyday. Gita inspires us eternally.

Let us discuss briefly the grandeur of the ten famous Upanishads.

1. **The Iśā-Upaniṣat** embodies in its very opening verse the central theme of all Upanishads namely the spiritual unity and solidarity of all existence.

It starts with the Peace Mantra (Pūrṇa madḥ), which says, "From Perfection every thing (Perfection) manifested, into perfection everything merges and the Perfection alone remains for eternity."

It tells, "The whole universe which is ever-changing is pervaded by the unchangable God (Eternal Divinity- the Perfection). Hence God owns everything and nothing is ours. So let us not selfishly covet others' wealth with greed, but enjoy life with detachment and awareness".

2. **The Kena- Upaniṣat** illumines the nature of knowledge by pointing out the eternal knower behind all acts of knowing. It purifies man's concept of ultimate reality by revealing its character as the eternal Self of the man and the Self of the universe.

The manifesting force, that our sense organs express, that our thoughts pour out, that our emotions bring out, all have their origin and roots in the self (the core of our being), the inherent power within us.

The Power of Self though inherent in us is all-pervading and ever-expansive. That is the real power that moves this universe. That is the Infinite Energy. That is the unlimited force, which makes us walk, talk, eat, run, feel, smell and think. That is the Godly power. That is divinity's expression that comes out through us.

3. **The Kaṭa- Upaniṣat** holds a special fascination for its profound Philosophy and charming Poetry. It is a dialogue between Yama, the god of death and the young spiritual aspirant Naciketā. He wanted to know, "What happens after death"? "Whether a person lives after Death"? Yama wonderfully explains the "Ātma Vidyā -The Science of Self" to Naciketā.

4. **The Praśna- Upaniṣat,** as its name implies, is an Upanishad of questions. Each of its six chapters comprises a question asked by each of a group of six disciples on various aspects of Vedanta-the spiritual science and answers were given by sage Pippalada.

5. **The Muṇḍaka-Upaniṣat** has classified all knowledge as "Aparā Vidyā" (Secular) and "Parā-Vidyā" (Spiritual). In the category of Aparā Vidyā, one finds all positive knowledge of Sciences, Arts, Politics, Economics, and Literature. Even Vedas have been included in the Aparā Vidyā by this Upanishad. The Parā Vidyā which reveals the ultimate truth the "one behind the many", "the changeless imperishable reality" is clearly dealt with.

> "The Power of Self though inherent in us is all pervading and ever expansive. That is the real power that moves this universe. That is the unlimited force, which makes us walk, talk, eat, run, feel, smell and think. That is the Godly power."
>
> **The Kena- Upanishad**

6. **The Māṇḍūkya-Upaniṣat** is a small Upanishad that contains twelve verses. It wonderfully explains the four states of human experience like Waking state (Jagrita), Dream state (Swapna): Dreamless sleep (Suṣhupta) and the fourth state "Turīya" a state of complete awareness of pure consciousness, the eternal and nondual self. It also reveals the nature of Self (Ātmā). It contains the one of four Mahā-Vākyas "Ayam Ātmā Brahma- "this Atman, the Self is Brahman".

7. **The Taittirīya- Upaniṣat** teaches the five sheaths (Pañca Kośas) that hide the Brahman, which is the ultimate spiritual reality. It demonstrates the technique of piercing though these five sheaths to reach the ultimate state of Eternal bliss. It also defines Brahman as "that from which all these beings are born, by which after being born, they live and into which they merge when they cease to be".

8. **The Aitareya- Upaniṣat** establishes the spiritual character of absolute through a discussion of the nature of the Self of the Man. It proclaims this truth in another of four Mahā-Vākyas "Prajñānaṁ Brahma- Brahman is pure consciousness".

9. **The Chāndogya- Upaniṣat** introduces us to the charming truth seekers like Satyakam Jabala, Svetaketu and Narada and the outstanding spiritual teachers like Aruni, Sanatkumara and Prajapati. Through illuminating teacher-student dialogues, the Upanishad helps us to discriminate the reality of being, from the appearance of becoming. It wonderfully explains the man's inquisitive search of reality. It explains the technique of transcending the worldliness into the domain of spirituality. It had revealed the great truth, one among the four Mahā-Vākyas "Tat- Tvam –Asi- "Thou art That" meaning, "that reality is none other than the human self".

10. **The Bṛhadāraṇyaka- Upaniṣat,** the longest of the Upanishads as the name implies, a big (Bṛhat), forest (Araṇya) of spiritual thought and inspiration. Four outstanding personalities illumine its page-

two men and two women –Janaka, the Philosopher- King, Yājñavalkya, the Philosopher-Sage, Maitreyi-the deeply Spiritual wife of Yājñavalkya and Gargī-the gifted woman speaker and philosopher who is foremost among the questioners of Yājñavalkya in philosophical debate. It contains another of the four Mahā-Vākyas, namely "Ahaṁ Brahmāsmi- I am Brahman".

The wonderful conversation between Yājñavalkya and his wife Maitreyi expounds the rationale of "Love & Self" and takes us to depth of our being. Modern couples can learn many a lesson from this mature conversation that happened 2500 years ago.

Swami Vivekananda says *"Strength, strength is what the Upaniṣads speak to me from every page....it has been the great one lesson I have been taught in my life. Strength, it says strength, O man, be not weak. ....Ay, it is the only literature in the world where you find the word "abhaya - fearless", used again and again; in no other scripture in the world is this adjective applied either to god or to man.... Upaniṣads are great mine of strength. Therein lies strength enough to invigorate the whole world. The whole world can be vivified, made strong, energized through them. They will call with trumpet voice upon the weak, miserable and the downtrodden of all races, all creeds, and all sects, to stand on their feet and be free. Freedom –Physical freedom, Mental freedom and Spiritual freedom are the watch words of Upaniṣads".*

"Upanishads are great mine of strength. Therein lies strength enough to invigorate the whole world.

- Swami Vivekananda"

67 Prophecies of Swami Vivekananda

Ages ago, a young Saint called Ādi Śaṅkara, travelled the length and breadth of India, and redeemed the Sanātana Dharma from its decay. He had shown the world, the point of convergence of various schools of religious thoughts. That oceanic thought of confluence was Advaita philosophy.

In the Nineteenth Century, another young monk from India travelled the length and breadth of the globe and glorified the universal message of Sanātana Dharma, by redeeming the world from decay. He was swami Vivekananda. His instrument was Advaita philosophy. He roared that India is the world's teacher.

Ancient India was replete with knowledge of material sciences and spirituality. Our ancestors could strike a balance between material and spiritual aspects of life. They enjoyed a life of discipline without compromising with the aspects of creating material wealth. Their lives were filled with bliss as they shared the bliss with other countries. India never invaded any country politically. India fascinated the world; Indians inspired the world; India contributed to world's progress and harmony with its gentle dew of Indian values- a confluence of material & spiritual aspects of life.

Let us listen to Swami Vivekananda's own words about the emerging giant wave that restores the balance between peace & prosperity for global harmony & progress.

"Whenever virtue subsides and vice prevails, I come down to help mankind," declares Kṛṣṇa, in the Bhagavad-Gitâ. Whenever this world of ours, on account of growth, on account of added circumstances, requires a new adjustment, a wave of power comes; and as a man is acting on two planes, the spiritual and the material, waves of adjustment come on both planes.

On the one side, of the adjustment on the material plane, Europe has mainly been the basis during modern times; and of the adjustment on the other, the spiritual plane, Asia has been the basis throughout the history of the world.

Today, man requires one more adjustment on the spiritual plane; today when material ideas are at the height of their glory and power, today when man is likely to forget his divine nature, through his growing dependence on matter, and is likely to be reduced to a mere money-making machine, an adjustment is necessary; the voice has spoken, and the power is coming to drive away the clouds of gathering materialism.

The power has been set in motion, which, at no distant date, will bring unto mankind once more the memory of its real nature; and again the place from which this power will start will be Asia.

This world of ours is on the plan of the division of labour. It is vain to say that one man shall possess everything. Yet how childish we are! The baby in its ignorance thinks that its doll is the only possession that is to be coveted in this whole universe. So a nation which is great in the possession of material power thinks that that is all that is to be coveted, that that is all that is meant by progress, that that is all that is meant by civilisation, and if there are other nations which do not care for possession and do not possess that power, they are not fit to live, their whole existence is useless! On the other hand, another nation may think that mere material civilisation is utterly useless. From the Orient came the voice which once told the world that if a man possesses everything that is under the sun and does not possess spirituality, what avails it? This is the oriental type; the other is the occidental type.

Each of these types has its grandeur; each has its glory. The present adjustment will be the harmonising, the mingling of these two ideals. To the Oriental, the world of spirit is as real as to the Occidental is the world of senses. In the spiritual, the Oriental finds everything he wants or hopes for; in it he finds all that makes life real to him.

To the Occidental he is a dreamer; to the Oriental the Occidental is a dreamer playing with ephemeral toys, and he laughs to think that grown-up men and women should make so much of a handful of

"The power has been set in motion, which, at no distant date, will bring unto mankind once more the memory of its real nature; and again the place from which this power will start will be Asia."

- Swami Vivekananda

matter, which they will have to leave sooner or later. Each calls the other a dreamer. But the oriental ideal is as necessary for the progress of the human race as is the occidental, and I think it is more necessary.

Machines never made mankind happy and never will make. He who is trying to make us believe this will claim that happiness is in the machine; but it is always in the mind. That man alone who is the lord of his mind can become happy, and none else. And what, after all, is this power of machinery? Why should a man who can send a current of electricity through a wire be called a very great man and a very intelligent man? Does not nature do a million times more than that every moment? Why not then fall down and worship nature? What avails it if you have power over the whole of the world, if you have mastered every atom in the universe? That will not make you happy unless you have the power of happiness in yourself, until you have conquered yourself.

Man is born to conquer nature, it is true, but the Occidental means by "nature" only physical or external nature. It is true that external nature is majestic, with its mountains, and oceans, and rivers, and with its infinite powers and varieties. Yet there is a more majestic internal nature of man, higher than the sun, moon, and stars, higher than this earth of ours, higher than the physical universe, transcending these little lives of ours; and it affords another field of study."

"Each of these types(Oriental and Occidental) has its grandeur; each has its glory. The present adjustment will be the harmonising, the mingling of these two ideals."

- Swami Vivekananda

Swami Vivekananda's words remain to us as eternal inspiration. Dharma, Artha, Kāma & Mokṣa, this was the majestic road of philosophy that ancient India travelled to remain at the zenith of its grandeur. Medieval India fell flat for one thousands years as a slave, when it ignored material prosperity. Swami Vivekananda foretells, modern India shall rise again by harmonising two aspects material and spiritual aspects and shines more glorious forever.

Let us aspire for a sublime India that is economically strong, ethically vibrant and spiritually grand.

Talented Nonresident Indians
Pravāsī Bhāratīya Pratibhā

68 Nonresident Indians – Scientists & Intellectuals

Swami Vivekananda prophetically said "as many Indians go to other countries, so rapid shall India develop".

Today, around two crore, nonresident Indians, who went to various countries had emerged successful in their pursuits and are making India feel proud. They have remitted 21 billon dollars into India last year. Today, they not only occupy vital positions, but also are working hard for the progress of various countries, in which they live. Let us know more about them.

Subrahmanyan Chandrasekhar

Subrahmanyan Chandrasekhar was an American Astrophysicist who was awarded the 1983 Nobel Prize in Physics (shared with William Alfred Fowler) for his theoretical work on the structure and evolution of stars.

He was in Lohore (then India) on October 19th 1910. He was a professor in Astro-physics in the University of Chicago. Chandrasekhar was a nephew of Nobel-prize winning physicist C. V. Raman.

Chandrasekhar's most famous success was the "Astrophysical Chandrasekhar Limit". The Limit describes the maximum mass (~1.44 solar masses) of a white dwarf star, or equivalently, the minimum mass for which a star will ultimately collapse into a Neutron star or black hole (following a Supernova). The Limit was first calculated by Chandrasekhar while on a ship from India to Cambridge, England.

He was a highly revered personality among the scientists of NASA. In 1999, NASA named the third of its four "Great Observatories'" after Chandrasekhar. The Chandra X-ray Observatory was launched and deployed by Space Shuttle Columbia on July 23, 1999.

The Asteroid 1958 Chandra is also named after Chandrasekhar. Chandrasekhar passed away in the year 1995.

Amartya Sen was born on 3 November 1933 in Śāntiniketan, Calcutta India. In the year 1998 he was awarded Nobel prize for Economics for his contribution on Human Development Theory & Welfare Economics.

From 1998 to 2004 he was Master of Trinity College at Cambridge University, becoming the first Asian academic to head an Oxbridge college. He is currently the Lamont University Professor at Harvard University. Amartya Sen's books have been translated into more than thirty languages.

Amartya Sen

Har Gobind Khurana is a Nobel Prize laureate and a Molecular Biologist from the Punjab. He was born in the year 1922. He is a professor of Biology and Chemistry at the Massachusetts Institute of Technology, America.

Khurana was awarded the 1968 Nobel Prize in Medicine (together with Robert W. Holley and Marshall Warren Nirenberg) for his work on the interpretation of the genetic code and its function in Protein synthesis. Dr. Khurana and his team had established that the mother of all codes, the biological language is common to all living organisms. It is spelled out in three-letter words. Each is a set of three nucleotides codes for a specific Amino acid.

These custom designed pieces of artificial genes are widely used in Biology labs for sequencing, cloning and engineering new plants and animals. This invention of Dr. Khurana has become automated and commercialized so that anyone now can order a synthetic gene from any of a number of companies.

Khurana also received the U.S. National Medal of Science in 1987.

Har Gobind Khurana

VS Naipaul

"Today, around two Crore, non-resident Indians, who went to various countries had emerged successful in their pursuits and are making India feel proud."

VS Naipaul, is a British novelist of Indian origin, born in the island of Trinidad. He was awarded Nobel Prize in the year 2001 for his contributions in the field of Literature. He had written many books on world civilizations, India's cultural uniqueness and history.

Balamurali Ambati: He is a child prodigy of Indian origin settled in USA. He completed his degree at the age of 13 and created a world record by becoming the youngest doctor at the age of 17. Today he is working at Harvard and is doing research in ophthalmology. He and his brother together had written a book on AIDS.

CS Kumar Patil: An eminent scientist who had invented the Laser Technology based on carbon-dioxide. This technology is being used in the field of surgery immensely. He was honoured by the then President of United States Mr. Bill Clinton with USA's highest award "National Medal of Science" for excellence in the fields of science and engineering in the year 1996.

Dr. Narendra Singh: He hails from Punjab. He has studied in England and now stays in USA. He is called Father of Fibre Optics. Today Fibre Optic Technology is playing a vital role in the fields of telecommunications, Medicine, Defence and IT. Forbes magazine in its issue on Nov 2nd 1999 had ranked him as the seventh important technology innovator and businessman in the world. He has established many industries in the field of Fiber Optics.

Mani Bhaumik is a reputed Physicist of Indian origin, hailing from Bengal, who helped to develop the first Excimer laser at the University of California.This is the kind of laser technology that would eventually eliminate glasses or contact lenses in many cases requiring vision correction. The surgical procedure takes less than a minute and is spreading like wildfire today.

He worked under the guidance of eminent Indian scientist Sayonara Nath Bose. Later he earned his Ph.D. from Indian Institute of Technology, Kharagpur. His biography, Mani the Jewel, is a current bestseller in Bengal. He has published over fifty papers in many scientific periodicals.

Dr. Bhaumik is the fellow of the American Physical Society as well as the Institute of Electrical and Electronics Engineers.

Raj Reddy, hails from Andra Pradesh . He is considered to be a genius and is the most revered personality in the field of Artificial Intelligence and Robotics. He is instrumental in establishing Carnegie Mellon Robotics Institute. In the year 1994, he had received the highest award for excellence in computer science called "Turing award".

Indian government had honoured him with Padma Bhushan in the year 2001. French Government had honored him with the highest civilian award for his contributions in the year 1994. He received the 2006 Vannevar Bush Award given by the National Science Board, America. He is also an adviser to many governments in the fields of Science and Technology.

Vinod Dham : The creator of Intel Pentium chip, today's most popular technology of personal computer's processor. He graduated from Delhi University in the year 1971 and completed his master's degree from Cinncennati. University,USA in 1975 and became successful in the domain of micro-electronics and semi-conductor industry. He worked with personal computer processor producing giants like AMD and Intel. He has inspired many young technocrats working in USA to innovate.

George Sudarshan hails from the state of Kerala; studied in Madras; established himself as eminent scientist at New York, USA. His extensive research in the field of Quantum optics had earned him many laurels. His theories, his research submissions, in this domain had been appreciated by many

Raj Reddy

Vinod Dham

George Sudharshan

scientists worldwide. He had propounded the subatomic particles called "Tachyons" that travel faster than light. He had been awarded Padma Vibushan in the year 2007 by the Government of India.

There was controversy for not awarding him the Nobel Prize in the year 2005 for his greatest contributions in the field of Quantum optics.

Neal Kumar Katyal is a Professor of Law at Georgetown University Law School. Katyal was born in America to immigrant parents. He was named "the Lawyer of the Year" by Lawyers USA for 2006, Runner Up for Lawyer of the Year by National Law Journal. He has been listed as one of the top 50 Litigators in the nation by the American Lawyer Magazine.

Anita Goyal : MIT's technology review magazine had recognized Anita Goyal hightech-innovator under 35 years,who heads the instituiton called " Nanobiosym"

Ranjit Manohar: He is working as the associate professor in Cornell university. He had invented clockless computer chip that is ten times more efficient than ordinary computer chips.

Narasimha Chari: NRI who had contributed for wireless meshnet technology working standards. He owns the company called Troops network. MIT' s review magazine had ranked him among less than 35 years-top technology innovators.

Adam Rashid: He is an Aeronautical engineer. He had invented, "Pulsed Detonation Engines". These engines had drastically reduced the intake of fuel in Aero-Engines.

Saladityasen Gupta: He is working as associate professor in Harward university's medical school. He had revolutionized the Chemo-Therapy of cancer treatment. This became possible because of invention of the instrument called Nanocell.

Vikram Sheel Kumar: He is the youngest scientist of Indian origin, who had received the prestigious American award "Toyo". MIT magazine had recognized him as the high technology innovator (less than 35 years) for his marvellous contributions in the field of Bio-technology.

Election to the National Academy of Engineering in USA is among the highest professional distinctions accorded to an engineer. Academy membership honours those, who have made outstanding contributions to engineering research, practice, or education, including, significant contributions to the engineering literature. There are many Indians who had become fellows of National Academy of Engineering. Here is the list of Indians who had been honoured with this distinction for the years 2004 & 2005.

Year	Name & Designation	Contributions
2005	**Subhash Mahajan,** chairman, department of chemical and materials engineering, Arizona State University.	For advancing our understanding of structure-property relationships in semiconductors, magnetic materials, and materials for light-wave communication
	Arunava Majumdar- He is a Almy and Agnes Maynard Professor of Mechanical Engineering, University of California, Berkeley	For contributions to Nano-scale Thermal Engineering and Molecular Nano-mechanics.
	R. Shankar Nair, senior vice-president, Teng & Associates, Chicago.	For contributions to the art and Science of Engineering through the design of innovative bridges and building structures.

"Like the gentle morning dew, our Indian scientists are creating wonders in Science & Technology and are contributing for the world's progress."

	Raja V. Ramani, Professor Emeritus, Mining and Geo-environmental engineering, Pennsylvania State University, University Park.	For improvements in the health and safety of miners through a better understanding of the nature and control of airborne particals.
	Subhash C. Singhal, Battelle Fellow and director of fuel cells, Pacific Northwest National Laboratory, Richland, Washington.	For the development and promotion of Solid Oxide Fuel Cells for clean and efficient power generation
Year 2004:	**Rakesh K. Jain,** director, Edwin L. Steele Laboratory, department of radiation oncology, Massachusetts General Hospital, Boston	For the integration of Bio-Engineering with Tumour Biology and Imaging Gene Expression and functions in Vivo for drug delivery in tumours.
	Pradman P. Kaul, chairman and chief executive officer, Hughes Network Systems. Germantown, MD.	For leadership in the development of satellite communication networks.
	Kishor C. Mehta, P.W. Horn Professor of Civil Engineering and director, Wind Engineering Research Center, Texas Tech University, Lubbock.	For systematic studies of structural damage caused by windstorms and leadership in the development of structural design standards for wind loads.

Rajagopal S. Raghavan, senior staff associate (retired), Philips Petroleum Co., Tulsa, Okla.	For pioneering contributions to the interpretation of pressure data in wells to improve the Definition, Engineering, and Production of complex oil and gas reservoirs.
Shivaji Sircar, professor of practice, chemical engineering department, Lehigh University, Bethlehem, PA.	For contributions to the fundamental Science and Technology of adsorption separations and their applications in process industries.
Vijay Vittal, Harpole Professor, department of electrical and computer engineering, Iowa State University, Ames	For improvements in real-time control and dynamic security assessment for electric power systems.
Darsh T. Wasan, vice-president and Motorola Chair, department of international affairs, Illinois Institute of Technology, Chicago.	For pioneering research, inspirational teaching, and the development of novel technology in colloidal processing and interfacial rheology.

Like the gentle morning dew, our Indian scientists are creating wonders in Science & Technology and are contributing for the world's progress. The names mentioned in the above article are not all inclusive and there are many un-sung heroes and heroines who are doing their best.

Innumerable feathers of the Indian Diaspora's contributions, crowd the cap of India's Talents, eternally.

69 NRI- Millionaires, Industrialists, Business & Political Leaders

LN Mittal :

Lakshmi Nivas Mittal, is resident of Britain, born in Sadulpur, Churu District of Rajsathan in India, and graduated from Calcutta.

In March 2006, he was reported the fifth wealthiest person in the world by Forbes Magazine with net worth, 25 billion US Dollars. The Mittal family owns 45% of Arcelor Mittal, the world's largest steel company.

LN Mittal

Today he is Chairman and CEO of Arcelor Mittal which is the world's largest producer of low and mid-grade steels, with assets in Romania, Bosnia-Herzegovina, South Africa, Poland, Czech Republic, and Indonesia.

Hindujas:

The Hinduja brothers — Srichand , Gopichand based in London, Prakash (PP), based in Geneva and Ashok (AP), based in Mumbai — are an Indian business family. They are believed to own assets worth more than 12 billion U.S. dollars.They are involved in many businesses, in various parts of the world. The Hinduja brothers have stakes in global finance, telecommunications, and film and oil (Gulf Oil) businesses. Indian Flagship Company of their group is Ashok Leyland. (Truck manufacturing company)

As many as 30 NRI's in the UK, including Lord Swaraj Paul, had fortunes worth over 60 million pounds each.

The combined wealth of top 1,000 rich people in the UK has soared by over 50 billion pounds in a single year to 300.9 billion pounds, The Sunday Times Rich List 2006 revealed.

(Source; http://www.nriinternet.com/NRI_Forbes/index.htm)

Shabeer Bhatia: A BITS Pilani graduate, born in Chandigarh, went for further studies in USA (Caltech) and became the founder of first free email service (1995) in the world. "Hotmail". He sold that to Microsoft for $400 million in the year 1997. His latest ventures are Blog everywhere, a new software concept and nano city project in India, which aims at replicating the Silicon Valley of USA.

Amar Bose (Born 1929) is the chairman and founder of Bose Corporation. A Bengali American electrical engineer, he was listed on the 2006 Forbes 400 with a net worth of $1.5 billion.

Assistant Professor of Electrical Engineering at MIT, Bose embarked on research in Acoustics that led him to invent a stereo loudspeaker that would reproduce, in a domestic setting, the dominantly reflected sound field that characterizes the listening space of the audience in a concert hall.

Vinod Khosla (Born 1955 in Poona) is an Indian American venture capitalist. He is an influential personality in Silicon Valley. He was one of the co-founders of Sun Microsystems and became a general partner of the venture capital firm Kleiner, Perkins, Caufield & Byers in 1986. He had graduated from Delhi IIT. Today he is funding various research projects and ventures including a project on ethanol fuel.

Sanjiv Siddhu: He is a software entrepreneur. He had established a company called I2 Technologies, which has pioneered innovations in supply chain management solutions. Today, he is one of among the richest Indian millionaires of USA.

Indians are on rise everywhere, Nonresident Indians are doing their best to make India proud about their achievements.

Shabeer Bhatia

Amar Bose

Vinod Khosla

Indian CEOs & Top business Leaders–Multi National Companies

Srimati Indira Noyoi

Name	Institution	Position held
Arun Netravilli	Bell Lab LucentTechnology	Former President CT0
Srimati Indira Nooyi	Pepsi/motorola	CEO/president/Director
Rajiv Gupta	HP	GM(technical)
Sanjay Jijurikar	Microsoft	WIN 2000 project director
Rana Talwar	Standard Chartered Bank Centurion Bank of Punjab	(former) CEO Chairman
Aurab Sarin	Vedophone	CEO
Kim Singh	IBM Portal Enterprise	(former) senior executive CEO
Ronadatta	United Air Lines, Air sahara	(former) President President
Rakesh Ganagawal	US Airways group	Former CEO
Rajit Gupta	Mackinsey &Co	Former (MD)-UN Secretary General's Advisor

Important Poltical leaders of Indian origin

	Country	Name of Leader	Designation	Tenure
1	Fiji	Mahendra Chaudary	Prime minister	1999-2000
2	Trinand	Vasudev Pandey	Prime minister	1995-2001
3	Mauritius	Shiv Sagar Ram Gulam	Prime minister	1968-1992
4	Mauritius	Anuruddin Jagnath	Prime minister	1992-1995/ 2000-2003
5	Singapore	SR Nathan	President	1999-
6	Gayana	Cheddi Jagan	President	1992-1997
7	Gayana	Bharat Jagdev	President	1999-
8	Singapore	Sri Devan Nayar	President	1981-1985
9	Malaysia	S. Swami Vel	Minister (Malayasian) Indian Congress President	Present

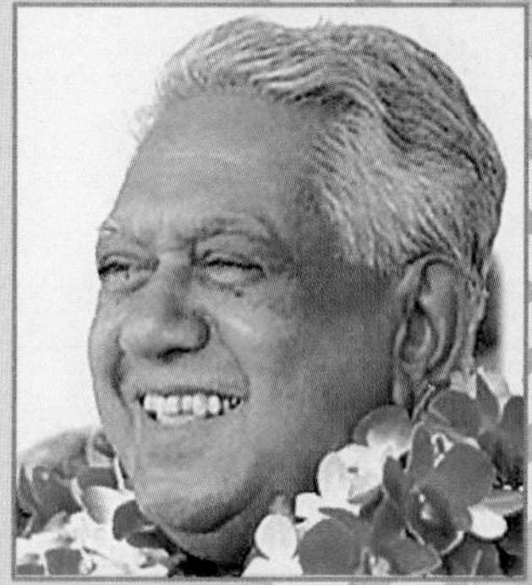

SR Nathan

70 NRI – Contributions to America's Progress

- There are 3.22 million Indians in USA (1.5% of population).
- 12% of the scientists in the USA are Indians.
- 38% of doctors in America are Indian.
- 36% of NASA scientists are Indians.
- 34% of Microsoft employees are Indians.
- 28% of IBM employees are Indians. 17% of INTEL scientists are Indians. 13% of XEROX employees are Indians.
- Biggest student communities in USA are Indians.
- Indians stand today as the largest community of millionaires in USA. (www.stephen-knapp.com)
- Today, Indian Americans are the second largest Asian American ethnic group following the Chinese American community in USA.
- Indians own 50% of all economy lodges and 35% of all hotels in the US, which have a combined market value of almost $40 billion. Source: Little India Magazine
- One in every nine Indians in the US is a Millionaire, comprising 10% of US millionaires. Source: 2003 Merrill Lynch SA Market Study
- A University of California, Berkeley, study reported that one-third of the engineers in Silicon Valley are of Indian descent, while 7% of valley hi-tech firms are led by Indian CEOs. Source: Silicon India Readership Survey
- Indians along with other Asians, have the highest educational qualifications of all ethnic groups in the US. Almost 67% of all Indians have a bachelor's or high degree (compared to 28% nationally). Almost 40% of all Indians have a master's, doctorate or other professional degree, which is five times the national average. Source: The Indian American Centre for Political Awareness

(Source : en.wikipedia.org/wiki/Non-resident_Indian)

Educational Talents
Vidyā Pratibhā

71 World's First Universities

Ancient India was the world's teacher - Jagat Guru or World's Guru. World looked at India for seeking knowledge. In India, we had world's first universities. Indian universities were replete with students, teachers and scholars. They came to India all the way from far of countries in search of learning.

Ruins of Takshila- University

Takshila (Taxila):

The oldest university known to the world is Takshila. It flourished around seventh century BC. Today the ruins of Takshila speak volumes about its past glory. The remnants of this once glorious university are situated in today's Rawalpindi district of Pakistan.

It was famed to lodge ten thousand students from all over the world in its campus. Every student used to spend eight years in this university. Education was imparted in sixty-eight faculties like Vedas, World Languages, Saṁskṛta, Fine Arts, and Professional skills, Grammar, Logic, Medicine, Mathematics, Astronomy, Warfare, Commerce, Politics and Governance etc.

Kauṭilaya (Chāṇakya), Panini, Jivaka, Vishnusarma and many others were the celebrated Gurus of this university. There are evidences to prove that the

Greek philosopher Pythagoras and others had been the pupils of this university.

Nalanda:

Nalanda was the crown jewel of universities. It had a long and checkered history of fame and riot. It existed from 5th century AD to 12th century AD. It was patronized by the Hindu kings and Buddhistic kings. It was famed as a Buddhist centre of learning. Yet the Hindu thought, culture and philosophy and wisdom prevailed there. Temple ruins and historical references of various visitors substantiate that fact.

Towards the Southeast of Patna, the Capital City of Bihar State in India, is a village called the 'Bada Gaon', in the vicinity of which, are the world famous ruins of Nalanda University.

A walk in the ruins of the university, takes you to an era that saw India leading in imparting knowledge, to the world - the era when India was a coveted place for studies.

More than two thousand gurus and 10,000 students were stationed in Nalanda.

The famous Chinese traveller and scholar, Hieun-Tsang stayed here and has given a detailed description of the situations prevailing at that time.

Careful excavation of the place has revealed many stupas, monasteries, hostels, staircases, meditation halls, lecture halls and many other structures, which speak of the splendour and grandeur of this place, enjoyed, when the place was a centre of serious study.

King Kumaragupta, Harshvardhan and Ashoka had patronized this centre of learning immensely. Nagarjuna- a Mahayana philosopher, Dinnaga- founder of the school of Logic and Dharmpala- the Brahmin scholar, taught here. Historians estimate that around 20 lakh manuscripts existed in the libraries of Nalanda.

Kasi and Kanchi were also regarded as highly revered centers of learning.

In the year 1194 AD, a Muslim invader Bhakitar Khilji, had invaded this university and had burnt its books of learning. India's glorious knowledge vanished into the flames of fire with this satanic event. Thousands of students, teachers and monks ran away to save themselves, as the grandeur of this university crippled.

Swami Vivekananda blames it as a historic blunder, for not resisting this barbaric act and letting this wealth of knowledge, consigned to blazes of fire.

Ruins of Nalanda University

Chinese traveller and scholar, Hieun-Tsang

72 Ancient Indian Libraries

Ancient India was a glowing beacon that radiated the light of knowledge. The centre of learning that emitted the fragrance of wisdom & intelligence. Many students bee lined to its universities and libraries to drink the nectar of knowledge.

If libraries are the abodes of learning, then ancient India was the abode of such libraries.

Indian manuscripts reveal ancient India's concern for documentation. Except Vedas all the knowledge of eternal India was meticulously documented and preserved.

Indian libraries were called as "Granthalaya", "Pustak Bhandar", or "Saraswati Bhandar" (Place where the goddess of learning Saraswati resides).

There existed three kinds of libraries in India,

1. Takshila, Nalanda & Kasi – Universities and centers of learning.
2. King's palaces.
3. Temples of India.

During the seventh century BC, Takshila, attracted students from all over the world and had a huge collection of various texts, not only of Saṁskṛta, but also of other world languages.

Nalanda flourished as a world-renowned University between fifth century AD and twelfth century AD. When Nalanda was ransacked by the Muslim invader Bhakthiyar Khilaji in 1194 AD, its greatest wealth the "Books of learning" was burnt and historians noted that the flames of Nalanada burned unabated for three months. It was estimated that 10 Lakh manuscripts would have been burnt during that brutal arson. With this single incidence India lost its seat of brilliance, world lost the wealth of knowledge.

Many famous temples patronized the Libraries. Especially, Kasi, Gaya, Puri, Kanchi, Sringeri, Nagi, Chidambaram and Sri Rangam temples of worship had Saraswati Bhandars.

In this connection it may be mentioned that libraries in ancient Cambodia were all located in temples and the inscriptions from some temples in the area bear evidence to that. "Library" is mentioned for the first time in the inscriptions of the king Indravarman at Preah Ko and Bakong (Cambodia). They were rectangular with gabled ends and at first with a single vaulted hall. The temples of Prasat Bantay Pir Chan, and Angkor Wat contained libraries.

Among the libraries established at King's palaces, "Saraswati Mahal library" at Thanjavur, (Tamil nadu), stands tall with grandeur.

The Nayaks of Thanjavur (1535 - 1675 A.D.) started and developed "Sarasvati Bhandar" (Collection place of Manuscripts). Maratha rulers developed the "Sarasvati Bhandar" into a Royal Palace Library, called Saraswati Mahal Library. The Maratha King Serfoji II (1798 - 1832) was an eminent scholar with extensive knowledge of various branches of learning and is instrumental in developing this library into a repository of Knowledge.

"Saraswati Mahal library" at Thanjavur, (Tamil nadu),

The Saraswati Mahal Library of Thanjavur is virtually a treasure house of knowledge. It contains one of the most extensive collections of oriental manuscripts in India - over 44,000 palm leaf and paper manuscripts in Indian (Sanskrit, Marathi, Tamil and Telugu) and European languages. They include treatises on medicine and commentaries on works from ancient times.

Other famous royal libraries include, the libraries established by Baroda Maharaja, Jaipur Maharaja, "Raja Man Singh" and Mysore Maharaja.

During the past one thousand years of foreign rule, ancient Indian manuscripts were stolen, robbed, burnt and destroyed by the Western and Islamic invaders. Many manuscripts had reached China and Tibet through Buddhist monks during those dark ages.

The height of mockery is, after plundering India's wealth of knowledge, Indians are ridiculed by the western scholars for not documenting its knowledge; if the Indian Libraries were saved from destruction, the world would have not lost the ancient knowledge that India (alone) possessed.

73 Pāṇini's Logic & Computer Languages

Sanskrit is the oldest prevailing language; the mother of all languages. It is a perfect language, rather a perfected language; a language that invokes the divine; an inexhaustible spiritual spring of inspiration. Indians called it as Devavāṇī- the language of gods.

The Most ancient language that remains eternally young & modern is Sanskrit. Eternal Vedas are revealed in that language; Modern computers adopt that language. Artificial intelligence inherits that language;

The greatness of this language can be understood when we read Panini's Grammar Rules (Vyākaraṇa Sūtras) called "Ashtadhyayi". This great sage who had lived around 500BC had postulated around 4000 sutras pertaining to Phonetics, Morphology, Grammar, Lexical lists and Verbal roots etc. It is highly systematic technical and logical in approach. The lexical lists are applied through structured algorithms. His sophisticated logical rules and techniques have been widely influential in ancient and modern linguistics of many languages within India and abroad.

Patañjali had written "Mahābhāṣya" (Commentary) for Panini's linguistic rules. It was with Pataṣjali that Indian linguistic science reached its definite form. The principles of Panini's grammar rules were lucidly enunciated by Patanjali from various perspectives like Śikṣa (Phonotics), Vyākaraṇa (Morphology), Nirukta (Etymology).

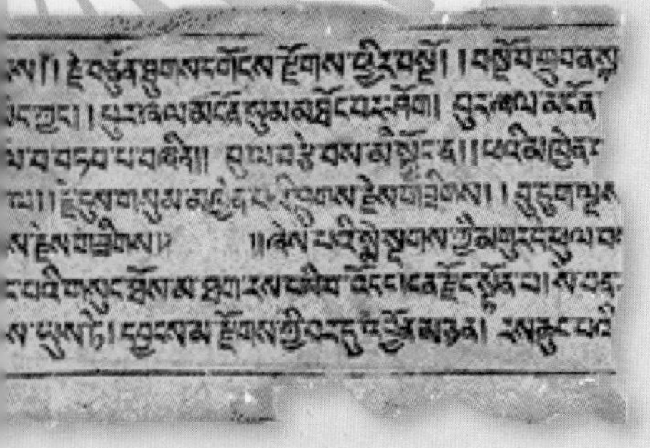

Panini's grammar uses a variety of formal techniques including recursion, transformations, and metarules. This in turn facilitates algorithmic computations. Hence Panini can be called father of computing machines.

For computer scientists, in the theory of formal languages, the word "formal" refers to the fact that all the rules for the language are explicitly stated in terms of what strings of symbols could occur, without any ambiguity and the need for interpretations based on mental skills. Sanskrit is the only language that has a very rich structure of grammar.

The formal structure of computer programming languages was introduced in the 1958-60 period by eminent scientists John Backus (1958), and Peter Naur (1963). They headed UNESCO conferences on International algorithmic language ALGOL 60, a language "suitable for expressing a large class of numerical processes in a form sufficiently concise for direct and automatic translation into the language of programmable automatic computers".

BNF is an acronym originally for "Backus Normal Form" that was later changed to Backus-Naur Form. BNF notation can be found in any book on programming languages.

Panini's rules of grammar follow a notation which is equivalent in its power to that of Backus, and has many similar properties: given the use to which the notation was put, it is possible to identify structures equivalent to Backus.

Proff. Subhash Kak, Scientist, Scholar on Indian Studies & Professor of Electrical Engineering and Professor of Asian Studies and Cognitive Science at Louisiana State University in Baton Rouge, reviews the Paninian approach to natural language processing (NLP) and compares it with the current knowledge representation systems of Artificial Intelligence, and argues that Paninian-style generative rules and metarules could assist in further advances in NLP.

Panini's grammar rules remain as the most marvellous contributions of ancient India to computing sciences.

In a Masjid, located in the town called "Dhar" of MadhyaPradesh, the Archeological department had excavated a cave, which contained a temple of Saraswati, the goddess of learning. On the walls of the temple, a big grammar chart and language rules of Panini had been chiseled. The temple seems to have been built during the King Bhoja's time. *(Source: Hindu Dharma, the universal way of life- By His holiness Chandra Sekhara Sarswati of Kanchi pīṭha).*

Today, that knowledge adorns the walls of the mosque. It remains unnoticed. Yet modern Indian brains, which dominate the domain of software development, had invoked the legacy of Paninian-logic.

"Panini's grammar uses a variety of formal techniques including recursion, transformations, and metarules. This in turn facilitates algorithmic computations. Hence Panini can be called father of computing machines."

74 Saṁskṛta Words in English

Sanskrit is called the mother of all languages. Sanskrit has contributed to the vocabulary of all languages in many ways. It has influenced the Greek and Latin immensely. Many western scholars had termed Sanskrit as the mother of Indo –European languages;

Here we may make a simple effort to correlate current English language, which was mostly influenced by Greek and Latin languages with some Sanskrit words. Please note this is not a scholastic attempt but a basic compilation to glorify the Sanskrit's influence on the western languages.

1. Parts of human body:

Dant- dental

Nasa-nose/nostril

Aksha- eye

Atma-auto

Hasta-hand

Naka-nails

Chati-chest

2. Human relations:

Naam- name

Pita- pater-father

Bhrathru- brother

Mata-mother

Mann-man

Sut-son

Swasar-sister

3. Numbers:

Nava- nine

Tri- three

Satam- centum-century

Sapta-seven

Pañca-penta(five)

Dwa- deo- two

Dasa-deca

4. Animals/kingdom etc

Nav-new

Sarpa-serpent

Yuva- youth

Raj- regal/rich/royal

Maha- mega/magnify

Manas-mental

Kri- create

“Sanskrit is called the mother of all languages. Sanskrit has contributed to the vocabulary of all languages in many ways.”

Kapala- cap/captain

Jana- generate/genetic/generations

Gau-cow

Ga-go

Kal- Caluculator (latin-caluculare)-calander

Dvār-door

Dham-domicile

Chakra- car

Band-band

Antar- Inter/anty

Vak-vocal/vocation/vocabulary

Pra- prey/ preface/presize/preview

Many are words that resemble the words of Sanskrit;
Many are the words that echo the words of Sanskrit;
Many are the words that speak volumes about Sanskrit's glory.

Corresponding English
Archaic Roman
Archaic Greek
Phoenician
Brāhma
Developments of Brāhma
Modern Nāgarī

"I feel with them, that it is impossible for us, with our limited means, to attempt to educate the body of the people. We must at present do our best to form a class who may be interpreters between us and the millions whom we govern; a class of persons, Indian in blood and colour, but English in taste, in opinions, in morals, and in intellect. To that class we may leave it to refine the vernacular dialects of the country, to enrich those dialects with terms of science borrowed from the Western nomenclature, and to render them by degrees fit vehicles for conveying knowledge to the great mass of the population.

- Lord Macaulay

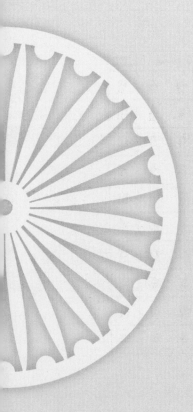

75 Macaulay's Game Plan of Westernizing Indian Generations

It was March 7th 1835, Governor General William Bentick with one pen stroke had doomed India's cultural and intellectual legacy. He had sealed the Indian giant of wisdom & knowledge into the bottle of obscurity. Let us look into the main aspects of that bad news in his ordinance...

- British government henceforth shall spend money only for the propagation of European culture and western knowledge, by adopting the medium of communication and instruction in English.
- All the scholarships that are being granted to propagation of local culture and languages especially Sanskrit and Arabic shall be stopped, henceforth.
- No funds shall be allocated to printing and translation of Sanskrit literature and Indian knowledge.
- Action plan to be evolved for popularizing the English language among natives.

Lord Macaulay

Lord Macaulay is the force behind this evil design. He was the honorable member in the supreme council of India. The minutes of the meeting held on February 2nd 1835, for implementing the English education in India is a historic document that one should read with all objectivity to know his game plan of westernizing future Indian generations....

"I feel with them, that it is impossible for us, with our limited means, to attempt to educate the body of the people. We must at present do our best to form a class who may be interpreters between us and the millions whom we govern; a class of persons, Indian in blood and colour, but English in taste, in opinions, in morals, and in intellect. To that class we may leave it to refine the vernacular dialects of the country, to enrich those dialects with terms of science borrowed from the Western nomenclature, and to render them by degrees fit vehicles for conveying knowledge to the great mass of the population."

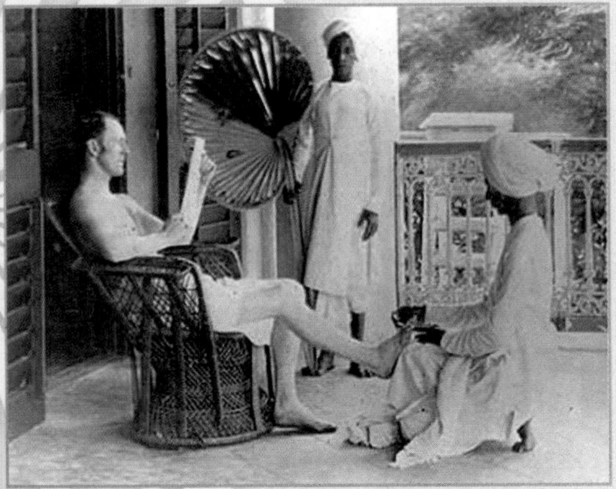

Oh! Indian Come out of the Painfull Past

"What then shall that language be? One-half of the Committee maintains that it should be the English. The other half strongly recommends the Arabic and Sanskrit. The whole question seems to me to be, which language is the best worth knowing?"

"I have never found one among them who could deny that a single shelf of a good European library was worth the whole native literature of India and Arabia."

"Nobody, I suppose, will contend that English is so difficult to a Hindu as Greek to an Englishman…Less than half the time which enables an English youth to read Herodotus and Sophocles, ought to enable a Hindu to read Hume and Milton."

"We are a Board for wasting public money, for printing books which are of less value than the paper on which they are printed was while it was blank; for giving artificial encouragement to absurd history, absurd metaphysics, absurd physics, absurd theology; for raising up a breed of scholars who find their scholarship an encumbrance and a blemish, who live on the public while they are receiving their education, and whose education is so utterly useless to them that when they have received it they must either starve or live on the public all the rest of their lives".

"But I would strike at the root of the bad system which has hitherto been fostered by us. I would at once stop the printing of Arabic and Sanskrit books; I would abolish the Madrassa and the Sanskrit college at Calcutta. Benares is the great seat of Brahmanical learning. Delhi of Arabic learning. If we retain the Sanskrit college at Benares and the Mahometan College at Delhi, we do enough and much more than enough in my opinion, for the Eastern languages.

Certain serious objections to Macaulay's strong views were raised by another member of the Supreme Council, H. T. Prinsep who was Secretary for matters pertaining to education. Prinsep's objections were cleverly tackled by adopting a game plan; Macaulay had already got the concurrence of the Governor General before H.T. Princep presented his objections;. However, Prinsep felt that Macaulay carried the day with him because of his name and fame as a literary figure. Prinsep wrote in his diary as follows: February 15, 1835:

"When the subject came under consideration in Council, there was a very hot argument between myself and Mr. Macaulay. The issue was the resolution that was published not abolishing existing colleges, but requiring them to teach English as well as native literature and making the former obligatory, also giving some encouragement to vernacular studies, but declaring that all Government pecuniary aid in future should be given exclusively to promote the study of European science through the medium of the English language. Lord W. Bentinck would not even allow my memorandum to be placed on record."

Chaining The Indian Future with Western Influence

Let us clearly question ourselves / whether India really benefited because of introduction of English?

Some people argue that...

Today, Indians are doing great jobs throughout the world; Poor India is becoming a very rich country, because of English educated youth. Even today people are crazy about learning English. English has become the window of knowledge. After independence we continued with patronage of English medium schools and colleges. Macaulay had done a great favour to us by introducing English.

But countries like... French, Germany, Japan, Russia, China ... and many others do not give prominence to the English at the cost of local culture and language. Yet they are as wealthy as India, as progressive as India, the youth of these countries are doing great jobs too.

Milton, Newton, Darwin, Shakespeare and Marx and Mao need not be our source of inspiration; instead Aryabhatta, Bhaskaracharya, Charaka, Shusruta, Varahamihira, Kalidasa, Panini, and galaxy of stalwarts can inspire us for generations;

Because of too much prominence given to English, world is unaware of the wealth of knowledge that is lying latent in our Sanskrit literature; culturally - our awareness about our own past glories had vanished; we are becoming slaves to western thought and culture shunning our individuality; these are the repercussions of great English education; let us learn English, but let us use it as only the communicative tool; and let us limit its usage there.

Milton, Newton, Darwin, Shakespeare and Marx and Mao need not be our source of inspiration; instead Aryabhatta, Bhaskaracharya, Charaka, Shusruta, Varahamihira, Kalidasa, Panini, Bharadwaj, Potana, Kabir, Shivaji, Bhagatsingh, Gargi, Sita, Maiytreyi, Jhansi Lakshmi, Mahatama Gandhi, Netaji Subash Chandra Bose…Swami Vivekananda… and galaxy of stalwarts can inspire us for generations;

Let our school books teach students more about India's greatest souls; Sanskrit is the mother of all languages; we should be proud of that and encourage younger generations to know more about our Sanskrit and Indian culture…. Then we shall not lose our individuality… other wise Macaulay's treacherous game plan comes true.

His great speech in British parliament is a recorded evidence and we can understand his open strategy to westernize India…

"It is scarcely possible to calculate the benefits which we might derive from the diffusion of European civilisation among the vast population of the East. It would be, on the most selfish view of the case, far better for us that the people of India were well-governed and independent of us, than ill-governed and subject to us; that they were ruled by their own kings, but wearing our broadcloth, and working with our cutlery, than that they were performing their salaams to English collectors and English magistrates, but were too ignorant to value, or too poor to buy, English manufactures. To trade with civilised men is infinitely more profitable than to govern savages. That would, indeed, be a doting wisdom, which, in order that India might remain a dependency, would make it a useless and costly dependency, which would keep a hundred millions of men from being our customers in order that they might continue to be our slaves."

(From Thomas Babington Macaulay, "Speech in Parliament on the Government of India Bill, 10 July 1833," Macaulay, Prose and Poetry, selected by G.M. Young (Cambridge, MA: Harvard University Press, 1957), pp. 716

In spite of Maculay's treacherous plan to make India a country of slaves and clerks, Indians survived only to prosper and shall surely turn the tables on its deceivers. Let us await for that bright day.

> "Far better for us that the people of India were well governed and independent of us, than ill governed and subject to us; that they were ruled by their own kings, but wearing our broadcloth, and working with our cutlery,
>
> - Lord Macaulay"

இத்தருணத்தில், சுமார் 170 ஆண்டுகளுக்கு முன்பு பிரிட்டிஷ் நாடாளுமன்றத்தின், பிரபல உறுப்பினரும், பிரிட்டிஷ் அரசாங்கத்தில் பல முக்கியப் பதவிகளை வகித்தவரும், 1834-ம் ஆண்டு பிரிட்டிஷ் அரசு அமைத்த 'சுப்ரீம் கவுன்ஸில் ஆஃப் இந்தியா' என்ற அமைப்பின் முக்கிய உறுப்பினருமான மெக்காலே பிரபு நான்காண்டுகள் நமது நாட்டைச் சுற்றிப்பார்த்துவிட்டு ஆங்கிலேய அரசுக்கு எழுதியதைக் கீழே தந்துள்ளோம்.

LORD MACAULAY'S ADDRESS TO THE BRITISH PARLIAMENT 2 FEBRUARY, 1835

"I have travelled across the lenght and breadth of India and I have not seen one person who is a begger, who is a thief. Such wealth I have seen in this country, such high moral values, people of such caliber, that I do not think we would ever conquer this country, unless we break the very backbone of this nation, which is her spiritual and cultural heritage, and therefore, I propose that we replace her old and ancient education system, her culture, for if the Indians think that all that is foreign and English is good and greater than their own, they will lose their selfesteem, their native culture and they will become what we want them, a truly dominated nation."

76 Indian Educational Scene When British Entered India

When the British came to India, there was flourishing Indian system of community schools, managed by the village communities- Gurukula system & Grama Pāthaśālās.

The agents of the East India Company and the Christian missionaries destroyed these village community schools, and took steps to replace education by introducing English and western system of education.

In October 1931 Mahatma Gandhi made a statement at Chatham House, London, that created a furor in the English press.

He said, "Today India is more illiterate than it was fifty or a hundred years ago, and so is Burma, because the British administrators, when they came to India, instead of taking hold of things as they were, began to root them out. They scratched the soil and left the root exposed and the beautiful tree perished".

Sir Thomas Munro, Governor of Madras, ordered a mammoth survey in June 1822, whereby the district collectors furnished the caste-wise division of students in four categories, viz., Brahmins, Vysyas (Vaishyas), Shoodras (Śūdrās) and other castes (broadly the modern scheduled castes).

	Vishakapatanam	**Tirunelveli**	**South arcot**
Brahmins+Vysyas	47%	21.8%	16%
Sudras	21%	31.2%	-
Others (including muslims)	32%	38.4%	84% (including Sudras)

The 'Survey of Indigenous Education in the Province of Bombay (1820-1830)' showed that Brahmins were only 30% of the total students 70% belonged to other castes.

What is more, when William Adam surveyed Bengal and Bihar, he found that Brahmins and Kayasthas together comprised less than 40% of the total students, and that forty castes like Tanti, Teli, Napit, Sadgop, etc. were well-represented in the student body.

It was the British, particularly Lord Wellesley in 1800AD who played a major role in giving prominence to Vedantic learning, it probably hadn't had for centuries. In the process, the cultural heritage of the lower castes was successfully marginalized, and this remains an enduring legacy of colonialism.

By reading the Dharampal's book "Indian science and Technology in the Eighteenth century," one can infer that most of the native skills and technologies that perished as a result of British policies were those of the Dalit and artisan castes.

Mr. Ernest Havell (formerly Principal of the Calcutta school of Art) has rightly said, the fault of the Anglo-Indian Educational System is that, instead of harmonizing with, and supplementing, National Culture, it is antagonistic to, and destructive, of it. (Source: Bharata Shakti: Collection of Addresses on Indian Culture - By Sir John Woodroffe p 75-77).

As Max Müeller, the propagator of the Aryan invasion Theory wrote to his wife, "It took only 200 years for us to Christianise the whole of Africa, but even after 400 years India eludes us, I have come to realize that it is Sanskrit which has enabled India to do so. And to break it I have decided to learn Sanskrit." The soul of India lies in Sanskrit. And Lord Macaulay saw to it that the later generations are successfully cut off from their roots.

(Source: Assaulting India's pluralist ethos - by D. Harikumar 'Th Hindu').

> "Today India is more illiterate than it was fifty or a hundred years ago, and so is Burma, because the British administrators, when they came to India, instead of taking hold of things as they were, began to root them out. They scratched the soil and left the root exposed and the beautiful tree perished .
>
> \- Mahatma Gandhi
> October 1931

Let us look into Swami Vivekananda's views about Indian Education system uttered one hundred and ten years ago,

"The education that you are getting now has some good points, but it has a tremendous disadvantage which is so great that the good things are all weighed down. In the first place it is not a man-making education, it is merely and entirely a negative education. A negative education or any training that is based on negation is worse than death. The child is taken to school, and the first thing he learns is that his father is a fool, the second thing that his grandfather is a lunatic, the third thing that all his teachers are hypocrites, the fourth that all the sacred books are lies! By the time he is sixteen he is a mass of negation, lifeless and boneless. And the result is that fifty years of such education has not produced one original man in the three Presidencies. Every man of originality that has been produced has been educated elsewhere, and not in this country, or they have gone to the old universities once more to cleanse themselves of superstitions. Education is not the amount of information that is put into your brain and runs riot there, undigested, all your life. We must have life-building, man-making, character-making assimilation of ideas."

(Source : Complete works of Swami Vivekananda-vol3 pg-301,302, in the year 1897)

77 Replicating Indian Teaching Methods in England

During the formative period of the modern educational systems in Europe and America, the pedagogy of the Hindus, especially on its elementary side, has played an important part.

It is well known that primary education was grossly neglected in America during the first half-century of her independence. In England even so late as 1845, 3.2 percent of men and 49 per cent of women had to sign their names on the marriage register with a cross. In the age of paucity of "public schools" private educational efforts naturally elicited the people's admiration. And none drew more sympathy and support than Andrew Bell's (1775-1823) "mutual-tuition" or "pupil teacher" or "monitorial" system of school management.

What, now, is the origin of this much-applauded mutual instruction or monitorial system, the so-called Bell-Lancasterain "discovery" in pedagogy. **Historians of education are familiar with the fact that the plan of making one boy teach others has been indigenous to India for centuries.**

Bell, himself, in his Mutual Tuition (pt.I.ch.I. V) describes how in Madras (combined state of Andhra and Tamilnadu) he came into contact with a school conducted by a single master or superintendent through the medium of the scholars themselves. And, in fact, in England the monitorial system or the method of making every boy at once a master and a scholar is known as the "Madras system". Bell, a Christian missionary in Madras took the Indian system of education back to England, and introduced it there. Until then, only the children of the nobles were given education there and he started education for the masses in England. So, we gather that it is from India that the British adopted the system for educating the masses.

England's debt to India in pedagogies has been fitly acknowledged in the tablet in West Minister Abbey, which describes Andrew Bell as "the eminent founder of the Madras System of Education, which has been adopted within the British Empire, as the national system of education for the children of the poor."

(Source: Creative India: From Mohen-jo-Daro to The Age of Ramakrishna-Vivekananda – By Benoy Kumar Sarkar p. 108-110 and Education in India Under The Rule of the East India Company – By Major B. D. Basu 1934 2nd edition. Calcutta and The Destruction of The Indian System of Education).

Simple Indian Teaching Methods

Ancient Indian Global Influence
Viśva vyāpta Bhārata Pratibhā

78 Ages ago Indians reached American Shores

Baffling Links to Ancient India: History is full of misnomers. One such term is the New World, as applied to the Americas. The landing of Columbus in 1492 undoubtedly created a new life on the continents, but it neither created nor discovered a new world. Many centuries ago Asian migrants had come to the western shore in substantial numbers.

Archeologists have unearthed in the capital a gigantic 12 ton stone slab - Aztec earth goddess, Tlaltecuhtli, at the site of the ancient Aztec Templo Mayor, Mexico City

The Māyans of Guatemala - representative of the Māyā civilization that flourished during the first millennium AD in Central America - believe their ancestors came from eastern continents, 20,000 years ago. One of the most dominant ethnic groups, Kekichi Maya, has always had special attraction for India in the past as their forefathers have told them that the "Nāgā tribes of Nāgāland" were one of the four original branches of the Māyā civilization. It is for these reasons and the similarities between the Aryan and Māyān civilizations, the people of Guatemala for long have been trying to establish contact with Indians and have a cultural dialogue.

World's leading anthropologists, Robert Heine Geldern and Gordon F. Ekholm have said:

"Ships of size that carried Fahien from India to China (through stormy China water) were certainly capable of proceeding all the way to Mexico and Peru by crossing the Pacific. One thousand years before the birth of Columbus Indian ships were far superior to any made in Europe up to the 18th century".

(Source: The Civilizations of Ancient America: The Selected Papers of the XXIX International Congress of Americanists - edited Sol Tax 1951).

The Archaeological remains of ancient Māyā civilization of Mexico have a spread of 125000 square miles and are lying scattered in the parts of Yucatan, Campeche, Tabasco and eastern half of Chiapas and adjacent highlands of Guatemala and practically in the whole of Honduras.

Māyan people seem to be highly advanced in art and architecture and had evolved good economic and political systems. Māyan calendar and their knowledge about celestial bodies were immensely superior.

The most important development of the ancient American or Asio-american culture took place in the south of the United States, in Mexico, in Central America, and in Peru. The early history of Asio-americans is shrouded in mystery and controversy due to the absence of definite documentary evidence, which was destroyed by the European conquerors in their misguided religious zeal.

Post-Columbus history of America for 300 years was the story of ruthless destruction. And fanatics like "Bishop Diego da Landa" burnt a huge bonfire of valuable documents. They destroyed huge temples and smashed idols. And others like Hernando Cortez are said to have slaughtered, in less than two hours, six thousand people who had gathered in a temple Patio. Destruction of Aztec cities was so complete that almost everything lay in ruins.

Aztec Ruins

To quote Glen Daniel from his books 'The First Civilizations', "within 15 years, (between 1519 to 1533), the Western world discovered and brutally destroyed three civilizations - the Aztecs of Mexico, Māyā of Yucatan and Guatemala and Incā of Peru."

Sir William Jones (1746-1794) judge of the Supreme Court at Calcutta was one who pioneered Sanskrit studies. His admiration for Indian thought and culture was almost limitless. He has remarked:

"Rama is represented as a descendant from the sun, as the husband of Sita, and the son of a princess named Kaushalya. It is very remarkable that Peruvians, whose Incās boasted of the same descent, styled their greatest festival Rama-Sitva; whence we may take it that South America was peopled by the same race who imported into the farthest parts of Asia the rites and the fabulous history of Rama."
(Source: Asiatic Researches Volume I. p. 426)

> The ancient Puranas and the Mahabharata make mention of the Americas as Kuruvarsha, lands rich with gold and silver. Argentina, which means, "related to silver", is thought to have been named after Arjuna (of silver hue).

Ephraim George Squire (1821-1888) was United States Charge d'affaires to Central America in 1849 and the author of Peru; Incidents of Travel and Exploration in the Land of the Incās and The Serpent Symbol, and the Worship of the Reciprocal Principles of Nature in America. Comparing the temples of India, Java and Mexico, he wrote nearly a hundred years ago:

"A proper examination of these monuments would disclose the fact that in their interior as well as their exterior form and obvious purposes, these buildings (temples in Palanque, Mexico) correspond with great exactness to those of Hindustan..."

Both the Hindus and Americans used similar items in their worship and rituals. They both maintained the concept of four Yuga cycles, or cosmological seasons, extending over thousands of years, and conceived of twelve constellations with reference to the sun as indicated by the Incān sun calendar. Royal insignias, systems of government, and practice of religious dance and temple worship all showed remarkable similarities, pointing strongly to the idea that the Americas were strongly influenced by the Aryans.

The ancient Purāṇas and the Mahābhārata make mention of the Americas as "Kuruvarsha", lands rich with gold and silver. Argentina, which means, "related to silver", is thought to have been named after Arjuna (of silver hue).

Dr. B. Chakravarti author of The Indians And The Amerindians has written:

It will be evident from a close study of the texts of Indian Astronomy that Latin America was known to ancient Indians, who called it Pataladesa.

The Surya Siddhanta, a textbook of Astronomy, composed before 500 BC. Identifies and describes Pataldesa in very clear and definite terms in the chapter of Geography (chapter xii).

The above book mentions four great cities situated on the opposite ends of the world, equidistant from one another. 1. Yamakotipura in Bhadrasvavarsa (Indonesia) in the East, Lanka in Bharatvarsa (India) in the South and 3. Rome in Ketumalavarsa (Europe) in the west and Siddhapura in Kuruvarsa (America) in the north.

The celebrated Astronomer Bhaskaracarya mentions the time difference between the important cities situated in different parts of the world in his Siddhanta Siromani (Goladhyaya) thus:" When the sun rises at Lanka, the time as at Yakakotipura to the East of Lanka will be midday. Below the earth at Siddhapura, it will be twilight then, and at Romakadesa in Europe, the time will be midnight."

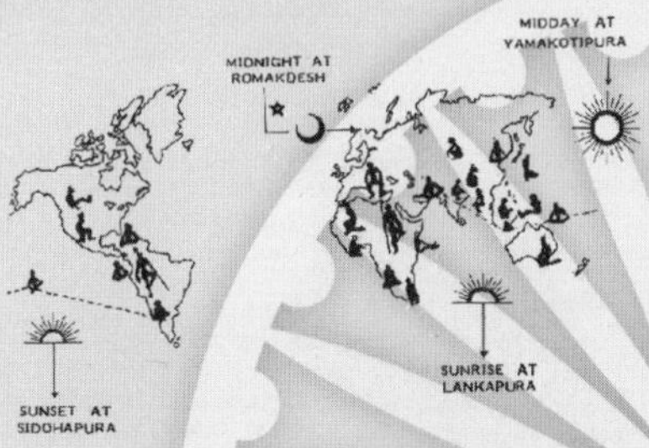

Bhaskaracarya mentions the time difference between the important cities situated in different parts of the world in his Siddhanta Siromani

Many similarities between two cultures suggest a link between Indus Valley and Māyans of Central America. A few studies focused on the calendars of the two advanced civilizations. The Indus Valley inhabitants followed a calendar based on the movements of Jupiter, and the Māyans followed one based on Venus. In the Purāṇas, a secondary Hindu scripture, Jupiter, Bṛhaspati, was acknowledged to be the leader of the gods, while Venus, Shukra, was the leader of the asuras. The texts further state that the devas and asuras lived on opposite sides of the Earth. Mexico and India are at opposite sides in longitude. The correspondences were pointed out by B. G. Siddarth, director of the B. M. Birla Science Centre in Hyderabad. He also said the Hindu story of the churning of the ocean has been found in carvings in Mexico (source Hyderabad, INDIA, April 29, 2002 & Deccan Chronicle and Hinduism Today)

The startling discoveries came during March 1995, when Sri Ganapati Sthapati the master builder visited the ancient Incan and Māyan sites of South and Central America. Ganapati Sthapati is India's foremost traditional temple architect and perhaps the first true expert in sculpture and stone construction to personally examine these ancient buildings.

The ruins of Machu Picchu site of Incas civilization, Peru, South America

It is Sthapati's theory that Māyan, the creator of Indian architecture, originated from the Māyan people of Central America. In Indian history, Māyan appears several times, most significantly as the author of Mayamatam, "Concept of Mayan" which is a Vāstu Shastra, a text on art, architecture and town planning. The traditional date for this work is 8,000 BC. Māyan appears in the Ramayana and again in the Mahābhārata. In the latter he designs a magnificent palace for the Pāṇḍava brothers.

The fundamental principle of Māyan's architecture and town planning is the "module". Buildings and towns are to be laid out according to certain multiples of a standard unit. Floor plans, door locations and sizes, wall heights and roofs, all are determined by the modular plan. More specifically, Māyan advocated the use of an eight-by-eight square, for a total of 64 units, which is known as the Vāstu Puruṣa Maṇḍala.

The on-site inspection by Sthapati was to determine if the Incan and Māyan structures did follow a modular plan and reflect the Vāstu Puruṣa Maṇḍala.

The moment Sthapati approached an ancient Incan residential building at Machu Picchu on March 15th, he pointed at the wall and said, "That is a thickness of one kishku hasta"-33 inches, a standard measure in South India first promulgated by Māyan.

Sthapati and his team visited Chichīn Itzá, Mexico's Yucatan peninsula, on the day of summer equinox on March 21st (1995). At the moment of sunset on the equinox, a shadow is cast by the steps of the Pyramid of the Castle where the shadow can be seen upon the side of the staircase to the top. The shadow creates the image of a serpent's body, which joins a stone carving of a serpent's head at the bottom of the staircase. It is a stunning demonstration of Māyan astronomical and architectural precision.

They measured and closely examined the Pyramid of the Castle. It too conformed to the Vāstu Vedic principles of Māyan. The temple structure at the top was exactly 1/4th of the base. And the stepped pyramid design derived from a three-dimensional extension of the basic eight-by-eight grid system. The temple room at the top was also modular in design, with the wall thickness determining the size of doorways, location of columns, thickness of columns and the width and length of the structure.

Most interesting was the name of this structure-chilambalam, meaning a sacred space. It is Sthapati's theory that the Māyans worshipped the very concept of space, specifically a space made according to the modular system. This same idea is found in Hinduism in the sacred room in the center of the Chidambaram Siva Temple in South India, where space or ākāśa is worshiped-there is no idol. Chidambaram, Sounds like chilambalam, means "hall of consciousness". The concept of sacred space is at the center of the mystical shilpi tradition of India.

The linguistic similarities had been pointed by the Sthapthi between yogic terminology and Māyan terminology; Text: "Chacla" in Mayan refers to force centers of the body similar to the chakras of Hinduism. K'ultanlilni in Māyan refers to the power of God within man which is controlled by the breath, similar in meaning to Kuṇḍalinī. Māyan Chilambalam refers to a sacred space, as does Indian word Chidambaram. Yok'hah in Māyan means "on top of truth," similar to yoga in Sanskrit.

The emigrant races of India took with them, wherever they went, (Southeast Asia or America) and their system of measurement of time, their local gods, their customs, including games, dances and ceremonials. They established their cultural empires in Java, Bali, Sumatra, Borneo, Philippines, Cambodia, Champa, Burma, and Thailand.

Ancient Indians were mighty navigators and pioneers of cultures, centuries before Columbus was born.

(Source: Adopted from the great website www.hinduwisdom.info)

> "Most interesting was the name of this structure-chilambalam, (Mexician Pyramid) meaning a sacred space. This same idea is found in Hinduism in the sacred room in the center of the Chidambaram Siva Temple in South India, where space or akasha is worshi ped-there is no idol."

79 India, The China's Teacher

A wall painting of Brahma, depicted in China

India was China's teacher. Cultural bonds existed between the two Asian giants. They could be traced from the times of Mahābhārata and later consolidated through the spread of Buddhism.

Lin Yutang (1895-1976) author of The Wisdom of China and India (p3-4): says "India was China's teacher in religion and imaginative literature, and the world's teacher in Trignometry, quandratic equations, grammar, phonetics, Arabian Nights, animal fables, chess, as well as in philosophy, and that she inspired Boccaccio, Goethe, Herder, Schopenhauer, Emerson, and probably also old Aesop."

Sir William Jones (1746-1794) came to India as a judge of the Supreme Court at Calcutta. He pioneered Sanskrit studies. His admiration for Indian thought and culture was almost limitless. He says that the Chinese assert their Hindu origin."

Hu Shih, (1891-1962), was a Chinese philosopher in the Republican China. He was an Ambassador to the U.S. (1938-42) and Chancellor of Peking University (1946-48). He said:

"India conquered and dominated China culturally for two thousand years without ever having to send a single soldier across her border".

The Sanskrit name for China is "Cina". Sir Rene Grousset, a French historian, says, the name China comes from Sanskrit name for the regions of the east;

Many other Scholars clearly mention that the Chinese word for lion, shih, used long before the Chin dynasty, was derived from the Sanskrit word, simha, and that the Greek word for China, Tzinista, used by some later writers, appears to be derivative of the Sanskrit Chinasthana.

Both Arnold Toynbee and Sir L. Wooley speak of a ready-made culture coming to China. That was the Vedic culture of India.

China (Cina)'s reference in Mahābhārata:

It is well-known that in the Mahābhārata the Cinas appear with the Kiratas among the armies of king Bhagadatta of Pragjyotisa or Assam.

In the Sabhaparva this king is described as surrounded by the Kiratas and the Cinas.

In the Bhishmaparva, the corps of Bhagadatta, consisting of the Kirtas and the Cinas of yellow color, appeared like a forest of Karnikaras.

In the Vanaparva of the Mahābhārata the Pāṇḍava brothers are said to have crossed the country of the Cinas in course of their trek through the Himalayan territory north of Badri and reached the realm of the Kirata king Subahu.

The Cinas are brought into intimate relationship with the Himalayan people (Haimavatas) in the Sabhaparva also.

In the **Nagarjunakonda** inscription of Virapurusdatta, China (Cina) is said to be lying in the Himalayas beyond Cilata or Kirata. These references to the proximity of China to the Himalayan regions, inhabited by the Kiratas, show that there were regular routes through the Tibeto-Burman territories, along which the Indians could reach China.

Some such land-route is implied in the remark of the Harsacarita of Banabhatta that Arjuna conquered the Hemakuta region after passing through Cina.

Trade & commerce:

India had contact with China from the early period through three routes. One was through the Central Asian region; the second was through Yunan and Burma. The third was by sea to the South Indian ports.

> "India conquered and dominated China culturally for two thousand years without ever having to send a single soldier across her border."
>
> - Hu Shih
> Chinese philosopher

The chronicle 'Sung-chu' states that all the precious things of land and water came from India. Gems made of rhinoceros' horns and kingfishers' stones, serpent pearls and asbestos cloths, or innumerable varieties of these curiosities, were imported into China from India.

Kalidasa mentions this silk fabric (Chinamsuka) as one of the most fashionable textiles among the richer sections of society. Silk and silk-products were also in much demanded luxury articles even in the reign of Harshavardhana.

Literature:

Sanskrit influenced the Chinese literature in many ways; Many Buddhistic works had been translated into Chinese; Phrases and words coined by Buddhist scholars enriched the Chinese vocabulary by more than thirty-five thousand words. Sanskrit dramas like Sakuntala, which were translated into Chinese, had become popular dramas.

"Sanskrit scholarship must have been fairly widespread in China. It is interesting to find that some Chinese scholars tried to introduce Sanskrit phonetics into the Chinese language. A well-known example of this is that of the monk Shon Wen, who lived at the time of the Tang dynasty. He tried to develop an alphabetical system along these lines in Chinese." (Source: The Discovery of India - By Jawaharlal Nehru p. 197-198).

Art : Indian art also reached China, mainly through Central Asia, although some works of Buddhist art came by sea. Monks and their retinues, and traders brought Buddha statues, models of Hindu temples, and other objects of art to China. Fa-hsien made drawings of images whilst at Tamralipiti. Hsuan-tsang returned with several golden and sandalwood figures of the Buddha; and Hui-lun with a model of the Nalanda Mahavihara. Wang Huan-ts'e, who went to India several times, collected many drawings of Buddhist images, including a copy of the Buddha image at Bodhgaya; this was deposited at the Imperial palace and it served as a model of the image in Ko-ngai-see temple.

Indian music was so popular in China, that Emperor Kao-tsu (581-595) tried unsuccessfully to proscribe it by an Imperial decree. His successor Yang-ti was also very fond of Indian music. In Chinese annals, references are found to visiting Indian musicians, who reached China from India, Kucha, Kashgar, Bokhara and Cambodia.

A major Buddhist influence on Chinese science was in scientific thought itself. Buddhist concepts, such as the infinity of space and time, and the plurality of worlds and of time-cycles or Hindu Kalpas (chieh) had a stimulating effect on Chinese inquiry, broadening the Chinese outlook and better equipping it to investigate scientific problems.

Tantric Buddhism reached China in the eighth century and the greatest Chinese Astronomer and Mathematician of his time, I-hsing (682-727), was a Tāntric Buddhist monk. While the work of Indian Mathematicians was carried Westward by the Arabs and transmitted to Europe, it was taken Eastward by Indian Buddhist monks and professional Mathematicians.

In the annals of the Sui dynasty, numerous Chinese translations of Indian Mathematical and Astronomical works are mentioned, such as Po-lo-men Suan fa (The Hindu Arithmetical rules) and Po-lo-men Suan King. These Dates from 2600 BC - A complete cycle takes 60 years, divided into 12 year elements. Each of these 12 years is named after an animal favored by the Buddha.

(Source: China welcomes the New Year - BBC). Chinese 60-year cycle has strong resemblance to Indian Hindu Calendars.

Medicine:

Indian medical texts were widely known in Central Asia, where parts of the original texts on Āyur Veda have been found as well as numerous translations.

The T'ang emperors patronized Indian Thaumaturges (Tāntric Yogīs) who were believed to possess secret methods of rejuvenation. Wang Hsuan-chao, who returned to India after the death of King Harsha, had been charged by the Chinese Emperor in 664 to bring back Indian medicines and physicians.

"Acupuncture therapy originated from India. It is a part of Ayurveda. Buddhist monks carried this knowledge of medicine to china."

Acupuncture:

Acupuncture therapy originated from India. It is a part of Āyurveda. The discovery of the vital bodily points began by the Indian kṣatrīya warriors in order to discover the vital (and deadly) points of the body, which could be struck during hand-to-hand encounters. It is said that they experimented upon prisoners by piercing their bodies with the iron and stone "needles' daggers called Suci daggers, common to their infantry and foot soldiers, in order to determine these points.

Buddhist monks carried this knowledge of medicine to China. In India, Herbal medicine had dominated the scene. Hence suchhi karma was not given much importance.

Charaka Saṁhitā and Suśruta Saṁhitā, mention about succhi Karma, and marma cikitsā. According to Chinese acupuncture, there are 24 pressure routes within the human body; Śuśruta had called them as 24 dhamanas.

Warfare studies:

Father and founder of Zen Buddhism (called C'han in China), **Bodhidharma,** was a Brahmin born in Kancheepuram of south India in 522 A.D. He arrived at the court of the Chinese Emperor Liang Nuti, of the 6th dynasty. He taught the Chinese monks Kalaripayattu, a very ancient Indian martial art, so that they could defend themselves against the frequent attacks of bandits. In time, the monks became famous all over China as experts in barehanded fighting, later known as the Shaolin.

The Shaolin temple, which has been handed back a few years ago by the communist Government to the C'han Buddhist monks, inheritors of Bodhi dharma's spiritual and martial teachings, is now open to visitors. On one of the walls, a fresco can be seen, showing Indian dark-skinned monks, teaching their lighter-skinned Chinese brothers the art of barehanded fighting. On this painting are inscribed: "Tenjiku Naranokaku" which means: **"the fighting techniques to train the body (which come) from India..."**

Kalari payattu was banned by the British in 1793. (Refer to chapter on European Imperialism).

Yoga:

Yoga has had an enormous influence on all forms of Indian spirituality, including Hinduism, Buddhist, and Jain and later on the Sufi and Christian. The teachings of Buddhism, which arose in India, are similar to those of yoga: striving towards Nirvāṇa and renouncing the world.

Education & learning:

The University of Nalanda built in the 4th century BCE (some historians say it was built in the fifth century AD) was one of the greatest achievements of ancient India in the field of education. The Chinese scholar and traveller **Hiuen Tsang** (600-654 AD) stayed at the Nalanda University in the 7th century, and has left an elaborate description of the excellence, and purity of monastic life practised here. **He found Indians to be "high-minded, upright and honorable.**

China received Mahāyānic Buddhism and Sanskrit texts from the Central-Asian provinces of India in 67 A.D. After that China became Hinduized not only in Theology and Metaphysics, but also in every department of thought and activity. Thousands of Hindus lived in Chinese cities, eg. at Changan in the N.W. and at Canton on the sea, as priests, teachers, merchants, physicians, sculptors and "interpreters."

India was China's teacher. Cultural bonds existed between the two Asian giants. They could be traced from the times of Mahabharata and later consolidated through the spread of Buddhism.

During his Indian tour the great Itsing (634-712) mastered Hindu medicine at the University of Nalanda. Hindu Mathematics and Logic were cultivated among the intellectuals of China, Sanskrit treatises on painting and art criticism, eg. Ṣaḍāṅga (six limbs of painting) in Vatsayayan's Kāmasūtra (erotics), Chitralaksana (marks of painting), etc. furnished the canons of the Chinese art during its greatest epoch (Tang and Sung Dynasties 600-1250).

Indian style of Architecture had influenced the Chinese Architecture in many ways; there were certain temples built during the Tang Period in China, which were the offspring of Indian and Chinese styles of Architecture. Those temples are however in ruins now, and so they cannot be studied properly. But the Chinese pagoda fortunately still exists. It is called Chinese, though the country of its origin was Nepal. The Newars, a people living in the Valley of Nepal, evolved it by making certain alterations in the Hindu temple.

Indian Education, Medicine, Religion, Literature, Technology, Martial Arts and Culture had a sublime effect and impact on China for the past two thousand years.

(Source: Adopted from the great website www.hinduwisdom.info)

80 Indians Inspired Greeks

India and Greece have many similarities; Ancient Western civilizations, known to India include Greece, Rome, Eygpt, Persia, and Mespatonia. Among all the western civilizations, Greeks are immensely and intimately connected to Indian thought and culture.

Professor Sir Flinders Patrie (1853-1942) British Archaeologist and Egyptologist, author of **"Egypt and Israel"** (1911) observes:

"The presence of a large body of Indian troops in the Persian army in Greece in 480 B.C. shows how far west the Indian connections were carried. And the discovery of modeled heads of **Indians at Memphis,** of about the fifth century B.C. shows that Indians were living there for trade. Hence there is no difficulty in regarding India as the source of the entirely new ideal of asceticism in the West."

(Source: **Eastern Religions and Western Thought - By Dr. Sarvepalli Radhakrishnan p. 150).**

Similarities in language, associated by similarities in religious beliefs, indicate that these two peoples must have either been in close contact at some early period or have had a common origin, even though neither had any recollection of those times. The Olympian religion of the Greeks and Vedic beliefs had a common background. The Greek concept of logos was very close to the Vedic Vāk, which corresponds to the Latin Vox.

Indians used to call Greeks as Yavanas; The brisk interaction between India and Greece is attested by the fact that a special rule was inserted in the great grammar of Panini to distinguish three feminine forms of yavana: a Greek woman was Yavani, the curtain was Yavanika, and the Greek script was Yavanani.

Ages before Alexander's interaction with north western Indian border, Pythagoras, Thales, Empedocles, Anaxagoras, Democritus and others undertook journey to the East to study philosophy and science at Taxilia, the ancient Indian university. Many historians testify the above fact.

According to Voltaire, "The Greeks, before the time of Pythagoras, travelled into India for instruction. The signs of the seven planets and of the seven metals are still almost all over the earth, such as the Indians invented: the Arabians were obliged to adopt their cyphers."

(Source: The Philosophy of History p. 527).

Swami Vivekananda also confirms the above view that, many a Greek philosopher had been influenced by Kapila's Sāṅkhya Śāstra; and Pythagorus came to India in search of learning the higher Knowledge;

Aristotle and Democratis had contributed the basic ideas of Atomic structure to the Western science. These theories are very similar to the Atomic theories propounded by Kanaad & Gautama. These two Indian legends lived two centuries before Aristotle.

Western Historians exaggerate Alexander's invasion on India. (325BC) Alexander had not even crossed the Punjab boarder; the vassal king called Porus resisted him. And Alexender turned back, citing the reasons of army mutiny; even the victory over Porus is not certain, according to many historians.

Jawaharlal Nehru in his book 'Discovery of India' says, " From a military point of view his invasion, was a minor affair. It was more of a raid across the border, and not a very successful raid at that." He met with such stout resistance from a border chieftain that the contemplated advance into the heart of India had to be reconsidered. If a small ruler on the frontier could fight thus, what of the larger and more powerful kingdom further south? Probably this was the main reason why his army refused to march further and insisted on returning."

(Source: **Discovery of India - By Jawaharlal Nehru p. 114-115**)

Professor H. G. Rawlinson writes: "It is more likely that Pythagoras was influenced by India than by Egypt. Almost all the theories, religions, philosophical and Mathematics taught by the Pythagoreans, were known in India in the sixth century B.C., and the Pythagoreans, like the Jains and the Buddhists, refrained from the destruction of life and eating meat and regarded certain vegetables such as beans as taboo". "It seems that the so-called Pythagorean theorem of the quadrature of the hypotenuse was already known to the Indians in the older Vedic times, and thus before Pythagoras (ibid). **(Legacy of India 1937, p. 5).**

Alexander on his return from India, took with him a sage called Kalanus (kalyana), during his last days, Alexander was influenced by this sage of India. Kalanus departed from life with the words 'Alexander, we shall meet again in Babylon'. Nobody understood why he said this, but in the end, the words proved true when Alexander died in Babylon.

Alexander appointed Selucus as his representative at Babylon; in a battle between Selucus and Chandra Gupta, Selucus gets defeated and gives his daughter in marriage to Chandra Gupta. Selucus further appoints Megesthenese as the ambassador in Chandra Gupta's kingdom.

Magesthenese' accounts about India, speak volumes of India's achievements in science, philosophy and political thoughts (especially democracy); He appreciates the Indian culture in every way;

Please note that Magesthenese adored India for its achievements, as early as, 2300 years ago.

(Source: Adopted from the great website www.hinduwisdom.info)

"From a military point of view his invasion, was a minor affair. It was more of a raid across the border, and not a very successful raid at that."

Jawaharlal Nehru
in his book Discovery of India
about Alexanders invasion

81 South Asian Cultural Bondage

Southeast Asia was closely allied to India culturally and commercially. The history of Indian connection covers a period of more than fifteen hundred years.

This region was broadly referred to by ancient Indians as *Suvarnabhumi* (the Land of Gold) or *Suvarnadvipa* (the Island of Gold), The Chinese called it Kin-Lin; Kin means gold **The Agni Purana, along with many other Puranas, calls India proper as Jambudvipa as distinguished from Dvipantara or India of the islands or overseas India.**

During the last two thousand years, this region has come under the influence of practically all the major civilizations of the world: Indian, Chinese, Islamic, and Western. Of these, Indian culture appears to have blended best with the indigenous culture.

In Ceylon, Burma, Siam (Thailand), Cambodia, Champa (Vietnam), and Indoensia, religion, art, the alphabet, literature, as well as whatever science and political organization existed, were the direct gift of Indians, whether Hindu or Buddhists.

Indonesia:

Islands of Java, Bali, Sumithra and Brunei are together called as Indonesia. It consists of 18,000 islands; Capital city of Indonesia is Jakarta.(Jaya kartā is the Sanskrit name) Most people of these Islands are Muslims. The language they speak is "bahasa", but niety percent of its vocabulary consists of Sanskrit language.

At traffic roundabout on one of the busiest arteries of the city stands a monumental sculpture facing the central bank on one side and the national monument on the other. It depicts Krishna and Arjuna in a chariot drawn by several horses. The sheer size and magnificence of this famous scene from the Mahābhārata has no parallel in India.

The mottos inscribed on government buildings are equally revealing. When you drive past the defence ministry -- called the Yuddha Graha -- you come across the following inscription engraved in marble on the archway: Chatur Dharma, Eka Karma. Further down the road is the ministry of sports known as the Krida Bhakti. The government has also named its national airlines after Garuḍa Airways.

An image of Lord Ganesha is printed on high denominational currency notes. Ganesha statues are seen everywhere, including a magnificent one at the entrance of the presidential palace.

Statues of dwarpalakas are to be found in front of both public and private buildings source: Hindu presence in Indonesia - media watch.org).

The textiles of Indonesia have, across time, also incorporated and integrated Hindu's symbols such as the Garuḍa, the nāga, the lotus, the elephant, the "maṇḍala diagrams" and so on.

Suharto Sukarno (1901-1970) Indonesian nationalist leader and the first President of Indonesia. He helped the country win its independence from the Netherlands. In a special article in 'The Hindu' on 4th January 1946, Sukarno wrote:

"In the veins of everyone of my people flows the blood of Indian ancestors and the culture that we possess is steeped through and through with Indian influences. Two thousand years ago people from your country came to Jawadvipa and Suvarnadvipa in the spirit of brotherly love. They gave the initiative to found powerful kingdoms such as those of Sri Vijaya, Mataram and Majapahit. We then learnt to worship the very gods that you now worship still and we fashioned a culture that even today is largely identical with your own. Later, we turned to Islam: but that religion too was brought by people coming from both sides of India".

India & Java

The name Java comes from the Sanskrit Jawadwip, which means, an (dvip) island (yawa) shaped like a barleycorn. The Vedic Indians must have charted Java, Yawadvip, thousands of years ago because Yawadvip is mentioned in India's earliest epic, the Rāmāyaṇa. The Ramayana reveals some knowledge of the eastern regions beyond seas; for instance Sugriva dispatched his men to Yavadvipa, the island of Java, in search of Sīta. It speaks of Burma as the land of silver mines. The Agni Purana, along with many other Puranas, calls India proper as Jambudvipa as distinguished from Dvipantara or India of the islands or overseas India.

Sir Stamford Raffles (1781-1826) the British Governor of Java, in his book, History of Java, II, p. 87, wrote:

"In the year 525 Saka era – 603 A.D., it was foretold to a king of Gujarat that his country would decay and go to ruin. He therefore, resolved to send his son to Java. He embarked with about 5000 followers in 6 large and about 100 small vessels, and after a voyage of four months reached an island. They supposed it to be Java; but finding themselves mistaken re-embarked, and finally settled at Matarem, in the center of the island they were seeking.... The prince then found that men alone wanted to make a great and flourishing state. He accordingly applied to Gujarat for assistance, when his father, delighted at his success, sent him reinforcement of 2000 people... From this period Java was known and celebrated as a kingdom; an extensive commerce was carried on with Gujarat and other countries, and the bay of Matarem was filled with adventurers from all parts". (Source: Periplus of the Erythrean Sea - W.H. Schoff p. 245

The construction of Prambanan temple, which was dedicated to Lord Shiva, was started in 856 AD and completed in 900 AD by King Dakṣa. Earlier Shiva temples were built in 675 AD on the Dieng mountain range, southwest of Medang Kamolan, the capital of the Mataram Kingdom.

The Barobhudur is the largest Buddhist Araama in Asia.

India & Sumatra

The geographical position of Sumatra marks it out as pre-eminently the earliest Hindu settlement in Indonesia. The earliest Hindu kingdom in Sumatra was Sri-Vijaya (Palembang). It was founded during or before the fourth century A.D. It rose to great eminence towards the close of the seventh century A.D. By that time, it had conquered another Hindu kingdom of Malaya and established its supremacy over the island of Banka. Thus, Singapore, which is a great city, now, was originally a settlement of the Sumatran colonists. The name, as you will notice, is a typical Indian name: Singhpur.

World's Largest Hindu Temple-Angkorwat complex of Cambodia

Bali or Balidvipa

Bali has been justly called the island of thousands of temples. Despite the loss of about 2500 temples due to earthquake, it still contains more than 4500 large and important temples. The most important is Pura Besakih, at the foot of the mountain Gunung Agung, and associated with the Hindu Trinity. It is said to have been founded by Warmadeva Keshari (Wira Dalem Kesari). The island of Bali possesses the unique distinction of being the only Hindu colony in the Far East, which still retains its old culture and civilization to a considerable extent. Islam has failed to penetrate into this island. The people are still proud of their Hindu connection. Vishnu, Shiva, Indra, Ganesh, Nandi, Krishna and the heroes of the Mahabharata are still known. The Vedas, the Mahabharata and the Ramayana are found there, although not in Sanskrit but in Kawi. The people call their deities as Devas. They have the temples of Durga and the images of Durga and Kaliki. The bodies of the dead are still burnt.

Borneo or Varunadvipa

Islands of Brunei are called as Varuna Dwipa.The earliest evidence of Hindu colonies of Borneo is furnished by inscriptions, which have been referred on paleographic grounds to about 400 A.D. These inscriptions refer to king Mula-varman, son of Asva-varman and grandson of king Kundunga. Mula-varman performed many Hindu sacrifices. The Sultan of Brunei (in Borneo) bore the title of Seri Bhagwan meaning Shree Bhagwan (Lord Almighty).

India & Cambodia or Khamboja - (Ancient Kamboja desa is today's Cambodia)

India is a country of temples with un-matched splendour, but there is a certain irony in that, one of the largest and most dramatic monuments to Hinduism rests not in India, but thousands of miles away from the subcontinent, amid the ruins of a metropolis hidden in the jungles of Cambodia (formerly known as Kamboja). One of the largest cities of the ancient world, Angkor was built by King Suryavarnam II to honour Lord Vishnu in the ninth century AD.

Cambodia boasts of the largest temple complex in the world, named Ankor, from the Sanskrit meaning "the capital city". It has become a symbol of Cambodia, appearing on its national flag, and it is the country's prime attraction for visitors.

Around the second century AD, Indians arrived in Funan (South Cambodia-Vietnam), and a Brahmin named Kaundinya married the daughter of the local Naga king and introduced Hindu religion and culture and Sanskrit to the region. The power center shifted to Angkor from the ninth to the fifteenth centuries A.D.

Sculptures on the great temple of Ankorwat depict the events of the Ramayana and the Mahabharatha. The main river of this country is called " Ma kang"- derived from the Indian name Maa-Ganga.

World's Largest Hindu Temple-Angkorwat Complex of Cambodia-another View

India & Burma

Burma was known as Indra-Dvipa. Hindu settlements began to established in Burma before the first century A.D

Literary and archaeological evidence shows that the entire culture and civilization of Burma was borrowed from India and not from China. Ptolemy, the geographer, tells us that in the 2nd century A.D. many places in Burma had Sanskrit names. Indian religions flourished in Burma. Many religious structures having the images of Indian gods and goddesses have also been found in Burma.

The names of its rivers are Sanskrit names - Irrawati, Brahmaputra and Chindwin. Her head of state is also known as Adipadi, which is the Sanskrit Adhaipati, meaning the chief executive.

Ganesh idol installed at the main crossroads - Thai Royal palace

India & Philipines

Even the national flower of Philippines is the Indian Champaka. The Indian influence on Philippines is explicable by the fact that it was for 150 years a colony of a Java-based Hindu Empire of Sri Vijaya.

When the Philippines drafted its Constitution, it placed the statue of Manu in the Assembly Hall with this inscription on its base: "The first, the greatest and the wisest law-giver of mankind.

Two Filipino scholars, Tavera and Paterno, have concluded that about 25% of the Philippine vocabularies can be traced to Indian influence.

For instance: bahagi (part, portion), in Tagalog is bhag in Hindi,

kathā (story, fiction) - kathā;
divatā (god or goddess) is devatā

dukha (poor, destitute) is duḥkha
guru (teacher) is guru
mukha (face) is mukha
yaya (nurse) is āyā and so on.

An adaptation of "The Ramayana, " the 4th century Indian epic, is preserved by the Maranao people of the South Philippines. A story of the battle between good and evil, filled with love, deceit, heroism and triumph is **Rajah Mangandiri" or "the Ramayana of the Philippines.**

Thailand – Siam

Hindu civilization spread to Siam in early times from about 2nd century A.D. The Hindus set up many colonies in Siam and the most important of them was Dvaravati, which ruled from Cambodia to the Bay of Bengal up to the 10th century A.D. when it was overthrown by the Kaundinya kingdom.

Although Thailand is today predominantly Buddhist, there are traces of Hindu influence, visible mostly in the court ceremonials. Until recently, the court Brahmins cast horoscopes, consulted omens, and performed worship of both Hindu and Buddhist deities.

Paintings depicting Ramayana in Thai Royal Palace

Even today, the kings of Thailand bear the royal title "Rama", a Hindu avatār, and the story of Ramayana is depicted on the palace and temple walls of Bangkok. Hindu festivals such as Daśaharā, commemorating the victory of Rama over the demon king Rāvaṇa, are still observed in Thailand. Famous Indian works, such as the Ramayana and the Mahabharata, and Shakuntala have formed the basis of some of the outstanding Siamese literature. The Ramayana, known in Siam as the "Ramakien" or "Ram-Akhyan" where "Akhya" is a Sanskrit word meaning "rendition or version of the story of". It is regarded as Siamese classic.

Indian influence is clearly seen on Siamese dance, drama, and music. Many of the themes of Siam's various dance-dramas (lakhon-ram) are drawn from Indian stories

The Siamese legal system has directly descended from the Manusmṛti. The Hindu Dharmaśāstras provided the framework for Siamese justice.

Malaya or Sri Vijaya

The greatest of the states was the Sailendra Empire, or the empire of Shri Vijaya, which became the dominant power both on sea and land in the whole of Malaysia by the eighth century. Malaysian peninsula derives its name from the Sanskrit word Malaya. Its other name was Vanga from its abundance of 'tin' because in Sanskrit 'Vanga' means tin.

The language and culture of Malaysia are still Sanskrit and Hindu. Take the name of Kuala Lumpur. The suffix 'Pur' is a Sanskrit termination used to signify a township. The original Sanskrit name was Cholanampuram. i.e. the city of the Cholas.

In Malaysia, the commander-in-chief is still called Lakṣmaṇa -- a remnant of the role played by Rama's brother in the battle of Lanka.

Kedah is by far the most important of Malayan sites. The Pallavas founded settlements in Kedah, on the Bujang River, whose temple ruins have yielded an image of Ganesha and other objects of Saiva faiths.

Malaya's literature and folklore are deeply influenced by the Hindu epics, the Ramayana, and the Mahabharata.

The Champa Today's Vietnam

Champa seems to have been mentioned under the name Angadvipa by the Vayu Purana.

According to Sir Charles Eliot, the Hindu dynasty of Champa was founded between 150 and 200 A.D. The conquerors were known as the Chams and hence the country came to be known as Champa. Vietnam, figures prominently as a stepping-stone in the story of India's cultural expansion to the Americas.

A Hindu dynasty was founded by Sri Mara in the second century A.D. A successor to Sri Mara was the famous king called Bhadravarma. He ruled over the Northern and Central portions of the kingdom comprising the provinces of Amravati and Vijaya and possibly also the Southern province of Panduranga. His greatest contribution to Hindu culture was the building of the temple of Bhadresvarasvamin (Shiva) at Myson, which became the national shrine of the Chams.

Champa passed through various dynasties and war with China continued in the 3rd and 4th century. This was a period of political unrest in China, and which gave Champa the opportunity to expand into Chinese territory. Shiva and Vishnu were worshipped by various names. Goddess Laxmi was known as Padma or Sri.

As regards literature, Sanskrit was the language of the learned. It was also the official language of the country. Many kings of Champa were Sanskrit scholars. Brāhmi script was used in inscriptions.

The books in use were the Vedas, Śāstras, the Epics, Buddhist philosophy, Saivism, Vaishnavism, Panini's grammar along with its commentary, Dharmaśāstras of Manu and Narada, the Puranas and classical Sanskrit literature including prose and Kāvya literature.

(Source: Adopted from the great website www.hinduwisdom.info)

82 Influencing East Asian Countries

Japan

"India is culturally, Mother of Japan. For centuries it has, in her own characteristic way, been exercising her influence on the thought and culture of Japan."Says Professor H. Nakamura of Japan (Source: India: Mother Of Us All - By Chaman Lal p. 25).

Buddhism stood as the bridge between India & Japan. Hinduism and Buddhism went from India to China and Korea to Japan.

India is called Tenjiku in Japan. Ancient India had direct sea contact with Japan and had strong trade links.

Images of Ganesha and Vishnu have been found throughout Japan. Numerous Buddhist deities were introduced into Japan and many of these are still very popular.

Ganesha is worshipped as **Sho-ten or Shoden** (literally, holy God) in many Buddhist temples, and is believed to confer happiness upon his devotees. There are some rare Ganesha bronzes as Vinayaka in Japan.

Even Shintoism adopted Indian gods, despite its desperate efforts after the Meiji Revolution (1868) to disengage itself from Buddhism. Today in Japan most people follow Shintoism, which consists of gods and deities like those of Hinduism.

The Indian sea **god Varuna** is worshipped in Tokyo as Sui-ten (water-God); the Indian goddess of learning, **Saraswati**, has become Benten (literally, goddess of speech), with many shrines dedicated to her along seacoasts and beside lakes and ponds.

Shiva is well known to the Japanese as **Daikoku** (literally, God of darkness), which is a Chinese and Japanese equivalent of the Indian Mahākāla, another name of Shiva. Daikoku is a popular god in Japan.

At the Kotohira shrine on the island of Shikoku, sailors worship a god called **Kompera**, which is a corruption of the Sanskrit word for crocodile, Kumbhira. The divine architect mentioned in the Ṛg Veda, Viśvakarmā, who designed and constructed the world, was regarded in ancient Japan as the god of carpenters, Bishukatsuma.

The Indian Yama, the god of death, is the most dreaded god of Japan, under the name of **Emmao**, the king of hell. There is considerable Indian influence on Japanese Art. A similarity between Shinto rituals and Hindu rituals - for example ringing the bell as one enters the temple.

The Indian script known as Siddham, called His-t'an in Chinese and Shittan in Japanese gained currency in Japan for writing Sanskrit from the 8th century. It was introduced by Kobo (a Buddhist monk) who was responsible for bringing Mantrayāna Buddhism from China to Japan.

In some Japanese temples, very ancient manuscripts in Sanskrit are preserved intact. It is significant that many of those manuscripts found in Japan are much older than those preserved in India.

(Source: India and World Civilization - By D. P. Singhal Part II p.20-27).

"Zen is the Japanese equivalent of Sanskrit Dhyāna (meditation) or Ch'an and is the name given to the sect founded in China by Bodhidharma". Says Sir Charles Elliot (1862-1931), British diplomat and colonial administrator, in his book, Hinduism and Buddhism, vol. I, p 405

Indian Jātaka stories, Indian Yoga, Indian Purāṇas, Indian legends, Indian samurāis, Indian deities, Indian Om are wonderfully integrated into the culture of Japan.

India & Korea

Korea was called Kaya deśa. Korean historians believe that Queen Huh was a princess of an ancient kingdom in Ayodhya.

"India is culturally, Mother of Japan. For centuries it has, in her own characteristic way, been exercising her influence on the thought and culture of Japan. Says Professor H. Nakamura of Japan

She went to Korea some two thousand years ago and started the Karak dynasty by marrying a local king, Suro. Today, the historians say, Queen Huh's descendant's number more than six million, including the South Korean president - Kim Dae Jung. (Source: Korean memorial to Indian princess - BBC.com).

Dr Seo Jeong-sun of Seoul National University and Kim Jong-il of Hallym University conducted a research and decoded the entire genetic code of ancient Korean remains. They have recently presented their findings at a meeting of the Korea Genome Organisation in Chuncheon, Gangwong province. The findings have gained interests in the backdrop of the popular Indian connection of Great Gaya dynasty.

(Source: Economic Times- Times News Network, Saturday, August 21, 2004 -As was reported by leading South Korean newspaper Joong Ang Daily on Friday)

Russia & Siberia

An ancient statue of Lord Vishnu has been found during excavation in an old village in Russia's Volga region, raising questions about the prevalent view on the origin of ancient Russia.

The statue found in Staraya (old) Maina village dates back to VII-X century AD. Staraya Maina village in Ulyanovsk region was a highly populated city 1700 years ago, much older than Kiev, so far believed to be the mother of all Russian cities. *(Source: Ancient Vishnu idol found in Russian town - Press Trust of India)*

Lake Baikal, which is in Siberia, was known to Hindus as lake "Vaikhanas"; there was a group of Ṛṣis known as "Vaikhanas", who meditated on the shores of the lake. Vaikhanas means deep and powerful thought.

According to official reports there are half a million people who adhere to their age-long faith, which is a mixture of Buddhism, Tāntrism and Śaivism and other `ways' (yāna) that have travelled there from India.

It is a syncretic faith, wherein India is the Holy Land, Sanskrit the divine language, and mantras are recited in Sanskrit, and every child has a certain `saṁskāra'. These half-a-million people look towards India for academic and cultural relations. They are keen to start Sanskrit studies in their colleges.

Some even want to study technical texts like the Aṣṭāṅga-hridaya of Vagbhatta in Āyurveda, which was translated into their language centuries ago.

Ayurveda is a living element of Buryat life. They term it 'national medicine'. From Siberia this national medicine (Ayurveda) travelled to European Russia. During the early part of the century, at Leningrad there was a famous Siberian doctor, Badmayef by name. His name is Sanskrit Padma with the Russian suffix-yef. He had also been summoned to treat Stalin

(Source: Cultural Relations of India and Siberia - Dr. Lokesh Chandra - Dialogue October - December 2001, Volume 3 No. 2).

It appears that a few years ago a Russian orientalist by name Prof. Ribakov from Moscow went to Kanchi to have the darshan and receive the blessings of the late Kanchi Paramācārya. The Paramacharya asked the Russian professor: 'Does not the northernmost part of Russia have more Sanskrit content in the language?' The professor was stunned. This scholar, who came to ask questions, shed tears of joy at the very sight of the Paramacharya and was dumbfounded at the depth of his scholarship. The Paramacharya further explained to the Russian that Russia was called 'Ṛṣi Varṣa' in ancient Indian Geography, because it was the land where our Ṛṣis like sage Yajñavalkya had their conference on the Vedas. This could further be corroborated by the fact that some women in the northernmost point of Russia have names like Lopamudrova, which is stunningly close to Lopamudra, wife of sage Agastya.

(Source: Adopted from the great website www.hinduwisdom.info)

“Ayurveda is a living element of Buryat life. They term it national medicine. From Siberia this national medicine (Ayurveda) travelled to European Russia.”

83 Ties with Rome & Egypt

Egypt

Indian contacts with the Western world date back to prehistoric times. Trade relations, preceded by the migration of peoples, inevitably developed into cultural relations. On the similar lines Indian **–Egyptian bond began ages ago.**

Egyptians claim to have migrated from a place called "Punth" from the mysterious land on the shore of Indian Ocean. Historians believe this land to be India.

Egyptians claim to have migrated from a place called "Punth" from the mysterious land on the shore of Indian Ocean. Historians believe this land to be India. Indian Terrocotta artifacts that were found in the region of sumar in Egypt reveal the Indian connection from second century BC.

In the Akkadian tongue, Indian cotton was expressed by ideographs meaning "vegetable cloth". Assurbanipal (668-626 B.C) cultivated Indian plants including the "wool-bearing trees" of India. Cotton is called "kapāsa" in Sanskrit. In Egypt it is called as "Karpus" According to the Skandha Purana, Egypt (Africa) was known as Sancha-dvipa continent mentioned in Sir Willliams Jones' dissertation on Egypt. At Alexandria, in Egypt, Indian scholars were a common sight: they are mentioned both by Dio Chrysostom (c. 100 A.D.) and by Clement (c. 200 A.D.)

Peter Von Bohlen (1796-1840) German Indologist compared India with ancient Egypt. He thought there was a cultural connection between the two in ancient times. There are elements of folk art, language, and rural culture of Bengal which have an affinity with their Egyptian counterparts and which have not been explained satisfactorily in terms of Aryan, Mongolian, or Dravidian influences. There are similarities between place names in Bengal and Egypt and recently an Egyptian scholar, El Mansouri, has pointed out that in both Egypt and India the worship of cow, sun, snake, and river are common.

Max Müller had also observed that the mythology of Egyptians (and also that of the Greeks and Assyrians) is wholly founded on Vedic traditions. Eusebius, a Greek writer, has also recorded that the early Ethiopians emigrated from the river Indus and first settled in the vicinity of Egypt.

The brightest evidence of India's direct relations with Egypt is, however, preserved in the Mauryan Emperor Ashok's thirteenth rock edict, inscribed in the early decades of the third century B.C. In it, Emperor Ashoka refers to his contacts with Ptolemy II Philadelphus of Egypt (285-246 BC), in connection with the expansion of his policy of the propagation of the Law of Righteousness (dharma).

Ashoka, in his second rock edict, refers to the philanthropic activities undertaken by him. He records that he had made arrangements for the medical treatment of men and animals in the territories of his own empire as well as in the region ruled by Antiochus Theos II of Syria (260-246 BC) and its neighbouring kingdoms, which also included Egypt. (Source: India and Egypt: Influences and Interactions - edited by Saryu Doshi).

"It is testified by many historians that Herdotus, Plato, Salon, Pythagoras, and Philostratus that the religion of Egypt proceeded from India...." source: India and Egypt: Influences and Interactions - edited by Saryu Doshi).

Historians have long known that Egypt and India traded by land and sea during the Roman era. Many European texts had clearly referred to the commercial exchange of luxury goods, including fabrics, spices and wine between the two.

Rome

Roman connection with India dates back to 23 AD that happened mostly through Egypt.Trade and commerce flourished between India and Rome; Romans used to buy Indian sesame oil. They purchased indigo-dyed clothes, silk, ivory tusk, perfumes and other valuable products from Kashmir.

Aryabhata, Indian Astronomer (5 AD) refers to the city in Rome as Romika, while describing the sunrise and sunset. Varahamihir (6 AD) in his text "Pañca siddhānta", describes the school of thought called "Romaka" siddhānta. India might have had connections with Rome through Egypt or through Greece during the early centuries of Christian era.

(Source: Adopted from the great website www.hinduwisdom.info)

The Father of the Modern India, a Rare Indian Genius

Mahatma Gandhi (1869-1948)

"Generations to come, it may be, will scarce believe that such one as this ever in flesh and blood walked upon this earth".

- Albert Einstein on Gandhi

"Mahatma Gandhi's life achievement stands unique in political history. He has invented a completely new and humane means for the liberation war of an oppressed country, and practiced it with greatest energy and devotion. The moral influence he had on the consciously thinking human being of the entire civilized world will probably be much more lasting than it seems in our time with its overestimation of brutal violent forces."

- Albert Einstein on Gandhi

(Collected works of Gandhi-Volume 54)

"........If humanity is to progress, Gandhi is inescapable. He lived, thought, acted and inspired by the vision of humanity evolving toward a world of peace and harmony............."

- Dr. Martin Luther King, Jr. on Gandhi

"We in South Africa brought about our new democracy relatively peacefully on the foundations of such thinking, (Gandhian) regardless of whether we were directly influenced by Gandhi or not."
"He dared to exhort nonviolence in a time when the violence of Hiroshima and Nagasaki had exploded on us; he exhorted morality when science, technology and the capitalist order had made it redundant; he replaced self-interest with group interest without minimizing self."

"At a time when Freud was liberating sex, Gandhi was reining it in; when Marx was pitting worker against capitalist, Gandhi was reconciling them; when the dominant European thought had dropped God and soul out of the social reckoning, he was centralizing society in God and soul; at a time when the colonized had ceased to think and control, he dared to think and control; and when the ideologies of the colonized had virtually disappeared, he revived them and empowered them with a potency that liberated and redeemed."

- Nelson Mandela on Gandhi

(January 3, 2000 issue of TIME magazine).

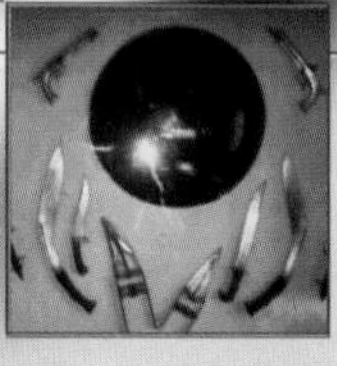

Indian Miltary Skills
Yuddha kalā - Pratibhā

84 Indian Science of Warfare

In India, Kshatra Dharma was very much prevailing during Vedic times. Kshatra Dharma is not limited to ruling the kingdom, but it includes protecting the kingdom too. Warrior caste in India assumed the responsibility of defending the country from enemies. They believed it to be the ordained duty to protect the Kingdom.

Indian science of warfare was a well-developed knowledge. Many ancient institutions in India had imparted that knowledge to the students. Yuddha Vidyā or Yuddha Śāstra had recognized two kinds of warfare. One is Dharma Yuddha. The Second kind is Kuṭila Yuddha.

Indians gave importance to the first school of warfare that is Dharma Yuddha. It was waged on the ethical principles pertaining to Kshtra dharma. Valour and righteousness were given equal importance in this style of warfare.

Warfare strategies, War laws, War ethics, guidance to building of armies, army operations and maintenance, building weapons and their operations, erecting arsenals and ordinance factories, were elaborately described and discussed in the literature related to two Upavedas.

These two Upavedas are

1. Dhanurveda- Upaveda to Yajur Veda.
2. Arthasastra- Upaveda to Atharva Veda.

Apart from the above two major works, Dharma Sastras, epics like Ramayana and Mahabharata, Puranas like Agni, Vishnu, Skandha deal with the knowledge of warfare.

Indian king was supposed to maintain Chaturaṅga bala (four kinds of armies). They are Ratha (war vehicles like chariots etc), Gaja (elephants), Turaga (Horses), and Padati (soliders). Three kinds of

Dalas (forces) were maintained by the kings. They are Vāyu Sena (Air force), Navka Sena (Naval force) and Padati sena (Military). Wars used to be waged in air, on the sea and on the ground.

During war times common people were never troubled. Winner never looted the subjects of the defeated king.

The above fact was described by the Greek ambassador and historian, Magasthenus who stayed in India during Chandra Gupta's regime (4th century BC).

In India, farmers ploughed the fields calmly, when warriors fought battles. Commoners were neither tortured nor looted. They remained in villages as usual, when fierce battles were waged in the battlefields. This is a unique feature of Indian wartime ethics. In other countries, there was loot, arson, anarchy and devastation during wartime. (A Brief history of India by Alain Danielou-p no 106)

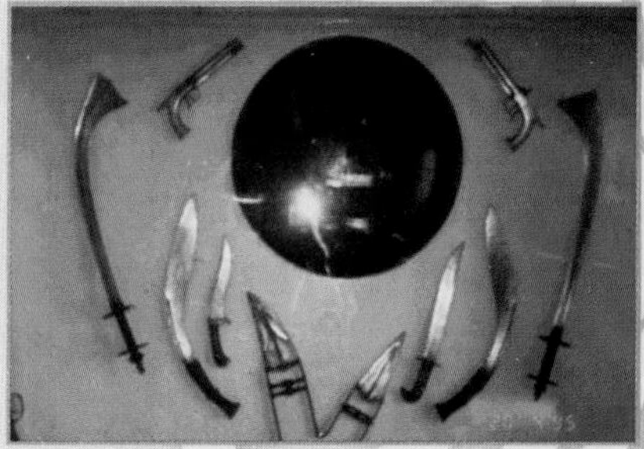

"Dhanuṣa Chandrodaya" and *"Dhanuṣa Pradīpa"* are the Sanskrit texts of Dhanurveda. There are around sixty thousand ślokas explaining the methods, techniques, strategies, and ethics of warfare.

Weapons:

Dhanurveda explains the four kinds of weapons. They are :

a) Mukta (that can be triggred or released) *b) Amukta c) Mukthamukta d) Yantramukta etc.*

"Niti prakāśaka", an artha śastra treatise describes three kinds,

a) Mukta b) Amukta c) Mantra Mukta.

"Yukta kalpataru" of Bhojarāja, had classified weapons into two categories, they are Mikam and Nirmayam.

Kauṭilya's Artha śāstra also had classified the weapons into various categories.

Indian weapons that were used to Attack – Dhanuṣa (Bow), Khaḍaga (Sword), Śūla (Spear), Gadā (Club), Chakra (Pointed disc) Nalika (Gun), Shathagni (Canon), Dhupha (Missile) etc;

Indian weapons that were used to defend –Sirathranam (Helmet), kavacham (Armour), kanṭha kavacham (Neck Armour), Kanchukam (Shield) etc.

Ancient Indians used machines (Yantras) during wars. Machines were of various kinds, Machines that were used in Vimānas (Aircrafts); Machines that throw huge boulders on the Enemies; Machines that make fierce war sounds; Machines that showered fire on the enemies.

The description about the various machines can be found in Sanskrit texts

a) *Samarangana Sutradhara- written by King Bhoja*
b) *Yantra Sarvaswam- written by Bharadwaja.*
c) *Artha Sastra- written by Kautilya*
d) *Sukraniti – written by Sukracharya*
e) *Sakti tantra/sutras- written by Agastya*

Agneyaastra: Kauṭilya had discussed various kinds of firearms and their manufacture. Fire arrows were powered with certain combustible material like Agni dharana, Viswasagati etc. The book describes the preparation of various combustible materials.

Sukraniti, describes Agni Bāṇas. It gives the recipe for preparing the Gunpowder. Gunpowder is called Agni chūrṇam. On the fort citadels, many war machines called "Sathagni" were placed in ancient times. Sukraniti describes the weapons called "Nalikas", (equal to modern guns), which were used to kill people through blasts from a distance. Two types of nalikas were described in Sukraniti, smaller one and larger one.

Swords: Indian swords were world famous. They were made of high quality steel. Indian swords were called, "Damascus" swords. Indians had the talents of engraving watermarks on the swords. The word wotez steel had been derived from Indian word "ukku" for steel.

Artha śāstra texts describe about various aspects of foreign policy, war strategy, making peace and treaty; etc; the famous adage "enemy's enemy is my friend" is a kauṭilyan exhortation.

The famous Artha sastra texts that are available today are :

1. *Cāṇakya's Artha Śāstra.*
2. *śukrācārya's Śukranīti*
3. *Kamandaka's Arthaśāstra.*

Ancient Indians respected the enemy's skills & valour. They had given importance to war ethics. They used advanced technology in warfare, yet human destruction was never aimed at.

India in its history of past ten thousand years, never invaded any country, inspite of having effective trade & cultural links with other countries. Kings within India fought wars among themselves, but never troubled the commoners. Looting and arson are foreign in origin; Indians never knew them.

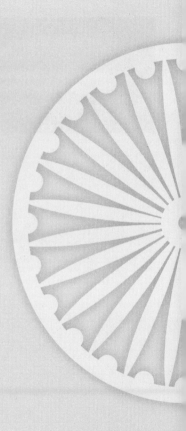

85 History's First Atomic Explosion at Harappa

It was 1920 AD, Archeologists excavated a great civilization called Indus valley civilization at the ruins of Harappa and Mohen-jo-daro (now in Pakistan).

World stood in awe & wonder by seeing the grandeur of advanced civilization and technology that existed 5000 years ago.

Eternal Indian talents are echoed in every excavated brick that stood for thousands of centuries. The underground drainage system that prevailed during those times, the town planning skills that were possessed by the citizens of these cities only reverberate the heights achieved by the ancient Indian genius.

But archeologists and many scientists were equally surprised to learn the facts about the sudden collapse or destruction of these mighty cities of great civilization.

Two European scientists Davenport and Vencenti put forward an amazing theory. They concluded that the cities had been ruined due to a nuclear explosion.

They found big stratums of clay & green glass. Similar layers of green glass can be found in Nevada and other deserts where nuclear explosions are tested.

The researchers estimated that ruins that exist today are fragments of the ancient city that had been melted at high temperatures of around 15000 Centigrate.

Dozens of Skeltons were found in the area of Mohenjodaro & Harappa, their radio activity exceeded the norm almost by 50 times.

Researchers also found the strictly outlined epicenter, where all buildings were razed to the ground. The calamity of destruction lessened towards the outskirts of the city. Explosion would have occurred for a very short duration.

Historian Kisari Mohan Ganguli says that Indian sacred writings are full of such descriptions, which sound like an atomic blast as experienced in Hiroshima and Nagasaki. He says references mention fighting sky chariots and finishing weapons. An ancient battle is described in the Droṇa Parva, a section of the Mahabharata. Ganguli further says "The passage tells of combat where explosions of finishing weapons decimate entire armies, causing crowds of warriors with steeds and elephants and weapons to be carried away as if they were dry leaves of trees"

Consider these other verses from the ancient (6500 BC) Mahabharata:

> *...a single projectile charged with all the power of the Universe.*
> *An incandescent column of smoke and flame, As bright as the thousand suns*
> *Rose in all its splendour... a perpendicular explosion with its billowing smoke clouds...*
> *...the cloud of smoke rising after its first explosion formed into expanding round circles*
> *like the opening of giant parasols...it was an unknown weapon,*
> *An iron thunderbolt, A gigantic messenger of death,*
> *Which reduced to ashes The entire race of the Vṛṣnis and the Andhakas.*
> *...The corpses were so burned as to be unrecognisable.*
> *The hair and nails fell out; Pottery broke without apparent cause,*
> *And the birds turned white.*
> *After a few hours all foodstuffs were infected... ...to escape from this fire*
> *The soldiers threw themselves in streams, To wash themselves and their equipment.*

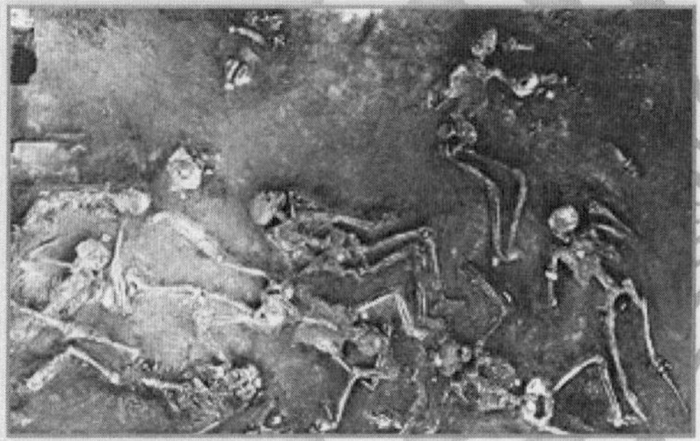

Pile of Skeletons found at Harappa Ruins

Until the bombing of Hiroshima and Nagasaki, modern mankind could not imagine any weapon as horrible and devastating as those described in the ancient Indian texts. Yet they very accurately described the effects of an atomic explosion. Radioactive poisoning will make hair and nails fall out. Immersing oneself in water gives some respite, though it is not a cure.

Interestingly, Manhattan Project chief scientist Dr J. Robert Oppenheimer was known to be familiar with ancient Sanskrit literature. In an interview conducted after he watched the first atomic test (conducted in Almogardo desert of America), he quoted from the Bhagavad Gita: "Divi sūrya sahasrasya", (light of thousand suns shinning at a time, -Gita 11th chapter-12th śloka), describing the illumination created by blast.

When asked in an interview at Rochester University seven years after the Alamogordo Nuclear test whether that was the first atomic bomb ever to be detonated? His reply was, "Well, yes, in modern history."

Another curious sign of an ancient nuclear impact in India is a giant crater near Bombay. The nearly circular 2,154-metre-diameter Lonar crater, located 400 kilometres northeast of Bombay and aged at less than 50,000 years old, could be related to nuclear warfare of antiquity. No trace of any meteoric material, etc. has been found at the site or in the vicinity, and this is the worlds only known "impact" crater in basalt. Indications of great shock (from a pressure exceeding 600,000 atmospheres) and intense, abrupt heat (indicated by basalt glass spherules) can be ascertained from the site. There are many indications of earlier nuclear holocausts that horrified the mankind. Indian example is only one such.

Indians give vital importance to spirituality. After experiencing the tragedies of war and dreadful weapons, Indians might have shunned these technologies ages ago.

Source: 1.www.ancientx.com 2. Towards Grand unification –Dilip Kulkarni. (Vivekananda Kendra Patrika-Aug1993-pg116) 3. Ancient Nuclear Blasts & leviating stones of Shivpur Alexander Pechersky

"Two European scientists Davneport and Vencenti put forward an amazing theory. They concluded that the cities (Harrappa and Mohen-jo-daro) had been ruined due to a nuclear explosion."

86 Inventing Gun Powder

The Chinese work of 1044 AD Wu-ching tsung-yao gives the earliest gunpowder formula in any civilization. Historians say so. Some of them also say that, during 1400 AD, Indians learnt the art of making gunpowder from the Chinese.

But, theTruth seems to be different. There are many evidences to substantiate the fact that Indian knowledge about Gunpowder, dates back to centuries before the birth of Christ.

Indians called gunpowder as *"Agni Cūrnam"*. In fact, Chinese and Arabs would have learnt the recipe of making Gunpowder from Indians.

The Agnicūrṇa or Gunpowder was composed of 4 to 6 parts of saltpetre, one part of sulphur, and one part of Charcoal of Arka, Sruhi and other trees burnt in a pit and reduced to powder. Here is certain evidence of the ancient rockets giving place to actual guns in warfare. From the description of the composition of gunpowder, the composition of the Śukra Niti can be dated at the pre-Gupta age.

(Source: War in Ancient India - By V. R. Ramachandra Dikshitar 1944. p. 103 -105).

We find from Indian medical books, that Indians were perfectly well-acquainted with the constituents of gun-powder - sulphur, charcoal, saltpetre - had them all at hand in great abundance. It is very unlikely that they should not have discovered their inflammability, either singly or in combination.

In *Dhanvantari Nigantu* (Medical lexicon) salt petre is termed as a medicine. It is called Sauvarcha Lavana or Krishna Lavana (Potassium nitrate). It is mostly used in indigestion. Even Śukra Niti refers saltpetre as sauvarcha lavana.

Letters written by Alexander to Aristotle say" Indians have showered the rain of fire on our armies" *(Dantes Inferno xiv-31-7).*

"Indians called gunpowder as Agni Churnam. In fact, Chinese and Arabs would have learnt the recipe of making Gunpowder from Indians."

In the 12th century, we find pieces of ordinance being taken to battlefields in the armies of Prithviraj. In the 25th stanza of Prithviraja Rasa it is said "The calivers and cannons made a loud report when they were fired off, and the noise which issued from the ball was heard at a distance of ten kosas".

It is said that the Turkish word "top" and the Persian "tupang" or "tufang" are derived from the Sanskrit word "Dhupa". The "Dhupa" of the Agni Purana means a rocket; the word Bāṇa is also called a missile or an arrow.

The Atharva Veda shows the employment of firearms with lead shots. The Aitareya Brahmana describes an arrow with fire at its tip. In the Mahabharata and Ramayana, the employment of Agneyaśastras is frequently mentioned.

Śukranīti often uses the word "Nalika", which can be nothing else, but the gun. Śukranīti while referring to firearms (Agneyaśastras) says that before any war, the duty of the minister of war is to check up the total stock of Gunpowder in the arsenal.

The installation of *"yantras"* (engines of war) inside the walls of the forts referred to by "Manasollasa". And the reference of **"Sataghni"** (killer of hundreds of men) pressed into service for the protection of the forts by *"Samaranganasutradhara"* clearly reveals the frequent use of firearms in the battlefield.

The above references only confirm Indian acquaintance of usage of gunpowder and firearms.

87 World's First Rocket Launches

We have substantial evidence to prove that in modern times, Indians are the first to fire rockets and missiles in the world.

Rockets helped the Mysore army to achieve a famous victory over the British in 1780. The army was led by Hyder Ali, a bold officer who had become the effective ruler of the Mysore state afterwards. The fortunes of the English in India had fallen to their lowest watermark, with this battle in the second Anglo-Mysore War.

Not many people know that the hero of Waterloo, Colonel Arthur Wellesley (1769-1852), (who defeated Napoleon at the famous battle of Waterloo (1815)), had to run away from the battlefield, when attacked by the rockets and musket-fire of Tipu Sultan's army. (Hyder Ali'son).

It happened at the time of the Fourth Anglo-Mysore war (April 1799). Col.Wellesley was advancing towards Srirangapatnam, (Tipu's capital city). The British army was attacked at Sultanpet after dark on the 5th April, by a tremendous fire of musketry and rockets. The men gave way and retreated in disorder.

Tippu's Rocket hitting British army-a painting

The 'Sultanpet incident' had a profound and traumatic effect on Arthur Wellesley. His biographer Guedalla tells us that, even late in his life, after Waterloo, the unpleasant night lived vividly in Arthur's memory.

Tipu Sultan met a hero's end on 4th May while defending his capital *Srirangapatanam.* Along with the enormous loot another precious gift from India arrived in England. It was the Mysorean rocket, two specimens of which can still be seen in the *Royal Artillery Museum,* Woolwich *Arsenal London.*

Our honourable Ex-President of India, Dr. APJ Abdul Kalam (then Director Defence Research & Development Laboratory Hyderabad, India) says in his essay The History of Indian Rocketry, **30th November 1991.**

"I learnt that two of the war rockets captured by the British at Srirangapatanam have been displayed in the Museum of Artillery at Woolwich in London. One of my missions during my visit to Europe in 1980 was to study this rocket. Dr.V.R.Gowarikar and I visited the museum. It was a great thrill especially for Rocket technologists like us, to see an Indian innovation in a foreign soil well-preserved and with facts not distorted.

Under the heading "India's War Rocket", the following details are recorded in the Woolwhich museum London. The motor casing of this rocket is made of steel with multi nozzle holes, with the sword blade as the warhead. The propellant used was packed gunpowder. Weight of the rocket is about 2 kg. With about 1 kg of propellant. 50 mm in dia about 250 mm length, the range performance is reported 900 mts to 1.5 km. our designers analyzed and confirmed their performance. What a simple and elegant design effectively used in war".

Missiles are not new to Indians, ages before Tipu's rockets; ancient Indians used missiles in wars.

Ancient Indian literature is replete with missile references. Purāṇas talk about " Agneya astra"; Mahabharata and Ramayana do mention about various missiles used during the war.

In "Śukranīti" written by Śukrācārya; Vyśampāyana's "Nīti Prakaśika"; Agni Purāṇa, and Kauṭilya's Arthaśāstra, we find reference of missile technology.

Governing Skills of Ancient India
Dharma Dīpti & Rājanīti Dakṣatā

88 Dharma Śāstras – The Science of Ethics

'Dharmo Rakṣati Rakṣitaḥa'
'Protect Dhaarma, Dharma Protects you'

What is Dharma or Righteousness? Fish swim in water. Birds fly in air. Plants grow but don't move. Man lives on the earth. Every being in this creation acts according to certain laws of nature. All beings are bound by charecteristic nature. Human being alone has freedom to use his intellect. Other beings do not have such freedom. Other beings float with nature's rhythm and cadence; Animal's life is a sensual experience; whereas human's life alone is an attitudinal expression. The independent intellectual expression of human being requires certain guiding principles from time to time to make him follow the laws of nature. These behavioural exhortations are called "Dharmas". Human being loses the rhythm of life, if he violates Dharma. He is in tune with it, if he follows Dharma; Dharma protects the person, who adheres to it.

This Dharma made Rāma win over Rāvaṇa. This Dharma had ensured victory for Pāṇḍavas over Kauravas. For protecting this Dharma, the Lord himself often descends on the earth; God supports them, who support Dharma.

Sanātana Dharma flourishes through *"Śruti"*, *"Smriti"* and *"Purāṇas"* and had gifted us the Dhārmic principles suiting various contexts and different times. Śrutis are Vedas; Smṛtis had adapted the essence of śrutis and conveyed to us the life guiding principles, which regulate and refine our lives. These Smṛtis are popularly called Dharma Śāstras.

Eighteen sages of yore, who had assimilated the essence of Vedas, had given us this knowledge of Dharma śāstras *(1) Manu Smṛti (2) Parāśara Smṛti (3) Yājñavalkya Smṛti (4) Gautama Smṛti (5) Harita Smṛti (6) Yama Smṛti (7) Viṣṇu Smṛti (8) Sanka Smṛti (9) Likhita Smṛti (10) Bṛhaspati Smṛti (11) Dakṣa Smṛti (12) Aṅgirasa Smṛti (13) Prasita Smṛti (14) Samavarta Smṛti (15) Apasthamba Smṛti (16) Atri Smṛti (17) Sathapata Smṛti (18) Akanas Smṛti*

For these eighteen smṛtis there are upa-smṛtis. If there are conflicts of opinion among smṛtis, then one has to refer to *"Dharma Śāstra Nibandhanas"*. These nibandhanas vary from place to place, region to region.

Every Dharma śāstra contains principles relating to three aspects; they are "Ācāra", "Vyavāhāra" and "Prāyaścitta".

- *Varṇa Āśhrama Dharma, (Guiding principles -relating to division of labour)*
- *Saṁskāra Dharma, (Guiding principles – relating to sanctifying ceremonies like Birth, marriage, death etc)*
- *Āśrama Dharma, (Guiding principles for various stages of life- studentlife, marriedlife, oldage and renunciation)*
- *Rāja Dharmas, (Guiding principles for the kings)*
- *Dāna Dharmas, (Guiding principles for making charity)*
- *Dharma Sūkṣmas, (Subtle Laws of ethics)*
- *Sikṣā, (Punishment and penal code)*
- *Pāpa-Parihāra, (Guiding principles for redemption of sins)*
- *Dīkṣā, (Guiding principles for following austerities)*
- *Varasatva Adhikāra, (Inheritance rights of various persons)*

Manu Smṛti had been popularized by Western scholars and often used by them to divide Indian society. Manu Smṛti offers more positive values than negative values, if one understands it from Indian perspective.

If there is conflict of opinion between the Srutis and Smritis, then one has to follow the dictates of Śrutis, the Vedic precincts. Smṛtis are man made; Śrutis are nature's laws (Not created by man).

The principles of Dharmaśāstras are the essence of Vedas and are refined and perfected quite often in every Yuga. When other parts of the world are struggling to exist, surviving on competition, India blossomed with laws of harmony and order to manifest human excellence; thanks to sages who had gifted dharma śāstras to Indians.

Sri PV Kafe published a book, "The History of Dharma Śāstras". This book gives us a clear perspective of Dharma śāstras.

"The independent intellectual expression of human being requires certain guiding principles from time to time to make him follow the laws of nature. These behavioural exhortations are called Dharmas. Human being loses the rhythm of life, if he violates Dharma."

89 Nyāya Śāstra–The Science of Logic/ Reasoning

Nyāya Śāstra remains as the ever-shinning Gem of Indian Crown of Talents. It reveals the heights achieved by Indian intellect in systematizing the Knowledge.

Every scholar of ancient Indian studies, masters *"The Ṣaḍ Dharśanas"*, (six schools of philosophy) which is more than today's M.phil. Nyāya Śāstra is one among the six schools of philosophy.

The other name for *Nyāya Śāstra* is *"Tarka Śāstra"* (The science of Reasoning/Logic). *Guatama Mahā Muni* was the author of *Nyāya Śāstra.* This book is unique in the world.

Guatama Maha Muni

The logical aphorisms described here, develop the reasoning faculty in the student, in a systematic way. This knowledge is not only used to interpret the Vedic meaning, but also applied to various sciences like *Astronomy, Mathematics, Botany, Āyurveda, Veda Mīmāṁsā* and *Upaniṣads* etc.

Kanād's Vaiśeṣika Śāstra is also read with *Nyāya Śāstra*, which reveals the physical laws of this universe.

The quest for truth compels a person to get into philosophical reasoning. *Nyaya Sastra* supports such enquiry with its four pillars of proofs or substantiation.

1.Pratyakṣa 2.Anumāna 3.Upamāna & 4.Śabda;

1. Pratyakṣa: The method of confirmation of truth, that is grossly visible to our eyes; that can be heard through our ears; that are tangible to our perceptions;

2. Anumāna: The method of confirmation of truth through inference and logic; for example: smoke viewed from a distance; one may not actually see the fire, yet concludes the existence of fire based on the visibility of smoke; The above inference is based on the logic that without fire there cannot be a smoke; The truth which is inferred is called" sādhya" and the reasoning or the object the truth is inferred is called "sādhana"; here fire is sādhya and smoke is "sādhana".

3. Upamāna: Upamāna is the method of revealing the truth through comparison or by the use of a simile. This method is quite popularly used in the field of literature.

4. Śabda: Śabda is the method of establishing the truth through Vedic reference or Vedic authority. The knowledge of applied sciences is always collaborated with Vedic authenticity.

For the sake of simplifying this complicated logic, many standard logical dictums were evolved. They are called by various names

1. *Kṣīra nīra nyāya-* water is mixed with the milk, not otherwise; in the milk of goodness, the mistakes get absorbed like water drops.

2. *Laghu Guru nyāya-* small object gets attracted towards the big object; disiciple goes in search of guru; Aryabhatta uses this Nyāya sūtra to describe the fact that earth goes round the sun, not otherwise.

Other maxims are like Kalpa kurma nyāya, Nukasakata nyāya, sthalipulaka nyāya & kakathaliya nyāya etc.

Hundreds of Nyāya sūtras are elaborately discussed by sage Gautama to instil the sense of logic and reasoning among the students.

The edifice of Ancient Indian knowledge was not built on the foundations of blind beliefs and figs of imagination, but was erected on the solid base of logic and reasoning. This science confers that truth.

“The logical aphorisms described here, develop the reasoning faculty in the student, in a systematic way. This knowledge is not only used to interpret the Vedic meaning, but also applied to various sciences like Astronomy, Mathematics, Botany, Ayurveda, Veda Mimamsa and Upanishads etc.”

90 India – The Cradle of Democracy

India is the bedrock of all Democracies. The most popular system of self-Governance was very much popular in ancient India. As popularly believed, it was not brain wave of the westerners.

Will Durant, an American Historian says: **" India is the mother of democracy".** He points out that the Greek Assembly, the Roman Agora or the German Moot, the antecedents of modern democracy, were derived from the Indian institution known as Samiti or Sabhā recorded in the Vedas. In fact, there was a democratic deity called Samajñāna to whom the last hymn of the Ṛg Veda makes salutation".

(Source: The Soul of India - By Satyavrata R Patel p.137).

Indian parliament at New Delhi

The Vedic terminologies like *Samiti, Sabhā, Saṅga, Vidhata, Pariṣad, Samudaya and Samana* are the various elected bodies or assemblies of people, who sat together to discuss varied issues relating to people etc.

Gaṇa Rājyas can be equated to present day Republics. Megasthenes, writing about political situation of India in 300 B.C., records that sovereignty (kingship) was dissolved and democratic governments were set up in a number of places. The historians of Alexander's campaign also mention that during his retreat, Alexander actually came across many Indian republics. Indeed, all the states with which he made contact on his way back appear to have been under republican form of government which are free, autonomous and independent.

Nysa, a city on the border of modern Afghanistan and Pakistan was ruled by a president named Aculphis and a council of 300.

The Buddha was born in a republican country, and it is not without significance that he should have called the monastic order he founded the Republic of the Bhikkus (Monks), the name "Republic" suggesting that he transferred the constitution of a political to a religious order. Thus, independent democratic and aristocratic republics seem to have flourished widely throughout the continent of India for a period of nearly a thousand years, a period that ended with the establishment of the Gupta Empire in A.D. 300. The outstanding feature of the republican system during this period is known as the "Gaṇa Rājya", or rule of numbers, that is to say, the rule of many persons.

(Source: The Story of Indian Civilization - By C. E. M. Joad p. 108-111).

Buddhist texts "Maha-parinibhana suthanthu", "Mahavagga", "kullavagga", describe byelaws and ways of conduct of Bouddha-saṅghas, voting methods, invalid votes, implementing the decisions of the majority etc.

The Marquis of Zetland former Viceroy of India, has written:

"And it may come as a surprise to many to learn that in the Assemblies of the Buddhists in India, 2,000 years and more ago, are to be found the rudiments of our Parliamentary practice of the present day. The dignity of the Assembly was preserved by the appointment of a special officer - the embryo of 'Mr. Speaker' in our House of Commons. A second officer was appointed whose duty it was to see that when necessary a quorum was secured - the prototype of the Parliamentary 'Chief Whip' in our own system. A member initiating business did so in the form of a 'motion', which was then open for discussion. In some cases this was done once only, in others three times, thus, anticipating the practice of Parliament in requiring that a Bill be read a third time before it becomes a law. If discussion disclosed a difference of opinion, the matter was decided by a vote of the majority, the voting being a ballot." ***(Source: The Legacy of India - edited By G. T. Garrett p. x-xii).***

"

Will Durant, an American Historian says: "India is the mother of democracy . He points out that the Greek Assembly, the Roman Agora or the German Moot, the antecedents of modern democracy, were derived from the Indian institution known as Samiti or Sabha recorded in the Vedas."

"

Pāṇini, the 5th century BC Grammarian, in his famous book "Aṣṭādhyāyī", had discussed words "Janapada", "Saṅghas", "Gaṇas"; he had also indicated the interactions between various elected bodies. He had described about votes, election, quorum etc and also explained the political situation prevailing in those times.

Pāṇini further says there was "a craze for constituting new republics" which "had reached the climax in the Vahika country and north-west India where clans constituting of as many as one hundred families only organized themselves as Gaṇas." Furthermore, power in some republics was vested in a large number of individuals. In a well-known Jātaka tale we are told that in the Licchavi capital of Vaishali, there were 7707 kings (Rajas), 7707 viceroys, 7707 generals, and 7707 treasurers.

(Source: Democracy in Ancient India - By Steve Muhlberger).

According to Kauṭilya there were two kinds of Janapadas,

1. Ayudhiya-praya, those made up mostly of soldiers.

2. Sreni-praya, those comprising guilds of craftsmen, traders, and agriculturalists.

When British entered India, the democracy was prevailing only at the grass root level i.e at village level "Gram pañcāyats". All other systems of Indian Governance had already become defunct before the advent of British.

Sir Charles Napier Metcalfe in an official report to the British Parliament writes, "The village communities are little republics having nearly everything they want within themselves. They seem to last when nothing else lasts. Dynasty after dynasty tumbles, revolution succeeds revolution, but the village community remains the same". *(Source: The Soul of India - By Satyavrata R Patel p.144).*

The inscriptions on the walls of the Sundaravarada temple in Uttiramerur, near Kanchipuram, show how democracy was practised 1,000 years ago in South India.

The village is known for its historic inscription of a written constitution that deals with elections to the village assembly, qualifications required of candidates contesting in elections, circumstances under which a candidate may be disqualified, mode of election, tenure of the elected candidates and the right of the public to recall the elected members when they failed to discharge their duties properly and so on.

It is interesting how in every aspect of life the highest standard of democracy was enforced in Uttiramerur.

(Source: DR. R. Nagaswamy the Director of Archaeology, Tamil Nadu in an article written in 'Hindu' dt: 10th October 2003)

91 Indian Governing Principles Through Ages

> While appointing people to various positions in your government, you might have appointed intelligent people for the high positions; mediocre people for the middle level positions; people with low intellect for lower positions; haven't you?
>
> - Lord Rama's Advice to Bharatha

The sciences of management, administration and governance were evolved into major subjects of learning, ages ago, in India.

Takshasila, an ancient Indian University, was the major centre for mastering political science. Acharya Chanakya was a renowned political scholar of that famed university. His treatise still remains to us as the source of authority to teach us administrative principles. Many kings, ministers and teachers, would come to such universities for studying the science of governance.

Today we find these governing principles elaborately discussed in Arthasastra texts like Kautilya's Arthasastra & Sukraniti. Sage Valmiki and Sage Vyasa had wonderfully inter-woven the knowledge of political thought and resource management techniques in the Ramayana & the Mahabharata.

Valmiki Ramayana- Ayodhya Kāṇḍa

Lord Rama teaches the secrets of administration & governing principles to his brother king Bharata, when the latter meets the former in the forest. Sage Valimiki had wonderfully composed 100 verses, which reveal the knowledge of good Governance.

100th Sarga of Ayodhya kanda of Valmiki Ramayana contains the 100 verses about the governing techniques. Let us discuss a few of them...

- Rama says to Bharata "You might have appointed your council of ministers, who are loyal to you, who are fearless, straight forward, highly ethical in their conduct, who are well-versed in the matters of political science & governance, who have good family background and come from a high lineage, who behave accordingly after understanding your intentions; Haven't you?"(Ay.K-100/16)

- "While appointing people to various positions in your government, you might have appointed intelligent people for the high positions; mediocre people for the middle level positions; people with low intellect for lower positions; haven't you?"(Ay.K-100/26)
- "Hope, your decisions are not agitating the people. Hope, you are being rightly advised in this regard by your ministers."(Ay.K-100/28)
- "You might have appointed an efficient person as your Army general, who knows the art of warfare, who is loyal to you and who is contented with your remuneration and honours; haven't you? (Ay.K-100/31)
- "Remuneration & Salaries are to be paid regularly to employees without delay and default. Otherwise they express disregard to the royal authority. Hope you are honoring your commitments from time to time". (100/34)
- "Persons who are native & born in your country, persons who can understand the feelings & opinions of other kings, persons who convey the message to other kings without distortion, who have tact & common sense, who exhibit a high degree of discrimination in matters pertaining to relations with other kings should be appointed as ambassador. Hope you have appointed such ambassadors for your kingdom". (100/35)
- "Have you appointed spies to monitor the 18 classes of people, who reside in other countries and fifteen categories of people who reside in your own country?" (100/37)
- "Do the People who depend on agriculture, cattle rearing and commerce feel happy about the state of affairs of your governance? In their happiness and wellbeing lies country's prosperity". (100/48)

- Are you protecting all kinds of citizens of your country? It is the fundamental duty of the king to protect his subjects at all times.
- Hope, you are not very intimate with your employees or subjects and at the same time you are not distancing them from meeting you. A king has to maintain a proper balance in his relationship with his sub-ordinates.

- Are you following the dictums of Rājanīti Śāstra (knowledge of Governing principles) without any deviation? Are you discussing the affairs of the state with your council of ministers through a formal meeting and also through private talk (one to one discussion)?
- I believe that you are not enjoying all alone the Wealth & delicious food. Hope you are sharing them with your kith and kin.
- Are you befriending senior citizens, intellectuals, and the youth of your country with your good words and good gifts? (100/62)
- Rama proceeds to exhort Bharata on the ways and means of protecting palaces, forts, water bodies etc and gives guidance for maintaining cities and villages. (Sarga-100)

Economics & Administration from Mahabharata

In the Mahabharata, we find an interesting conversation between King Yudhisthira (Dharma Rāja) and Grand seer Bhīṣhma (Edited from The Mahabharata, Śānti Parva, section LXXXVIII, Translated by Sri Kisari Mohan Ganguli)

Dharma Raja asks Bhishma, What plans & strategies, a king should adopt to increase his wealth?

Bhishma exorts

A King, who is bound by righteousness, uses all his faculties and resources according to time and situation and seeking the wellbeing of his subjects, protects them.

A King should adopt one of the following methods to collect taxes from the people:

A) Like a bee collecting honey from flowers;

B) Like milking a cow without troubling the cow & calf.

C) Like a leech that sucks the blood without people knowing it.

A King should handle the people very gently. He should conduct himself towards his subjects like a tigress in the matter of carrying her cubs, touching them with her teeth but never piercing them therewith.

The King should never impose taxes unreasonably and on persons unable to bear them. He should impose them gradually and with conciliation, in proper season. These contrivances that I declare unto thee are legitimate means of kingcraft. They are not reckoned as methods fraught with deceit. One who seeks to govern steeds(horses) by improper methods only makes them furious.

Liquor shops, public women, pimps, actors, gamblers and keepers of gambling houses, and other persons of this kind, who are sources of disorder to the state, should all be checked. Residing within the realm, these afflict and injure the better classes of the subjects and so they are to be checked.

If all men were to live by asking or begging and abstaining from work, the world would doubtless come to an end. The king alone is competent to restrain and check.

> "A King should adopt one of the following methods to collect taxes from the people
> Like a leach that sucks the blood without people knowing it."
>
> - Bhishma's Advice to Yudhisthira

Let there be no beggars or robbers in thy kingdom. Robbers (not virtuous men) offer alms to wash off their sins, not out of compassion. Such givers are not real benefactors of men.

Those (corrupt) officers, O king, who take from the subjects more than what is due should be punished. You should appoint sincere officers.

If a person engaged in agriculture, cattle rearing or trade, develops a sense of insecurity (due to thieves and tyrannical officers), the king, as a consequence, incurs infamy.

The king should always honour his subjects who are rich and should say unto them 'Do be, with me and advance the interest of the people'.

For these reasons, O monarch, do thou love all creatures, and display the qualities of truth, sincerity, absence of wrath, and abstention from injury! Thou shouldst, thus, wield the rod of chastisement, and enhance thy treasury and support thy friends and consolidate thy kingdom thus, practising the qualities of truthfulness and sincerity and supported by thy friends, treasury and forces.

Protection of the subject, O Yudhiṣṭhira, is the very cheese of kingly duties.

Subdue thy foes, protect thy subjects, worship the deities in sacrifices, and fight battles with courage, O delighter of the Kurus! A king should protect those that deserve protection. The king who does this is the best of rulers. Those kings that do not exercise the duty of protection live a vain life. For the benefit of all his subjects the king should always seek to ascertain the acts and thoughts of all, O Yudhishthira; and for that reason he should set spies and secret agents. Protecting others from thy own, and thy own from others, as also others, and thy own from thy own, do thou always cherish thy people. Protecting his own self first from everyone, the king should protect the earth.

The king, even if possessed of strength, should not disregard a foe, however weak. A spark of fire can produce a conflagration and a particle of poison can kill.

King should not tolerate the self-centered people or flatterers around him.

Every thing in the world is obtained through exertion or hard work. Education, wealth and penance are obtained through hard work.

Hard work or exertion is controlled by intellect, yet hard work is superior to intelligence.

This body gives the energy required for the hard work or exertion; intelligent person considers the body as the "Godly embodiment" and never neglects the body.

A greedy person can always be won by showering gifts and bribes; such kind of people should not be appointed for important posts like chief minister or minister.

★ ★ ★

Vidura's, exhortations to Yudhishthira (Dharma Raja) are called Vidura Niti. He had explained the subtleties of kingcraft at many instances.

Management Philosophy in Bhagvad Gita

Bhagvad Gita, is considered to be the essence of Indian philosophy ,which was revealed to Arjuna by Lord Kṛṣṇa on the battle field, when the former went into depression and declared to withdraw himself from waging the war.

Great western thinkers, writers and scientists are fascinated by the essence of the Gita. Millions of Indians chant the Gita verses everyday. Many scholars have written commentaries on the Gita. Many Gurus give Gita discourses as thousands listen and comprehend it.

Modern management gurus are using the Gita verses to explain the management concepts. Here a few verses of Gita are discussed from the point of efficiency in management.

Efficient Manager/Worker- Sāttvika Kartā **(18Ch-26 śloka)**

A person, who is

- free from ego and attachment while performing the work;
- and is having clarity & resolve about his goals;
- ever enthusiastic and energetic;
- even-minded in success or failure; is called a satvika worker /manager.

Emotional Manager/ Worker- Rājasika Kartā **(18Ch-24 śloka)**

A person who

- gives importance to the (end) result;
- and neglects the means of achieving the end;
- and does the work with over-exertion;
- and always carried away by emotions like anger, attachment and passions, is called a Rājasika worker/manager.

Idiotic Manager / Worker – Tāmasika Kartā **(18Ch-25 Śloka)**

A person who

- over-estimates his capabilities and performs the work with ignorance
- and whose acts always end in violence or cause disturbance to the people around him ,
- who procrastinates the work without honoring the commitments, is called a Tāmasika worker / manager.

Kṛṣṇa reveals about the ways to obtain Communication Skills.... (17Ch-15 śloka)

The words that are not provocative, that are truthful, spoken with good intention, words that produce soothing effect in others are considered to be the effort for communicative ability (Vāk tapas). This skill can be obtained by consistent study of great literary works and continuous practice with awareness.

Kautilya

Kauṭilya's Artha śāstra- Highlights of Foreign Policy.

Kauṭilya had explained in his treatise called *"Artha Sastra"* on various aspects like administration, politics, governance, foreign policy & others. Though written in the 4th century BC, it contains the advanced management techniques. It contains fifteen chapters (adhikaraṇas). Many of the terms used in this treatise represent a position in administration and powers & responisbilites assigned to that position. Various revenue divisions of administration from village level to the confederation of Republics had been extensively dealt with. It explains the systems of Governance including Democracy, elections etc. The beauty of Artha Sastra is that, it also deals with Agriculture, Metallurgy, measuring the Rainfall, Business cartels, Ports management, ways & means of controlling the Armies & a few

War strategies etc. It reflects the political maturity of Ancient Indians.

We have herewith culled out certain viewpoints of Kauṭilya on foreign policy. The policy of dealing with the neighbouring kingdoms is called "Ṣaḍ Guṇyam" (Six Aspects of Foreign Policy).

1. Sandhi 2.Vigraham 3.Asanam 4.Yaanam 5. Samsrayam 6. Dvaidhibhavam

- Sandhi, making peace, by concluding a treaty.
- Vigraha, hostilities could mean a conventional war, a secret war or a proxy war as is known today and an undeclared war.
- Asana means staying quiet and
- Yaana is preparing for war.
- Samsraya is seeking protection from a stronger king
- Dvaidhibhava is the policy of making peace with a neighboring king in order to pursue, with his help, the policy of hostility towards another.

"The welfare of a state depends on an active foreign policy". *(Ref: 6.2.1)*

"An enemy's destruction shall be brought about even at the cost of great losses in men, material and wealth". *(Ref: 7.13.33)*

"A King weak in power shall endeavour to promote the welfare of his people. For the power comes from the countryside, which is the source of all activities". *(Ref: 7.14.18,19)*

"One should never submit spinelessly; nor sacrifice oneself in foolhardy valour. It is better to adopt such policies as would enable one to survive and live to fight another day". *(Ref: 7.15.13-20,12.1.1-9)*

"When there is a choice between two allies, the one amenable to control, though temporarily is preferred because he remains an ally as long as he helps. The real characteristic of friendship is help". *(Ref: 7.9.9-12)*

Treaties - "Non-intervention, negotiating a peace treaty and making peace by giving a hostage-all mean the same thing, since the aim of all the three is to create confidence between the two kings". *(Ref: 7.17.1,2)*

Choosing an ally or forming an alliance:

The constant ally giving small help shall be preferred. The temporary friend giving substantial help is likely to withdraw for fear of having to give more or will expect it to be repaid. The constant ally, giving small help continuously, does in fact give great help over a period of time". *(Ref: 7.9.13-17)*

"An ally mobilizing quickly, even if he is less mighty, is preferable because he does not allow opportune time for action to pass". *(Ref: 7.9.18-21)*

"An ally who helps monetarily is preferable because one can always use money but troops only sometimes". *(Ref: 7.9.26-30)*

"An ally who is likely to grow in power after defeating the enemy and thus, become uncontrollable shall be embroiled in a conflict with his own neighbour. Such actions would be taken as would oblige the ally to remain obedient, in return for the help received". *(Ref: 7.18)*

Kautilya lists eight factors to decide when to wage a war, when to abstain from planning a Campaign.

"One should never submit spinelessly; nor sacrifice oneself in fool hardy valour. It is better to adopt such policies as would enable one to survive and live to fight another day."

- Kautilya's Artha sastra

1. Power or strength: They are of three kinds

   a) Intellectual Strength b) Military might c) Self-Confidence

2. Place or terrain
3. Timing
4. Right kind of use of force & resources
5. Internal revolts
6. Clear objectives of mission
7. Benefits and losses
8. Possibility of treachery

"Before taking a decision, the king should discuss all these factors thoroughly with his council of ministers. After taking a decision, he should implement it thoroughly. King should never fight with a stronger foe."

Kauṭilya had extensively discussed various aspects of exceptional foreign policy and war strategy.

Source: Kauṭilya's Artha śāstra- Pollala Ramachandra (7th adikaraṇam)
www.esamskriti.com

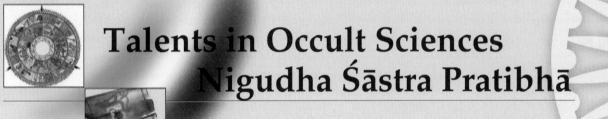

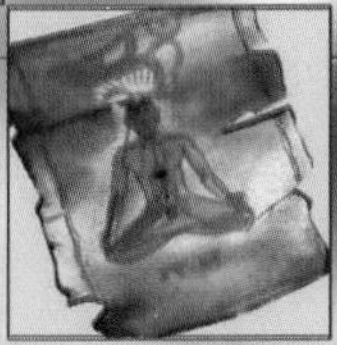

Talents in Occult Sciences
Nigudha Śāstra Pratibhā

92 The Science of Vāstu for Harmonious Living

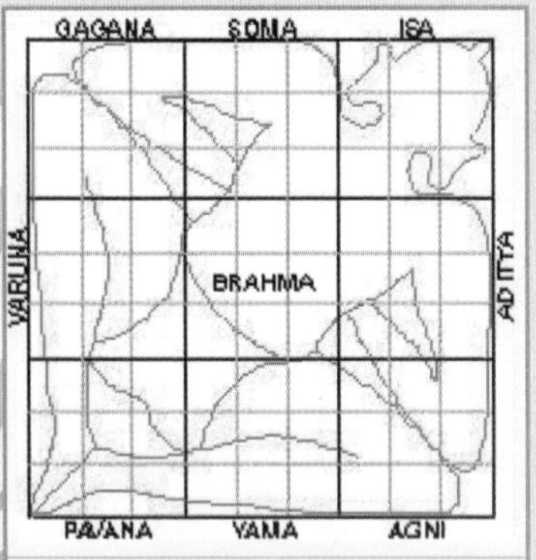

Vasthu Purusha

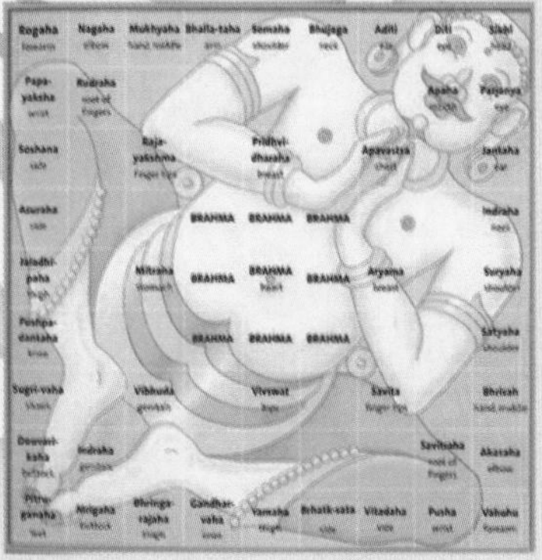

Today Western world is crazy about many Indian sciences. Among them Yoga, Āyurveda and Vāstu occupy the central stage of attraction & importance.

Advanced Building technology has recognized the importance of green-building concepts and eco-friendly houses. Engineers, Architects and environmentalists are building pressure on various governments to bring suitable amendments to building laws & statutes wherein houses and buildings are built in tune with the nature & environment.

Ancient Indian Knowledge never went against the nature but always understood the nature and synchronized itself with nature.

Nature is made up of Pañca Bhūtas, five elements. They are earth, water, fire, air and space. Indian building technology, the knowledge of Vāstu reveals the interconnection between the five elements of the nature, dwelling place and harmonious living with the nature. Vāstu Śāstra is a 5,000-year-old Indian science of dwelling place wisdom. It is found in the Atharva Veda as Sthāpatya Vidyā.

Ancient Indian intellect had not limited its analysis to this material world (Gross Tangible world). But it extended its in-depth study of understanding to the subtle world and subtle forces that control the material world.

Vāstu Śāstra synchronizes various energy points, energy lines and energy grids of Mother Nature with energy feilds of the dwelling house. It balances the energy flow by adhering to certain Vāstu principles.

Ancient Indians recognized the dwelling place as the living organism and evolved the knowledge of Vāstu. Vas meaning "to be" or "to live".

Hindu temples are built according to Āgama Śāstra, Vāstu Śāstra and Jyotiṣā Śāstra. Hindus consider the temples as a place of "Divine vibrations". They go to temple not just to worship the diety but also to get charged themselves with divine vibrations. So the above-mentioned Indian sciences deal with the knowledge of it.

Matsya Purana names eight scholars of Vāstu śāstra

They are *1.Bhṛgu 2. Atri 3. Vasiṣṭha 4. Viśvakarma 5. Māyā 6. Nārada 7.Nagnajit 8.Viśāla.*

The famous Mayasabhā, the mystic palace of Mahabharata was built by Maya, which had been built according to the principles of Vāstu Sāstram. Sage Vyāsa described it as a building that was built in form of equi-angled quadrilateral (with 10000 "hasthas" as its circumference).

In the Mahabharata it is said that a number of houses were built for the kings who were invited to the city of Indraprastha for the Rājasūya Yajña of King Yudhisthira. Sage Vyasa says that these houses were as high as the peaks of Kailaśa Mountains, perhaps meaning that they stood tall and majestic. The houses were free from obstructions, had compounds with high walls and their doors were of uniform height and inlaid with numerous metal ornaments. It is said that the site plan of Ayodhyā, the city of Lord Rama was similar to the plan found in the great architectural text "Manasara".

Lord Hanuman, while looking at the city of Lanka for the first time, exclaims that every house was built according to the Vāstu Śāstra.

References are also to be found in Buddhist literature, of buildings constructed on the basis of Vaastu.

Matsya Purana, Skanda Purana, Agni Purana, Garuda Purana, Vishnu Purana had dealt with many aspects of Vāstu Śāstra.

Important Vaastu sastra treatises, which are available to us, are:

1. *Kashyapa Shiapam- Kashyapa Mahamuni*
2. *Bruhit Samhita- Varahamihira.*
3. *Mayamata-Vaastu sastram- Maya*
4. *Vishwakarma Vaastu sastram- Viswa karma*
5. *Samarangana sutradhara- Bhoja kavi*

"Vaastu Sastra synchronizes various energy points, energy lines and energy grids of Mother Nature with energy feilds of the dwelling house. It balances the energy flow by adhering to certain Vaastu principles."

Other Vaastu sastra texts are Aparajitha Pruthya, Jayapruthya.

According to the Vaastu Sastra, the dwelling place is considered to be a living being called Vaastu Puruṣa or Vaastu Purusha Maṇḍali. It is an energy grid of 64 energy points of intersections (8*8)or (9*9) 81 points of intersections.

The following aspects are considered while designing the dwelling place or a building:

1. Nature of the soil.
2. Design layout of the building in synchronization with Vaastu Purusha Mandali.
3. Owner's birth chart (Astrology/Jyotiṣa Śāstra).
4. Number of thresholds and windows.
5. Brahma- central place of the house.
6. Placement of functional utilities for receiving the grace of Aṣṭa Dik Pālakas (lords of eight directions).
7. Heights to be of definite proportions.

If at the North and Eastern directions lot of empty space is provided – prosperity is assured. Similarly there are a few fundamental Vaastu rules that are generally adhered to

North east corner – Water source and Pooja mandir.
South east corner – cooking and fire related aspects.
South west corner – place of owner and should be in an elevated position.
North west corner - for bathroom, guestroom, childrenroom etc.

Central place of the house or central courtyard is kept open to the sky. This is called Brahma Sthāna. This place absorbs the divine vibrations and is considered to be auspicious to the owner of the house, if kept open.

93 Yoga–The World's Craze of the Day

Modern man's mechanical life, invited many problems for him. Tension, depression and pressure of commitments, drive him from pillar to post, as he is being heavily dosed with medicines. Bodies react, minds distract and lives burst out; what is the way out? Ancient Indian system of Yoga comes to their rescue.

Yoga is a craze in the Western world today. Yoga is giving them a pause of relaxation to their fast pace of life. CEOs, Managers, Professionals, Politicians, students and housewives are religiously pursuing courses in Yoga for stress-free life. Modern India is no exception to this; Indians do suffer from the so-called "civilized" stress and diseases and Yoga is the panacea for their problems too.

What are the secrets behind Yoga's attraction? Yoga is the invaluable gift, our Ṛṣis of yore, had bequeathed to us. Yoga is not limited to performing a few āsanas for toning up the body muscles and mind relaxation.

Yoga is a way of life. It is not a therapy to cure diseases. Yoga is the basis for the Indian culture and civilization. The word yoga means, "joining together" or "yoking together". It is merging of "Jīvātmā" (self–consiciousness) with "Paramātmā" (Cosmic Consciousness). That is the goal of yoga and the life had been designed to achieve that goal.

Lord Kṛṣna exhorted the depressed Arjuna to fight the battle and that wonderful conversation is the Knowledge of Yoga. Yoga gives the strength of mind to face the battles of life. Arjuna became a Yogī, won the battle and enjoyed the kingdom and finally merged with the divinity. Lord Krishna deals with yoga in eighteen chapters from various points of view. Krishna defines Yoga as "Samatvaṁ Yoga Ucyate"(Gītā : 2.48) obtaining the evenness of mind is called Yoga, or obtaining balance in life is called Yoga. He further says *"Yogaḥ karmasu Kauśalam"(Gītā : 2.50)* -Achieving work excellence is yoga.

The science of yoga had been explained by Sage Patañjali through his Yoga Sūtras.

According to Patañjali Yoga had been defined as "Citta vṛtti nirodhaḥ"(PYS:1.2) - freeing the mind stuff from the vortex of thoughts.

Usually people follow many paths of yoga. Among them Karma yoga, Bhakti yoga, Jñāna yoga, Rāja yoga, Haṭha yoga and Tantra yoga are very popular.

Bhakti Yoga: Loving God and creation and becoming one with God is called Bhakti yoga.

Karma Yoga: Shunning the ego of doer-ship while performing actions and getting not perturbed by the results of action is called Karma yoga.

Jñāna Yoga: Through self-inquiry, discrimination and renunciation, leading a life of oneness with awareness is Jñāna yoga.

Rāja Yoga: By control of breath and through it control of senses, the mind is stilled and made free from attachments and aversions and then it is called Rāja yoga.

Haṭha Yoga: Obtaining the longevity the life without any ailments and diseases through body and mind control is called Hatha yoga.

Tantra Yoga: Through chanting of mantras and performing rituals with the aid of yantras, rousing the self-consciousness hidden in the body (in the form of Kuṇḍalinī) to the cosmic consciousness and thus obtaining siddhis (powers) is called Tantra yoga.

Patañjali's Yoga Sūtras reveal to us more about Rāja yoga methods. Today we call them simply as yoga. According to Patanjali, there are eight steps to be followed for becoming a yogi. They are called Aṣṭāṇga yoga method.

1. **Yama- The five moral disciplines** : a) Ahiṁsā (non-injury) b) Satya (truthfulness) c) Brahmacarya (rising above the sexual gratification) d) Aparigraha (not acquiring or not accepting, than what is required for one's austre life) e) Asteya (not coveting others wealth).
2. **Niyama- The five Physical & Mental disciplines:** a) Śauca-Maintaining purity of body & mind b) Santoṣa-To be happy always with a positive approach to life (without any negativity) c) Tapasyā–Controlling Body, Mind and speech through severe austerities d) Svādhyāya-Self study d) Iśvara Praṇidhānam–surrending oneself to the divine power –God.
3. **Āsanas:** Āsanas are performed for obtaining a blissful body posture. There are many kinds of Āsanas. Body and senses are brought into control through āsanas.
4. **Prāñāyāma:** Control of breath and thereby controlling the mind. Recaka, Pūraka and Kumbhaka are methods of exhalation, inhalation and holding of breath.
5. **Pratyāhāra:** Controlling the senses and mind from vacillations.
6. **Dhāraṅā:** Fixing the mind on an object for obtaining concentration.
7. **Dhyāna:** Meditation; there are many methods of meditations and many states of meditation; in meditation there would be continuous awareness with the absence of ego. Even work can be a meditation; Cooking can be a meditation.
8. **Samādhi:** Complete merger with divine consciousness, a state of oneness.

   Patañjali had combined the last three stages of Dhāraṅā, Dhyāna and Samādhi, which is called as "saṁyama". If a yogi practices saṁyama, he obtains the power to perform miracles (vibhūtīs or siddhis)

Paṭañjali had described forty kinds of siddhis. A few of them are mentioned here.

1. Yogī can know about past and future of others.
2. Yogī can understand the languages of birds and animals.
3. Yogī can know about his own previous births.
4. Yogī can read other's thoughts.
5. Yogī can vanish his body.
6. Yogī can control his death.
7. Yogī can understand cosmic secrets.
8. Yogī can materialize things.
9. Yogī wins over hunger & thirst.
10. Yogī obtains telepathy.
11. Yogī obtains the state of weightlessness.

Patañjali cautions the yoga Sādhakas (Practitioners of yoga) about pitfalls of getting stagnated with the power of miracles. He abundantly cautions everybody that one cannot reach the ultimate state of divine consciousness, if one gets trapped with the power of siddhis.

According to Tantra Yoga in human body, there are seven yogic centers or cakras. As a yogī progresses in his pursuits, these yogic centers or cakras get activated.

Human vertebra consists of three yogic nāḍis they are "iḍā", "piṅgalā" and "suṣumnā". Among the three, suṣumnā nāḍī joins these seven yogic cakras.

1. Mūlādhāra cakra - base cakra - where the kuṇḍalinī (yogic power) is coiled and placed at the bottom of vertebra.
2. Svādhiṣṭhāna cakra - located near genital organs
3. Maṇipurā cakra – located in the naval region.
4. Anāhaṭa cakra - located in the heart
5. Viśuddha cakra - located in the throat
6. Ājñā cakra - located in between the eyebrows.

Kuṇdalinī after passing through the six cakras reaches the top of the head of person, this centre or location is called Sahasr Kamalam, where the blossoming of consciousness takes place and the yogic merger with divine consciousness is fructified.

Varied are the methods of yoga; vast is the science of yoga; Indians had cultured the yo gic principles with day-to-day life and the river of Indian culture is eternally flowing with yogic consciousness. Kudos! To our ancestors, who had gifted us, with the ultimate science of living.

Kundalini energy passing through the Six Yogic Chakras

94 Mantra Science & its Application

Mantra or sacred incantation is a gift from the scientific wisdom of India to the world. By receiving these sacred incantations (hymns), arrows were darted and diseases were also cured. With the help of mantras there are many welfare activities performed.

Seeking the wellbeing of the entire universe, Indians had been accustomed to reciting sacred hymns and mantras. Today in the modern medical world, the power of the mantra is best utilized as sound therapy.

What is a mantra? It is nothing but a collection of sanctified sounds uttered for a specific purpose and fulfilment. It does have a meaning and it should be said in a proper cadence, rhythm, intonation and pitch with purity of heart.

The power of the mantra gets multiplied in proportion to the unselfish use of the utterer.

It is not a mere collection of serene sounds. It is also a subtle science. Depending upon the user's intensity of feeling and accuracy of expression, the incantation gains efficacy and success. The gross body has no power, but the subtle mind is all-powerful. It is the power of the mind that drives the body into action. This mind is a subtle body. In other words, subtle always governs the gross, like an elephant governed by, a puny person on its top.

Powers of the mind are enormous. The concentrated mind is still more powerful. As the concentrated rays of sun, when focused, gain the power to burn a paper. The concentrated power of the mantra can do good and evil. In the warfare, the mantras were used to kill and in the social life they were used to help and heal.

By rousing the inner powers through a mantra, impossible will become possible.

Each deity has a cosmic function and duty to perform. Every cosmic function has a form associated with it. The respective deity is the repository of the required energy to perform that function. That energy can be obtained from the energy source by propitiating it with appropriate mantra. The sound vibrations produced while reciting the mantra are not only capable of pleasing the deity but can show us the form and benevolence of the invoked Godly being.

In the sounds of Sanskrit, both the meaning and pitch are essential. Properly arranging them and expressing them can achieve extraordinary results.

Some of the letters in Sanskrit are considered to be the root sounds of great energy. By ceaselessly repeating them, we can generate electrifying results, thereby mantras have fulfillment. Some such sounds are "Iym", "Kleem", "Sow", "Hreem", "Sreem".

In the scriptures pertaining to mantras, the utility and power of these sounds are well-explained. "Iym" – is the sound, which can make us rich. "Kleem" is other powerful sound, which can make us irresistibly attractive. The entire Vedic lore is a treasure house of these sacred syllables and sounds.

We have to be very careful while using them. Our pronunciation must be precise and pure. By reciting these sounds, the whole body and nerves within get charged. They then become Divine. Thereby desires get fulfilled.

Those who are able to visualize and compose the propitious sounds and syllables are called Ṛṣis.

Behind every mantra there is great sage of intuition. Before making use of that mantra we have to invoke the blessings of that great composer. The Deity, invoked by that mantra is to be worshipped mentally. By worshipping the Rishi and the deity, the mantra becomes more energetic.

Each mantra has prosody (Chandas); the root sound of the mantra is its life spirit. (Bīja Akṣara). It is the source of all energy, divinity and psychic power. The other root syllable (śakti), which is potential and pregnant with energy, should be prevented from diffusion, miscarriage, misuse and abuse. The

> "Seeking the wellbeing of the entire universe, Indians had been accustomed to reciting sacred hymns and mantras. Today in the modern medical world, the power of the mantra is best utilized as sound therapy."

root syllable, which prevents this diffusion, is called "Kilakam". By properly reciting the said sounds, we succeed in the right use and in getting the desired benefits. This repeated recitation is called "Viniyoga".

This "Viniyoga" is very often augmented by japa, homa and purity of heart. The entire potential energy of the mantra is divided into six parts while being directed towards the chosen deity during contemplation. This division and utilization is called "Nyasa".

When it is applied on the hands of the Diety, it is called Karan- nyasa. Similarly, the mantra is usually applied on the six parts of the deity (aṅga nyasa).

Before reciting any hymn, there is a mantra exclusively meant to keep our minds directed and fixed on the chosen deity. It is called Dhyāna mantra. By reciting that hymn, the mind gets the ability to meditate on the God. By constantly pouring forth our mind, to the accompaniment of Hymns in mediation is called Dhyāna.

The gross form of the mantra takes us to the subtle energetic expression of sound. This subtle energy elevates us to the heights of the sublime Kuṇḍalinī awakening.

The chanting of the mantra has to be learned from a master or guru. He only can initiate that energy into us.

For the total fulfilment, initiation is essential. In the Vedic lore of India, many a mantra is still lying hidden. They are all to be unearthed and fully utilized for the cosmic welfare.

From the ancient Hindu faith, the science of mantras had spread to foreigners and other faiths like Jains, Buddhists, Sufis and even Christians.

Almost everybody now evinces interest in the hidden energies of the ancient knowledge of mantras.

95 The Sāmudrika Śāstra–The Science of Body Language

Face is the index of mind. We often use this adage. By seeing the face of a person we predict his wellbeing. Brilliance or dullness is indicated by the facial expressions. We analyze the face and often conclude about the person's state of mind and pour out questions about his health & welfare. This is a typical experience of everyone & a common habit.

Some doctors diagnose a disease by looking at the body symptoms. Some look at the face to foretell the future. Some others read the thoughts by looking at us. Some others analyze our body gestures and reveal our character & personality. There is a science behind these interpretations. This knowledge had been wonderfully evolved by Indians ages ago and is called as *Samudrika Sastra.*

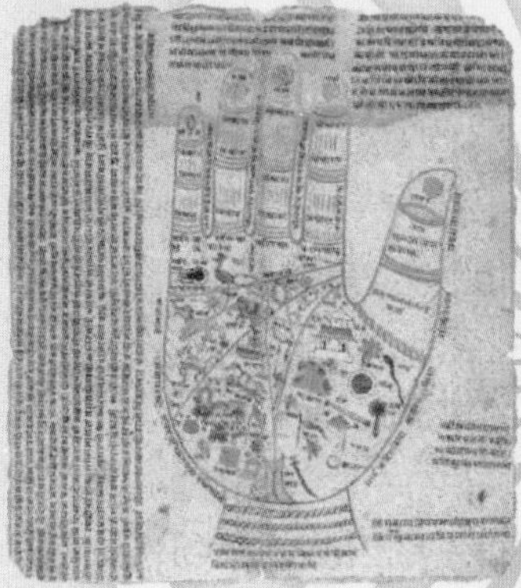

Legend says *Samudra* had revealed this *Samudrika Sastra*, hence the name. Samudra had meticulously noted the indications and auspicious marks on the body of Lord Vishnu, when he was resting on Adisesha (serpent king) on the milky ocean (the abode of samudra). He had evolved his observations as knowledge and had passed it on to the later generations. Afterwards sages like Narada, Mandavya, Varaha and Kartikeya had developed this knowledge of body gestures and marks.

Today, bits and pieces of this knowledge are available to us. We also find its applications in traditional Sanskrit literature and Indian languages. Ramayana and Mahabharatha do contain references of this knowledge.

In Ramayana, Sage Valmiki wonderfully describes the physical features of Sri Rama, indirectly hinting to us that Sri Rama was the incarnation of Lord Vishnu. Sage Valmiki would have considered Samudrika Sastra as authority to substantiate his views about Rama, as *Samudrika Sastra* indicates auspicious marks of Lord Vishnu.

Valmiki chooses the episode of Sri Hanuman's search for Sita in AshokaVana, as the former answers the questions of later about Sri Rama's features.

> Some analyze our body gestures and reveal our character & personality. There is a science behind these interpretations. This knowledge had been wonderfully evolved by Indians ages ago and is called as Samudrika Sastra.

The Sundara Kāṇḍa, 35th Sarga, Ślokas 15 to 20 of Vālmikī Rāmāyaṇa contains the description of Rama from head to toe.

There are many modern commentaries available on the Samudrika Sastra. Among them books written by Gopesh Kumar Ahuja and RG Rao are considered to be an authority.

This science is called "Siang-mein" in China. Palmistry or Hasta Samudrika is also a part of Samudrika Sastra.

There are many methods of observations mentioned in Samudrika Sastra. Some of them are given below...

a) Human faces and bodily features are compared with animal faces and animal bodies and thus revealing the character of a person.

b) By recognizing the brilliance in the face of a person, one analyzes a person's aura or energy field around that person. The observations mentioned in Samudrika Sastra tally with the observations by modern sophisticated instruments.

c) Birth chart of a person is prepared, based on the physical features of that person.

The methods of making birth charts can be obtained from the Jyotish texts. For example

Second house of the birth chart indicates the face of the person. Third house indicates the shoulders. Fourth house indicates chest & mother. If a person is short, it is said he is more influenced by mercury. If a person appears black and tall, he is said be influenced by Saturn. If a person is handsome or beautiful, then that person is said to be influenced by Venus. Structured, well-built body indicates the influence of Mars; stout and tall persons are influenced by Jupiter.

If a person has attractive eyes then that person is said to be influenced by sun and shall be the leader in his walk of life. Similarly right eye indicates father. Left eye indicates mother; nose brothers etc.

Samudrika sastra discusses the kingly qualities & physical features.

In Ayurvedic texts like Charaka & Sushruta, the methods of diagnosis are explained by looking at the characteristic features of the human body. Pulse reading is an effective technique of āyurveda.

Hastha Samudrikam

Palmistry is a branch of Samudrika Sastra. But the hand reading or palmistry is an independent study, very popular throughout the world.

By reading the lines on the palm, human character and man's future are predicted. It is a great mystic art globally mastered & admired.

Today this science has become an effective tool in the hands of psychiatrists. Fingerprints & analysis had originated from Samudrika Sastra only. Today fingerprints are analysed by police and used as an effective identification methodology.

Though this science originated from India, we do not find many authoritative texts. This science is kept alive by traditional families who took it as profession. Tribal people of India are wellversed in this subject.

Westerners and Chinese had patronized this art of Palmistry and developed the Science of it.

Today Palmistry is mixed with Astrology and a new branch called Astro-palmistry came into being. Palmistry is mixed with medicine and health palmistry is being studied.

Cakras in fingers, sizes of hand, colour of the hand, shape of hand, various lines on the Palm, the mounts on the Palm and complexion of the lines are considered while analysing the hand . Health, life, life partner, children, wealth, travel, accidents and major events of the person's life are predicted with the help of Palmistry.

It is a great art and knowledge. This great art has been developed as the science of Palmistry. Unfortunately some people shun Palmistry as a blind belief. If we analyze and assimilate the knowledge of Palmistry, the world gets benefited by it.

96 Jyotiṣa-The Science of Light – *(That Correlates Planetary Influence on Human Behaviour)*

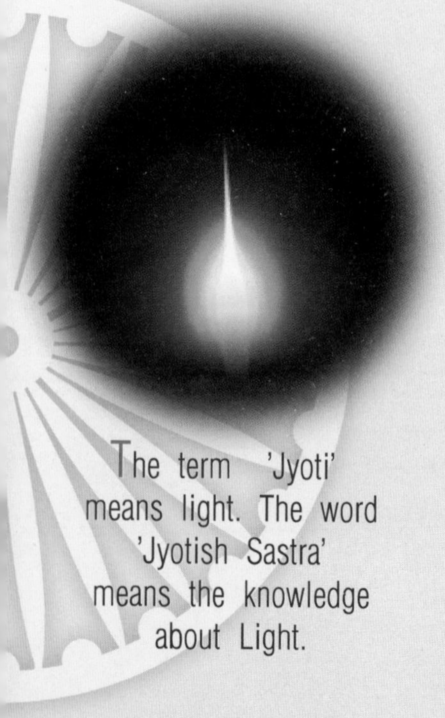

The term 'Jyoti' means light. The word 'Jyotish Sastra' means the knowledge about Light.

"Jyotiṣa", is one among the Vedāṅgas. It is like an eye to the Veda Puruṣa. It means, one should obtain mastery in this subject, before assimilating the knowledge of Vedas. Vedic karmas or Vedic rites are required to be performed according to the precision of timings. The knowledge of Jyotiṣa had originated for performing the Vedic yagnas or Vedic sacrifices.

The term *"Jyoti"* means light. The word *"Jyotiṣa Śāstra"* means the knowledge about Light. But unfortunately it is being used today as the knowledge to know the future. *Jyotiṣa Sastra* is a wonderful science. It is not a blind belief. Foretelling the future events is a small part of the oceanic science of light.

Modern Science describes the distance between the planets in terms of light years. Light year means distance travelled by the light in one year. If we are able to see a star in the sky, the light emitted from that star takes hundreds and thousands of years to reach us on the earth.

Similarly ancient Indians took the sun's light as the basis to find the planetary motions and scaled the eternal time. By measuring the light, they evolved the system of time and its calculations. They even estimated with precision, favourable time and unfavourable time, natural calamities and catostrophes. By co-relating the planetary movements with human behaviour on the earth, they predicted the future events of human life.

Varahamihira, one of the greatest Indian Astronomical scientists in his classical text, *"Bruhit Jataka"* explains in the very first verse that, Jyotish Sastra is only a device which guides us to sail the ocean of life. A compass gives us direction, so also Jyotish predicts the favourability or un-favourability of the forthcoming events.

According to Jyotish, there are nine planets and 27 constellations of stars. One complete cycle is calculated as 360 degrees. And this is divided into 12 Rāśi divisions of 30 degrees each. The effects of planetary motions on human beings are studied from various perspectives based on the 12 primary Rasi divisions.

For every individual a Jyotish chart is prepared based on the time of birth and place of birth. The planetary positions at the time of birth are noted and analyzed. This chart is called *Janma-Kuṇḍalī*.

Jyotish Sastra is a vast ocean of knowledge, Indian Astronomy (Khagola sastra) and predicting the future (Astrology) is a part of it; Gaṇita (various principles of Mathematics) evolved from this science. Beauty of Jyotish sastra is, that it is linked with every branch of Indian knowledge. Ayurveda analyses birth chart of the patient and accordingly treats him for effective results. In Building houses, agriculture, travel, wars, marriages and other sanctifying rituals and in many aspects of day-to-day life, Indians consult the almanac (Panchanga) for knowing the favourability of time. This science of Jyotish got intermingled with India's culture and life stream.

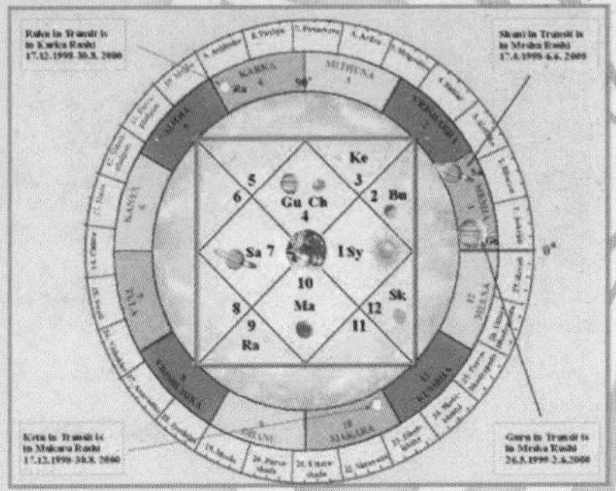

The ocean of Indian Jyotish can be assimilated from the books that are available to us today,

1. Parasara's Hora Sastra. 2. Varahamihira's Bruhit Jataka 3. Kalyana varma's Saravali. 4. Jaimini Maharshi's Jaiminiya Siddanta. 5. Mantreswara's phaladeepika and Brughu maharshi's Bhṛgu Samhita.

There are many works of Jyotish sastra. Each work is a lifetime experience of this great knowledge.

Many (so called) rationalists criticize this science of Jyotish as a big fraud committed on Human mind. They debase it as a mere blind belief. In spite of severe criticism, Jyotish Sastra is becoming popular everyday. With the advent of computer programming, Jyotish charts are being analyzed with great precision.

Today, we are very much advanced in medical knowledge. Does modern medicine give guarantee to cure all the diseases? Do doctors concur or differ in their views regarding diagnosis and treatment of various diseases? Every doctor follows certain school of thought in the treatment of disease. Each school of thought differs from other school of thought. Are we calling medicine as blind belief or Science? Please note that, we go to a doctor, believing in his competency and efficiency. Irrespective of results or advancement of knowledge, we develop a positive faith in the practitioner of that knowledge.

So is the case with Jyotish Sastra. Infinite is the knowledge. Varied are the schools of thoughts. Many are the predictive analysis. People are getting benefits and knowledge is prospering. Long live Jyotish, the science of light.

Nāḍī Jyotiṣa

Certain ancestral families of South India are preserving certain palm leaves, which contain the past, present and future of human lives. They are codified as the conversation between the Mother Goddess Parvathi and Lord Siva. These events are codified by noble souls called "Siddhas". This knowledge is called "Nadi Jyotish".

The familes hail from a village called Vaidhieswaran koil near Chidambaram of Tamilnadu, south India. Even today these families hold them. But many of the palm leaves were lost with the passage of time. Hence, today we don't have the palm leaves for every individual. The then ruler of Tanjore, Serfoji-2 had preserved them in the Saraswati Mahal Library. British government took them away from the library and these palm leaves had reached international shores. There are fakes and counterfeits available today and it is now a roaring business.

Method of Nadi Jyotish

Fingerprints of the individual are obtained first. Based on the fingerprints, the matching palm leaves are selected. The primary information codified in the palm leaves is revealed to the individual. If the data like, father's name and mother's name and name of the individual match and then other aspects are looked into, otherwise not.

Out of one hundred persons, only two or three persons get the correct palm leaves and future and past are perfectly revealed to them.

Only a few traditional families maintain sanctity and reveal the codified knowledge in those palm leaves.

It is a great art to codify the future & past with precision. We should always be indebted to these great Siddhas, who had revealed this knowledge of Nadi Jyotish.

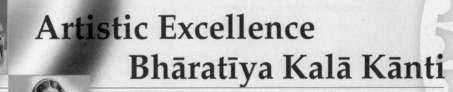

Artistic Excellence
Bhāratīya Kalā Kānti

97 Indian Sculpture & Painting

Indian art has evolved not for mere entertainment, but for enlightenment. The pen of the Indian poet, the brush of the Indian painter, the chisel of the Indian sculptor, the dancing legs and singing voices of India, all stand focussed on one centre, the divine Consciousness. Yet, one cannot grade them as substandard stuff, without any emotive appeal.

The Indian art stands *par excellence*. It has stood the test of time. This old art of India remains eternally young, inspiring generation after generation, without losing its classical elegance.

The perfection that our ancient artists exhibited belittles the so-called modernists in art and architecture. The intricacies, the details, the depth of our traditional artisans, subtleties and maturity in their presentation brings out their spiritual zeal and vigour, yet making their works, the eternal master pieces of aesthetic elegance.

Music emitted from the granite pillars, courtesy the artistic exuberance of Indian sculptors. Every design, every functional placement in Indian architecture or sculpture was linked to cosmic form of Godliness. Ages pass by, yet the traditional buildings stand tall and strong, echoing the divine vibrations, testing the patience of ever diminishing time.

Indian sculptors vanished with the passage of time, but their sculptures live vibrantly; Granites are brought to life by giving their lives to them. Ages pass by, yet beauty never leaves the chiseled rocks.

The sciences of Indian arts were called "Śāstras". The Śilpa śāstra is a part of Vāstu Śāstra. The knowledge of making sculptures is extended as part of Indian Architecture.

Ancient Temples & cave sculptures that stand today in our midst are living evidence of India's sculptural glory and talents.

The stone chariots of Mahabalipuram, near Madras stand unique on the seashores braving the oceanic waves.

Brihadeswara temple of Tanjavur, Tamilnadu built by Chola kings and renovated by Vijayanagar kings has the highest temple tower of the world called Gopuram. Its erection is an engineering marvel, 81 tonne stone structure moved on to the 216 ft tall tower. Another feat of this temple construction is that the shadow of the tower never falls on the ground on any day of the year. This temple has the biggest Nandi carved on a single stone.

Meenakshi Temple of Madurai, Tamilnadu is the abode for sculptural excellence. This massive temple with magnificent pillars, thousand pillar mandapams, beaming temple towers, well built temple tanks, all speak volumes of perfected sculptural art of India. This temple has sapta svara pillars made of rock, which reverberates with seven musical notes.

Lepakshi temple of Andhra Pradesh and its sculptural elegance display the heights achieved by the Indian sculptures. Ruins of Hampi speak about Vijayanagar kings' artistic mindset and monumental glory.

Rameswaram temple of Tamilnadu is famed for its largest corridor in the world. It has around 1212 pillars. Temple towns of Kanchi, Tirupati & Kalahasti eternally remind us of ancient building skills, our ancestors possessed.

Rock cut caves of Ajanta; Ellora and Elephanta caves in Maharashtra reflect the maturity obtained by Indian artists in painting, sculpture and architecture.

Gomatheswara statue of the tenth century AD stands tall in the world at Śravaṇabelgola in Karnataka.

Chenna Kesava temple of Belur in Karnataka exposes the artistic splendour of Hoyasala architecture. The meticulous details carved by sculptors bring the beauty of women statutes alive. The grandeur of Lord Narasimha Swamy's granite statute is inexpressible in words.

The Sun temple of Konark in Orissa is an architectural marvel built in the 12th century. Rock cut chariot wheel had become Indian artistic symbol of excellence. The design of the temple, naṭa mandir, bogh mandir, walls, corridors and detailed sculptural beauty are unparallelled in world of Art.

Buddhagaya's Buddistic temples of Bihar too remind us of the Buddistic contribution to artistic exuberance of India.

Khajuraho temple in Madhaya Pradesh built during 950 AD-1050 AD is a complex of 85 temples. Among them twenty alone remain to us. Most of the temples were made of granite or sandstone. These temples are world famous for their erotic idols chiseled on the walls. Most of them are chiseled according to the science of sex –Kāmasūtra of Vātsyāyana. Even the Jain complex of these temples does have sexual images.

In the states of Gujarat & Rajasthan we find marble marvels chiselled to perfection. Jaipur architecture stands testimony to it.

The Dwarakamukh temple and Somanath temple (rebuilt) of Gujarat, glorify the eternal art of India.

Many Indian temples were destroyed during foreign invasions in the last thousand years. Temples of Kasi, Ayodhya, Mathura, the very cultural springs of Indian Ganges plain remain to us as redeemed structures after destruction. The golden temple of Amritsar, Punjab still shines with golden aura of yester year's sculptural excellence.

Temples, towns, tanks, and forts, all were manifesting beauty & splendour during ancient times. The architectural marvels of India achieved by our ancestors shall eternally puzzle future generations. Ages ago they achieved perfection in erecting structures without the aid of cranes, bulldozers and JBCs.

Indian Paintings

Indian painting skills still remain on the walls of temples, on the rocks of caves. Tanjavur, Lepakshi, Kalankari, Rajasthan, Ajanta & Ellora and Mughal paintings reflect the unique Indian style of artistic presentation.

In Ancient India every housewife was a seeming painter. From making the wonderful drawings on the ground at the threshold of the house every morning to painting the sarees and clothes with magnificient dyes; from beautifully decorating the idols of deities with colours and puja rooms to furnishing the house with attractive paintings, Indian women excelled in the art of painting.

Great Indian painters; Raja Ravi varma, Amṛta sherrgil and Bapu do stand as the legends of Indian Painting.

Trimurthi - Elephanta Caves Bombay

Ajantha Painting

Bapu's Ramayana Painting

98 Nāṭya Śāstram

āṅgikaṁ bhuvanaṁ yasya vācikam sarva vāmmayaṁ
āharyaṁ candra tārādi taṁ vande sāttivikaṁ śivaṁ

(Nandikeswara's Abhinaya Darpana)

I worship the benevolent God Siva,
the movement of whose limbs is the movement of the universe,
whose speech is the literary expression of the entire world,
whose decorative ornaments are the moon and the stars.

Our Ṛṣis of yore visualized the Cosmic motion as the Creator's Dance; From a tiny atom to a gigantic planet, all are moving with a rhythm; From a baby's tumbling gait to a Peacock's scintillating play, all are dancing with a cadence; Every step & every beat of every being is resonating to the tunes of nature. The wonderful science of dancing art swayed from the ecstatic hearts of those great souls into a blissful *"Nāṭya śāstra"*.

Indian science of dancing art is a classical gift of Bharata Muni's treatise *"Nāṭya Śāstra"* ; it evolved from the *"Gandharva Veda"*, which is an Upaveda of Sāmaveda. This book was supposed to have been written during the fifth century BC. It contains thirty-six chapters.

Indian classical dance is generally classified into Nṛta or pure dance and Abhinaya or portrayal of feeling and expression. Abhinaya is of four kinds, namely *"Sāttvika"*, *"Vācika"*, *"Aṅgika"* and *"Aharya"*.

Sāttvika Abhinaya means dance expressions of mind soothing feelings; *Vācika Abhinaya* means expression through power of speech or song; *Aṅgika Abhinaya* –dance expression through gestures and rhythmic body movements; *Aharya Abhinaya* means dance expression with an aid of dress and decoration.

The domain of *Nāṭya Śāstra* is not limited to the arena of dance alone. It is also a science of Indian theatre. After discussing the above mentioned four Abhinayas, it proceeds to discuss the various aspects of stage making, stage maintenance, the methodology of beginning a play and ending it, entry of roles and characters in a play.

It contains the literary aspects like Chandas (Prosody); Kāvya lakṣaṇa (charectristics of dance drama); Bhāṣā Lakṣaṇa (the refinement of the language that has to be used in the writing the script; It even discusses the aspects of music like composition of music such as tālas (beats) & rāgas (tunes of melody) etc.

We find the advanced aspects of acoustics discussed in Bharata's Nāṭya Śāstra. The second chapter ślokas 85-87 reveal the knowledge of sound management in a theatre. The Auditorium had to be built in a semi-circular fashion and the control of movements of air in theatre for clear audibility had been explained therein.

Indian dance theatre is mainly based on the facial expressions called Nava Rasas. The expressions of the artists evoke feelings in hearts of viewer and the viewer's emotional response to the expressions of artist is called 'Rasa". Each rasa experienced by the audience is associated with a specific bhāva portrayed on the stage.

For example, in order to give the audience an experience of śriṅgāra (the 'erotic' rasa), the playwright, actors and musician work together to portray the bhāva called rati (love).

Smt Śobhā Nāidu world famous Kuchipudi Exponent

Today Nava rasas are popular for portraying the artistic feelings but the Nāṭyaśāstra identifies eight rasas and eight corresponding bhāvas:

Rasa	***Bhava***
Adbhuta (Marvelous)	*Vismaya (Astonishment)*
Hāsya (Comic)	*Hasya (Mirth)*
Śriṅgāra (Erotic)	*Rati (Love)*
Bibhatsa (Odious)	*Jugupsa (Disgust)*
Vīra (Heroic)	*Utsaha (Energy)*
Karuna (Pathetic)	*Soka (Sorrow)*
Bhayaṅaka (Terrible)	*Bhaya (Terror)*
Raudra (Furious)	*Krodha(Anger)*

A ninth rasa, called *Śānta* (Peace), was later extrapolated from the eight identified in the Nāṭya Śāstra.

Kathakali

After Bharata wrote his *Nāṭya Śāstra,* abhinaya assumed such importance that Nandikeswara, a legendary figure, wrote a separate treatise called *Abhinaya Darpaṅa* (A mirror of gestures).

'Hasta Lakṣaṇa Dīpikā', *'Kohala Bhāratam'*, *'Dathilam'* and *'Saṅgīt Ratnākara'* are other classical books of Indian dance theatre.

Indian Dance Forms

Bharata Nāṭyam: It is a famous dance expression of South India, now very popular in Tamil Nadu. It owes its origin to Bharata's Nāṭya Śāstram. It contains various aspects like Alarimpu, Varnam, Pada, and Tillānā etc. It was patronized as a temple art of dance. The famous artists of this dance theatre are Smt. Rukmini Arundale, Smt. Bala Saraswati, Smt. Yamini Krishnamurthy, Smt. Mrinalini Sarabhai, Smt. Padmasubramanyam & Smt. Vyjayanthimala etc.

Kuchipudi Nātyam: It symbolizes Andhra's cultural excellence & expression. It evolved from the village called Kuchipudi, hence the name. Siddhandra yogī had developed this theatre of dance drama into a wonderful art of expressive feelings (Abhinaya) based on classical foundation of Bharata's Nāṭya Śāstra. Earlier men alone used to perform these dance ballets. Today, women outnumbered men and even excelled them in every aspect of its presentation.

Famous gurus of this dance form are *Sri Vedantham Satyanarayana, Sri Vempati Chinna Satyam, Smt & Sri Radha Raja Reddy* couple, Smt Sobha Naidu. The efforts of Smt Sobha Naidu, (the prime disciple of Guru Vempati Chinna Satyam) in chiseling more than two thousand dancers throughout the world are highly admirable.

Kathākali: This is Kerala's dance expression. Prime importance is given to the movement of eyes and decorative unique dress. Mostly males perform it. Famous dance gurus are Guru Gopi Chand; Champakulam Parama Pillai; Vallathoal Narayanan Menon.

Kathak

Mohini Attam: It evolved as a dance form of Kerala in the 16th century AD. King Swati Thirunal of Kerala patronized this art form. Famous dance gurus are Vallathoal Kavi, Kalyani Amma etc.

Odissy: It is the cultural dance expression of Orissa. It is a very traditional dance form evolved in the second century BC. Later this dance style was patronized at Puri Jaganath temple and performed by a sect of women dancers called " Mahirs". Only women performed this dance style.

Famous Gurus; Samyukhta Panigrahi; Kolacharan Mahapatro; Gurupankaj Charana Das. Etc.

Manipuri

Maṇipuri: North Eastern India's classical dance form. It originated in the 15th century AD. Most of the dance episodes are built around the stories of Radha & Kṛṣṇa. It contains a dance style called "Punj" performed by carrying drums mostly by males.

The famous dancers are Juvari sisters, Savitā Mehta, Nirmala Mehta, Gurubinusinha & Sanghajit Singh etc.

Katthak: Famous dance style of Northern India. The dance episodes revolve round the stories of Radha & Kṛṣṇa and do contain erotic expressions and appeal.

Famous dance Gurus; Birju Maharaj; Sundara Prasad; Sitara Devi; Bindarin Maharaj; Kumudini Gopikrishna; Damayanti Joshi; Bharaheya Gupta etc.

Yakṣa ganam: Karnataka's classical dance expression. Its dance episodes are composed from Purāṇas. It has a history of 600 years. Dr Shivram Karanth had modernized this art into a classical form of dance.

There are folklore dance theatres spread throughout India. On every aspect of Indian dance style whether classical or folklore, the impact of Nāṭya Śāstra is immense.

As all rivers merge into ocean, so do all dance forms merge at the holy feet of Naṭarāja, the cosmic dancer.

99 Musical Melody of India

"Gitaṁ vadhyamca nirtyamca triyaṁ saṅgītaṁ ucyate"

Lyrical melody, instrumental music & rhythmic tdance;
these three aspects put together become sangeet, the Art of Music.

Music is the artistic expression of emotions through systematic & aesthetic combination of sound patterns.

Indian music originates from the *Samaveda*. The Samaveda had to be rendered in a Musical way. Indians through their art of music could win over Nature. Through music they used to cure many a disease. Animals are charmed and tamed by the power of music.

Indian music is classified into two schools, Hindustani (Northern India) & Carnatic (South India). During Vedic times or in Samaveda there is no mention about this division. This division prevailed from the 11th century AD. Hindustani music has more Persian influence and Mughal patronage during the medieval period.

Music is an aesthetic combination of frequencies lying in the audible range. *Swara* (note), which is fundamental to a *Raga* (melody), is an audible frequency. There are seven basic notes called *Sapta Swaras*. They are classified based on the increasing order of their frequency.

There are many evidences to prove that seven notes of Indian music form the basis for Western classical music.

Smt. MS Subba Lakshmi
The Icon of Modern India's Classical Music

Indian Svara	Western note
• *Shadja – Sa*	C
• *Riṣabha – Ri*	D (flat)
	D (sharp)

● *Gandhāra – Ga*	E (flat)
	E (Sharp)
● *Madhyama – Ma*	F (flat)
	F (sharp)
● *Pañcama – Pa*	G
● *Dhaivata – Da*	A (flat)
	A (sharp)
● *Niṣada – Ni*	B (flat)
	B (sharp)

Indian classical music is based on the maxim *"Srutir Maata Layah Pita"*. Three pillars of Carnatic classical music are :

- Melody – concept of *Rāga*
- Rhythm – concept of *Tāla*
- Lyrical beauty- *Pallavi*

Rāga

Rāga is the very profound concept in Carnatic music (in Hindustani as well). Rāga is a melodious entity arising out of the combination of notes (musical scale), with ornamentation (Gamaka). It is created by the permutation and combination of notes rendered in a particular sequence in ascent (Ārohaṇa) and descent (Avarohaṇa). Various combinations of swaras that are possible is the key to the Raga system in Carnatic music.

Rāga possesses the power to create different moods. Ex: Khamas rāga is sung to evoke erotic feelings; Mukhari- compassion; Sarangaraga- heroic mood. It prescribes a set of rules to build melody. Rāga Lakṣaṇa is the technical boundary of the rāga. There are two kinds of rāgas 1. Janaka Rāgas

2. Janyu Ragas. There are 72 Janaka ragas called as Melakarthari Ragas, the parent scales. Janyu Ragas are derived from Melakarthari ragas.

Tāla

The rhythmic aspects in Carnatic music are arguably among the most developed and sophisticated across the world. The patterns range from the simple to the complex. Laya refers to the inherent rhythm in anything. Tāla is only a time scale, and is highly mathematical, characterized by internal coherence, logical rigidity and numeric accuracy. There are six parts (Aṅgas - limbs) of a Tāla, but the following three are used more frequently than the others - *Anudhruta, Dhruta* and *Laghu.*

There are seven basic Tālas with the combinations of *Dhrutam* and *Laghu.* Every letter of lyric has to be in tune with the Tāla. Otherwise rythm cannot be maintained.

There are 108 derivations of the basic seven Tālas.

- Dhruva tala: a laghu, a dhrutam followed by two more laghus. Symbol - 1 O 1 1
- Mattya tala: a laghu, a dhrutam followed by another laghu. Symbol - 1 O 1
- Rūpaka tala: a dhrutam followed by a laghu. Symbol - O 1
- Jhampa tala: a laghu followed by an anudrutam and a dhrutam. Symbol - 1 U O
- Triputa Tala: a laghu followed by two drutams. Symbol - 1 O O
- Ata tala: two laghus followed by two drutams. Symbol - 1 1 O O
- Eka tala: consists of just a laghu. Symbol - 1

"Indian music is classified into two schools, Hindustani (Northern India) & Carnatic (South India). During Vedic times or in Samaveda there is no mention about this division. This division prevailed from the 11th century AD."

Pallavi (Lyrical Beauty)

Lyrics form the basis of music. Music derives its strength from the poetic grandeur. Lyrical beauty is mingled with the heart stirring melody and enticing rhythm to create musical bonanza. Sublime integration of various themes, religion, devotion, philosophy, emotions, intellect (science), entertainment and others with music, has created a vibrant life and tradition in this art form.

Indian lyrics adhere to the system of strict prosody called Chandas. Sage Pingala wrote "Chandas Sastra", 2500 years ago, wherein the world's first musical notation was clearly mentioned. There are many forms of lyrical composition among them Gitam, Swarajati, Varnam, Kriti, Padam, Jaavali & Tillana are popular.

Famous Texts on Indian Music

Bharata's Natya Sastra has reference to Ragas, Talas, and Instruments. The work of *Matanga* (6th - 7th Century A.D.), *Brihaddesi,* is the first to mention the word, Raga. *"Sangeet Ratnakara"* - an important musical treatise was written by *Sarangadeva* (1210-1247). It talks of Swaras, Ragas, Prabandhas (musical form of this period), Tala-Vadyas (Percussion Instruments), Gamakas (ornamentations) and other such aspects. The SangeetaSara, attributed to Vidyaranya (1320-1380) was the first to classify ragas as Melas (Parent) and Janya ragas - a milestone in the scientific development of our music. The well-structured **72 Melakarta Scheme** was formulated by *Venkatamukhi* in his treatise *"Chaturdandi Prakasika"* in 1660 AD.

Famous Musical Composers of Carnatic Music:

- *Purandaradasa (1484 - 1564 AD) is known as the Sangeet Pitāmaha (the grandfather of Carnatic music).* ***18th century – Era of the musical trinity-Sri Syama Sastri (1762 - 1827), Sri Tyagaraja (1767-1847), Sri Muthuswami Dikshitar (1776-1835).***

- *Annamayya (1408-1503); Bhadrachala Ramadas (16th century); Kshertrayya (17th century), Narayana Tirtha (17th century) Swati Tirunal (1813-1847), Veena Kuppayyar, Subbaraya Sastri, Gopalakrishna Bharati, Ghanam Krishna Iyer, Patnam Subramanya Iyer, Koteeswara Iyer, Muthaiah Bhagavatar, Mysore Vasudevachar and Papanasam Sivan.*

Most Celebrated Artists: Aryakudi Ramanujam Iyengar, Maharajapuram Viswanath Iyer, Tiger Vardachari, Chemmangudi Sreenivasa Iyer, GN Balasubramanyam, Madurai Mani Iyer, Chembai Vaidyanath Bagavathar, Veena Danammal, Dk Pattaammal, MS Subbalakshmi, ML Vasantha kumari, MangalampalliBalamuraliKrishna, Sripada Pinakapani, Nadanuri Krishnamurthy, NukalaChinna Satyanarayana, Balakrishna Prasad & Sobha Raju.

Hindustani Music: In the school of Hindustani Music, many Gharānās were formed. Among them Gwalior Gharānā, Jaipur Gharana, Agra Gharana are popular. Among the Hindustani style of renderings "Khayal" is very famous. There are many similar rāgas in both Hindustani and Carnatic music; but the names of them are different. Popular Hindustani Musical forms are *Tumarai, Ghazal, Bhajan, Tappa & Khawali.*

Famous Hindustani Music Composers: Tansen, who flourished in the court of Akbar stands as the greatest luminary . Another great legend was Santh Haridas.

Most Celebrated Artists: Aamirkhan, Bade Gulam Alikhan, Vinayak Rao Pattawardhanay, Mallikarjuna Mansoor, Kumara Gandharwa, Bhimsenjoshi, BasavarajRajaguru, Pandit Jasraj, GangubaiHangal, NoorjhahanBegum, BegumAktar(GazalRani), KishoriAmolkar, Ninadevi, Girijadevi, Siddheswari & Parvin Sultana.

"Indian music was rendered more for enlightenment than for entertainment. It enhances the Satvik quality of the listener; whereas the western music enhances the Rajasik quality of the listener. This fact was proved through certain experiments."

Indian music was rendered more for enlightenment than for entertainment. It enhances the Satvik quality of the listener; whereas the western music enhances the Rajasik quality of the listener. This fact was proved through certain experiments.

Instrumental Music- Indian Stalwarts

1. **Violin:** *VG Jog, T.K Dattar, Dwaram Venkatswami Naidu, T.Chowdaiah, Lalgudi Jayaraman, MS Gopala Krishnan, TN Krishnan, Ponnukudi Vaidyanathan, N.Rajam, L Subramanianan.*
2. **Sitar:** *Ravishankar, Nikel banerji, Vilayath khan, MustarAli khan, Shamid Pravin.*
3. **Sarod:** *Ali Akbar khan, Anjad Ali khan, SaradaRani, Afiz khan.*
4. **Veena:** *Veena Danammal, Tumarada Sangameswara Sastri, Yamani Sankar Sastri, S.Balachander, Mysore Doraiswami Iyengar, KK Bhagavatar, Chitti Babu, SadikAlikhan.*
5. **Shahanai:** *Bismillahkhan, Umashanker Misra.*
6. **Tabala:** *Allarakha, Zakir Hussian, Santhi Prasad.*
7. **Nadaswaram:** *Kumbakonam Rajratnam Pillai, Daliparti Picchahari, Sheik China Moulana, Karukuchi Arunachalam, Namagiripettiah Krishnan, Veeraswami Pillai.*
8. **Mṛdaṅgam:** *Palani Subramanya Pillai, Palghat Mani Iyer, Palghat Raghu, Umayalpuram Sivaraman, Yalla Venketswarulu.*
9. **Flute:** *TR Mahalingam, Pannalal Gosh, Hariprasadchaurasiya, N.Ramani.*
10. **Sarangi:** *Ramnarayan Sarangi, Usthad Sabrikhan, SultanKhan;*

The names mentioned above are only an indicative list and not an all inclusive list. There are many more stalwarts who make the flag of Indian artistic talents flutter at its excellent heights forever.

100 Beauty of Saṁskṛta Literature

Saṁskṛt is the mother of all languages; the Oldest prevailing language, yet very modern in its content and utility. Even Computer programming logic had been derived from the grammatical syntax and structure of Saṁskṛt.

Sanskrit is called as Devabhāṣā or Vedabhāṣā. The grandeur, beauty and complexity of the Sanskrit language is very much evident in Vedic verses.

Our Rishis of yore had wonderfully depicted the highly technical concepts with wonderful similes and presented them in compact verses with indepth meaning. These Vedic verses were intuitively comprehended by them by their Power of penance. They are not figment of imaginations but perceived truths.

The Upaniṣadic truths are replete with poetic grandeur. The Indian epic, The Ramayana is considered to be the Ādikāvya, written by Ādikavī, Valmiki in Anushtubh metre. The story of Ramayana was not just limited to India. It had a great cultural impact on south Asian countries. The content of Ramayana depicts the cultural aspects, ethical aspects, governing principles and inspires everybody who reads it. Inspired by Valmiki Ramayana, there came many works at later stage in many languages on the story of Lord Rama. The beauty of literature, usage of language and comparisons all are unique to Ramayana. It remains to be an eternal inspiration not only to the Indians, but also to the world at large.

The Mahabharata, the largest literary work of the world with 1,00,000 verses, was authored by sage Vyasa. Vyasa himself had said about Mahabharata that, "The subject matter discussed in his book can be found elsewhere, but subjects not discussed in Mahabharata cannot be found anywhere else."

Every aspect of human personality had been interestingly dealt with. It is a Cultural, Social and Historical Encyclopedia.

As long as world exists, these two Indian epics the Ramayana & the Mahabharata inspire mankind and guide them. The language, poetry and similes used in Mahabharata, stand exemplary in their renderings.

The *"Pañcatantra"* is India's Classical contribution to the world of literature. It contains stories told by Vishnu Sharma a scholar to educate the dullard princes of a king. He educates them in kingcraft and worldly dealings by introducing animated characters. This book was attributed to the second century AD. It was translated into Persian and Arabic languages in the seventh century AD. Europe had learnt it as "The Fables of Vinpay". Panchatantra contains five parts.

1. *Mithra labha* (benefiting from the friendiship) 2. *Mitrabheda* (various kinds of friendship and their usefulness) 3. *Sruhudh Bheda* (Creating differences between the friends and its consequence) 4. *Vigraham* 5. *Sandhi* (making a compromise).

Buddhist Jataka stories written in Pali language were translated into Sanskrit with classical elegance.

In the 5th century AD, *"Bṛhit Kathā"*, a compendium of 1000 stories was written in Paichachika bhasa (the language spoken in the then central India) by Gunadiya. This was later translated into Sanskrit by Somadeva with the name *"Kathā Saritā Sāgara"*.

These stories had been instrumental in evolving the stories of Arabian Nights. Most of the Arabian night stories are similar to the stories of Kathā Saritā Sāgara.

Panini's Ashtadhyayi (5th century BC) is a grammar text .Yet it deals with science of sounds and rules of pronunciation etc. It had influenced the evolution of many Indian languages and is still influencing the syntax code for Artificial intelligence (speaking to a machine). *Pingala's Chandas Sutra deals* with the prosody to the Sanskrit language.

Sanskrit plays were world famous in ancient days. These plays are reflected in the literature of China, Greece, Germany and South Asian countries. India has a rich tradition of theatrical arts, much longer than that of the Western world. Famous Sanskrit dramatists include Sudraka, Bhasa, Asvaghosa and Kalidasa. Though numerous plays were written by these playwrights only a few are available; very little is known about the authors themselves.

Mṛcchakaṭikā (The Little Clay Cart) is the one of the earliest known Sanskrit plays in the post-Vedic age. This play is thought to have been composed by Shudraka in the 2nd century BC. Rife with romance, sex, royal intrigue and comedy, the juicy plot of the play has numerous twists and turns. The main story is about a young man named, Charudatta, and his love for a rich courtesan, Vasantasena. The love affair is complicated by a royal courtier, who is also attracted to Vasantasena.

Bhasa's most famous plays are *Svapna Vasavadatta* (Vasavadatta's dream), *Pancharātra* and *Pratijna Yaugandharayaanam* (The vows of Yaugandharayana).

Bhasa is considered to be one of the best Sanskrit playwrights, second only to Kalidasa. Kalidasa in his many plays tells about Bhasa.

Kalidasa (3rd-4th cent AD) is the greatest poet and playwright in Sanskrit, and occupies the same position in Sanskrit literature that Shakespeare occupies in English literature. The famous plays by Kalidaṣa

"Sanskrit is the mother of all languages; the Oldest prevailing language, yet very modern in its content and utility. Even Computer programming logic had been derived from the grammatical syntax and structure of Sanskrit."

are *Vikramorvaśīya* (Vikrama and Urvashi), *Mālavikāgnimitra* (Malavika and Agnimitra), and the play that he is most known for: *Abhijñānaśākuntala* (The Recognition of Shakuntala). The last named play is considered to be greatest play in Sanskrit.

Kalidasa also wrote two large epic poems, *Raghuvamsham* (The Genealogy of Raghu) and *Kumarasambhavam* (Birth of Kumara), and two smaller epics, *Ritusamhaara* (Medley of Seasons) and *Meghadutam* (The Cloud Messenger), another perfect work.

Palm Leaves of Geeta Govinda

Kalidasa's writing is characterized by the usage of simple but beautiful Sanskrit, and by his extensive use of similes. His similes have earned him the saying, Upamana Kalidasasya (Kalidasa owns simile).

Other important plays written in this period include *Ratnavali* and *Nagananda*, by Sri Harsha in the 7th century.

All the Sanskrit plays were very popular and were staged in ancient times all over India. Now the only surviving ancient Sanskrit drama theatre is Koodiyattam. It is being preserved in Kerala by the Chakyar community. Padma Shri Māni Mādhava Chākyār choreographed and directed plays like *Kalidasa's Abhijñānaśākuntala, Vikramorvaśīya* and *Mālavikāgnimitra; Bhasa's Swapnavāsadatta* and *Pancharātra* for the first time in the history of *Koodiyattam*. He popularized Koodiyattam and rejuvenated the only surviving Sanskrit drama theatre in India.

Bharata's Natya Sastra deals with the science of Indian theatre (both play & dance drama)

The greatest works of poetry in this period are the five Mahākāvyas, or great epics:

- *Kumarasambhavam by Kalidasa*
- *Raghuvamsham by Kalidasa*
- *Kiratarjuniya by Bharavi*
- *Shishupala Vadha by Sri Maagha*
- *Naishadiya Charitam by Sri Harsha*

Other major literary works of this period are Kadambari by Bana Bhatta, the first Sanskrit novelist (6th-7th centuries),

The *Geeta Govinda* (The song of Govinda) by Jayadeva (11th century AD) is the story of Krishna's love for Radha, and is written in spectacularly lyrical and musical Sanskrit. The *Ashtapadis* of the Geeta Govinda also form a staple theme in Bharatanatyam, Kuchipudi and Odissi classical dance recitals.

Sanskrit influenced literary works of all the Indian languages. Hindi, Telugu, Kannada, Tamil, Bengali & other Indian languages derived the structure and terminology from Sanskrit. Since 11th century AD, many Sanskrit works were translated into regional languages. But usage of Sanskrit in technical studies continued till great Macaulay introduced English in the year 1835. Even today usage of Sanskrit remains supreme in religious literature and religious rituals.

Sanskrit is a perfected language. Sanskrit existed for more than 5000 years. Richness of human thought and culture is still preserved with its pristine glory only in Sanskrit language.

101 Avadhanam –The Language Gymnastics

Indian literary genius manifests itself in a language feat called "Avadhanam". After Sanskrit, most of the Indian languages have adopted this exposition of literary talent called Avadhanam. It is a very popular literary feat in Telugu & other regional languages.

The concentrated mind gets focussed on a particular aspect. If the poetic mind gets concentrated on many aspects simultenously it is called *Avadhanam.* If a poet is able to concentrate fully on the eight varied aspects of literature, then it is called *Ashta-Avadhanam.* The poet or person who does this feat is called Avadhani. Other Scholars who pose questions on the various aspects of the language are called *"Pruchyakas".* The Avadhani answers all the questions posed by each Pruchyaka. If there are one hundred Pruchyakas it is called sata-avadhanam. If there are 1000 pruchyakas, then it is called shasra- avadhanam.

"Avandhanam is the literary feat and is unique to India. It requires subtle and sharp intellect to deal with language gymnastics."

What are the various aspects of Avadhanam?

Nishidha-Akshari: The questioner restricts the Avadhani by asking him not use a particular letter or syllable while the poet starts composing a poem in a particular chandas (prosody).

Niyantha-Akshari: The questioner defines the letter or syallable to be used by the poet in each stanza, while composing a poem.

Datta Padi: The questioner brings in a funny word or irrelevant word and asks the poet to use that word while composing the poem without losing the context & meaning of the composition.

Samasya Puranam: The questioner brings in a poetic riddle and the poet has to build upon the poetic problem and provide solution to the riddle while composing the poem. For example "the sun rises in midnight"- for this kind of poetic riddle the avadhani has to use his litrary talent and common sense to build upon the problem.

Varnana: Questioner asks the poet to describe poetically any thing in a most difficult chandas .It may vary from a small bit of waste paper to a mighty star in the sky.

Asuvu: Poet or avadhani has to compose a poem instantaneously in full with quickness and alterness.

Purana Patanam: Questioner poses a question from puranas and famous literary classics and requests the avadhani to repeat verbatim the said poem of a particular purana.

Aprasthutha Prasangam: Silly interference by a questioner in every aspect of avadhana to divert the attention of the avadhani appears lively and provides entertainment to the listeners. The avadhani is supposed to answer the silly interference with tact, satire and fun.

The beauty of the Avadhanam is that, regarding the first six aspects from *"Nissidhakshari"* to *"Varnana"*, the poet or Avadhani had to compose a single line of each aspect or question and finally repeat the entire poem at once after the round while simultaneously withstanding the hurdles created by the questioner of *"Asuvu"* and *"Aprasthutha Prasangam"*, questioner.

The process of Avadhanam requires a lot of creativity, sense of humour, concentration, command on the subject and the language and the Avadhani should be well-versed in Scriptures and Puranas.

Avandhanam is the literary feat and is unique to India. It requires subtle and sharp intellect to deal with language gymnastics.

"The process of Avadhanam requires a lot of creativity, sense of humour, concentration, command on the subject and the language and the Avadhani should be well versed in Scri ptures and Puranas."

Womanhood West vs East ?

-In the words of Swami Vivekananda

The ideal of womanhood in India is motherhood — that marvelous, unselfish, all-suffering, ever-forgiving mother.

In the West, the woman is wife. The idea of womanhood is concentrated there — as the wife. To the ordinary man in India, the whole force of womanhood is concentrated in motherhood. In the Western home, the wife rules. In an Indian home, the mother rules. If a mother comes into a Western home, she has to be subordinate to the wife; to the wife belongs the home. A mother always lives in our homes: the wife must be subordinate to her. See all the difference of ideas.

Now, I only suggest comparisons; I would state facts so that we may compare the two sides. Make this comparison. If you ask, "What is an Indian woman as wife?", the Indian asks, "Where is the American woman as mother? What is she, the all-glorious, who gave me this body? What is she who kept me in her body for nine months? Where is she who would give me twenty times her life, if I had need? Where is she whose love never dies, however wicked, however vile I am? Where is she, in comparison with her, who goes to the divorce court the moment I treat her a little badly? O American woman! where is she?" I will not find her in your country. I have not found the son who thinks mother is first.

Exemplary Indian Womanhood
Mahilā Pratibhā Prabhā

102 Women Ṛṣis

Yatra nariṣu pūjyate tatra ramyate devatāḥ

(Manusmṛti)

Whereever women are respected and worshipped, there dwell the Devatās-
(the Godly beings who shower grace, prosperity and peace on us)

> "Women in India are Goddesses, great mothers, valorous queens and noble teachers (gurus); Women studied Vedas; Women Performed yagnas-vedic sacrifices; women even visualized Vedic mantras:"

Women in India are goddesses, great mothers, valorous queens and noble teachers (gurus); Women studied Vedas; Women performed yajñas-vedic sacrifices; women even visualized Vedic mantras:

This need not surprise us, for most of the hymns of the Ṛg Veda are the composition by twenty-one sage-poetesses. **Women-sages were called Ṛṣikas and Brahmavādinīs.**

Certain Rig Veda hymns were composed by following Ṛṣikas

1. Romasa 2. Lopamudra 3. Apala 4. Kadru 5. Visvavara 6. Ghosha 7. Juhu 8. Vagambhrini 9. Paulomi 10. Jarita 11. Sraddha-Kamayani 12. Urvasi 13. Saranga 14. Yami 15. Indrani 16. Savitri 17. Devajami 18. Nodha 19. Akrishtabhasha 20. Sikatanivavari 21. Gaupayana.

Here are a few references of women's education during Vedic times. Brahmavādinīs means women – spiritual seekers and scholars in Vedas; Gargi, and Maiteriyi were the towering references. Brahmavadins used to marry after their education was over, some of them like Vedavati, a daughter of sage Kusadhvaja, would not marry at all. A verse in Yajur Veda (xxvi, 2) substantiates the women learning Vedic knowledge along with all classes.

Upanayana is mandatory for learning Vedas; hence women ought to have undergone Upanayana ceremony before mastering vedas. The Atharva Veda (xi. 5.8) expressly refers to maidens undergoing the Brahmacarya discipline and the Sūtra works of the 5th century B.C.Manusmrithi too refers to Upanayana among the saṁskāras (rituals) obligatory for girls (II.66).

103 Women Rulers Through Ages

- Many Centuries before the birth of Chirst, Chandra Gupta Maurya had ruled his kingdom along with queen **" Kumara Devi".**
- In the second century AD, a Queen named **" Naganika"** ruled the mighty kingdom of Sathavahana dynasty, in central and southern India.
- In Kashmir, a queen called **"Sugandhi"** had ruled the kingdom after the demise of king Sankar Rao.
- The great empress, **"Rani Karnavati"** had fought with the invader Bahudur Shah and protected the Chittore Fort of Rajasthan.
- During the sixteenth century AD, **"Rani Durgavati"** had ruled the Bundel Khand Kingdom.
- Warrior queen **"Karunadevi"** had defeated Muhammad Gori's General Kutbuddhin.
- **"Rani Rudramadevi"**, (13th century) had ruled the Kingdom of Kakateeeyas (Telugu) in Southern India, with Warangal as her capital.
- Telugu queen **"Ganapamba"** had ruled the Kingdom of Madhura (South India); **Mangamma, Nagaamma, Manchala, Cheenaamma,** were the Chieftains of many provinces of Andhra Pradesh, Karnataka, Kerala and Tamilnadu.
- **Rani Chandra Prabha**; ruled the Khachar Kingdom of Bengal and Assam, when her husband had been captivated by the rival kings, she got him released through tact and strategy; She patronized the development of Sanskrit in the areas of Bengal & Assam.

Divine Mother- Mahā Durgā

Rani of Janshi

- **Rani Ahilya Bai** (1735-95), the Maharastrian queen, ruled the great Maratha empire; She protected many Hindu temples, patronized them and renovated them; Kasi's Shiva temple; Gaya's Vishnu temple; Tirupati's Venketswara temple were supported by her and she had even renovated them; She even constructed the roadway between Kasi and Calcutta.
- None can forget the contribution of **Rani of Jhansi –Lakshmi Bai,** in the freedom struggle-the first war of Indian independence against British during 1857, the great Sepoy Mutiny.

Muslim Queens of India

- **Chandbibi** ruled a part of Bijapur Kingdom (Ahmedabad province) after the death of her brother;
- During the 13th century AD, Queen **Razia Sultana** ruled Delhi, for a period of four years;
- During the regime of Moghul emperor, "Jahangir", the de-facto power had been wielded by his Queen **Nurjahan** (1611-1627)

Modern India

- Our Prime Minister Late **Smt Indira Gandhi** stands tall, as the symbol of women's valour, intellect and efficiency;
- Today there are galaxies of women stalwarts.... Indian Chief Ministers, Governors, Ministers, State Secretaries & District collectors, who are efficiently managing the affairs of the country;
- Look at the countries of Indian subcontinent, which were part of once united India. Women had occupied top positions within a few years of these countries becoming independent,

Smt. Srimaobandara Naike, the first president of SriLanka, *Mrs. Bhutto*, the Prime Minister of Pakistan, *Mrs. Khalida Zia, Mrs Rehaman* of Bangladesh.

Look at the American democracy, which is considered to be the greatest of all prevailing democracies, even today (as on today-Aug, 2007), there is no woman who had been appointed to the highest post of President.

The above facts substantiate that, it is the inbuilt culture of India to respect womanhood; Queen of the Kingdom had been always referred to as **"Rājamātā"** or **"Rāni-mā"**; Not just queens of India were considered as an embodiment of mothers; every thing related to Power or Śakti is equated with "Womanhood" in India.

Hence the river Ganga is called Ganga Mātā; our country is called **"Bhārata Mātā";** the land on which we live is called **"Bhū Mātā";** Power of learning is called **Saraswati Mātā**; Power of valour is equated with **"Durgā Mātā";** Power of prosperity and wealth is called as **"Śrī Mātā";** Cow, the embodiment of all celestial powers is called **'Gomātā'.**

Indian culture regards womanhood as "Motherhood"; Western culture considers the relationship with women as "Partnership" and women are appreciated as an object of "Beauty"; as the cultural gap remains forever. The Indian womanhood shines forever more glorious than the West; History reveals it too.

Ravi Varma's Painting

Four Great Foreign Women who were Inspired by India and served it.

Annie Besant
(1847 - 1933)

Besant was a British social reformer, who settled in India and became a leading light in Theosophy,aspiritualmovement based on Indian doctrines, She was a campaigner for women's rights and a supporter of Indian nationalism and core member of Indian National congress and founding member of Indian Home rule league.

Sister Nivedita
(1867-1911)

Sister Nivedita, earlier known as Margaret Elizabeth , a British national, dedicated her life in service of India. Her work among women of India , her support to the cause of national education and her contributions in the field of national awakening, her service to the poor and the needy and, above all, her love for our motherland endeared her among all Indians

Having inspired by Swami Vivekananda, the day Margaret landed in Kolkata(1898), she started working among the poor and destitute. Nivedita plunged into action in Kolkata to save the city from the grip of the plague in 1899. She started sweeping the streets and clearing the drains.

The Mother. *(1878-1973)*

Mirra Alfassa, a French woman, respectfully called as the Mother, became the guiding light of great spiritual movement, which was ignited by MahaYogi Aurobindo of Pondichery. Today millions of foreign nationals come to Aurovilli, the global spiritual township envisaged by the mother. She has become the spiritual mother, who nurtures the spiritual child with supra mental divine consciousness. Her work continues as spiritual being in us evolves.

Mother Teresa
(1910 –1997)

Agnes Gonxha Bojaxhiu was an Albanian Roman Catholic nun, whose photo inspiringly adore many Indian homes today. She founded the Missionaries of Charity and won the Nobel Peace Prize in 1979 for her great humanitarian work. For over forty years she served the poor, sick, orphaned, and dying in Calcutta and in may remote parts of India . She inspired millions to undertake Social work in name of God. Except for the criticism of converting many innocent poor Indians into Christianity, and her accepting donations even from criminals, her services to poor and downtrodden remain ever in the heart of Indians.

Talents in Sports
Krīḍā- Pratibhā

104 Indian Sports & Sports Legends

Indian genius was not confined to knowledge & wisdom. Ancient India was equally talented in recreation – sports & games. Many of today's popular games originated from India. Games like, Chess, Snakes and Ladders, Playing Cards, Polo, the martial arts of Judo and Karate had originated in India and were transmitted to foreign countries, where they were further refined & developed.

Chess- Caturaṅga

A game very similar to modern Chess and Ludo was played in ancient India. In this game there used to be four participants due to which it was named Caturaṅga meaning 'four bodies'. This four-bodied game was played with counters and a dice (aksha). Another name for this game was Astapada meaning 'eight steps'. This game was perhaps the progenitor of both modern day games of Chess and Ludo. There are instances in Indian history of this game being played.

The Indian origin of the game of chess is supported even by the Encyclopedia Britannica according to which, "About 1783-89 Sir. William Jones, in an essay published in the 2nd Vol. of Asiatic Researches, argued that Hindustan was the cradle of chess, the game having been known there from time immemorial by the name Caturaṅga, that is, the four angas, or members of an army, which are said in the *Amarakośa* (an ancient Indian Dictionary - S.B.) to be elephants, horses, chariots and foot soldiers. As applicable to real armies, the term Chaturanga is frequently used by the epic poets of India

He further says that chess, under the Sanskrit name Chaturanga was exported from India into Persia in the 6th century of our era; that by a natural corruption, the old Persians changed the name into *"Chatrang"*; but when their country was soon afterwards taken possession of by the Arabs, they altered it further into "Shatranj", which name has found its way presently into Europe.

"H.J.R. Murry in his monumental work "A History of Chess", comes to the conclusion that chess is a descendant of an Indian game played in the 7th century.

The other term Ashtapada meaning eight steps, which was also used to describe this game in ancient India, perhaps was a description for the eight steps (Squares), which the modern Chessboard, has. The modern Chessboard is chequered with 64 (8 x 8) squares in all, with eight squares on each side. The old English word for chess which is Esches, possibly stems from this eight squared aspect of the game as did the Sanskrit word Astapada.

Playing Cards

The game of playing cards was also one of the favourite pastimes of Indians in ancient times. This game was patronised especially by the royalty and nobility. This game was known in ancient times as "Krīḍāpatram", in the Middle Ages, it was known as Ganjifa. In medieval India Ganjifa cards were played in practically all-royal courts. This game is recorded to have been played in Rajputana, Kashyapa Meru (Kashmir), Utkala (Orissa) the Deccan and even in Nepal. The Mughals also patronised this game, but the Mughal card-sets differ from those of the ancient Indian royal courts.

But according to Abul Fazal author of the Ain-e-Akbari, the game of cards was of Indian origin and that it was a very popular pastime in the Indian (Hindu) courts when the Muslims came into India.

Themes from the Ramayana and Mahabharata are painted on these cards. The largest numbers of such cards are to be found in Orissa.

All these cards were hand-made and were painted in the traditional style. This required considerable patience and hard meticulous work. The kings usually commissioned painters to make cards as per

> "Games like, Chess, Snakes and Ladders, Playing Cards, Polo, the martial arts of Judo and Karate had originated in India and were transmitted to foreign countries, where they were further refined & developed."

their preference. Some cards were also made of ivory, tortoiseshell, and pearls in laid or enamelled with precious metals. The cards were of different shapes; they were circular, oval rectangular, but the circular cards were more common.

Judo & Karate

Martial arts of India Kalaripayate

Many eyebrows would be raised when an Indian lays claim to the martial arts of Judo and Karate.

But in the distant corner of India a dying martial art exists which comes significantly close to Karate. This art form is called ***Kalaripayate***. The practitioners of ***Kalaripayate*** have to develop acrobatic capabilities and use swords or knives to attack an opponent. This art form seems to have travelled from India to the countries of the far-east alongwith the Buddhist religion. Buddhist monks who travelled barefoot and unarmed to spread the gospel of Buddha seem to have accepted this art with alterations.

The Father and founder of Zen Buddhism (called C'han in China), ***Bodhidharma***, a Brahmin born in Kacheepuram in Tamil Nadu, in 522 A.D. arrived at the courts of the Chinese Emperor Liang Nuti, of the 6th dynasty. He taught the Chinese monks Kalaripayattu, a very ancient Indian martial art, so that they could defend themselves against the frequent attacks of bandits. In time, the monks became famous all over China as experts in barehanded fighting, later known as the Shaolin boxing art.

The Shaolin temple, which has been handed back a few years ago by the communist Government to the C'han Buddhist monks, inheritors of Boddhidharma's spiritual and martial teachings, is now open to visitors. On one of the walls, a fresco can be seen, showing Indian dark-skinned monks, teaching their lighter-skinned Chinese brothers the art of barehanded fighting. On this painting are inscribed: "Tenjiku Naranokaku" which means: "the fighting techniques to train the body (which come) from India…"

Kalaripayate was banned by the British in 1793. (Refer to chapter on European Imperialism).

(Source: A Western Journalist on India: a ferengi's columns - By Francois Gautier p. 155-158).

Polo

Polo was an ancient Indian game. Mostly royal clan used to play this game. Indian kings used to play polo sitting on the horsebacks, camel backs and elephant tops.

There are many games native to India, they are Kabaddī, Malcom, Hockey (Indian stick game), stick wielding, sword plying, Indian wrestling, Top playing, kite flying, etc.

Modern India & Sports

India could not achieve much in sports after independence. It is not because of lack of Talent in India. It is because of not recognizing the genuine talent and due to lack of encouragement. If India excelled today in any game or sport, it is because of individual efforts of that particular sports person. If necessary infrastructure and equipment are provided to our sports persons, they shall certainly bring glory to India.

"India could not achieve much in sports after independence. It is not because of lack of Talent in India. It is because of not recognizing the genuine talent and due to lack of encouragement."

Let us atleast remember the names of sports legends who brought Indian glory.

Olympics

Name	Year	Event	Award/Honour
1. Narman	Olympics1900	200m hurdles 200m Run	Silver Silver
2. KS Javed	Olympics 1952	wrestling	Bronze
3. Leander peas	Olympics 1996	Lawn tennis	Bronze
4. Karanam Malleswari	Olympics 2000	Weight lighting (69 kgs)	Bronze

Chess

Viswanathan Anand - 2000 world champion, today is being called as chess king and top-seeded player. In junior chess champion master Harikrishna and Koneru Hampi had won many International trophies.

Badminton

Prakash Padukone - 1981 world Cup victor. Gopichand had won prestigious "all England championship". He had won many victories at international tournaments.

Tennis

Men: Vijay Amṛta Raj, Ramesh Krishnan, Leander Peas, Mahesh Bhupati.

Women: Sania Mirza, the shining star of India today.

Motor Racing

Naveen Kartikeyan had won world class racing events.

Hockey

Hockey was once India's national game. Today cricket had taken over its position.

Indian hockey star "Dhyan Chand"'s statue was honorably erected as a mark of respect in Vienna with four hockey sticks in four hands. Other stalwarts of of Hockey were Dhan Raj Pillai, Mukesh Kumar etc.

Billiards

Michael Ferreira, Geeth Sethi, Pankaj Advani stood tall to bring glory to India.

Shooting

Jaspal Rane had won many international championships.

Athletics /Running

The Indian legendary athletes are Millka Singh, PT Usha, and Aswani Nachappa.

Foot Ball

IM Vijayan, Baichung Bhutia remain to us as a source of inspiration.

Cricket

India won 1983 World Cup under the Captainship of Kapildev, 20-20 World Cup in 2007 under the Captainship of Dhoni and won 2011 World Cup again under the Captainship of Dhoni. India has a reputation of being a cricket superpower, with a galaxy of Indian cricketers bringing fame to the country. A Few Personalities 1. Sir Ranji 2. CK Naidu 3. Nari Contractor 4. Pataudi 5. Kapildev 6. Gavaskar 7. Tendulkar 8. Chandra Sekhar 9. Ravi Sastri 10. Viswanath.

Only thing that has to be done in the field of sports is to stop politicians from interfering in the selection process. The genuine talent has to be recognized; corporate sector has to be involved in providing sports related infrastructure & for patronizing vigrous training courses to sports personnel.

Indians are talented in sports, but the Indian sports plants are to be nurtured regularly. Then the flowers of Indian sports talents blossom in full.

Other Indian Glories
Anya Pratibhā Dīpti

105 Taj Mahal – A Wonderful Mystery

An Indian Edifice remains even today as the Symbol of Romance. It stands magnificently as one of the Seven Wonders of the World. It attracts millions of visitors and holds them with awe by its charm, beauty, grandeur and resplendence. That marble marvel is Taj Mahal. It was built by great Moghul emperor Shahjahan.

An Indian historian, by name PN Oak, had written a book called "Taj Mahal –The True Story". Facts mentioned therein are as under.

He claims that as the world believes, the Taj Mahal is not Queen Mumtaz Mahal's tomb, but an ancient Hindu temple of Lord Shiva (then known as Tejo Mahalaya), located in a Palace complex and worshipped by the Rajputs of Agra city.

In the course of his research, Oak discovered that the Shiva temple palace had been usurped by Shah Jahan from the then Maharaja of Jaipur, Jai Singh. It seems that Mughal emperor Shah Jahan then remodelled the palace into his wife's memorial.

To substantiate his claim, he gives more than 100 evidences in his book. Here we try to reproduce a few of them…

Shahjahan's own court-chronicle, the Badshahnama, admits (on page 403, Vol. I), that a grand mansion of unique splendour, capped with a dome (imaarat-e-alishan wa gumbaze) was taken from the Jaipur Maharaja Jaisingh for Mumtaz's burial, and that the building was then known as Raja Mansingh's palace.

Prince Aurangzeb's letter to his father, emperor Shahjahan, belies the Archaeological Department's reliance on Tavernier. Aurangzeb's letter is recorded in at least three chronicles titled 'Aadaab-e-Alamgiri' 'Yaadgaarnama' and the 'Muraqqa-I-Akbarabadi' (edited by Said Ahmad, Agra, 1931, page 43, footnote 2) In that letter Aurangzeb records in 1652 A.D. itself that the several buildings in the fancied burial place of Mumtaz were all seven-storeyed and were so old that they were all leaking, while the dome had developed a crack on the northern side. Aurangzeb, therefore, ordered immediate repairs to the buildings at his own expense while recommending to the emperor that more elaborate repairs be carried out later. This is proof that during Shahjahan's reign itself the Taj complex was old requiring immediate repairs.

The ex-Maharaja of Jaipur retains in his secret personal Kapad Dwara collection two orders from Shahjahan dated December 18, 1633 (bearing modern numbers R. 176 and 177) requisitioning the Taj building complex. That was so blatant a usurpation that the then ruler of Jaipur was ashamed to make the documents public.

The word Tasimacan is Taz-I-macan, ie. Royal residence, which is synonymous with Taj Mahal. That is to say, the Hindu palace was known as Tasimacan alias Taj mahal even before Mumtaz's burial, according to Tavernier.

French merchant Jean Baptiste Tavernier, who visited India during Shah Jahan's reign, has said in his book, Travels in India, the cost of the scaffolding exceeded that of the entire work done regarding the mausoleum. This proves that all Shah Jahan had to do was engrave Koranic texts on the walls of a Hindu palace; that is why the cost of the scaffolding was much more than the value of the entire work done.

Tombs ofMumtaj & Shahjahan

Even Encyclopedia Britanica states that Tavernier undertook a journey (1638-43) as far as Agra and Golconda. His purpose was to visit the Great Moghul emperor and to the diamond mines.

Tavernier has recorded: " Of all the tombs which one sees at Agra that of the wife of Shahjahan is the most splendid. He purposely made the tomb near the Tasimacan (which had six large courts) where all foreigners come, so that the whole world should see and admire it".

"Mahal" is exclusively used in India. It is not of Arabic or Persian origin. Therefore, it is not of the Mughal period. It is of Sanskrit origin. One can easily identify "Mahal" as a contraction of the Sanskrit "Mahalaya" or "Maha-alaya" meaning "Grand Residence" and "Tejas" is also the Sanskrit term for "resplendence" and "light". "Teja Mahalaya" also means "Resplendent Shrine".

The people who dominate the Agra region are Jats. Their name for Shiva is Tejaji. The Jat special issue of the Illustrated Weekly of India (June 28, 1971) mentions that the Jats have Teja Mandirs i.e. Teja Temples. This is because Teja Linga is one among several names of Shiva Lingas. From this it is apparent that the Taj Mahal is Tejo Mahalaya, the Great Abode of Tej.

The Taj Palace is located in the twin township of Jaisinghpura and Khawaspura, which are Rajput words, not Muslim.

The entire Taj building consists of many sealed rooms along its corridors, in the two basements, on the upper floors and in its numerous towers, which clearly proves the contention that it was meant to be a temple-palace.

Many rooms in the Taj Mahal have remained sealed since Shah Jahan's time, and are still inaccessible to the public. Oak asserts they contain a headless statue of Shiva and other objects commonly used for worship and rituals in Hindu temples

The sanctum in the Taj Mahal had silver doors and gold railings as Hindu temples still have. It also had nets of pearl, and gems stuffed in the marble lattices.

Radiocarbon dating was performed on some door samples taken from the Taj Mahal by Prof Marvin Mills of the Pratt Institute Archaeological History Department, New York, who with Dr. Evan Williams of the Brooklyn College radiocarbon laboratory, thereby determined that the monument pre-dates Shah Jehan by at least three centuries.

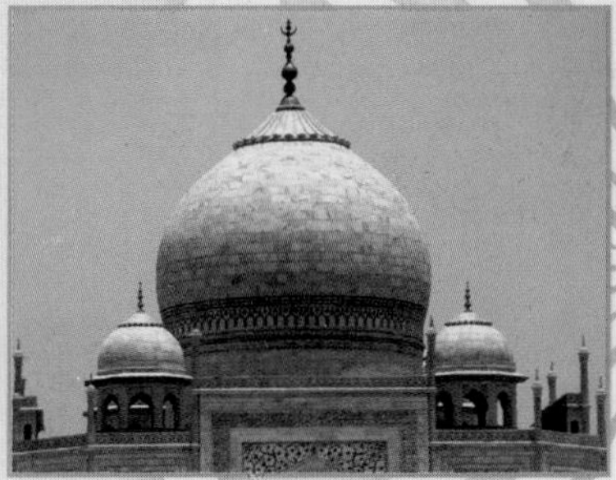

Trishul & kalash, Lotus petals and Jaipur style of domes of Taj architecture

Dr. Ernest Binfield Havell (1861-1934 (principal to the Madras College of Art in the 1890s and left as principal of the Calcutta College of Art some 20 years later)) has observed: in his book, Indian Architecture - Its Psychology, Structure and History from the First Mohammedan Invasion to the Present Day. **'there is one thing which has struck every writer about the Taj Mahal and that is its dissimilarity to any other monument in any other part of the world" and observes that Islamic architecture in India is influenced by Hindu**

Please Note that A public interest Litigation filed by PN Oak in Supreme Court had been dismissed in the year 2002. Many historians of India donot authenticate the version of PN Oak.

It is evident that Taj mahal stands unique in many aspects, being born as Hindu temple palace, metaphorshised into Muslim Tomb and today stands as symbolic edifice of Romance, and being preserved as world heritage site, manifesting Indian glory and talents for eternity. Let us say Indians built it may be by 20 thousand or 20 lakh people, who knows?

106 Eternal Fragrance of Indian Perfumes

Since ancient times, India's perfume fragrance reached the western noses and was in great demand. Greeks, Romans, Arabs, Egyptians, were all crazy about Indian scents and the aroma trade between India and these countries. It dates back to 500 BC.

A Greek historian of 1st century BC called "Pariplus" recorded that Greeks imported sandalwood from India in large quantities.

Etymology of word sandal in English had its roots in Latin word *"santulam"* and Sanskrit word *"Chandanam"*. This "Chandanam" was widely available in south India. *Vanaspati Sastra* is a branch of Āyurveda and *Vṛkṣa Āyurveda,* which mentions about three varieties of sandalwood

1. White sandalwood – *Srikanda Chandanam or Sweta Chandanam.*
2. Yellow sandalwood - *Peeta Chandanam.*
3. Red Sandalwood - *Rakta Chandanam.*

Oil was extracted from the sandalwood, Indians called it as Chandana tailam. Arabs called it as Theyl peshani. Romans and Arabs used to purchase this oil from India.

The Musk Deer

Musk Perfume

Musk: Musk is a widely used perfume today. This is a liquid extracted from musk deer. This liquid is used in perfumes and toiletries. English "Musk" had Sanskrit origin. In Sanskrit **Muska** means deer's testicals. Hence **Muska** had become *Musk.*

Spikenard: It is a rarest herb only available in the mountain ranges of Himalayas. Romans used to import this herb from India. An aura of fragrance encircles a person who smears it on his body. This is also used as a medicine to blacken the hair. In Sanskrit it is called as "Nardostachys jatamansi".

Apart from these, Indians had the knowledge of making perfumes from herbs and rare animal extracts, flowers, always bloomed with fragrance on Indian bodies?

Perfume making requires the knowledge of Chemistry. Ancient India had abundant expertise of it. Eternally talented India's fragrance always attracted the Western bees, at all times, in all ages.

107 Natural Dyes – Eternal India in Flying Colours

The world today is turning back to age old natural dyes as they are environment-friendly, less toxic, less polluting, non-carcinogenic and non-poisonous, gentle, soft and subtle.

From the indigo `ikat' fabric found in a Pharoah's tomb to the rose madder scrap dug up at Mohenjodaro, from Biblical references to 17th century literature testify Europe's fascination with Indian dyes and other art forms.

India's heritage of natural dye fabrics has been synonymous to excellence. The Vedas have mentioned many herbs that give dyes. For example, Indigo dye and turmeric dye. Turmeric dyeing to cotton cloth is considered auspicious while performing yagnas.

The 2000 year old paintings of Ajantha caves in Maharastra stand testimony to the brilliant colouring technology of ancient India. The charm of Indian dyes attracted many foreign kings, merchants and travelers to India. Traditional Artisans, Tribals and Ayurvedic experts use natural dyes. With the wide spread awareness of harmful effects of chemical dyes,the west are exploring various options of utilizing ancient India's dye making technology.

Kalamkari Traditions of India

Kalamkari, the unique style of artistic cloth painting of Ancient India, flourished at Kalahasti and Machilipatnam in Andhra Pradesh. In this style, vegetable dyes are used to colour the designs on themes from Hindu mythology and epics (Ramayana, Mahabharata), images of Gods and heroes. The artists use a bamboo or date palm stick as the brush or pen. The Kalamkari work was a further embellishment to the gold brocade work in the woven fabric, which was used as sarees & dhotis by the royal family.

Tanjore Paintings

Karrupur is a style of Kalamkari that developed in the Thanjavur region during the Maratha rule.

Traditionally, Natural dyes in India can be divided into three categories: dyes obtained from plants, animals and minerals.

Plant Dyes

Although plants exhibit a wide range of colours, not all of these pigments can be used as dyes. Some do not dissolve in water, some cannot be absorbed by fibres, whereas others fade when washed or exposed to air or sunlight. Almost all parts of the plants like root, bark, leaf, fruit, wood, seed, flower, gums and resins etc. produce dyes. Over 2000 pigments are synthesized by various parts of plants, of which only about 150 have been commercially exploited. Well-known ancient India dyes obtained from herbs & plants include red madder, blue indigo yellow saffron turmeric, Pomegranate rind.

Animal/Insect Dye-LAC

Lac taken from insect Kerria Lacca is probably most ancient of all Animal Dyes. Atharva Veda says that both lac as well as lac dye served as effective & valuable medicine. Cochineal is a brilliant red dye produced from insects living on cactus plants.

Minerals dyes: Iron, copper and tin were used as dyes as well as mordant. E.g. Ocher obtained from iron.

Mordant

Although some fabrics such as silk and wool can be coloured simply by being dipped in the dye, cotton requires a mordant. Natural dyes require a mordant to fix to the fabric, and prevent the colour from either fading with exposure to light or washing out. Common mordants are Alum, Iron, Tin etc.

Natural dyes preparations

The dye is generally prepared by boiling the crushed powder with water, but sometimes it is left to steep in cold water. The solution then obtained is used generally to dye coarse cotton fabrics. Alum is generally used as a mordant.

Limitations

Although India possesses large plant resources, only little has been exploited so far. With the increasing of using natural products, there is a great demand for naturally dyed products. But this is getting limited to hand loom textiles. Moreover, even in India, the techniques of preparing natural dyes are fast disappearing. This tradition has to be revived among weaving communities and Tribals.

Scientific investigations, Biotechnological and other modern techniques are required to improve the quality and quantity of dye production, to assess the real potential and availability of natural dye-yielding resources and for propagation of species.

Ajanta paintings – The Testimonial for Natural Colours

Let us colour the modern technology with age old wisdom of India, to give the brightest hue to life. Let the Natural dye industry of India, come back with flying colours.

108 Sugar's Sweet History

Producing sugar from sugarcane is an Indian invention. Since Vedic times, Indians know this art of producing sugar. In Sanskrit sugar is called *"Syakarah"*, in Arabic it had become *"Shaker"*, in Latin it is called *"Sacrum"* in German it is called *"Zucker"* in French it is *"Sucere"* in English it had become sugar. And thus India's syakarah had finally become sugar.

Greeks had first come to know from Indians the usage of sugar. Greek Chronicles during Alexander's interaction with India, had decribed sugarcane as a crop that produces honey without honeybees. Till the advent of the 13th century, sugar was a luxurious item in Europe and was heavily imported from India. Chinese also had learnt the skills of producing sugar from the sugarcane crop of Indians.

Pourtugeuse, Spanish & Italian merchants had introduced sugarcane crop in the countries of Africa, South America and West Indies, after learning it in India

HIS VISION - OUR MISSION

" But one vision I see clear as life before me that the ancient Mother has awakened once more, sitting on her throne- rejuvenated, more glorious than ever. Proclaim her to the entire world with the voice of peace and benedicition. Arise, Awake! Stop not till the Goal is reached"

- *Swami Vivekananda*

Om Shanti